# ULTIMATE
# GERMAN

## ADVANCED

WRITTEN BY

**BIRGIT NIELSEN**

EDITED BY

**HELGA SCHIER, PH.D., AND**

**ANA SUFFREDINI**

D1615160

LIVING LANGUAGE®
A Random House Company

Copyright © 1998 by Living Language, A Random House Company

Content revised and updated in 2003

Living Language is a member of the Random House Information Group

Living Language and colophon are registered trademarks of Random House, Inc.

Maps © Fodors LLC
Fodor's is a registered trademark of Random House, Inc.

The publisher gratefully acknowledges permission to reprint the article *DER EURO STREIFT DIE PARITÄT ZUM DOLLAR* © 2002 by Claus Tigges, from the November 2, 2002 issue of *Frankfurter Allgemeine Zeitung*. Reprinted by permission of *Frankfurter Allgemeine Zeitung* and Claus Tigges.

Published in the United States by Living Language, A Random House Company

www.livinglanguage.com

Editors: Helga Schier, Ph.D. and Ana Suffredini
Production Editor: John Whitman
Production Managers: Helen Kilcullen and Heather Lanigan
Cover Design: Sophie Ye Chin

First Edition

ISBN 1-4000-2058-1

Library of Congress Cataloging-in-Publication Data available upon request.

PRINTED IN THE UNITED STATES OF AMERICA

10 9 8 7 6 5 4

# ACKNOWLEDGMENTS

Thanks to the staff at Living Language: Kathy Mintz, Jessica Frankel, Chris Warnasch, Julie A. Lewis, Lenny Henderson, Mark McCauslin, Erin Bekowies, and Lois Berkowitz. Special thanks also to Emanuel Bergmann, Steele Burrow, Cheryl Hodgson, Andreas Kasper, Chris Leibundgut, Wilm Pelters, Astrid Ronke, as well as Jack Schroeder and Stefan Kloo from the Goethe-Institut Los Angeles.

The following organizations have provided us with a wealth of crucial information: the *Frankfurter Allgemeine Zeitung; Die Zeit;* the *Süddeutsche Zeitung;* the *Lübecker Nachrichten; Der Stern;* the *Neue Zürcher Zeitung;* the German American Chamber of Commerce, Los Angeles; the Goethe-Institut, Los Angeles; the German Information Center, New York; the *Ausstellungs- und Messeausschuß der Deutschen Wirtschaft e.V.,* Köln; the *Senatsverwaltung für Wirtschaft und Technologie,* Berlin; the Press and Information Office of the Federal Government, Bonn; the press offices of the Hansestadt Rostock, Landeshauptstadt Magdeburg, and Stadt Zwickau; the Swiss National Tourist Office; the Swiss Consulate General; the Tourist Office Bern; the *Verkehrshaus Luzern;* the *Gemeinschaft Autofreier Schweizer Tourismusorte;* the Austrian National Tourist Office; the Vienna Tourist Board, Vienna; *Wiener Messen & Kongress GmbH;* CDS International Inc.; and the Smithsonian Institution.

Additional thanks to Elizabeth Bennett, Helen Tang, Zviezdana Verzich, Suzanne McQuade, Sophie Chin, Denise DeGennaro, Linda Schmidt, Alison Skrabek, Arlene Aizer, Helen Kilcullen, and Heather Lanigan.

Thanks to all of the above. Without their help this book would not have been possible.

# FREE ACCESS TO
# MORE PRACTICE ONLINE

Enhance your *Ultimate German Advanced* learning experience with free extra practice online! Go to **www.livinglanguage.com/bonus/ultimateadvanced/german** to get access to 100 additional exercises and answers.

# CONTENTS

# LIVING LANGUAGE®

## ULTIMATE

# GERMAN

## A D V A N C E D

# INTRODUCTION

*Living Language™ Ultimate German Advanced* is a continuation of the beginner-intermediate *Ultimate German* program. If you have already mastered the basics of German in school, while traveling abroad, or with other *Living Language™* courses, then *Ultimate German Advanced* is right for you.

The complete course consists of this text and eight hours of recordings. However, if you are confident of your pronunciation, you can also use this manual on its own.

With *Ultimate German Advanced* you'll continue to learn how to speak, understand, read, and write idiomatic German. The program will also introduce you to some of the more interesting aspects of German culture and business. You'll be able to participate in engaging conversations about a variety of topics, as well as recognize and respond to several styles of formal and informal speech.

The course will take you everywhere, from vineyards to investment banks, while teaching useful vocabulary and expressions. You'll get practice deciphering newspaper articles, classified ads, and legal papers. You'll also learn about subtle cultural distinctions in personal interaction, such as when to insist on paying for dinner and when to stop, that will help smooth your way abroad.

# COURSE MATERIALS

## THE MANUAL

*Living Language™ Ultimate German Advanced* consists of twenty lessons, four reading passages, and two review sections. The reading passages appear after every five lessons, and the review sections after Lesson 10 and Lesson 20. It's best to read and study each lesson in the manual before listening to it on the recordings.

*DIALOG* (DIALOGUE): Each lesson begins with a dialogue in standard, idiomatic German presenting a realistic situation—a job interview, a news report, a meeting with a lawyer—set in a different German-speaking locale. All dialogues are translated into idiomatic English.

*IN KÜRZE* (IN BRIEF): The notes in this section refer to specific expressions and phrases used in the dialogue. They'll introduce you to the cultural and historical background relevant to a particular expression, and allow you to see grammar rules and vocabulary "in action."

*GRAMMATIK UND GEBRAUCH* (GRAMMAR AND USAGE): After a brief review of basic German grammar, you'll concentrate on more advanced grammatical forms and their usage. You'll also learn how to express yourself more accurately and appropriately by using idiomatic German. For easy reference, the heading of each topic corresponds to its listing in the table of contents.

*REIN GESCHÄFTLICH* (STRICTLY BUSINESS): In this section you'll explore different areas of the German, Austrian, and Swiss economy, as well as cultural and historical information relevant to business etiquette and procedures. Discussing topics such as dress codes, import and export, the government and its involvement in the economy, this section will enable you to conduct business in Germany, Austria, and Switzerland with confidence.

*ÜBUNGEN* (EXERCISES): This section allows you to review the grammar and vocabulary covered in the lessons. You can check your answers in the *Lösungen* (Answer Key), which appears after the last *Lesestück* (Reading).

*LESESTÜCK* (READING): The four reading passages—appearing after Lessons 5, 10, 15, and 20—are not translated. The material covered in the preceding lessons, along with the vocabulary notes on the more difficult words and phrases, will enable you to infer the meaning, just as you would when reading a newspaper article or business report abroad.

*WIEDERHOLUNGSAUFGABE* (REVIEW QUIZ): The two review quizzes appear after Lessons 10 and 20. Similar in structure to the *Übungen,* these sections will allow you to integrate and test your mastery of the material covered in the preceding lessons.

APPENDIXES: There are three appendixes—a pronunciation guide, a grammar summary, and a letter-writing section.

GLOSSARY: The extensive two-way glossary will prove an invaluable reference as you work through this program and as you apply your knowledge when meeting Germans, Austrians, or Swiss abroad.

INDEX: The manual ends with an index of the major grammar points covered in the lessons.

The appendixes, glossary, and index make this manual an excellent source for future reference and study.

## RECORDINGS (SETS A & B)

This program provides you with eight hours of audio instruction and practice. There are two sets of complementary recordings: the first is designed for use with the manual, while the second may be used independently. By listening to and imitating the native speakers, you'll improve your pronunciation and comprehension while learning to use new phrases and structures.

## RECORDINGS FOR USE WITH THE MANUAL (SET A)

This set of recordings gives you four hours of audio practice in German only, and features the complete dialogues of all 20 lessons. The recorded material appears in **boldface** in your manual. You'll first hear native German speakers read the complete dialogue, without interruption, at normal conversational speed. Then you'll have a chance to listen to the dialogue a second time and repeat each phrase in the pauses provided.

If you wish to practice your comprehension, first listen to the recordings of the dialogue without consulting the translations in the manual. Write down a summary of what you think the dialogue was about, and then listen to the recordings a second time, checking how much you understood with the translations in the manual.

After you study each lesson and practice with Set A, go on to the second set of recordings (Set B), which can be used on the go—while driving, jogging, traveling, or doing housework.

## RECORDINGS FOR USE ON THE GO (SET B)

This set of recordings gives you four hours of audio instruction and practice in German and English. Because they are bilingual, these recordings may be used 'on the go' without the manual, wherever it's convenient to learn.

The 20 lessons on Set B correspond to those in the manual. A bilingual narrator leads you through the four sections of each lesson.

The first section presents the most important phrases from the original dialogue. You will first hear the abridged version of the dialogue without interruption at normal conversational speed. You'll then hear it again, phrase by phrase, with English translations and pauses for you to repeat after the native German speakers.

The second section reviews and expands upon the most important vocabulary introduced in the lesson. You will practice the most important words and phrases selected from the *Dialog* (Dialogue), *In Kürze* (In Brief), and *Rein geschäftlich* (Strictly Business). Additional expressions show how the words and phrases may be used in other contexts. Again, you are given time to repeat the German phrases after the native speakers.

In the third section you will explore the lesson's most important grammatical structures. After a quick review of the rules, you can practice with illustrative sentences.

The conversational exercises in the last section integrate what you've learned and help you generate sentences in German on your own. You'll take part in brief conversations, ask and respond to questions, transform sentences, and occasionally translate from English into German. After you respond, you'll hear the correct answer from a German native speaker.

The interactive approach on this set of recordings focuses on the idiomatic spoken word and will teach you to communicate and *think* in German.

Now let's begin.

3

# LEKTION 1

ANKUNFT.   Arrival.

## A. DIALOG (Dialogue)

*In München[1] bei Obermeiers zu Hause. Musik spielt im Hintergrund.*

ANNA OBERMEIER: **Bernd, es hat geklingelt. Geh doch mal bitte zur Tür. Unser Gast ist da.**

BERND OBERMEIER: **Oh, das habe ich gar nicht[2] gehört.**

ANNA OBERMEIER: **Kein Wunder, du spielst die Musik ja auch so laut.**

BERND OBERMEIER: **Ja, ich weiß, aber das ist doch Gabrieles[3] Lieblingsstück.**

*Er öffnet die Wohnungstür.*

BERND OBERMEIER: **Grüß Gott.[4] Schön, dass Sie da sind.**

*Der Gast aus den USA, Kevin Milton, tritt ein. Bernd Obermeier reicht ihm die Hand zur Begrüßung.*

BERND OBERMEIER: **Legen Sie doch bitte ab.[5] Hier ist die Garderobe.[6]**

KEVIN MILTON: **Ich habe Blumen mitgebracht.**

*Anna Obermeier kommt aus der Küche und nimmt die Blumen.*

ANNA OBERMEIER: **Das ist aber nett. Vielen Dank. Willkommen in München, Herr Milton.**

BERND OBERMEIER: **Meine Frau, Anna.**

KEVIN MILTON: **Ich freue mich, Sie kennen zu lernen.[7]**

*Bernd begleitet Herrn Milton ins Wohnzimmer. Eine Bekannte der Obermeiers, Gabriele Schlosser, sitzt auf dem Sofa.*

BERND OBERMEIER: **Ich stelle mal kurz vor, Kevin Milton. Er ist extra für die Konferenz aus Amerika gekommen.**

*Gabriele Schlosser steht auf und gibt Kevin Milton die Hand.*

GABRIELE SCHLOSSER: Schlosser.[8] Schönen guten Abend. Woher in den USA kommen Sie denn?

KEVIN MILTON: Aus Boston.

GABRIELE SCHLOSSER: Das ist ja interessant. Ich war letztes Jahr in den USA and habe auch Boston kurz besucht. Eine sehr schöne Stadt.

BERND OBERMEIER: Wie wär's[9] mit einem Glas Wein? Oder ein Bier?

KEVIN MILTON: Ein Bier, bitte.

ANNA OBERMEIER: Wie lange bleiben Sie denn in München?

KEVIN MILTON: Leider nur fünf Tage. Morgen beginnt die Konferenz. Am Freitag fliege ich nach Rom, und dann geht[10] es schon wieder zurück.

ANNA OBERMEIER: Nur so kurz? Waren Sie schon mal in Deutschland?

KEVIN MILTON: Nein, ich war noch nie in Europa.

GABRIELE SCHLOSSER: Wann sind Sie denn angekommen?

KEVIN MILTON: Gestern nachmittag.

GABRIELE SCHLOSSER: Erst gestern? Dann haben Sie ja gar keine Zeit für eine Stadtrundfahrt.

KEVIN MILTON: Doch, Bernd hat mir gestern gleich die wichtigsten Sehenswürdigkeiten gezeigt.

GABRIELE SCHLOSSER: Was hat Ihnen denn am besten gefallen?

KEVIN MILTON: Oh, ich habe so viel gesehen. Die Frauenkirche und der Marienplatz sind sehr schön, und der Viktualienmarkt[11] hat mir gut gefallen. Wir sind dort echt bayerisch essen gegangen. Wie heißt es doch gleich? Brotzeit?[12]

ANNA OBERMEIER: Genau. Ich hoffe, es hat Ihnen geschmeckt, denn bayerische Spezialitäten gibt es in zehn Minuten gleich nochmal.

GABRIELE SCHLOSSER: Sie interessieren sich also für historische Gebäude?

KEVIN MILTON: Ja, vor allem für Kirchen aus dem Mittelalter. Ich habe einen ganzen Stapel Bücher über das Thema.

GABRIELE SCHLOSSER: Das ist ja interessant. Regensburg hat einen schönen Dom. Na ja,[13] in Rom sehen Sie sich ja bestimmt den Vatikan und die Sixtinische Kirche an.

KEVIN MILTON: **Ja, natürlich. Entschuldigen Sie, wie war Ihr Name gleich nochmal? Ich fürchte,[14] ich habe ihn nicht verstanden.**

GABRIELE SCHLOSSER: **Ach, das macht nichts.[15] Schlosser ist mein Name.**

BERND OBERMEIER: **Noch einen Wein für die Frau Doktor?[16]**

*Gabriele Schlosser schüttelt den Kopf.*

KEVIN MILTON: **Oh, Sie sind Ärztin?**

GABRIELE SCHLOSSER: **Nein, ich unterrichte Geschichte an der Münchener Uni.**

ANNA OBERMEIER: **Ich glaube, das Essen ist fertig. Ich hoffe, ihr habt Hunger.**

BERND OBERMEIER: **Noch ein Bier, Herr Milton?**

KEVIN MILTON: **Nein, danke, und bitte nennen Sie mich doch Kevin.[17]**

BERND OBERMEIER: **Gern. Ich bin der Bernd. Frau Schlosser heißt mit Vornamen Gabriele, und das ist Anna, meine Frau, die beste Köchin[18] an der Isar.[19]**

ANNA OBERMEIER: **Ach, erzähl kein' Schmarr'n![20] Echter bayerischer Kartoffelsalat, Radis, Brez'n,[21] Käse und Kalbshax'n mit Knödel und Blaukraut. Ich hoffe, ich habe keine Vegetarier unter meinen Gästen.**

GABRIELE SCHLOSSER: **Zu spät. Guten Appetit.**

---

## TRANSLATION

At the Obermeiers' home in Munich. Music is playing in the background.

ANNA OBERMEIER: Bernd, that was the doorbell. Can you please answer the door? Our guest has arrived.

BERND OBERMEIER: Oh, I didn't hear that.

ANNA OBERMEIER: I'm not surprised. You're playing the music really loud.

BERND OBERMEIER: Yes, I know, but that's Gabriele's favorite piece.

He opens the door.

BERND OBERMEIER: Hello. How nice of you to come.

The guest from the U.S.A., Kevin Milton, enters. Bernd Obermeier greets him with a handshake.

BERND OBERMEIER: Please take off your jacket. The coatrack's right here.

KEVIN MILTON: I brought some flowers.

Anna Obermeier comes out of the kitchen and takes the flowers.

ANNA OBERMEIER: How nice of you. Thank you. Welcome to Munich, Mr. Milton.

BERND OBERMEIER: My wife, Anna.

KEVIN MILTON: Nice to meet you.

Bernd shows Mr. Milton into the living room. A friend of the Obermeiers, Gabriele Schlosser, is sitting on the sofa.

BERND OBERMEIER: Let me introduce you: this is Kevin Milton. He came from America just to attend our conference.

Gabriele gets up to shake Kevin's hand.

GABRIELE SCHLOSSER: Schlosser. Good evening. Where in the U.S.A. are you from?

KEVIN MILTON: Boston.

GABRIELE SCHLOSSER: How interesting. I was in the U.S.A. last year and visited Boston for a short while. A very beautiful city.

BERND OBERMEIER: How about a glass of wine? Or a beer?

KEVIN MILTON: A beer, please.

GABRIELE SCHLOSSER: How long are you staying in Munich?

KEVIN MILTON: Unfortunately only five days. The conference starts tomorrow. I'm flying to Rome on Friday and then it's already time to go back.

ANNA OBERMEIER: Only such a short stay? Have you ever been to Germany before?

KEVIN MILTON: No, I've never been to Europe.

GABRIELE SCHLOSSER: When did you arrive?

KEVIN MILTON: Yesterday afternoon.

GABRIELE SCHLOSSER: Only yesterday? Then you'll hardly have any time for a sightseeing tour.

KEVIN MILTON: Oh yes, Bernd already showed me all major sights yesterday.

GABRIELE SCHLOSSER: What did you like best?

KEVIN MILTON: Oh, I saw so much. The *Frauenkirche* and the *Marienplatz* are very beautiful and I liked the *Viktualienmarkt* a lot. We had a traditional Bavarian meal there. What was it called again? *Brotzeit?*

ANNA OBERMEIER: Exactly. I hope you liked it, because there'll be more Bavarian specialties in about ten minutes.

GABRIELE SCHLOSSER: So you are interested in historic buildings?

KEVIN MILTON: Yes, especially medieval churches. I have a whole stack of books on the subject.

GABRIELE SCHLOSSER: How interesting. Regensburg has a beautiful cathedral. Well, I'm sure you'll go and see the Vatican and the Sistine Chapel in Rome.

KEVIN MILTON: Yes, of course. Excuse me, what was your name again? I'm afraid I didn't understand it.

GABRIELE SCHLOSSER: Oh, that doesn't matter. Schlosser is my name.

BERND OBERMEIER: Another wine, doctor?

Gabriele Schlosser shakes her head.

KEVIN MILTON: Oh, you're a physician?

GABRIELE SCHLOSSER: No, I teach history at the University of Munich.

ANNA OBERMEIER: I think dinner is ready. I hope you're hungry.

BERND OBERMEIER: Another beer for you, Mr. Milton?

KEVIN MILTON: No, thank you, and please call me Kevin.

BERND OBERMEIER: With pleasure. My name's Bernd. Frau Schlosser's first name is Gabriele and this is Anna, my wife, the best cook on the Isar.

ANNA OBERMEIER: What hokum! Authentic Bavarian potato salad, radish, *Brez'n,* cheese, and then we have leg of veal with dumplings and red cabbage. I hope none of my guests is vegetarian.

GABRIELE SCHLOSSER: Too late. *Guten Appetit.*

# B. IN KÜRZE (In Brief)

1. *München* (Munich) is the capital of *Bayern* (Bavaria). *Bayern* is the largest German state, well known for its beer, food, and traditions. The *Schuhplattler,* for example, a traditional Bavarian dance, and the traditional folk costumes, the *Dirndl* and the *Lederhosen,* are considered to be typically Bavarian. *Bayern* has a number of dialects that differ greatly from each other: the Munich dialect, for example, is very different from the Northern Bavarian *Fränkisch.* For more information, go to www.München.de.

2. *Gar* is a stress marker used for emphasis with the negation *nicht* or *kein.*

*Ich habe gar keine Zeit.*
   I have no time (at all).

3. As in English, names take a genitive *-s* to indicate possession. Unlike in English, however, no apostrophe is added.

*Herrn Miltons Blumen waren sehr schön.*
   Mr. Milton's flowers were very beautiful.

4. *Grüß Gott* (literally: Greet God) is the common greeting in the South of Germany. The most popular greetings in Germany are:

*Guten Tag./Tag.*
   Good day.

*Guten Morgen./Morgen.*
   Good morning.

*Guten Abend./'n Abend.*
   Good evening.

   You may of course hear variations on these greetings, such as *Schönen guten Tag* (literally: [Have a] beautiful good day) or *Grüß Gott mit'nand* (Good day to you all). The Swiss use *Grüezi* and the Austrians use *Grüß Gott* any time of the day. In all three countries young people use *Hallo* in informal settings.

5. *Ablegen* (to take off) generally refers to leaving the outdoor, climate-protective clothing including hat or umbrella in the hallway before proceeding into the living or waiting area, the office, or restaurant.

*Bitte legen Sie hier Ihren Mantel und ihre Taschen ab, bevor Sie die Ausstellung betreten.*
   Please leave your coat and bags here before proceeding into the exhibition.

In other contexts *ablegen* means "to put down, to file."

*Die Sekretärin hat die Korrespondenz schon abgelegt.*
The secretary already filed the correspondence.

*Ablegen* is a verb with a separable prefix (see Lessons 10 and 14).

6. Most theaters, opera houses, and restaurants have a *Garderobe* (cloakroom) to check in your coat. Sometimes the establishment will charge a small amount. In private homes, the *Garderobe* is the coatrack in the hallway.

7. *Sich freuen* (to be glad, to look forward to) is a reflexive verb (see Lesson 5).

*Ich freue mich, Sie kennen zu lernen.*
Nice to meet you.

Infinitives after a main verb are preceded by *zu* (see Lesson 11). In combinations of two verbs, such as *Kennen lernen, zu* is inserted between the two verbs.

*Er freut sich darauf, bei schönem Wetter segeln zu gehen.*
He looks forward to sailing during nice weather.

8. In formal situations it is most common to introduce oneself by one's last name.

9. *Wie wär's (wäre es) mit . . . ?* (How about . . . ?) is a fixed phrase. *Wäre* is the subjunctive II of *sein* (see Lesson 16). The expression is always followed by the dative because of the dative preposition *mit*.

*Wie wär's (wäre es) mit einem Bier?*
How about a beer?

10. The idiomatic expression *es geht zurück* implies travel plans in which the traveler takes a passive role. It is only used with the third person singular pronoun *es*. In other contexts, *zurückgehen* means "to go back."

*Ich muss zurückgehen, denn ich habe etwas vergessen.*
I have to go back, because I forgot something.

11. *Die Frauenkirche, der Marienplatz,* and *der Viktualienmarkt* are famous historical sights in the center of Munich. The *Frauenkirche* is a late Gothic two-spire cathedral completed in 1494. Its actual name is *Dom zu unserer lieben Frau* (Cathedral to Our Dear Lady). The twin towers of the cathedral are a trademark of Munich, commonly found on brochures and postcards. The *Marienplatz* is a picturesque town square, closed to traffic, framed by the old and the

new town hall and Saint Peter's church. The *Mariensäule,* a commemorative column erected in 1638, stands in its center. The *Viktualienmarkt* is one of the oldest open-air farmers' markets, with cafés and beer, and snack bars serving Bavarian specialties.

12. *Brotzeit* (literally: bread time) is the Bavarian term for a cold dinner. *Brotzeit* traditionally involves bread, sausages, cold cuts, cheese, and large soft pretzels (*Brez'n*). The main meal is traditionally eaten at lunchtime.

13. *Na ja* (oh well, anyway) is a conversational term used at the beginning of a sentence, as a concessive connection or lead-in to the following statement.

14. The verb *(sich) fürchten* (to be afraid/to fear something) is mostly used as a reflexive verb with the preposition *vor.*

*Ich fürchte mich vor Gewittern.*
I'm afraid of thunderstorms.

Without the reflexive pronoun and the preposition, it is a polite admission that you have failed to do something.

*Ich fürchte, ich habe es vergessen.*
I'm afraid I forgot.

15. *Das macht nichts.* (That's quite all right/It doesn't matter) is an idiomatic expression. In other contexts *(nichts) machen* means "to do (nothing)."

*Was machst du denn?*
What are you doing?

*Im Moment mache ich nichts.*
I'm not doing anything right now.

16. The German title *Doktor* is equivalent to the Ph.D. and the M.D. In academic and political circles, as well as in formal settings, people who have introduced themselves with their titles should be addressed as *Frau Doktor Niemann* or *Doktorin Niemann,* or *Herr Professor,* or *Professor Steiner.* In semiformal and informal social situations it is acceptable to address a *Dr. Gabriele Schlosser* as *Frau Schlosser.*

17. In some situations Germans address each other by their first name while still using the formal *Sie.* The use of the first name acknowledges that the parties involved have most likely known each other for a long time, whereas the continued use of *Sie* keeps a certain distance. The offer to use first names, however, may be a first step from formality to friendship. First name and *Sie* is the customary address at schools for students above the age of sixteen. Here it is a sign of respect rather than formality.

18. Note how the noun has changed from *Koch* to *Köchin* in the feminine. Some nouns don't only add *-in,* but also change the stem vowels in the feminine:

MASCULINE | FEMININE
--- | ---
*der Koch* | *die Köch-in*
*der Bauer* | *die Bäuer-in*
*der Freund* | *die Freund-in*
*der Architekt* | *die Architekt-in*

The plural of *-in* becomes *-innen.*

19. The Isar river runs through Munich. In summer its banks are crowded with sunbathers and swimmers.

20. *Schmarr'n* is Bavarian for a scrambled pancake served with powdered sugar, raisins, and/or fruit. In the phrase *Erzähl kein' Schmarr'n* it is used figuratively and best translated as "What hokum!"

21. *Brez'n* is Bavarian for *die Brezel* (pretzel). While the noun is feminine in standard German, in a dialect such as Bavarian it can change to masculine, *der Brez'n. Brez'n* are always large, soft pretzels and are eaten fresh, rather than dried.

# C. GRAMMATIK UND GEBRAUCH (Grammar and Usage)

## 1. *FRAGEN* (QUESTIONS)

The German word order in a normal sentence is subject-verb-object. In questions, subject and verb change position. There are three ways of forming questions in German.

a. Inversion

The subject and verb are inverted. Compare:

*Barbara ist Vegetarierin.*
Barbara is a vegetarian.

*Ist Barbara Vegetarierin?*
Is Barbara a vegetarian?

b. Questions with question pronouns

The verb immediately follows the question word.

*Wo liegt München?*
Where is Munich?

*Wer ist Vegetarierin?*
Who is a vegetarian?

The most common question words are:

| | | | | | |
|---|---|---|---|---|---|
| *wer* | who | *wo* | where | *wie* | how |
| *was* | what | *woher* | where from | *wieviel* | how much |
| *wen* | who(m) | *wohin* | where to | *warum* | why |
| *wem* | to who(m) | *wann* | when | *wessen* | whose |

The German equivalent of "who(m)" changes depending on its function within the sentence. Use *wer* if you are asking for the subject.

*Wer ist eingeladen?*
Who is invited?

*Kevin Milton ist eingeladen.*
Kevin Milton is invited.

Use *wen* if you are asking for the direct object (accusative).

*Bernd stellt Gabriele Schlosser vor.*
Bernd is introducing Gabriele Schlosser.

*Wen stellt Bernd vor?*
Who(m) does Bernd introduce?

Use *wem* if you are asking for the indirect object (dative).

*Wem gibt er die Blumen?*
Who(m) does he give the flowers to?

Please note that verb and subject switch position after a question word, unless the question word itself is the subject.

*Wer kommt zum Essen?*
Who is coming for dinner?

c. Intonation

A third possibility to form questions in German is by raising your voice at the end of the sentence. Compare:

*Kevin Milton ist nur 4 Tage in München.*
Kevin Milton is in Munich for only four days.

*Er ist nur 4 Tage in München?*
He is in Munich for only four days?

## 2. *DIE VERNEINUNG* (NEGATION)

To change a positive statement or a question into a negative, add *nicht* after the conjugated (finite) verb in the present, past, and future tenses.

*Ich weiß nicht, wie spät es ist.*
I don't know what time it is.

*Wird er nicht fahren?*
Will he not go?

In compound tenses *nicht* stands between the auxiliary and the past participle.

*Wir sind nicht zur Konferenz gegangen.*
We didn't go to the conference.

*Nicht* usually precedes the part of the sentence that is negated, unless the whole sentence is negated.

*Das Olympia-Stadion interessierte ihn nicht.*
The Olympic stadium didn't interest him.

Time expressions or time adverbs always precede *nicht*.

*Er ist gestern nicht zum Essen gekommen.*
He didn't come home for dinner yesterday.

*Ich bin ab 15 Uhr nicht mehr im Büro.*
I'm not at the office anymore after 3 P.M.

If the sentence has both a dative (indirect) and an accusative (direct) object,* *nicht* precedes the part it negates, or, if negating the whole sentence, moves to the end.

NEGATING WHOLE SENTENCE
*Er hat Anna das Glas <u>nicht</u> gegeben.*
He didn't give Anna the glass.

NEGATING INDIRECT OBJECT
*Er hat nicht <u>Anna</u> das Glas gegeben (sondern Bernd).*
He didn't give the glass to Anna (but to Bernd).

NEGATING DIRECT OBJECT
*Er hat Anna nicht das <u>Glas</u> gegeben (sondern den Teller).*
He didn't give Anna the glass (but the plate).

*Kein* is used to negate nouns that have no articles or indefinite articles.[†] It means "not any," "not a," "no," or "none." *Kein* is declined like the indefinite article.

*Heute ist kein Markt.*
There is no market today.

*Dann haben Sie ja gar keine Zeit für eine Stadtrundfahrt.*
Then you won't have any time (at all) for a sightseeing tour.

## 3. *DAS PRÄSENS* (THE PRESENT TENSE)

In the present tense all verb forms take endings that are attached to the stem. These endings are:

| PRONOUNS | ENDING | REGULAR VERBS *kaufen* | VERBS WITH *-d/-t* STEM *antworten* | VERBS WITH *-s/-ß/-z* STEM *reisen* |
|---|---|---|---|---|
| *ich* | *-e* | *kauf-e* | *antwort-e* | *reis-e* |
| *du* | *-st* | *kauf-st* | *antwort-est* | *reis-t* |
| *er/sie/es* | *-t* | *kauf-t* | *antwort-et* | *reis-t* |
| *wir* | *-en* | *kauf-en* | *antwort-en* | *reis-en* |
| *ihr* | *-t* | *kauf-t* | *antwort-et* | *reis-t* |
| *sie* | *-en* | *kauf-en* | *antwort-en* | *reis-en* |
| *Sie* | *-en* | *kauf-en* | *antwort-en* | *reis-en* |

* The position of direct and indirect objects is discussed in Lesson 5.
† See appendix for the declension of the indefinite article.

Some verbs change their stem vowel in the first and second person singular.

| | |
|---|---|
| *a* becomes *ä* | *schlafen* (to sleep) |
| | *du schläfst, er/sie/es schläft* |
| | *waschen* (to wash) |
| | *du wäschst, er/sie/es wäscht* |
| *au* becomes *äu* | *laufen* (to run) |
| | *du läufst, er/sie/es läuft* |
| *e* becomes *i* | *geben* (to give) |
| | *du gibst, er/sie/es gibl* |
| *e* becomes *ie* | *sehen* (to see) |
| | *du siehst, er/sie/es sieht* |
| | *lesen* (to read) |
| | *du liest, er/sie/es liest* |

Unlike English, German has only one present tense. Therefore the following sentence can be translated in various ways.

*Ich fahre nach München.*
I drive to Munich./I'm driving to Munich./I do drive to Munich.

## 4. *DAS PERFEKT UND DAS IMPERFEKT* (THE PRESENT PERFECT AND THE SIMPLE PAST)

To describe events in the past, German uses either the present perfect or the simple past. The present perfect is most commonly used in conversation, whereas the simple past is mainly used in writing, particularly in literary prose, newspapers, and magazines.

The auxiliaries *haben* and *sein* are exceptions to the rule above. They are mostly used in the simple past, even in conversation. Their past tense forms are irregular:

| SEIN | TO BE | HABEN | TO HAVE |
|---|---|---|---|
| *ich war* | I was | *ich hatte* | I had |
| *du warst* | you were | *du hattest* | you had |
| *er/sie/es war* | he/she/it was | *er/sie/es hatte* | he/she/it had |
| *wir waren* | we were | *wir hatten* | we had |
| *ihr wart* | you were | *ihr hattet* | you had |
| *sie waren* | they were | *sie hatten* | they had |
| *Sie waren* | you were | *Sie hatten* | you had |

Most German verbs are weak. They form their past tense by adding endings to the stem, and their past participle by adding *ge-* and *-t*: *glauben* (to believe), *er glaubte, geglaubt*. Irregular weak verbs (or 'mixed verbs') show additional stem-vowel changes: *denken* (to think), *er dachte, gedacht*. Strong verbs often show stem-vowel changes in the second and third person singular simple past, and their past participle always ends in *-en: fahren* (to drive), *er fuhr, gefahren*.

a. The Present Perfect

The present perfect is a compound tense, consisting of the conjugated form of either *haben* or *sein* plus the past participle. Weak verbs form their past participle with the prefix *ge-* + stem + *-t*.

*KAUFEN* (REGULAR)

*ich habe gekauft*
*du hast gekauft*
*er/sie/es hat gekauft*
*wir haben gekauft*
*ihr habt gekauft*
*sie haben gekauft*
*Sie haben gekauft*

*DENKEN* (IRREGULAR)

*ich habe gedacht*
*du hast gedacht*
*er/sie/es hat gedacht*
*wir haben gedacht*
*ihr habt gedacht*
*sie haben gedacht*
*Sie haben gedacht*

Strong verbs form their past participle with the prefix *ge-* and *-en*. Since the strong verbs either form their past participle with the infinitive (to see: *sehen - gesehen*) or with vowel (to write: *schreiben - geschrieben*) and/or consonant changes (to take: *nehmen - genommen*) in the past participle, it is best to learn them separately.*

*ESSEN* (STRONG)

*ich habe gegessen*
*du hast gegessen*
*er/sie/es hat gegessen*

*wir haben gegessen*
*ihr habt gegessen*
*sie haben gegessen*

*SEHEN* (to see)
*Er hat die Frauenkirche gesehen.*
  He saw the Frauenkirche.

*SCHREIBEN* (to write)
*Kevin Milton hat seiner Familie geschrieben.*
  Kevin Milton wrote to his family.

---

* Please see the list of strong verbs in the appendix.

*NEHMEN* (to take)
*Anna Obermeier hat die Blumen genommen.*
  Anna Obermeier took the flowers.

Verbs with separable prefixes add *ge-* between prefix and stem:

*MITBRINGEN* (to bring)
*Kevin hat den Obermeiers Blumen mitgebracht.*
  Kevin brought flowers for the Obermeiers.

Other verbs, such as those with inseparable prefixes, do not add *ge-*.

*GEFALLEN* (to like)
*Der Viktualienmarkt hat mir sehr gefallen.*
  I liked the Viktualienmarkt very much.

*VERSTEHEN* (to understand)
*Kevin hat Frau Schlossers Namen nicht verstanden.*
  Kevin did not understand Frau Schlosser's name.

Verbs that end in *-ieren* in the infinitive do not take *ge-* prefixes. Instead their past participles are formed from stem + *-iert* ending.

*RESTAURIEREN* (to restore)
*Die Stadt München hat die Kirche restauriert.*
  The city of Munich restored the church.

While most verbs take *haben* as the auxiliary, some verbs of motion like *kommen* (to arrive, to come), *fahren* (to drive, to travel), *laufen* (to run), *gehen* (to go), *schwimmen* (to swim), *steigen* (to climb), as well as a few verbs of being (*sein, bleiben*) or dying (*ertrinken, sterben*), or verbs indicating a change of situation (*aufstehen, einschlafen, wachsen*) take *sein* as the auxiliary for the compound tenses.

*ANKOMMEN* (to arrive)
*Kevin Milton ist gestern angekommen.*
  Kevin Milton arrived yesterday.

*FAHREN* (to drive)
*Bernd Obermeier und Kevin Milton sind durch München gefahren.*
  Bernd Obermeier and Kevin Milton drove through Munich.

*BLEIBEN* (to stay)
*Frau Schlosser ist nicht lange in Boston geblieben.*
  Frau Schlosser did not stay long in Boston.

### b. The Simple Past

Strong verbs in the simple past tense show stem vowel changes. In addition, the first and third person singular take no endings. The second person singular (*-st*) and all plural forms (*-en, -t, -en*) have regular endings.

Verbs with *-e-* in the stem in the infinitive usually change to *-i-* or *-a-* in the simple past tense.

| | | | |
|---|---|---|---|
| *gehen* | to go | *wir gingen* | we went |
| *treffen* | to meet | *wir trafen* | we met |

Verbs with *-a-* or *-ei-* in the infinitive usually change to *-u-, -ie-,* or *-i-* in the simple past tense.

| | | | |
|---|---|---|---|
| *tragen* | to carry | *wir trugen* | we carried |
| *schlafen* | to sleep | *wir schliefen* | we slept |
| *greifen* | to grab | *wir griffen* | we grabbed |

Verbs with *-ie-* in the infinitive usually change to *-o-* in the simple past tense.

| | | | |
|---|---|---|---|
| *verlieren* | to lose | *wir verloren* | we lost |

Here are three example conjugations:

| *GEHEN* (TO GO) | *TREFFEN* (TO MEET) | *SCHREIBEN* (TO WRITE) |
|---|---|---|
| *ich ging* | *ich traf* | *ich schrieb* |
| *du gingst* | *du trafst* | *du schriebst* |
| *er/sie/es ging* | *er/sie/es traf* | *er/sie/es schrieb* |
| *wir gingen* | *wir trafen* | *wir schrieben* |
| *ihr gingt* | *ihr traft* | *ihr schriebt* |
| *sie gingen* | *sie trafen* | *sie schrieben* |
| *Sie gingen* | *Sie trafen* | *Sie schrieben* |

Weak verbs add *-te-* between stem and ending in the simple past.

*KAUFEN* (TO BUY)

| | |
|---|---|
| *ich kaufte* | *wir kauften* |
| *du kauftest* | *ihr kauftet* |
| *er/sie/es kaufte* | *sie kauften* |
| | *Sie kauften* |

Weak irregular verbs take vowel changes in addition to the *-te*.

*BRINGEN* (to bring)
*Kevin Milton brachte Blumen.*
    Kevin Milton brought flowers.

*KENNEN* (to know)
*Er kannte Bernd Obermeier.*
    He knew Bernd Obermeier.

# D. REIN GESCHÄFTLICH
## (Strictly Business)

## 1. QUICK TIPS FOR THE BUSINESS TRAVELER

An American citizen must have a valid U.S. passport to enter and travel in *die Bundesrepublik Deutschland* (Federal Republic of Germany), *die Schweiz* (Switzerland), and *die Republik Österreich* (Austria). When entering the country of your destination you must declare what you are bringing in beyond allowable limits and, upon request, open your luggage for inspection by the customs officers. Please consult your travel agency or the local embassy for specific customs regulations.

Public transportation is well developed throughout Europe. At the *Flughafen* (airport) you will find a fast and convenient *Bus-, Zug-,* or *U-Bahnverbindung* (bus, train, or subway connection) to the *Stadtzentrum* (city center) and the *Hauptbahnhof* (major train station), where you will find further connections to anywhere within the railway network. In addition, most airports and train stations have an *Autoverleih* (car rental desk).

When driving, please remember that Europe uses the metric system to measure distance: 1 kilometer is approximately 0.621 miles. The *Autobahnnetz* (highway system) is extremely well developed in Germany, Austria, and Switzerland, as driving is by far the most common method of travel. The *Geschwindigkeitsbegrenzung* (speed limit) on the *Autobahn* in Austria is 130 km/h, and in Switzerland 120 km/h. Unless otherwise noted, there is no speed limit on the German *Autobahn*.

Every city and most smaller towns offer a wide assortment of hotels and pensions. Advance reservations are advised, especially for rooms in cities where international trade fairs are held during the major trade fair seasons, from February to June and October to November.

While hotels and pensions are open twenty-four hours a day, seven days a week, don't be surprised to find stores closed when arriving on a Saturday afternoon or a Sunday. Restaurants, even in large cities, are closed one day a week, mostly on Mondays, for their *Ruhetag* (literally: quiet day).

While larger cities may offer 24-hour convenience stores at the airport, around train stations, or as part of gas stations, most areas strictly enforce the *Ladenschlussgesetz* (set store hours). Stores close at 8 P.M.

on weekdays and 4 P.M. on Saturdays. On Sundays all stores are closed. The *Ladenschlussgesetz* is likely to change and offer more liberal store hours.

Usual business hours at offices are from 9 A.M. to 5 P.M. On Fridays many offices close early, around 4 P.M. Public administration offices are open from 8:00 A.M. through 4 P.M. On one day a week they will stay open until 5 or 6 P.M. to accommodate the needs of the working population. On Fridays public administration offices close as early as 1 or 2 P.M.

## 2. DOS AND DON'TS

## SPEAKING GERMAN

Your knowledge of German may be one of the most effective tools when doing business in Germany, Austria, and Switzerland. While most Germans, Austrians, and Swiss speak English very well, addressing your business partners in German will help to establish a positive relationship from the start. Don't be surprised or insulted if they respond in English—this is not meant as a reflection on your fluency, but rather an eagerness to practice their English. Feel free to continue in German, and don't be embarrassed about your mistakes.

Your knowledge of German will enable you to read the local papers, watch television, enjoy the theater, and get an inside look into the social fabric of society. Germans enjoy discussions and appreciate well-informed "opponents," although arguments should be avoided in an office environment.

Furthermore, try to use your hosts' measurement system. Talk in *Euro* (abbreviated as EUR), *Liter,* and *Meter* or *Kilometer* instead of dollars, gallons, and yards or miles. And, while blocks are a very common measurement of distance in the U.S.A., no such concept exists in Europe. Instead, try to translate everything into minutes, meters, or kilometers.

*Meine Wohnung ist 10 Minuten von hier.*
My apartment is ten blocks from here.

Things are different abroad. Your familiarity with the German culture will impress your partners, and keeping an open mind to a different way of life will unlock many doors for you.

Social etiquette in German-speaking countries is somewhat more formal than in the U.S.A. Introduce yourself by your last name, or by your first *and* last name in business or formal settings. It is common to shake hands at initial encounters in both formal and informal situations. A kiss or a hug is only appropriate among friends or relatives. Unless explicitly asked to use the first name, use *Herr* or *Frau* and the last name. Do not use the term *Fräulein* for young or unmarried women, as it is considered outdated and politically incorrect.

A first step from formal to informal address is a combination of first name and formal *Sie*. If you wish to take this step, say so:

*Bitte, nennen Sie mich doch Horst.*
*Bitte, sagen Sie doch Horst zu mir.*
  Please, call me Horst.

Moving from the formal *siezen* (using *Sie*) to the informal *duzen* (using *du*) is slightly more complicated. In general, unless explicitly asked to use *du*, use the formal *Sie* when addressing adults (and teenagers over sixteen) you are not close or related to. The person to initiate the *du* is usually the older person, regardless of social or professional status, or, among people of the same age, the person of higher social or professional rank. Common phrases to initiate this change include:

*Sie können mich ruhig duzen. Ich heiße Martin.*
  You may address me with *du*. My name is Martin.

*Warum duzen wir uns eigentlich nicht?*
  Why don't we use *du* with each other?

If someone offers to use a more familiar form of address, either first name plus *Sie* or even *du,* you should always accept. It is considered an affront to refuse such an invitation, as it often coincides with an invitation to friendship and closeness.

## BUSINESS DINNERS

If you are planning to take someone out to dinner, ask the waiter when ordering or at the time of payment to give the bill to you. Should you still have trouble convincing your guest that you intend to settle the bill, use any of the following phrases:

*Das geht auf meine Rechnung.*
  It's my bill.

*Ich möchte Sie gerne einladen.*
  I would like to treat you.

*Ich lade Sie ein.*
I'm buying./I'm treating you.

Service charge and tip are included in the bill, yet additional tipping is welcome. Ask the waiter or waitress to round up (*aufrunden*) to the next 5- or 10-EUR sum when giving you change. It is not customary to leave a tip in change or small notes on the table as it is in the U.S.A.
  Although Germans like to protect their privacy, you may be invited to someone's home for dinner or drinks. If so, try to be on time. Punctuality is a virtue in Germany. If you are running more than fifteen minutes late, call your host. Otherwise people might be offended or think something has happened. Apologize if you do come late:

*Entschuldigen Sie die Verspätung.*
I'm sorry for being late.

It is customary to bring either flowers or a bottle of wine. Flowers should always be given in uneven numbers and are usually presented to the host unwrapped. Don't bring red roses, as they have clear romantic overtones.

*Das ist für Sie!*
This is for you.

*Ich habe Ihnen etwas mitgebracht.*
I brought something for you.

It is considered polite to comment on the meal. A few common phrases may be helpful.

*Ich hoffe, es hat Ihnen geschmeckt.*
I hope you enjoyed your meal.

*Danke, es war ausgezeichnet.*
Thanks, it was excellent.

*Das hat ausgezeichnet geschmeckt.*
This dish/meal was excellent.

*Das schmeckt aber hervorragend.*
This dish/meal is wonderful.

Once you've been welcomed into a German home, you will find that the Germans are better than their reputation: Germans, often stiff and reserved on a first encounter, are actually very hospitable and social, and your business connections may lead to lasting friendships.

# ÜBUNGEN (EXERCISES)

**1.** *Fragen Sie bitte nach dem unterstrichenen Teil des Satzes.* (Form a question asking for the underlined part of the sentence.)

*BEISPIEL: Die Party war in <u>München</u>.*
    *Wo war die Party?*

 a. <u>*Anna Obermeier*</u> *hat das Essen gekocht.*
 b. *Kevin Milton hat* <u>*Blumen*</u> *mitgebracht.*
 c. *Die Frauenkirche ist in* <u>*München*</u>.
 d. *Kevin Milton ist* <u>*gestern*</u> *angekommen.*
 e. <u>*Zwei*</u> *Gäste sind eingeladen.*
 f. *Die Bekannte der Obermeiers heißt* <u>*Gabriele Schlosser*</u>.
 g. *Kevin Milton besucht* <u>*eine Konferenz*</u> *in München.*
 h. *Herr Milton kann nicht lange in München bleiben.* <u>*Er fliegt am Freitag nach Rom*</u>.

**2.** *Setzen Sie die folgenden Sätze ins Imperfekt.* (Rewrite the following sentences in the simple past.)

 a. *Ich bin gestern zum Marienplatz gegangen.*
 b. *Nach einer halben Stunde ist Bernd gekommen.*
 c. *Wir sind am Viktualienmarkt essen gegangen.*
 d. *Wir sind dann ins Büro gefahren und haben auf dem Weg Blumen für seine Frau gekauft.*
 e. *Abends bin ich zu den Obermeiers gegangen und habe Anna die Blumen gegeben.*

**3.** *Setzen Sie die folgenden Sätze ins Perfekt.* (Rewrite the following in the present perfect.)

 a. *Er fuhr mit dem Zug nach Regensburg.*
 b. *Abends traf er sich mit einem Geschäftskollegen.*
 c. *Sie gingen spazieren.*
 d. *Er sah die vielen alten Häuser in der Innenstadt.*
 e. *Am nächsten Tag besuchte er den Dom und kaufte Geschenke für seine Freunde.*

**4.** *Verneinen Sie die folgenden Sätze.* (Negate the following sentences.)

 a. *Ich war letztes Jahr in Regensburg.*
 b. *Er hat Herrn Obermeier angerufen.*
 c. *Waren Sie in München?*
 d. *Wir sind ins Museum gegangen.*
 e. *Bayern ist klein.*
 f. *Ich fahre gerne mit dem Auto.*
 g. *Die gothische Kathedrale gefällt mir.*

25

**5.** *Setzen Sie „kein"\* ein.* (Fill in *kein.*)

    a. *Es gab _____ Taxi.*
    b. *Im Museum waren _____ Bilder.*
    c. *_____ Mensch ist in die Kirche gegangen.*
    d. *Wir hatten _____ Besucher letztes Jahr.*
    e. *Sie hat _____ zum Essen eingeladen.*
    f. *Wir essen _____ Fleisch.*
    g. *Heute ist _____ Markt auf dem Viktualienmarkt.*

**6.** *Suchen Sie die richtige Antwort.* (Find the correct answer.)

    1. *Wer hat Kevin Milton den Viktualienmarkt gezeigt?*      a. *An der Uni München.*

    2. *Wo lebt Kevin Milton?*      b. *Gut.*

    3. *Was hat Gabriele Schlosser getrunken?*      c. *Nach Rom.*

    4. *Warum hat Bernd Obermeier die Klingel nicht gehört?*      d. *Gestern.*

    5. *Wo arbeitet Dr. Schlosser?*      e. *In Boston.*

    6. *Wann ist Kevin Milton angekommen?*      f. *Ein Glas Wein.*

    7. *Wohin fliegt er nach seinem Besuch in München?*      g. *Bernd Obermeier.*

    8. *Wie hat ihm das bayerische Essen geschmeckt?*      h. *Die Musik war sehr laut.*

---

\* In German, the quotation marks at the beginning of a quotation are placed just below the line.

# LEKTION 2

WOHNUNGSSUCHE.  Looking for an Apartment.

## A. DIALOG

*Richard Söhnke sucht eine Wohnung in Frankfurt am Main.[1] Er hat einige Wohnungsanzeigen in der Samstagsausgabe[2] der Zeitung angestrichen. Eine Anzeige interessiert ihn besonders.*

*Schöne 2½ Z. Whg.[3] mit gr.[4] Balkon, sonnig, Parknähe.[5] 900 EUR kalt.[6] 1.000 EUR Kaution.[7] Tel 254 78 96.*

VERMIETER: **Lange.**

HERR SÖHNKE: **Söhnke, guten Tag. Ich rufe wegen der Anzeige in der Zeitung an.**

VERMIETER: **Tut mir leid, die Wohnung ist schon vergeben.[8]**

HERR SÖHNKE: **Oh, wie schade. Vielen Dank. Auf Wiederhören.[9]**

*Herr Söhnke versucht es mit einer anderen Anzeige.*

*3 Z. Whg., zentrale Lage. Ruhig. 89 m²,[10] Gemeinsch. Dachterr.[11] Frühest.[12] zum 1.6 beziehbar. 1.500 EUR & 2.000 EUR Kaution. Tel. 987 57 56.*

VERMIETERIN: **Schaller.**

HERR SÖHNKE: **Guten Tag. Ist die inserierte[13] Wohnung noch frei?**

FRAU SCHALLER: **Ja. Wollen Sie sich die Wohnung anschauen?**

HERR SÖHNKE: **Ja, gern.[14] Können Sie mir vorher vielleicht noch ein paar kurze Fragen beantworten?**

FRAU SCHALLER: **Ja, natürlich.**

HERR SÖHNKE: **Warum ist die Wohnung erst Anfang Juni beziehbar?**

FRAU SCHALLER: **Wir renovieren gerade.**

HERR SÖHNKE: **Ist es eine Altbauwohnung?[15]**

FRAU SCHALLER: **Ja. Aber wir haben einige Umbauten vorgenommen. Das Haus hat jetzt eine große Dachterrasse. Wir werden neu tapezieren und die Wohnung bekommt neue Fenster.**

HERR SÖHNKE: **Ist es sehr laut in der Straße?**

FRAU SCHALLER: Nein, das Haus liegt in einer ruhigen Seitenstraße, nur 10 Minuten vom Hauptbahnhof entfernt. Die Straßenbahn- und Bushaltestellen[16] sind direkt um die Ecke. Die Wohnung liegt wirklich zentral und ist sehr praktisch[17] für Geschäftsleute.

HERR SÖHNKE: Könnte* ich die Wohnung für 6 Monate mieten?

FRAU SCHALLER: Unter Umständen ja. Normalerweise stelle ich Mietverträge zwar nur für mindestens 12 Monate aus, aber ich könnte mal eine Ausnahme machen. Aber das müssten[†] wir noch genauer besprechen.

HERR SÖHNKE: Natürlich. In welchem Stockwerk[18] ist die Wohnung denn?

FRAU SCHALLER: Im 3. Stock.[19] Ich werde die Wohnung wahrscheinlich nächsten Mittwoch zeigen.

HERR SÖHNKE: Kann ich die Wohnung vielleicht schon morgen sehen?

FRAU SCHALLER: Leider bin ich am Wochenende nicht hier. Ich werde erst Montag im Laufe des Tages zurückkommen.[20] Passt es Ihnen,[21] wenn wir uns Montag um 17.30 vor dem Haus treffen?

HERR SÖHNKE: Ja, das passt mir gut. Wie ist die Adresse?

FRAU SCHALLER: Hofgartenstraße 19.

HERR SÖHNKE: Und wie finde ich vom Hauptbahnhof dorthin?

FRAU SCHALLER: Von der Breiten Straße gehen Sie in Richtung[22] Opernplatz. An der linken Ecke ist eine Bank und eine Apotheke. Biegen Sie dort links ein. An der nächsten Kreuzung gehen Sie dann rechts in die Hofgartenstraße. Wie ist denn Ihr Name?

HERR SÖHNKE: Oh, entschuldigen Sie, ich habe mich ja noch gar nicht vorgestellt. Söhnke, Richard Söhnke.

FRAU SCHALLER: Das macht nichts. Wir werden uns ja am Montag kennenlernen. Mein Name ist Schaller.

HERR SÖHNKE: Vielen Dank, Frau Schaller. Ja, dann bis Montag um halb sechs.[23] Ich wünsche Ihnen ein schönes Wochenende.

FRAU SCHALLER: Danke, gleichfalls.

---

\* *könnte* is a subjunctive form of *können* (see Lessons 13 and 16).
[†] *müssten* is a subjunctive form of *müssen* (see Lessons 13 and 16).

# TRANSLATION

Richard Söhnke is looking for an apartment in Frankfurt am Main. He has marked several rental ads in the Saturday edition of the local paper. He is particularly interested in one of them.

Apt. with 2½ rooms and large balcony. Sunny, near park. €900 (excl. heating). €1,000 security deposit. Phone 254 78 96.

LANDLORD: Lange.

MR. SÖHNKE: Söhnke, hello, I'm calling about the advertisement in the paper.

LANDLORD: I'm sorry, the apartment is gone already.

MR. SÖHNKE: Oh, too bad. Thank you. Good-bye.

Mr. Söhnke tries another ad.

3 rm apt., central location, quiet, 89 m², communal roof terrace. Earliest move-in June 1st. €1,500 and €2,000 security deposit. Phone 987 57 56.

LANDLADY: Schaller.

MR. SÖHNKE: Hello, is the apartment advertised in the paper still available?

MS. SCHALLER: Yes. Would you like to see it?

MR. SÖHNKE: Yes, I'd love to. Could you possibly answer some quick questions first?

MS. SCHALLER: Yes, of course.

MR. SÖHNKE: Why won't the apartment be ready for move-in before early June?

MS. SCHALLER: We're currently renovating.

MR. SÖHNKE: Is it an old building?

MS. SCHALLER: Yes, it is. But we've made several alterations. The house has a large roof terrace now. We'll hang new wallpaper in the apartment and put in new windows.

MR. SÖHNKE: Is the street very noisy?

MS. SCHALLER: No, the building is on a quiet side street, only ten minutes from the train station. There are tram and bus stops just around the corner. The apartment is really right in the center of town and very convenient for businesspeople.

MR. SÖHNKE: Could I rent the apartment for six months?

MS. SCHALLER: Possibly. I usually issue rental agreements for a minimum of twelve months, but I could make an exception. But we'd have to talk about that in more detail.

MR. SÖHNKE: Of course. Which floor is the apartment on?

MS. SCHALLER: On the fourth floor. I'll be showing it on Wednesday.

MR. SÖHNKE: Can I possibly see the apartment tomorrow?

MS. SCHALLER: Unfortunately I'm not here over the weekend. I won't be back until sometime Monday. Is it convenient for you to meet me on Monday at 5:30 P.M. in front of the building?

MR. SÖHNKE: Yes, that's perfect. What's the address?

MS. SCHALLER: Hofgartenstraße 19.

MR. SÖHNKE: And how do I get there from the main station?

MS. SCHALLER: Take the Breite Straße and walk toward the Opernplatz. On the left-hand corner are a bank and a pharmacy. Turn left there. At the next intersection make a right into Hofgartenstraße. What is your name?

MR. SÖHNKE: Oh, excuse me, I didn't even introduce myself yet. (It is) Söhnke, Richard Söhnke.

MS. SCHALLER: It doesn't matter. We will meet on Monday. My name is Schaller.

MR. SÖHNKE: Thank you, Ms. Schaller. I'll see you Monday at 5:30, then. Have a nice weekend.

MS. SCHALLER: Thanks, you too.

# B. IN KÜRZE

1. *Frankfurt am Main* is the financial capital of Germany. Frankfurt also hosts several large international trade fairs such as the Frankfurt Book Fair and the Frankfurt Music Fair. Frankfurt lies on the banks of the river *Main*. Because of the city's financial status, the importance of the Frankfurt Stock Exchange, and its skyline with more high-rise buildings than any other German city, it is often jokingly called *Mainhattan*. For more information, please consult www.Frankfurt.de.

2. Unlike in the U.S.A., it is the *Samstagsausgabe* (Saturday edition) of most daily newspapers in Germany, Austria, and Switzerland that runs all classified ads.

3. The apartment size is defined by the number of rooms, including the living room, but not including bathroom and kitchen. Therefore a *2½-Zimmer-Wohnung* corresponds to a 1½ bedroom apartment, and always includes a separate kitchen and bathroom. *Z.* is the

abbreviation for *das Zimmer* (room) and *Whg.* is the abbreviation for *die Wohnung* (apartment).

4. *Gr.* is the abbreviation for *groß*.

5. *Parknähe* identifies the apartment as being close or adjacent to a park. Try not to confuse the term with "parking availability."

6. *900 EUR kalt.* The words *kalt* (cold) or *warm* (warm) in this context refer to heating costs that either are included in the rent *(warm)* or have to be paid extra *(kalt)*. Most apartments in Germany have central heating. Heating costs are either paid by the landlord and included in the rent, or paid by the tenant directly (gas/electric/fuel/coal).

7. *Die Kaution* (security deposit) is fully refundable, unless the apartment shows damages beyond the usual wear and tear. Often tenants have to renovate the apartment themselves (painting, hanging wallpaper, cleaning rugs and wall-to-wall carpeting) when moving in. The frequency of required renovations is stated in the *Mietvertrag* (rental agreement) or agreed upon between landlord and tenant individually. It is also common that the landlord requires that the apartment be renovated when moving out.

8. Please note the synonyms:

*Die Wohnung ist schon vergeben/vermietet/weg.*
The apartment is already taken/rented/"gone."

9. *Auf Wiederhören* is the telephone equivalent to *Auf Wiedersehen*.

10. The apartment size is most often measured by the overall space available. Germany, like most other European countries, uses the metric system and therefore uses *Quadratmeter* (square meters) rather than square feet. *89 $m^2$* approximately corresponds to 950 ft.$^2$

11. *Gemeinsch. Dachterr.* stands for *Gemeinschaftsdachterrasse* (communal roof terrace).

12. *Frühest.* is an abbreviation of *frühestens* (at the earliest).

13. In German two words can refer to advertisements: *die Anzeige* and *das Inserat. Die Anzeige* is either a commercial or a classified ad, whereas *das Inserat* can only be a classified ad.

14. *Gern/gerne* (gladly, with pleasure) is used in many different contexts. The *-e* ending is usually dropped.

| | | |
|---|---|---|
| As short answer: | *Möchten Sie einen Kaffee? Ja, gern (e).* | Would you like some coffee? Yes, please. |
| with *mögen:* | *Ich mag ihn gern.* | I like him quite a bit. |
| with a verb: | *Ich spiele gern Tennis.* | I enjoy playing tennis. |
| In set expressions: | *Gern geschehen.* | Don't mention it. |
| | *Er ist hier gern gesehen.* | He is welcome here. |
| | *Das glaube ich gern.* | I quite believe it. |

15. The term *der Altbau* refers to buildings from the time prior to World War II. It is not necessarily a disadvantage to live in an *Altbau,* because they may have more character and charm than modern buildings. The term may also refer to buildings from the nineteenth century. In most cities they are nicely renovated and restored.

16. *Straßenbahn- und Bushaltestellen* (tram and bus stops). Note how the two compound nouns have been connected to the noun they share. The first of the prefix nouns drops the shared noun *die Haltestelle* and uses a hyphen instead. This prevents repetition of the shared noun. Note that the gender of compound nouns is determined by the second noun *(die Haltestelle): der Bus + die Haltestelle = die Bushaltestelle.*

17. Beware of false friends: *praktisch* not only is "practical," but can mean many different things.

*Der Werkzeugkasten ist wirklich sehr praktisch für kleine Reparaturen.*
The toolbox comes in really handy for small repairs.

*Wie praktisch, dass du ein Telefon dabei hast.*
How convenient that you have a telephone with you.

*Es hat praktisch nichts zu bedeuten.*
It is virtually meaningless.

> *Der praktische Arzt* is a general practitioner and *die praktische Aus-bildung* is a practical training program.

18. The term "floor" can be translated with several different words: *das Stockwerk, der Stock,* or *die Etage.*

19. In Germany the ground floor (or first floor) is referred to as *das Erdgeschoß* (ground level). Therefore *der erste Stock* in Germany is the second floor in America, *der zweite Stock* is the third floor, and so on.

20. The expression *im Laufe* (during the course of) requires the genitive: *im Laufe des Tages, im Laufe des Monats, im Laufe der Woche, im Laufe des Jahres.*

21. *Passen* (to suit, to fit) can be used both literally and figuratively. *Passen* always takes the dative.

*Das passt mir nicht.*
That's not good for me./I can't make it./It doesn't suit me.

*Das Jackett passt mir sehr gut.*
The jacket fits really well.

22. The expression *in Richtung* (literally: in the direction of) requires no article.

*Wir fahren in Richtung Frankfurt.*
We are driving toward Frankfurt.

23. Germany uses the 24-hour clock for official time. 5:30 P.M. is therefore *17:30 Uhr* or *siebzehn Uhr dreißig.* Colloquially, the 12-hour clock is used and 5:30 P.M. is *5:30 abends* or *halb sechs.* Note that the half hour past the hour is not counted backward but forward, and therefore 9:30 is *halb zehn,* and 5:30 is *halb sechs.*

# C. GRAMMATIK UND GEBRAUCH

## 1. *DAS FUTUR* (FUTURE TENSE)

a. The simple future

The simple future is formed with *werden* and the infinitive of the main verb. The auxiliary verb *werden* is conjugated and the infinitive moves to the end of the sentence.

*Ich werde Montag arbeiten.*
I will work on Monday.

*Wir werden uns wiedersehen.*
We will see each other again.

In sentences with modal auxiliaries, the auxiliary takes the last position.

*Er wird umziehen müssen.*
He will have to move.

*Du wirst im Juli einziehen können.*
You will be able to move in July.

Events that are neither determined nor certain are expressed in the future tense.

*Ich werde wahrscheinlich 6 Monate in Frankfurt bleiben.*
I will probably stay 6 months in Frankfurt.

*Ich glaube, wir werden nächstes Jahr umziehen müssen.*
I believe we will have to move next year.

*Er wird in Zukunft vermutlich weniger Zeit haben.*
He will probably have less time in the future.

Adverbs such as *vermutlich* (probably, supposedly) and *wahrscheinlich* (probably) are often used to express the uncertainty of the future action.

b. The present tense as expression of the future

Conversational German often uses the simple present to express the future. This is particularly common for imminent events.

FUTURE
*Nächste Woche werde ich bereits in der Hofgartenstraße wohnen.*

PRESENT
*Nächste Woche wohne ich bereits in der Hofgartenstraße.*
Next week I'll be living at Hofgartenstraße.

FUTURE
*Im September werde ich in Köln sein und kann deswegen nicht kommen.*

PRESENT
*Im September bin ich in Köln und kann deswegen nicht kommen.*
I'll be in Cologne in September, and therefore I won't be able to come.

c. *Werden* as expression of probability

Probability in the present is often expressed with *werden* and the adverb *wohl* (well) or *wahrscheinlich* (probably).

*Wo ist Herr Söhnke? Er wird wohl eine Wohnung besichtigen.*
Where is Mr. Söhnke? (I imagine) He's probably looking at an apartment.

d. *Werden* in other contexts

*Werden* also appears as auxiliary in the passive voice (see Lesson 6).

ACTIVE
*Die Maler streichen die Fenster.*
The painters are painting the windows.

PASSIVE
*Die Fenster werden (von den Malern) gestrichen.*
The windows are being painted (by the painters).

*Werden* is the German equivalent of "to become."

*Er will Rechtsanwalt werden.*
He would like to become a lawyer.

# 2. *DEKLINATIONEN* (DECLENSIONS)

Nouns change the case according to their position in the sentence. The direct object takes the accusative case; the indirect object takes the dative.

NOMINATIVE
*Das Haus ist alt und die Wohnung ist schön.*
The house is old and the apartment is beautiful.

ACCUSATIVE
*Herr Söhnke rief den Vermieter an.*
Mr. Söhnke called the landlord.

DATIVE
*Ich zahle dem Vermieter die Kaution.*
I pay the security deposit to the landlord.

GENITIVE
*Das Haus der Frau Schaller wurde 1910 gebaut.*
Ms. Schaller's house was built in 1910.

Adjectives take on particular endings depending on gender and case of the noun they define. The chart below lists adjectives preceded by the definite articles *der, die, das,* as well as by the indefinite articles *ein, eine, ein.* Note the way the adjective endings change according to the article used.

|  | MASCULINE | FEMININE | NEUTER |
|---|---|---|---|
| NOM. | *der nette Vermieter* | *die schöne Wohnung* | *das alte Haus* |
|  | *ein netter Vermieter* | *eine schöne Wohnung* | *ein altes Haus* |
| ACC. | *den netten Vermieter* | *die schöne Wohnung* | *das alte Haus* |
|  | *einen netten Vermieter* | *eine schöne Wohnung* | *ein altes Haus* |
| DAT. | *dem netten Vermieter* | *der schönen Wohnung* | *dem alten Haus* |
|  | *einem netten Vermieter* | *einer schönen Wohnung* | *einem alten Haus* |
| GEN. | *des netten Vermieters* | *der schönen Wohnung* | *des alten Hauses* |
|  | *eines netten Vermieters* | *einer schönen Wohnung* | *eines alten Hauses* |

*Sie wohnt sehr gerne in der schönen Wohnung.*
She is very happy living in the beautiful apartment.

*Wir warten vor dem alten Haus auf den netten Vermieter.*
We are waiting for the nice landlord in front of the old house.

Adjectives in the plural always take *-en* endings, except when they precede a noun without an article.

|  | MASCULINE | FEMININE | NEUTER |
|---|---|---|---|
| NOM. | *die netten Vermieter* | *die schönen Wohnungen* | *die alten Häuser* |
|  | *nette Vermieter* | *schöne Wohnungen* | *alte Häuser* |
| ACC. | *die netten Vermieter* | *die schönen Wohnungen* | *die alten Häuser* |
|  | *nette Vermieter* | *schöne Wohnungen* | *alte Häuser* |
| DAT. | *den netten Vermietern* | *den schönen Wohnungen* | *den alten Häusern* |
|  | *netten Vermietern* | *schönen Wohnungen* | *alten Häusern* |
| GEN. | *der netten Vermieter* | *der schönen Wohnungen* | *der alten Häuser* |
|  | *netter Vermieter* | *schöner Wohnungen* | *alter Häuser* |

*Schöne Wohnungen sind schwer zu finden.*
  Nice apartments are hard to find.

*Ich habe von netten Vermietern gehört, aber noch nie einen getroffen.*
  I've heard of nice landlords, but never met one.

The negation *kein* (no) and the possessive adjectives (*mein, dein, sein, ihr, unser, euer,* etc.) are so-called *ein*-words, as they take the same endings as the indefinite article.

|  | MASCULINE SINGULAR | FEMININE SINGULAR | NEUTER SINGULAR | PLURAL ALL GENDERS |
|---|---|---|---|---|
| NOM. | *kein* | *keine* | *kein* | *keine* |
| ACC. | *keinen* | *keine* | *kein* | *keine* |
| DAT. | *keinem* | *keiner* | *keinem* | *keinen* |
| GEN. | *keines* | *keiner* | *keines* | *keiner* |

## 3. *KOORDINIERENDE KONJUNKTIONEN* (COORDINATING CONJUNCTIONS)

Main clauses are connected with coordinating conjunctions. The most common are *und* (and), *aber* (but), *oder* (or), *denn* (because, since, as), *sondern* (rather, but instead). Note that the word order with coordinating conjunctions does not change in the second clause.

*Herr Söhnke interessierte sich für die 2½-Zimmer-Wohnung in Parknähe, aber sie war leider schon vermietet.*
  Mr. Söhnke was interested in the 1½ bedroom apartment near the park but unfortunately it was already rented out.

*Die Wohnung ist noch nicht fertig, denn die Fenster werden gestrichen.*
The apartment isn't available yet because the windows are being painted.

Either clause in this construction could stand by itself as an independent sentence.

*Die Wohnung ist noch nicht fertig. Die Fenster werden gestrichen.*
The apartment isn't available yet. The windows are being painted.

If the two main clauses have the same subject, you can improve the style if you drop the repetition of the subject after the conjunction.

*Er verdient viel Geld und (er) hat eine schöne Wohnung.*
He makes a lot of money and (he) has a nice apartment.

*Sie können bis zum 1. Juni warten oder (Sie können) schon vorher einziehen.*
You can wait until June 1st or (you can) move in earlier.

*Tagsüber ist er im Büro und abends (ist er) zu Hause. ***
He is at the office during the day and at home in the evening.

If the subject remains the same, but the verb changes and is preceded by an adverbial construction, it is necessary to repeat the subject to prevent misunderstanding.

*Tagsüber ist er im Büro und abends trifft er den neuen Vermieter. ***
He is at the office all day and in the evening he will meet the new landlord.

If *sondern* is used by itself, the preceding part of the sentence is always negative.

*Er will nicht im Hotel wohnen, sondern eine eigene Wohnung haben.*
He doesn't want to live at a hotel, but wants to have his own apartment.

*Wir fahren nicht nach Italien sondern nach Österreich.*
We are not going to Italy but to Austria (instead).

*Sondern* also appears as part of the expression *nicht nur . . . sondern auch* (not only . . . but also).

*Er hat nicht nur eine neue Wohnung gefunden, sondern auch ein neues Auto gekauft.*
He didn't only find a new apartment, but he also bought a new car.

---

\* Note that both main clauses start with an adverbial construction, *tagsüber* and *abends*. These adverbs affect the word order and the verb moves before the subject.

Two main clauses linked with a coordinating conjunction usually take a comma.

*Er braucht eine Wohnung, denn er will nicht im Hotel wohnen.*
He needs an apartment because he doesn't want to live in a hotel.

If, however, the main clauses have the same subject and are linked by *und* or *oder* no comma is necessary.

*Heute abend schaue ich mir eine Wohnung an und dann bin ich zu Hause.*
Tonight I'm going to look at an apartment and after that I'll be at home.

## 4. *ZAHLEN* (NUMBERS)

The cardinal numbers *(Kardinalzahlen)* are *eins, zwei, drei* (one, two, three), etc. To form the ordinal numbers, add *-te* to all numbers up to and including 19.

*Heute ist der dreizehnte März.*
Today is the thirteenth of March.

*Morgen ist der sechste Dezember.*
Tomorrow is the sixth of December.

Exceptions are:

*eins → erste*          *drei → dritte*          *sieben → siebte*

*Sie sind der siebte Mieter.*
You are the seventh tenant.

All numbers from 20 on take *-ste* endings.

*Wir treffen uns immer am 25. (fünfundzwanzigsten) des Monats.*
We always meet on the 25th of each month.

*Es war ihr fünfzigster Geburtstag.*
It was her fiftieth birthday.

Ordinal numbers take adjective endings.

*Die Wohnung ist im dritten Stock.*
The apartment is on the fourth floor.

*Sie hat immer an fünfter Stelle gestanden.*
She always took fifth place.

## 5. *BEKOMMEN* VERSUS *WERDEN*

The verb *bekommen* (to get, to receive) is a false friend, as it is very often mistaken for the German translation of the English "to become" (*werden*). Please compare:

| | |
|---|---|
| *Herr Gersen bekommt zwei Faxe pro Woche von Frau Albert.* | Mr. Gersen gets two faxes per week from Ms. Albert. |
| *Was bekommen Sie?* | What can I get you? |
| *Was möchten Sie werden?* | What do you want to be? |
| *Seine Tochter ist Buchhalterin geworden.* | His daughter became an accountant. |

When used with the verb *werden,* professions and nationalities do not take articles in German.

*Sie ist Krankenschwester geworden.*
  She became a nurse.

*Nach 25 Jahren hat er sich entschieden, amerikanischer Staatsbürger zu werden.*
  After twenty-five years he decided to become an American citizen.

*Werden* is used in many different expressions.

*Er ist 50 geworden.*
  He turned fifty.

*Wir wurden müde.*
  We became tired.

*Ich bin krank geworden.*
  I became ill.

# D. REIN GESCHÄFTLICH

## 1. APARTMENT HUNTING

In general, Germans tend to move less frequently than Americans. Although many invest in *Immobilien* (real estate) and end up buying *eine Eigentumswohnung* (apartment, condominium) or *ein Eigenheim* (house), it is still rather common to rent an apartment or a house.

Inner-city living is very popular in Germany, Austria, and Switzerland, because there you often find beautifully restored and renovated historical buildings. Apart from the obvious charm of living in a medieval building, inner-city areas are popular because they offer convenient transportation, shopping, and entertainment. Urban areas all over Europe continue to see a large amount of new residents flocking in, as the cities offer employment opportunities and a wide variety of educational facilities. Therefore many major cities suffer from *Wohnungsnot* (housing shortage). It is not unusual to find people, desperate for an apartment, offering large sums as *Belohnung* (reward, finder's fee).

As the search for an apartment can be tedious and time-consuming, many people will contact a *Makler* (rental agent) to find the apartment they are looking for. The rental agent will charge *Maklergebühren* (broker fees), sometimes as much as two or three times the monthly rent.

Tenant rights are protected by law. Tenant rights organizations *(der Mieterbund)* exist all over Germany. As in the United States, certain buildings in urban areas, especially *Altbauten,* are subject to *Mietpreisbindungen* (rent control).

A lot of apartment buildings have *der Hausmeister* (a caretaker) living on the premises. (S)he will clean common hallways and staircases and take care of standard repairs. In some parts of Germany, particularly in Baden-Württemberg, Rhineland-Palatinate, Hesse, and North Rhine-Westphalia, the tenants themselves are required to take turns cleaning common spaces such as hallways and stairs, even though a *Hausmeister* lives on the premises.

All rentals require a *Mietvertrag* (rental agreement), which is available at most stationery and convenience stores. It must be signed by both the tenant and the landlord prior to moving in. Here are a few typical sentences and vocabulary of such a *Mietvertrag.*

*Die Miete ist am 1. des Monats fällig.*
The rent is due on the first of the month.

*Die Miete beträgt monatlich . . . EUR.*
The monthly rent is €. . . .

*Miete und Nebenkosten sind monatlich im Voraus, spätestens am 3. Werktag des Monats, zu zahlen.*
Rent and any additional charges are payable in advance, at the latest on the third business day of the month.

*Die Schönheitsreparaturen trägt der Vermieter/der Mieter.*
Renovation will be made by the landlord/the tenant.

*Nichtzutreffende Teile des Mietvertrages sind zu streichen.*
All parts of the rental agreement that are not applicable are to be crossed out.

*Das Mietverhältnis beginnt am . . . und es läuft auf unbestimmte Zeit.*
The rent period begins on . . . and will run for an indefinite time.

*Die Kündigungsfrist beträgt 3 Monate, wenn seit Überlassung des Wohnraums weniger als 5 Jahre vergangen sind.*
Notice is to be given three months in advance if less than five years have elapsed since the beginning of the rent period.

## 2. MAKING PHONE CALLS

While the telephone is considered a lifeline in Europe as well, personal contact is much preferred. As people do not live and work as far apart from each other in Europe as they do in the U.S.A., people will rather go visit a friend or a business partner personally than negotiate on the telephone. Cellular phones, voicemail, and answering machines, while increasing constantly, are still far less common, and certain automated services, such as requesting bank information over the phone, are unusual.

If you do use the phone, however, try to abide by the following rules. When answering the telephone in Germany, state your last name rather than just saying *Hallo?* And when calling someone, state your name before requesting to be connected or asking for information.

*Berger, guten Tag. Könnten Sie mich bitte mit Frau Schmitt verbinden?*
Berger, good afternoon. Could you please put me through to Ms. Schmitt?

*Handys* (cell phones), so called because they are hand-held, are increasing in popularity every day. Most car rental companies offer *Handy* rentals for a reasonable fee, and it is usually not necessary to order them in advance. Most American cell phones (and their calling plans) cannot be used in Europe. Please check with your provider prior to your trip abroad.

The *Telekom* issues *Telefonkarten* (telephone cards) for use with a *Kartentelefon* (card telephone booth). Contrary to American telephone cards, they are not based on your private or business telephone. They are available to anyone and can be purchased at any post office in several Euro-denominations. When all the units are used up, you simply throw the card away or return it to the post office for recycling.

While *Kartentelefone* are the norm, there are still a few coin-operated phone booths. Credit card telephones are gradually being introduced, and they are already readily available in airports and train stations of major cities.

American long-distance cards can be used in Germany, Austria, and Switzerland. Call the access code on your card and follow the instructions. Should you have problems, call the local operator and ask him or her to connect you to the international operator.

*Können Sie mich mit der internationalen Vermittlung verbinden?*
Can you connect me with the international operator?

*Wie ist die Nummer für die internationale Auskunft?*
What's the number for international directory inquiries?

41

The following is a list of phrases commonly used on the telephone.

*Gruber* (this is a family name).
Hello.

*Firma Schlosser & Co. Schmitt am Apparat.*
Schlosser & Co. Schmitt speaking.

*Roth, guten Tag. Kann ich bitte mit Herrn Schlosser sprechen?*
Roth, good morning. May I speak with Mr. Schlosser?

*Am Apparat.*
Speaking./This is he.

*Moment, ich verbinde.*
One moment, I'll put you through/connect you.

*Tut mir leid, aber die Leitung ist besetzt.*
I'm sorry, but the line is busy.

*Kann er Sie zurückrufen?*
Can he call you back?

*Nein danke, ich rufe später nochmal an.*
No thanks, I'll call back later.

*Frau Heinrich ist nicht da? Kann ich eine Nachricht für sie hinterlassen?*
Ms. Heinrich is not available? May I leave a message for her?

*Richten Sie ihr bitte aus, dass Herr Berger angerufen hat.*
Please tell her that Mr. Berger called.

*Kann sie mich zurückrufen? Meine Nummer ist 76 89 45.*
Can (s)he call me back? My number is 76 89 45.

*Bleiben Sie bitte einen Moment am Apparat.*
Please hold./Just a moment, please.

*Könnten Sie bitte etwas lauter sprechen? Die Verbindung ist sehr schlecht.*
Could you speak a little louder, please? We have a bad connection.

*Bitte wiederholen Sie das nochmal. Ich habe Sie leider nicht verstanden.*
Please repeat. I didn't catch it unfortunately.

*Einen Moment bitte, ich habe nichts zu schreiben.*
Just a second/one moment, please. I don't have anything to write with.

# ÜBUNGEN

1. *Verbinden Sie die folgenden Sätze mit den Konjunktionen „und, oder, aber, sondern, denn".* (Combine the following sentences by using the conjunctions *und, oder, aber, sondern, denn.*)

BEISPIEL: *Sie haben Glück. Die Wohnung ist sehr schön und billig.*
           *Sie haben Glück, denn die Wohnung ist sehr schön und billig.*

    a. *Er will den Vermieter treffen. Er hat die Adresse vergessen.*
    b. *Ich habe eine Wohnung gefunden. Ich kann sofort einziehen.*
    c. *Ich wohne nicht in der Stadt. Ich wohne auf dem Lande.*
    d. *Er kann mit dem Taxi fahren. Er kann den Bus nehmen.*
    e. *Sie sucht eine Wohnung in Heidelberg. Sie wird in Heidelberg studieren.*
    f. *Herr Walker hat eine Wohnung gefunden. Er muss zwei Wochen warten, bis sie fertig ist.*

2. *Übersetzen Sie.*

    a. I will probably buy a house in 2006.
    b. He is in Bonn tomorrow.
    c. When are you coming back?
    d. He will probably fly back to the States in December.
    e. I think I'll be at the hotel on the weekend.

3. *Setzen Sie den Text ins Futur.*

    *Ich brauche viele Möbel. Ich weiß nicht, wo ich Möbel billig kaufen kann, aber Herr Meier hilft mir. Vielleicht wohne ich hier lange. Ich brauche einen Kühlschrank, denn die Wohnung hat keinen. Die Kaution beträgt 2.000 EUR, aber Herr Schaller gibt mir einen Mietvertrag für 6 Monate und sagt, er berechnet nur 1.000 EUR. Er gibt mir einen Schlüssel für die Wohnung und einen Hausschlüssel. Wir besuchen dich in der neuen Wohnung.*

4. *Setzen Sie die richtigen Ordinalzahlen ein.* (Fill in the correct ordinal numbers.)

    a. *Die Miete ist immer am _____ (1) des Monats fällig.*
    b. *Sie wohnt im _____ (7) Stock.*
    c. *Heute ist der _____ (15) August.*
    d. *Das ist das _____ (3) Taxi.*
    e. *Morgen ist der _____ (30). Du musst die Miete zahlen.*
    f. *Meine Großmutter war das _____ (11) Kind von 12.*
    g. *Der Fahrstuhl hält im _____ (6) Stock.*

**5.** *Setzen Sie die richtigen Adjektivendungen ein.* (Fill in the correct adjective endings.)

    a. *Er hat ein _____ (alt) Haus in Bamberg gekauft.*

    b. *Sie will morgen schon in die _____ (neu), _____ (schön) Wohnung ziehen.*

    c. *Wir wollen das _____ (blau) Auto sehen.*

    d. *Haben Sie _____ (modern) Wohnungen in der Innenstadt?*

    e. *Ich wohne in dem _____ (weiß) Haus am Ende der _____ (lange) Straße.*

**6.** *Schreiben Sie den Text neu und benutzen Sie unbestimmte Artikel.* (Rewrite the text with indefinite articles.)

    a. *Der alte Mann stand an der großen Ecke.*

    b. *Vor dem kleinen Fenster stand der weiße Kühlschrank.*

    c. *In den modernen Häusern wohnt er nicht lange, er lebt gerne in der alten Wohnung.*

# LEKTION 3

BANKGESCHÄFTE.   Banking.

## A. DIALOG

*Kathrin Meier und Martin Walker arbeiten beide bei DUS Trading.\**
*Frau Meier begleitet ihren amerikanischen Kollegen, der für einige*
*Monate in Frankfurt bleiben wird, zu einer Filiale der Deutschen*
*Bank.*

FRAU MEIER: **Guten Tag, Herr Weber. Haben Sie einen Moment**
**Zeit?**

HERR WEBER: **Aber selbstverständlich, Frau Meier. Was kann ich**
**für Sie tun?**

FRAU MEIER: **Vielen Dank. Ich möchte Ihnen meinen**
**amerikanischen Kollegen, Herrn Walker,[1] vorstellen.[†]**

*Herr Weber steht auf, gibt Herrn Walker die Hand und begrüßt*
*ihn.*

HERR WEBER: **Willkommen in Frankfurt. Bitte nehmen Sie doch**
**Platz.**

HERR WALKER: **Danke. Ich werde einige Monate in Frankfurt**
**verbringen[‡] und möchte ein Konto eröffnen. Ich brauche**
**Schecks und möchte monatlich[2] etwas Geld auf mein Konto in**
**den USA überweisen.**

HERR WEBER: **Das ist kein Problem. Sie eröffnen am besten ein**
**Girokonto.[3] Beziehen Sie Ihr Gehalt aus Amerika oder werden**
**Sie von der deutschen Zweigstelle der DUS bezahlt?**

HERR WALKER: **Von der deutschen Zweigstelle.**

HERR WEBER: **Prima. Dann wird Ihr Gehalt ja sicherlich jeden**
**Monat automatisch auf Ihr Konto überwiesen. Das Girokonto**
**ist sehr praktisch, denn Sie können alle regelmäßigen**
**Zahlungen, z.B.[4] Ihre Miete, oder die Telefonrechnung, direkt**
**von Ihrem Konto abbuchen lassen.**

HERR WALKER: **Muss ich die nicht per[5] Scheck bezahlen?**

---

\* The *DUS Trading* is a fictional company.

[†] *vorstellen* is a verb with separable prefix (see Lesson 10). Other separable verbs appearing
in this dialogue are *abbuchen, angeben, ausfüllen, abgeben, eingehen, abheben, einrichten,*
*ansprechen.*

[‡] *verbringen* is a verb with inseparable prefix (see Lessons 10 and 14). Other verbs with
inseparable prefix appearing in this dialogue are *eröffnen, überweisen, begleiten, beziehen,*
*bezahlen, berechnen, vergessen, überziehen.*

HERR WEBER: Nein. Sie geben Ihrem Vermieter, oder der Telefongesellschaft einfach Ihre Kontonummer, und dann wird der Betrag per Dauerauftrag[6] von Ihrem Konto abgebucht.

HERR WALKER: Für Daueraufträge berechnen Sie sicher eine Gebühr.

HERR WEBER: Nein, alle Daueraufträge innerhalb der Bundesrepublik[7] sind gebührenfrei.

HERR WALKER: Dann sind Schecks also überflüssig?

FRAU MEIER: Nein, das nicht. Du[8] wirst Sie sicherlich benutzen, besonders wenn du auf Geschäftsreise gehst. Du bekommst Euroschecks für dein Girokonto. Damit kannst du fast überall in Europa bezahlen.

HERR WALKER: Das ist ja praktisch. Jetzt[9] habe ich noch eine Frage. Ich muss nächste Woche 1.000 EUR[10] Kaution an meinen Vermieter zahlen. Er hat mir den Namen seiner Bank und seine Kontonummer gegeben. Was mache ich in so einem Fall?

HERR WEBER: Bei einmaligen Zahlungen gehen Sie einfach[11] in eine unserer Filialen, füllen einen Überweisungsauftrag aus und geben den am Schalter ab. Das Geld geht dann innerhalb eines Geschäftstages auf dem Konto des Empfängers ein.[12]

HERR WALKER: Und ab wann kann ich Geld von meinem Girokonto abheben?

HERR WEBER: Frau Schmitt am Schalter 7 richtet Ihnen gleich ein Girokonto ein.[13] Sie brauchen dafür nur Ihren Pass. Dann können Sie sofort Geld einzahlen und ab morgen abheben.

FRAU MEIER: Und nicht vergessen: die Kontonummer musst du auch der DUS angeben, damit du bezahlt wirst.

HERR WALKER: Kann ich den Dauerauftrag für die Auslandsüberweisungen auf mein amerikanisches Konto schon heute bei Ihnen abgeben?

HERR WEBER: Selbstverständlich. Frau Schmitt wird Ihnen auch dabei[14] behilflich sein.

HERR WALKER: Prima.

HERR WEBER: Hier ist meine Karte. Wenn Sie Fragen haben, rufen Sie mich jederzeit[15] an.

HERR WALKER: Danke. Das war ja einfach. Dein Kollege im Büro machte ein ängstliches Gesicht, als ich ihm sagte, daß wir zur Bank gehen.

**FRAU MEIER: Na, kein Wunder! Er hat sich ein neues Auto gekauft und hat sein Konto weit überzogen.[16] Die Bank hat seine Euroscheckkarte gesperrt.[17]**

---

## TRANSLATION

Kathrin Meier and Martin Walker both work at DUS Trading. Ms. Meier accompanies her American colleague, who will be staying in Frankfurt for a few months, to a branch of the *Deutsche Bank*.

MS. MEIER: Hello, Mr. Weber. Do you have a moment?

MR. WEBER: Of course, Ms. Meier. How can I help you?

MS. MEIER: Thank you. I'd like to introduce you to my American colleague, Mr. Walker.

Mr. Weber rises, shakes Mr. Walker's hand, and greets him.

MR. WEBER: Welcome to Frankfurt. Please, take a seat.

MR. WALKER: Thanks. I'll be staying in Frankfurt for a few months and would like to open a bank account. I will need checks and I'd also like to transfer some money to my account in the U.S.A. on a monthly basis.

MR. WEBER: No problem. The best thing to do would be to open a checking account. Will you receive your salary from America or the German DUS branch?

MR. WALKER: From the German branch.

MR. WEBER: Good. Then you will probably receive your monthly salary by direct deposit. The checking account is very convenient because you can make all regular payments, such as your rent or telephone bill, automatically via standing order from your account.

MR. WALKER: Don't I have to pay these by check?

MR. WEBER: No. You simply give your account number to your landlord, or the telephone company, and the amount is debited from your account on a monthly basis.

MR. WALKER: You probably charge a fee for these direct debits.

MR. WEBER: No, all direct debits within the Federal Republic are free of charge.

MR. WALKER: So checks are unnecessary?

MRS. MEIER: Not quite. You will use them, especially on business trips. You will get Eurochecks with your account and can pay with them almost everywhere in Europe.

MR. WALKER: That's very convenient. I have one more question. Next week I'll have to transfer €1,000 security deposit to my landlord. He has given me the name of his bank and account number. What do I do in such a case?

MR. WEBER: For one-time-only payments, all you have to do is go to one of our branch offices, fill out a transfer form, and hand it to a teller. The amount will go to the recipient's account within one business day.

MR. WALKER: And when can I withdraw money from my account?

MR. WEBER: Ms. Schmitt at position 7 will open the account for you immediately. All you need is your passport. Then you can make a deposit immediately, and you may withdraw money as early as tomorrow.

MS. MEIER: And don't forget to give your account number to the DUS so you'll get paid.

MR. WALKER: May I give you the direct debit for the transfers to my account in the U.S.A. today?

MR. WEBER: Certainly, Ms. Schmitt will assist you with that as well.

MR. WALKER: Great.

MR. WEBER: Here is my card. If you have any questions, please don't hesitate to call me at any time.

MR. WALKER: Thanks. Well, that was easy. Your colleague at the office looked a little worried when I told him we were going to the bank.

MS. MEIER: I'm not surprised! He bought a new car and far overdrew his account. The bank froze his *Euroscheckkarte*.

# B. IN KÜRZE

1. Note that the accusative of *Herr* adds an *-n*. *Der Herr* belongs to the group of masculine *n*-nouns, which have *n*-endings in all cases except the nominative singular. Other such nouns include *der Mensch* (man, mankind), *der Bauer* (the farmer), and *der Architekt* (the architect).

2. *Monatlich* (monthly) is the adjective of *der Monat*. *Das Jahr* (one year), *der Tag* (day), and *die Stunde* (hour) form similar adjectives: *jährlich* (yearly), *täglich* (daily), and *stündlich* (hourly).

3. The *Girokonto* (checking account) is one of the most popular private banking accounts. It allows for frequent bank transfers, withdrawals, and the use of checks without limitation or additional charges.

4. *Z.B.* is an abbreviation of *zum Beispiel* (for example). It is used at the beginning of a list of examples or alternatives. *Z.B.* appears in formal and informal writing as an abbreviation, yet has to be fully pronounced when speaking: *zum Beispiel*.

5. An alternative to *per Scheck* (by check, with a check) is *mit (einem) Scheck* (with a check).

*Kann ich per Scheck bezahlen?*
*Kann ich mit (einem) Scheck bezahlen?*
Can I pay by check?/Do you take checks?

6. *Der Dauerauftrag* is a standing order, a permanent direct debit from one's bank account. If the account holder gives permission, all regular, recurring payments such as rent or loan payments are handled this way.

7. *Die Bundesrepublik (Deutschland),* the Federal Republic (of Germany), has been Germany's official name since 1949. The name was retained after reunification in 1990 for both former East and former West Germany. The name signifies that Germany consists of several *Bundesländer* (federal states).

8. Note that Frau Meier and Herr Walker address each other with the informal *du*. This suggests that the two have known each other in a professional relationship for years.

9. The regular word order in a sentence is subject-verb-object:

*Ich sah Herrn Walker.*
I saw Mr. Walker.

The use of adverbs at the beginning of a sentence reverses the position of subject and verb.

*Jetzt habe ich noch eine Frage.*
Now I still have one more question.

10. German punctuation for currency amounts differs from the American system:

US $24.95          *24,95 EUR*          $1,564.35          *1.564,35 EUR*

The currency used in the European Union is the euro. When the € sign is used in writing, it stands before the amount, i.e., €24,95. It is also customary for Germans to use the abbreviation EUR, which is usually placed after the amount, i.e., 24,95 EUR. Compare:

*Das Buch hat €10, 50 gekostet.*          *Das Buch hat 10,50 EUR gekostet.*
The book cost €10.50.          The book cost 10.50 EUR.

This book will use EUR in German sentences, and the € symbol in English sentences, so that you are used to seeing both.
For more information on the euro, go to www.europa.eu.int/euro.

11. *Einfach* is used as either an adjective or an adverb:

*Das war eine einfache Arbeit.*
That was an easy job.

*Gehen Sie einfach in eine unserer Filialen, und stellen sie dort einen Scheck aus.*
Simply go to one of our branches and write out a check.

Sometimes *ganz* is added as a stress marker.

*Das war ganz einfach*
That was really easy.

12. *Eingehen* is a banking term for the receipt of funds in an account. It is a verb with a separable prefix (see Lesson 10).

13. *Einrichten* is a separable prefix verb (see Lesson 10). *Ein Girokonto einrichten* is a bank term meaning to open a checking account (for someone). In other contexts, *einrichten* means to decorate, to furnish.

14. *Dabei* is a *da*-compound: *da* replaces the object and *bei* is the relevant preposition (see Lesson 6).

15. *Jederzeit* (always, anytime) is a synonym for *immer* (always, anytime). It is frequently used in marketing or promotional material to assure the customer politely that the service is available to him at any time.

16. *Das Konto überziehen* is a bank term meaning to overdraw the account. In other contexts, *überziehen* has an entirely different meaning:

*Ich will den Pullover überziehen.*
I want to put on the pullover.

*Hast du das Bett schon überzogen?*
Did you already put the sheets on the bed?

17. *Sperren* can take on different meanings:

*Die Bank hat alle meine Konten gesperrt.*
The bank froze all my accounts.

*Wir müssen mit der U-Bahn fahren, die Straßen sind gesperrt.*
We have to take the subway; the streets are closed (to traffic).

*Wir haben den Hund ausgesperrt.*
We locked out the dog.

*Der Bankräuber wurde verhaftet und eingesperrt.*
The bank robber was arrested and put in jail.

Note that *einsperren* and *aussperren* are verbs with a separable prefix (see Lesson 10).

# C. GRAMMATIK UND GEBRAUCH

## 1. *MODALE HILFSVERBEN* (MODAL AUXILIARY VERBS)

Modal auxiliary verbs indicate a wish, an ability, urgency, obligation, or permission relevant to the action expressed by the main verb (the verb of action). The modal verb is conjugated and follows the subject. The main verb is used in the infinitive and moves to the end of the sentence.

*Ich muss Herrn Walker 300 EUR überweisen.*
I have to send Mr. Walker €300 by bank transfer.

*Er darf bis zu 300 EUR pro Tag vom Geldautomaten abheben.*
He may withdraw up to €300 per day from the automated teller machine.

Note the position of the modal auxiliary verb and the infinitive in each of the above sentences.

|  | DÜRFEN (MAY) | KÖNNEN (CAN) | MÜSSEN (MUST) | WOLLEN (WANT TO) | SOLLEN (SHOULD) |
|---|---|---|---|---|---|
| ich | darf | kann | muss | will | soll |
| du | darfst | kannst | musst | willst | sollst |
| er/sie/es | darf | kann | muss | will | soll |
| wir | dürfen | können | müssen | wollen | sollen |
| ihr | dürft | könnt | müsst | wollt | sollt |
| sie | dürfen | können | müssen | wollen | sollen |

*Mögen* is used in two different conjugations: indicative and subjunctive. The indicative form of *mögen* is used when stating likes or dislikes. The subjunctive form, on the other hand, is used when stating an intention, a request, or a wish.

### *MÖGEN* (TO LIKE)

| INDICATIVE | SUBJUNCTIVE | INDICATIVE | SUBJUNCTIVE |
|---|---|---|---|
| ich mag | möchte | wir mögen | möchten |
| du magst | möchtest | ihr mögt | möchtet |
| er/sie/es mag | möchte | sie mögen | möchten |

*Ich mag Herrn Weber.*
I like Mr. Weber.

*Ich möchte Herrn Weber kennenlernen.*
    I'd like to meet Mr. Weber.

LIKES/DISLIKES
*Ich mag keine Schlagsahne.*
    I don't like whipped cream.

*Wir mögen Erik sehr gerne.*
    We like Erik very much.

    If the context makes it clear what is meant, the infinitive can be
    omitted (in parentheses).

ABILITY
*Ich kann Russisch (sprechen).*
    I can speak Russian.

*Mit der Euroscheckkarte können Sie sich auch jederzeit Kontoauszüge*
*abholen.*
    With the checking card you are able to obtain account statements
    anytime.

WISH
*Ich möchte morgen nicht arbeiten.*
    I don't want to work tomorrow.

INTENTION
*Er möchte Geld in die USA schicken.*
    He wants to send some money to the U.S.

POLITE REQUEST
*Ich möchte Sie bitten, nicht zu rauchen.*
    I'd like to ask you to refrain from smoking.

NECESSITY
*Muss ich die nicht per Scheck bezahlen?*
    I don't have to pay these by check?

OBLIGATION
*Sie soll mir jeden Monat 50 EUR überweisen.*
    She's supposed to send me €50 each month.

PERMISSION
*Er darf nicht mehr soviel arbeiten, hat sein Arzt gesagt.*
    He is not allowed to work as much anymore, said his doctor.

*Darf ich mehr als 500 EUR abheben?*
    May I withdraw more than €500?

WISH
*Er will Bankangestellter werden.*
He wants to become a bank clerk.

*Wollen Sie schon wieder Urlaub nehmen?*
You want to take a vacation again?

## 2. *KONDITIONALSÄTZE* (CONDITIONAL CLAUSES)*

As in English, conditional subclauses, or *wenn-Sätze* (if-clauses), introduce a condition upon which the main clause depends. If the conditions stated in the subclause present current or future possibilities, i.e., if the conditions are not contrary to fact, the indicative is used.

*Wenn[†] er ein Konto eröffnen will, (dann) muss er seinen Pass mitbringen.*
If he wants to open an account, (then) he has to bring his passport.

Note that, as in English, the main clause can or cannot be introduced by *dann* (then).

*Falls er nicht bezahlen kann, (dann) sperren Sie bitte seine Euroscheckkarte.*
If he can't pay, (then) freeze his checking card, please.

Note that the order of subject and verb is reversed in the main clause, and that the conjugated verb in the conditional subclause moves to the end of the conditional clause.

*Wenn Sie Ihren Ausweis dabei haben, (dann) richtet Ihnen Frau Schmitt am Schalter 7 gleich ein Girokonto ein.*
If you have your ID with you, (then) Ms. Schmitt at position 7 can open an account for you immediately.

In German, several items can be used to introduce conditional subclauses. In formal and business situations, expressions such as *vorausgesetzt, dass* (provided that), *gesetzt den Fall, dass* (in case, given the fact that), *unter der Voraussetzung, dass* (under the condition that), *unter der Bedingung, dass* (under the condition that), and *angenommen, dass* (assuming that) are used more frequently than *wenn* or *falls*.

*Vorausgesetzt, dass sein Gehalt jeden Monat pünktlich auf seinem Konto ist, können wir ihm einen Kredit anbieten.*
Provided that his salary arrives on time each month, we can offer him a loan.

---

* This lesson deals only with conditional sentences that are not contrary to fact. For contrary-to-fact conditions, please refer to Lesson 16.

[†] *wenn* is also used to introduce temporal subclauses (see Lesson 5).

53

It is also possible to use these expressions without the *dass* clause. Please note the change of word order.

*Wir können Ihnen kurzfristig Reiseschecks bestellen, gesetzt den Fall Sie fliegen nächste Woche nach London.*
We can order traveler's checks at short notice, in case you travel to London next week.

*Unter der Voraussetzung, dass* always needs the *dass* clause.

*Unter der Voraussetzung, dass Herr Walker jeden Monat den gleichen Betrag auf sein amerikanisches Bankkonto überweisen will, können wir das automatisch per Dauerauftrag erledigen.*
Provided that Mr. Walker wishes to transfer the same amount each month to his American bank account, we can arrange this transfer as a standing order.

Another way to express a condition in a subclause is by using the modal auxiliary *sollen* in the subjunctive II plus infinitive.

*Sollten Sie noch Fragen haben, so rufen Sie mich bitte jederzeit an.*
Should you have any further questions, please give me a call anytime.

# D. REIN GESCHÄFTLICH

## 1. BANKING IN GERMANY

Germany has the capital markets and credit machinery of any modern economy, including a central banking system, commercial and savings banks, building and loan associations, and special credit institutions. The three largest commercial banks are the *Deutsche Bank, Dresdner Bank,* and *Commerzbank.* Commercial banks primarily serve the investment needs of private industries, engaging in any kind of banking business. Local savings banks operate closely with municipal and regional authorities, contributing greatly to a geographically balanced development of the economy. The credit unions' principal purpose is to promote retail trade, handicrafts, and agriculture.

The *Bundesbank* is the central bank of the Federal Republic of Germany and, like other central banks in member states of the European Union, an integral part of the European system of central banks. Austria's member bank is the *Österreichische Nationalbank.* The main objective of the European Central Bank is to maintain price stability. In doing so, the European Central Bank aims to support the general economic policies effective throughout the European Union. Both the *Bundesbank* and the European central Bank are located in Frankfurt/Main.

## 2. COMMON FORMS OF PAYMENT

Although in the 1980s the use of credit cards became popular, Europeans still use cash far more frequently than Americans. The currency used in Germany, Austria and all other member states of the European Union is the Euro. The Euro (€, EUR) consists of 100 cent, and is available in 7 bills and 8 coins of different denominations. Unlike Germany and Austria, Switzerland is <u>not</u> a member of the European Union, and uses its own currency, the *Schweizer Franken (SF)*, which consist of 100 *Rappen*. In trade and industry, payment of invoices is usually done via *Überweisung* (bank transfer): the client will fill out a debit form, advising his/her bank to transfer x-amount from his/her account to the account xyz of his/her supplier. The supplier will then receive a copy of a *Gutschrift* (credit), notifying him/her of the amount received at his bank. The client keeps a copy of this *Überweisung*—the *Lastschrift* (debit notice).*

All recurring payments of a set amount are transferred via *Dauerauftrag* (standing order). These are arranged by supplying the payment details of the beneficiary to the bank. With regular payments such as telephone bills that vary from month to month, the customer supplies his/her bank details (account number, sorting code, account name, and bank) to the supplying company and authorizes them to debit the customer's account directly. This system guarantees timely payment, and thus saves administrative work involved with late payments.

The *Bundespost* (German Federal Post Office) also offers banking services, such as the *Postgirokonto* (Post Office checking account) and the popular *Postsparbuch* (Post Office savings account). As with *Euroschecks,* the *Postsparbuch* and *Girokonto* are easily accessible throughout most of Europe.

German banks operate an automatic overdraft allowance. Any working person may overdraw the *Girokonto* by at least the amount of his/her monthly salary. The overdraft limit is, of course, determined at the bank's discretion. The interest on overdrafts is significant, but to many people the convenience of having a permanent loan at their disposal makes up for the interest expense.

## 3. BUSINESS TRANSACTIONS

Standard letterheads and invoices differ most significantly from American samples in two ways: References (usually a line directly underneath the address) are always given to provide necessary information to the customer to facilitate an easy match-up of invoices or correspondence. Bank details at the bottom of the page ensure that each customer or business partner knows where, when, and how to effect payment. Other information included at the bottom of the page, such as names of the owners, head offices, and the like, is considered legally significant.

* Please refer to the sample shown on page 56.

Study the following example.
DUS Trading receives the following bill:

FRANKFURT BÜROMATERIAL G.m.b.H.*
Großer Ring 123
69023 Frankfurt a.M.1
Tel 069-44-36-70
Fax 069-44-36-7774

DUS Trading GmbH
z.Hd. Herrn Meier
Alte Allee 21
69022 Frankfurt a.M. 1
RECHNUNG Nr. 4789

| Datum | Ihr Auftrag vom | Auftrag Nr. | Ihr Zeichen | Unser Zeichen |
|---|---|---|---|---|
| 4.5.2003 | 2.3.2003 | 759 | MEI/sil | Baumann |

Wir berechnen Ihnen für die Lieferung von 2 Fotokopier-
geräten, Hersteller Rank Zerox, Marke XL2000
(nach Vereinbarung inkl. Lieferkosten und Installierung),                  7.950, - EUR
sowie für die Reparatur Ihres Telefaxgerätes, Hersteller
Telefunken, Marke XYZ, Gerät Nr. 12367894                                    467,50 EUR
                                                                          8.417,50 EUR
                                        zzgl. 14% MWSt.                    1.178,45 EUR
                                        Gesamtbetrag                       9.595,95 EUR

Zahlbar bei Rechnungseingang.

Wir danken Ihnen für Ihren Auftrag.

| Geschäftsführer: | Hessische Landesbank | Deutsche Kommerzbank | Öffnungszeiten: |
|---|---|---|---|
| Karl-Heinz Müller | Konto Nr. 0879437 | Konto Nr. 048908 | Mo-Fr 08.00-18.00Uhr |
| Inhaber: | BLZ 620 280 760 | BLZ 622 490 720 | Sa 08.00-12.30Uhr |
| Markus Müller | | | |

* The letters *GmbH* are an abbreviation for *Gesellschaft mit beschränkter Haftung* (private limited liability company).

In response to the bill above, DUS Accounts Payable will then fill out the following *Überweisungsauftrag:*

Unterschrift des Auftraggebers

Überweisungsauftrag
durch Frankfurter Bank für Handel & Industrie

Empfänger

Frankfurt Büromaterial GmbH
Konto-Nr. des Empfängers
048908

Bankleitzahl
622 490 720

bei Kreditinstitut
Deutsche Kommerzbank

Betrag: EUR
9.595,95 EUR

Verwendungszweck (z.B. Kunden-Referenznummer - nur für Empfänger)
Rechnung Nr. 4789
Unser Auftrag Nr. 759

Auftraggeber
DUS Trading GmbH/Meier

Konto Nr. des Auftraggebers
444889

# 4. BANK TERMINOLOGY

| | |
|---|---|
| *der Überweisungsauftrag* | bank transfer form |
| *die Lastschrift* | debit (form) |
| *die Gutschrift* | credit (form) |
| *die Buchung* | booking (here: transaction) |
| *die Abbuchung* | debit |
| *zu Ihren Lasten\** | debit on your account |
| *zu Ihren Gunsten* | credit to your account |
| *berechnen* | to charge (interest or fees) |
| *(Geld) überweisen* (+ dat.) | to transfer money |
| *(Geld) anlegen* | to invest money |
| *(Geld) abbuchen* | to debit the account |
| *(Geld) einzahlen* | to pay in, to deposit |
| *(Geld) abheben* | to withdraw |
| *(Scheck) einreichen* | to present a check for payment |
| *(Konto) überziehen* | to overdraw (an account) |
| *der Dauerauftrag* | automatic bank transfer |
| *die Bankleitzahl (BLZ)* | sorting code |
| *der Kontostand* | account balance |
| *der Kontoauszug* | bank statement |
| *das Sparkonto* | savings account |
| *die Sparkasse* | savings and loan |
| *die Anlage* | investment |
| *das Terminkonto* | account with fixed due date |
| *die (Euro-)Scheckkarte* | checking card |
| *die Bearbeitungsgebühr* | bank fee |
| *die Umrechnungsgebühr* | bank charge (for conversion of currency) |
| | |
| *die Rechnung* | invoice |
| *zuzüglich (zzgl.)* | plus, in addition |
| *Mehrwertsteuer (MWSt.)* | value added tax, sales tax |
| *der Gesamtbetrag* | total (amount) |
| *zahlbar* | payable, due |
| *der Rechnungseingang* | receipt of invoice |
| *zahlbar bei Rechnungseingang* | due/payable upon receipt of invoice |
| *zahlbar bei Empfang* | payable upon receipt |
| *der Auftrag* | order |
| *der Auftraggeber* | person authorized to sign on account |
| *das Zeichen* | sign, reference |
| *der Betrag* | amount |
| *die Lieferung* | delivery |

\* *zu Ihren Lasten/zu Ihren Gunsten* are expressions usually found on a bank statement.

| | |
|---|---|
| *das Kreditinstitut* | credit union |
| *die Öffnungszeiten* | opening/business hours |
| *der Verwendungszweck* | here: for, in payment of (otherwise: purpose of use) |
| *nach Vereinbarung* | as agreed |

---

# ÜBUNGEN

---

1. *Bitte beantworten Sie die Fragen zum Text.* (Please answer the questions about the text.)

   a. *Kosten Daueraufträge etwas?*
   b. *Wie lange wird Herr Walker in Frankfurt bleiben?*
   c. *Warum braucht Herr Walker keine Reiseschecks für seine Reise nach London?*
   d. *Wie oft will Herr Walker Geld auf sein Konto in den USA überweisen?*

2. *Übersetzen Sie.*

   a. I would like to open a checking account.
   b. I would like to send some money to my family in the U.S.A.
   c. I would like to transfer €500,75 to a company in Hamburg.
   d. Can you give me a bank transfer form?
   e. I would like to exchange $600 into euros and pay the money into my account.
   f. Can you tell me the account balance?
   g. May I see your passport?

3. *Schreiben Sie die Sätze neu oder stellen Sie eine Frage mit dem Modalverb in Klammern.* (Rewrite the sentences or form a question where indicated using the modal auxiliary in parentheses.)

   BEISPIEL: *Er zahlt die Rechnung nächsten Monat. (können)*
   *Er kann die Rechnung nächsten Monat bezahlen.*

   *Wir nehmen Platz. (dürfen?)*
   *Dürfen wir Platz nehmen?*

   a. *Ich helfe Ihnen beim Ausfüllen des Formulars. (können)*
   b. *Er geht morgen zum Arzt. (sollen)*
   c. *Sie hebt heute nachmittag schon Geld von ihrem neuen Konto ab. (können)*
   d. *Mein Kollege unterschreibt den Überweisungsauftrag (dürfen?)*
   e. *Herr Meier und Herr Walker gehen zur Bank. (wollen)*
   f. *Ich bezahle schon wieder 500 EUR für mein Auto. (müssen)*

**4.** *Benutzen Sie das passende Adverb: leider, selbstverständlich, jetzt, zusätzlich, gestern.* (Use the correct adverb: *leider, selbstverständlich, jetzt, zusätzlich, gestern.*)

BEISPIEL: *Ich treffe Herrn Meier bei der Post. (heute nachmittag)*
*Heute nachmittag treffe ich Herrn Meier bei der Post.*

    a. *Sie bekommen noch eine Euroscheckkarte.*
    b. *Ich weiß, wo die Bank ist, denn Herr Meier hat mir den Weg gezeigt.*
    c. *Ich war nicht im Büro.*
    d. *Er kann Geld abheben, er hat doch 500 EUR eingezahlt.*
    e. *Ich muss unsere Verabredung verschieben, mein Auto ist kaputt.*

**5.** *Verbinden Sie die folgenden Sätze.* (Combine the following sentences.)

BEISPIEL: *Hast du Hunger? Wir können essen gehen. (wenn)*
*Wenn du Hunger hast, können wir essen gehen.*

    a. *Carola bringt mir heute abend den Scheck. Ich kann morgen zur Bank gehen und den Scheck einzahlen. (wenn)*
    b. *Mein Gehalt ist morgen auf meinem Konto. Ich kann dir die 300 EUR zurückzahlen. (wenn)*
    c. *Ich treffe ihn morgen. Ich sage ihm Bescheid. (falls)*
    d. *Sie fahren nach Paris. Sie müssen mir ein Photo von der Notre Dame mitbringen. (wenn)*
    e. *Herr Walker schickt das Geld rechtzeitig in die USA. Es kommt pünktlich an. (wenn)*
    f. *Die Bankgebühren sind sehr niedrig. Ich möchte auch ein Konto bei der Bank eröffnen. (falls)*
    g. *Sein Gehalt geht rechtzeitig ein. Wir bieten ihm einen Überziehungskredit von 8.000 EUR an. (vorausgesetzt, dass)*
    h. *Du kannst mein Auto leihen. Du bist um 23 Uhr wieder zurück. (unter der Bedingung, dass)*

# LEKTION 4
ANTIQUITÄTEN.   Antiques.

## A. DIALOG

*Kirsten Bauer, die einen Antiquitätenladen in Düsseldorf[1] leitet,
besucht Christian Schwert, einen Sammler, von dem sie oft
Antiquitäten kauft. Christian ist gerade von einer Auktion in Zürich
zurückgekehrt.*

KIRSTEN: Hallo, Christian.

CHRISTIAN: Kirsten, da bist du ja! Ich warte schon seit einer
halben Stunde auf dich.

KIRSTEN: Entschuldige die Verspätung.[2] Ich habe keinen
Parkplatz[3] gefunden und musste gegenüber der Post parken.

CHRISTIAN: Komm, ich will dir zeigen, was ich mitgebracht habe.

KIRSTEN: Wie war die Auktion?

CHRISTIAN: Phänomenal. Der ganze Raum war voll. Die
Glanzstücke der Auktion waren dieses Jahr das Porzellan aus
dem 18. Jahrhundert und die Jugendstilmöbel.[4]

KIRSTEN: Die Lampen, die dort hinten in der Ecke stehen, sind ja
schön. Sind die auch aus Zürich?

CHRISTIAN: Möchtest du nicht lieber die Teekannen sehen? Das
sind Raritäten, die du nie wieder findest!

KIRSTEN: Die kosten doch ein Vermögen. Wo hast du die denn
her?

CHRISTIAN: Sammlerstücke aus Familienbestand. Es ist die beste
und vollständigste Sammlung, die ich in den letzten 20 Jahren
gesehen habe.

KIRSTEN: Die blaue Teekanne und die Tassen mit den
Goldhenkeln finde ich am schönsten. Aber die sind bestimmt
sündhaft[5] teuer.

CHRISTIAN: Hast du die Stehlampe gesehen, die hinter dem
grünen Sessel steht? Echt Jugendstil, wahrscheinlich von
1915. Du kannst sie für 400 EUR haben.

KIRSTEN: Ach, du bist ja komplett verrückt.

CHRISTIAN: Nein, ganz im Gegenteil. Jugendstil feiert gerade
wieder ein Comeback.[6]

KIRSTEN: Die kleine Lampe neben dem Sofa passt ja genau zu der, die du mir eben andrehen wolltest.[7]

CHRISTIAN: Liebe Kirsten, ich meine es nur gut mit dir.

KIRSTEN: Ja, ja, ich weiß. Was hast du noch Sehenswertes?[8]

CHRISTIAN: Pfeifen, Tabaksdosen, Krimskrams. Aber die Porzellansammlung ist wirklich ein Juwel.

KIRSTEN: Die wird weggehen wie warme Semmeln. 250 EUR für beide Lampen.

CHRISTIAN: Völlig ausgeschlossen. Hier sind zwei französische Schnupftabakdosen, 1790.

KIRSTEN: Die sehen so ähnlich aus wie die, die ich im Laden habe.

CHRISTIAN: Ach, wirklich?

KIRSTEN: Die Dosen im Laden gefallen[9] mir aber besser.

CHRISTIAN: Hier haben wir eine Leselampe aus der Jahrhundertwende.

KIRSTEN: Das Glas ist viel durchsichtiger als das der Lampe, die ich vorhin gesehen habe.

CHRISTIAN: Schön, nicht wahr?[10] Ein echtes Schmuckstück. Der Ständer ist ganz und gar unbeschädigt. Besser geht's nicht.[11]

KIRSTEN: Wieviel kostet die kleinere Lampe, die auf dem Regal steht?

CHRISTIAN: Ich gebe dir einen guten Preis, das weißt du doch. Wie gefällt dir denn der Schreibtisch, auf dem die Leselampe steht?

KIRSTEN: Der ist mir zu groß.

CHRISTIAN: Der sieht größer aus, als er ist. Und er ist sehr wertvoll.

KIRSTEN: Der ist garantiert[12] doppelt so groß wie meiner und kostet bestimmt dreimal soviel.

CHRISTIAN: Ich gebe dir den Schreibtisch, die Stehlampe und die kleine Lampe für einen unschlagbaren Preis.

KIRSTEN: Den Schreibtisch kannst du behalten. Wie wär's, kannst du mir ein paar Uhren[13] anbieten?

CHRISTIAN: Taschenuhren oder Standuhren?

KIRSTEN: Beides.

*Christian zieht eine Schublade auf, in der alte Taschenuhren liegen.*

KIRSTEN: **Ach, das Beste[14] kommt immer zuletzt.**

CHRISTIAN: **Na komm', du machst immer ein gutes Geschäft bei mir.**

*Kirsten nimmt eine Uhr heraus und klappt den Deckel auf.*

KIRSTEN: **Seit fünf Jahren suche ich schon nach dieser Uhr.**

CHRISTIAN: **Na, also. Ich habe noch etwas besseres, eine Perlmuttuhr von demselben[15] Uhrmacher.**

KIRSTEN: **Du hast immer die besten Sachen.**

CHRISTIAN: **Nein, ich habe nur die besten Kontakte.[16] Die Uhr, die zwei Lampen und der Schreibtisch: 1.400 EUR.**

KIRSTEN: **500 EUR für die Uhr und die Lampen.**

CHRISTIAN: **Na gut, aber nur weil du es bist.**

---

## TRANSLATION

Kirsten Bauer, who manages an antiques store in Düsseldorf, visits Christian Schwert, a collector, from whom she often buys antiques. Christian has just returned from an auction in Zürich.

KIRSTEN: Hello, Christian.

CHRISTIAN: Kirsten, there you are. I've been waiting for you for half an hour already.

KIRSTEN: Sorry I'm late. I couldn't find parking and had to park across from the post office.

CHRISTIAN: Come, I want to show you what I got.

KIRSTEN: How was the auction?

CHRISTIAN: Phenomenal. The room was full. The most remarkable items this year were the china from the eighteenth century and the Art Nouveau furniture.

KIRSTEN: The lamps that are standing in the corner over there are terrific. Are those from Zürich too?

CHRISTIAN: Wouldn't you rather see the teapots? Those are rarities you'll never find again.

KIRSTEN: But they cost a fortune. Where did you get them?

CHRISTIAN: A private family collection. It's the best and most complete collection I have seen in the last twenty years.

KIRSTEN: The blue teapot and cups with the gold handles I find most beautiful. But I'm sure they're terribly expensive.

CHRISTIAN: Did you see the floor lamp standing behind the green armchair? Real Art Nouveau, probably around 1915. You can have it for €400.

KIRSTEN: You're completely out of your mind.

CHRISTIAN: No, quite the contrary. Art Nouveau is making a comeback.

KIRSTEN: The small lamp next to the sofa perfectly matches the big one you tried to lure me into buying a minute ago.

CHRISTIAN: Dear Kirsten, I have only your best interests in mind.

KIRSTEN: Yeah, yeah, I know. What else do you have that is worth seeing?

CHRISTIAN: Pipes, snuffboxes, knickknacks. But the china collection is definitely a gem.

KIRSTEN: It'll sell like hotcakes. €250 for both lamps.

CHRISTIAN: Absolutely out of the question. Here are two French snuff boxes, 1790.

KIRSTEN: They look similar to the ones that I have in the store.

CHRISTIAN: Oh, really?

KIRSTEN: But I like the ones in the store better.

CHRISTIAN: Here we have a reading lamp from the turn of the century.

KIRSTEN: The glass shade is much more transparent than that of the lamp I saw before.

CHRISTIAN: Beautiful, isn't it? A real gem. The stand is completely unscathed. It won't get any better than that.

KIRSTEN: How much is the smaller lamp sitting on the shelf?

CHRISTIAN: I'll give you a good deal; you know that. How do you like the desk the reading lamp is on?

KIRSTEN: It's too big.

CHRISTIAN: It looks bigger than it is. And it's very valuable.

KIRSTEN: I guarantee you it's twice as big as mine in the store and probably costs three times as much.

CHRISTIAN: I'll give you the desk, the floor lamp, and the small lamp for an unbeatable price.

KIRSTEN: You can keep the desk. How about it? Can you offer me some watches and clocks?

CHRISTIAN: Pocket watches or clocks?

KIRSTEN: Both.

Christian opens the desk drawer in which old pocket watches are kept.

KIRSTEN: Always saving the best for last.

CHRISTIAN: Come on, you always cut a good deal with me.

Kirsten picks out one watch and flips open the lid.

KIRSTEN: I've been looking for this watch for five years.

CHRISTIAN: Well, there you go. I have something even better, a mother-of-pearl watch from the same watchmaker.

KIRSTEN: You always have the best pieces.

CHRISTIAN: No, I just have the best connections. The watch, the two lamps, and the desk for €1,400.

KIRSTEN: €500 for the watch and the lamps.

CHRISTIAN: All right, but only because it's you.

# B. IN KÜRZE

1. *Düsseldorf* is the capital of *Nordrhein-Westfalen* (North Rhine-Palatinate). It lies on the banks of the Rhine, close to Duisburg and Essen, in the center of the *Ruhrgebiet* (Ruhr area), an industrial area in the western part of Germany. Düsseldorf is famous for its role in the fashion, design, and advertising industries. The website www.Düsseldorf.de offers valuable information on Düsseldorf.

2. German uses a pronoun phrase instead of a verbal phrase as in English.

*Entschuldige die Verspätung. (familiar)*
*Entschuldigen Sie die Verspätung. (polite)*
   Sorry (that) I'm late. (lit.: Excuse the tardiness.)

3. As most European cities were never designed for automobile traffic, a chronic lack of parking spaces afflicts all inner-city areas. It is not uncommon for people to have to drive around for up to an hour to find parking. Unless you absolutely have to drive, take public transportation when visiting German cities. It will save you time and headaches.

4. *Jugendstil* (Art Nouveau) is an important and prolific style period around the turn of the century. It became very popular again in the 1970s, when much was unearthed and sold on flea markets or by antiques dealers and in estate sales.

5. *Sündhaft teuer* literally means "wickedly expensive" and is a common expression for luxury items that tend to be overpriced, or far too expensive for one's budget.

6. *Das Comeback* is one of several English words that have been adopted into German. Other words include *der Computer, das Marketing, die Publicity, der Cocktail. Ein Comeback feiern* (to celebrate a comeback) can also be expressed as *in sein* (to be in), another English expression adopted into German.

7. *Jemandem etwas andrehen* is a colloquial expression and difficult to translate. It implies selling something under false pretenses.

*Er hat mir seinen alten Fernseher angedreht.*
He tricked me into taking his old TV.

8. *Wert* (worth) is a rather common suffix: *preiswert* (price-worthy), *erwähnenswert* (worth mentioning). *Wert* also appears in other contexts:

*Das ist nicht der Rede wert.*
Don't mention it. (It's not worth talking about.)

9. *Gefallen* (+ dative) literally translates as "to be pleasing to someone." Thus in sentences with *gefallen* the subject is the thing(s) liked, and the person becomes an indirect dative object.

*Das gefällt mir.*
I like that. (It is pleasing to me.)

Another verb that takes a dative construction is *schmecken* (to taste good).

*Dieser Kuchen schmeckt mir aber sehr gut.*
This cake tastes very good.

10. *Nicht wahr* literally means "not true?" and translates into "isn't it?", "don't you think?" or "right?" It is as common as English tag questions.

*Das ist ihr Sohn, nicht wahr?*
That's your son, right?

11. The opposite expression of *Besser geht's nicht.* (It doesn't get any better than that) would be *Schlimmer kann's nicht werden.* (It couldn't be worse.) Note that both expressions use the impersonal *es.*

12. *Garantiert* is the past participle of the verb *garantieren* and is frequently used as an adverb.

*Sie hat garantiert mehr Geld als sie sagt.*
I'm sure she has more money than she says (she does).

13. German uses the word *die Uhr, -en* for any type of time-telling instrument. It distinguishes between different types by making compound nouns such as *die Taschenuhr* (pocket watch), *die Standuhr* (grandfather clock), *die Wanduhr* (wall clock), *die Digitaluhr* (digital clock).

14. Note how the word *das Beste* (the best), originally an adjective, has become a noun. As such it has to be capitalized.

15. German differentiates between *gleich, -e, -er, -es* and *derselbe/dieselbe/dasselbe*. While both are translated as "the same," there is a nuance of difference in meaning. *Gleich* signifies the same type of thing, but a different piece. *Derselbe* signifies something that is absolutely identical.

*Das ist dasselbe Auto, das ich gestern fuhr.*
That's the same car I drove yesterday. (same, identical vehicle)

*Du hast den gleichen Wagen wie ich.*
You have the same car as I. (same make)

16. Although contact and *Kontakt* are used in the same way in German as in English, the word is used in different idiomatic expressions.

| | | |
|---|---|---|
| *Kontakt aufnehmen* | *Ich muss mit der Firma in Singapur Kontakt aufnehmen.* | I have to contact the company in Singapore. |
| *Kontakt haben* | *Haben Sie noch Kontakt zu Sabine Niemann?* | Are you still in touch with Sabine Niemann? |
| *Kontakt abbrechen* | *Nein, sie hat den Kontakt abgebrochen.* | No, she no longer keeps in touch. |
| | *Ich habe guten Kontakt zu meinen Nachbarn.* | I have a great relationship with my neighbors. |

# C. GRAMMATIK UND GEBRAUCH

## 1. *RELATIVSÄTZE* (RELATIVE CLAUSES)

A relative clause is a subordinate clause that gives additional
information about a noun, either subject or object, in the sentence. A
relative pronoun relates to the noun it defines and can never stand by
itself. Unlike in English, German can never omit the relative pronoun.
In a relative clause the verb always moves to the end.

*Der Mann, der den schwarzen Mantel hier vergaß, kommt morgen wieder.*
The man who forgot the black coat is coming back tomorrow.

The relative pronoun changes according to gender and case of the
noun it refers to.

*Die Frau, die im Zimmer steht, hat rote Haare.* (Nominative)
The woman (who is) standing in the room has red hair.

*Der Verkäufer, den Sie ja kennen, ist bei einem Kunden.* (Accusative)
The salesperson (who[m]) you know is visiting a customer.

*Die Firma, der die Bilder gehören, ist in Hamburg.* (Dative)
The company (who[m]) these pictures belong to is in Hamburg.

Dative is used here because *gehören* always takes the dative.

*Der Sessel, dessen Sitz aus grünem Leder ist, steht in der Ecke.* (Genitive)
The armchair whose seat is made of green leather stands in the
corner.

The relative clauses above all relate to the subject of the sentence. If
you form a relative clause relating to the object of the main sentence,
the word order changes. The relative subclause no longer immediately
follows the noun it relates to. Sometimes the verb of the main clause
follows the noun and precedes the relative subclause.

*Ich habe die Lampen gesehen, die du gestern gekauft hast.*
I have seen the lamps (that) you bought yesterday.

*Der Mann, der ja nie Geld hat, hat sich gestern Lampen gekauft, die er nicht
bezahlen kann.*
The man, who never has any money, bought lamps (that) he can't
afford yesterday.

Here is a summary of the relative pronouns:

|  | MASCULINE | FEMININE | NEUTER | PLURAL |
|------|-----------|----------|--------|--------|
| NOM. | der | die | das | die |
| ACC. | den | die | das | die |
| DAT. | dem | der | dem | denen |
| GEN. | dessen | deren | dessen | deren |

## 2. *KOMPARATIV UND SUPERLATIV* (COMPARATIVE AND SUPERLATIVE)

a. Adjectives

Adjectives take an *-er* ending in the comparative, and an *-st-* ending in the superlative.

| ADJECTIVE | COMPARATIVE | SUPERLATIVE |
|-----------|-------------|-------------|
| schön | schöner | schönst- |
| neu | neuer | neuest- |
| groß | größer | größt- |

Adjectives in the comparative and superlative take regular adjective endings depending upon the case and number of the noun they describe.

*Das neuere Auto steht zu Hause in der Garage.*
The newer car is in the garage at home.

*Das ist die schönste Teekanne, die ich je gesehen habe.*
This is the most beautiful teapot I've ever seen.

Most one-syllable adjectives, such as *kalt* or *jung* or *groß,* add an umlaut in the comparative and superlative form.

| ADJECTIVE | COMPARATIVE | SUPERLATIVE |
|-----------|-------------|-------------|
| kalt | kälter | kältest- |
| jung | jünger | jüngst- |
| groß | größer | größt- |

*Der größere Schreibtisch steht in meinem Laden.*
The bigger desk is at my store.

*Ich mag das wärmere Wetter.*
I like the warmer weather.

b.  Adverbs

The comparative of adverbs is formed in the same way as that of adjectives. The superlative is formed by adding the word *am* to precede it and the suffix *-sten*.

*Sein Auto fährt am schnellsten.*
His car drives the fastest.

*Die Stehlampe von 1915 ist am schönsten.*
The floor lamp from 1915 is most beautiful.

If using the verb *sein* either the adjective or the adverb form of the superlative can be used.

*Die Stehlampe ist am schönsten.*
The floor lamp is most beautiful.

*Die Stehlampe ist die schönste.*
The floor lamp is the most beautiful.

c.  Comparative Sentence Structures

When drawing comparisons between two items or two people that are not alike, *als* is used.

*Er fährt ein neueres Auto als sein Vater.*
He drives a newer car than his father.

*Die Lampe ist teurer als die Uhr.*
The lamp is more expensive than the watch.

To make comparisons between objects that are not equal use either *weniger . . . als* (less than) or *mehr . . . als* (more than).

*Sie hat weniger Geld bei der Auktion ausgegeben als Christian.*
She spent less money at the auction than Christian did.

*Die Lampe auf dem Tisch kostet weniger als die Stehlampe.*
The lamp on the table costs less than the floor lamp.

*Ich habe mehr als genug.*
I have more than enough.

*Wir haben mehr Zeit als ihr.*
We have more time than you.

When comparing two equal things or people, *so . . . wie* or *genauso . . . wie* is used.

*Das Auto meines Vaters ist so alt wie ich.*
My father's car is as old as I am.

*Hast du eine rote Teekanne, die so schön ist wie die blaue?*
Do you have a red teapot that is as beautiful as the blue one?

*Der Stuhl ist genauso alt wie das Sofa.*
The chair is just as old as the sofa.

The following adjectives and adverbs have irregular comparatives and superlatives.

| ADJECTIVE | COMPARATIVE | SUPERLATIVE |
|-----------|-------------|-------------|
| *gut* | *besser* | *best-* |
| *gern*\* | *lieber* | *liebst-* |
| *viel* | *mehr*† | *meist-* |
| *hoch* | *höher* | *höchst-* |

*Ich mag Art Deco lieber.*
I prefer Art Deco.

*Er hat dich gern.*
He likes you.

*Er hat am meisten für die Picasso-Zeichnungen bezahlt.*
He paid the most for the Picasso drawings.

*Ich möchte am liebsten nach Australien fahren.*
I would most like to go to Australia.

*Nein, ich möchte lieber an die Ostsee.*
No, I'd rather go to the Baltic.

*Haben Sie noch mehr von diesen Bildern?*
Do you have more of these pictures?

*Sie hat jetzt mehr Zeit.*
She has more time now.

## 3. *DATIVPRÄPOSITIONEN* (DATIVE PREPOSITIONS)

Most prepositions take the accusative (see Lesson 8). Some are two-way prepositions and take either dative or accusative depending on the context in which they are used (see Lesson 7). Relatively few in comparison always take the genitive case (see Lesson 13). Prepositions always taking the dative are:

*BEI* (at)
*Ich war gestern bei einer Auktion.*
I was at an auction yesterday.

---

\* *gern* and its comparative and superlative are used only as adverbs.
† *mehr* never takes adjective endings.

*ZU* (to, at)
*Sie gingen zur\* Post.*
    They went to the post office.

*Ich bin abends immer zu Hause.*
    I'm always at home in the evening.

*Du bist schon zum[†] zweiten Mal hier.*
    You're here the second time already.

*Die Jugendstilmöbel sind z.Zt.[‡] sehr billig.*
    The Art Nouveau furniture is currently very cheap.

*NACH* (after, toward)
*Nach dem Abendessen möchte sie fernsehen.*
    After dinner she wants to watch TV.

*Er fährt nach Köln und dann fliegt er nach Guatemala.*
    He drives to Cologne and after that he'll fly to Guatemala.

*Nach der Arbeit bin ich nach Hause gegangen.*
    After work I went home.

*Er ging um 23 Uhr nach Hause.*
    He went home at 11 P.M.

*AUS* (from)
*Wir kommen aus dem Süden. Und ihr?*
    We are from the South. And you?

*Ich komme gerade aus der Schule.*
    I'm just back from school.

*MIT* (with, by means of)
*Kirsten Bauer hat mit dem Händler verhandelt.*
    Kirsten Bauer negotiated with the dealer.

*Er ist mit der Familie in den Urlaub gefahren.*
    He went on vacation with his family.

*Hier wird mit Erdgas geheizt.*
    We are using natural gas for heating.

*Wir fahren mit dem Auto nach Heidelberg.*
    We are traveling to Heidelberg by car.

*Ich spreche mit dir.*
    I'm talking with you.

---

\* *zu + der = zur.*
† *zu + dem = zum.*
‡ *z.Zt.* (at the moment, currently) is always abbreviated in writing. In conversation it is pronounced *zur Zeit.*

*Kommst du mit mir nach Hause?*
    Are you coming home with me?

GEGENÜBER (opposite)
*Sie hat gegenüber der Bank geparkt.*
    She parked opposite the bank.

VON (from, from . . . to)
*Er kam von der Arbeit.*
    He came from work.

*Vom 17. bis zum\* 19. ist das Büro geschlossen.*
    From the 17th until the 19th the office will be closed.

*Vom Opernplatz bis zur Wohnung ist es nicht weit.*
    It's not far from the Opernplatz to the apartment.

SEIT (for, since)
*Er ist seit drei Wochen in Frankfurt.*
    He has been in Frankfurt for three weeks.

*Seit Januar wohne ich in der neuen Wohnung.*
    I have been living in the new apartment since January.

AUßER (except)
*Ich habe außer den Uhren nichts gefunden.*
    I didn't find anything except the watches.

*War außer dir noch jemand da?*
    Was anybody else there except you?


## 4. *DEMONSTRATIVPRONOMEN* (DEMONSTRATIVE PRONOUNS)

---

Demonstrative pronouns are used to refer to an item or a person that
has previously been mentioned.

*Wie gefällt dir denn der Schreibtisch?*
    How do you like the desk?

*Der ist mir zu groß.*
    It's too big.

*Wie verkaufen sich deine Bilder?*
    How are your pictures selling?

*Die gehen weg wie warme Semmeln.*
    They are selling like hotcakes.

\* *von + dem = vom* and *zu + dem = zum.*

Demonstrative pronouns share the same form as the definite articles, except in the dative plural. Their usage is entirely different. While definite articles always appear in front of the noun, demonstrative pronouns stand by themselves referring to a noun previously mentioned. The repetition of the noun is thus made superfluous. As they often take the first position, they "demonstrate," or emphasize, the noun under discussion. Demonstrative pronouns are far more effective for emphasis than personal pronouns.* Compare:

*Wie gefällt dir der Schreibtisch?*

PERSONAL PRONOUN
*Er gefällt mir nicht.*
I don't like it.

DEMONSTRATIVE PRONOUN
*Der gefällt mir nicht.*
I don't like that one.

# D. REIN GESCHÄFTLICH

## 1. AUCTIONS

An auction, where items are sold by *versteigern* (bidding), is referred to as either *die Auktion* or *die Versteigerung*. Despite the dominance of Sotheby's in London among collectors throughout Europe, most major cities hold auctions, which you will find advertised in collectors' magazines or daily newspapers. While most auctions will do the bidding in the national currency, they are nonetheless international affairs and will accept other currencies, such as the euro (if in Switzerland or other non-EU countries), or the US $. Before you go, check the exchange rate and acceptance of credit cards and other currencies.

Major auction houses are *Dorotheum & Dorotheum Kunst-Palais, Wien; Wiener Kunstauktionen, Wien; Nagel, Stuttgart & Leipzig; Villa Grisebach, Berlin; Bassenge, Berlin; Lempertz, Köln; Fischer, Luzern (Schweiz)*.

## 2. TO BID OR NOT TO BID

The following vocabulary will be helpful at auctions.

| | |
|---|---|
| *bieten* | to bid, in other contexts: to offer |
| *der Interessent* | the interested buyer |
| *der Auktionär* | auctioneer |
| *der Käufer* | buyer |
| *der Höchstbietende* | the highest bidder |
| *der Meistbietende* | the one who bids the most |

* The demonstrative adjectives *dieser, diese, dieses* are dealt with in Lesson 6.

| | |
|---|---|
| *das Gebot* | bid |
| *das Telefongebot* | bid (via telephone) |
| *das Original* | original (artwork, piece) |
| *die Kopie* | copy |
| *die Reproduktion* | reproduction |
| *die Schätzung* | estimate |

After the basic price has been stated, the auctioneer will say:

*Wer bietet mehr?*
Who bids higher/more?

After the last and possibly final bid has been made, the auctioneer will say:

*Zum Ersten, zum Zweiten und zum Letzten/zum Dritten.*
Going, going, gone!

*Das Bild geht an den Käufer zu 1.350 EUR.*
The picture goes to the buyer at €1,350.

If a bid is closed, the auctioneer will say:

*Keine Gebote mehr./Es werden\* keine Gebote mehr angenommen.*
No more bids./No more bids will be accepted.

When negotiating you might need to use any of these phrases:

| | |
|---|---|
| *die Verhandlung* | negotiation |
| *verhandeln* | to negotiate |
| *in Verhandlung stehen mit* | to negotiate with |
| *Wir stehen in Verhandlung.* | We are currently negotiating. |
| *Der Handel ist abgeschlossen.* | The deal went through./The deal closed. |
| *Der Handel ist geplatzt.* | The deal fell through. |
| *Das ist mein letztes Angebot.* | This is my last offer. |
| *Den Preis kann ich nicht bezahlen. Wie können wir uns denn einigen?* | I can't pay that price. How can we come to an agreement? |
| *Können Sie mir ein besseres Angebot machen?* | Can you make me a better offer? |
| *An welchen Preis dachten Sie denn?* | What price were you thinking of? |

\* The passive voice with *werden* is discussed in Lesson 6.

# ÜBUNGEN

**1.** *Verbinden Sie die Sätze mit einem Relativpronomen.* (Combine the sentences with a relative pronoun.)

*BEISPIEL: Kirsten Bauer ist eine Händlerin. Kirsten Bauer hat einen Antiquitätenladen.*
*Kirsten Bauer, die einen Antiquitätenladen hat, ist eine Händlerin.*

   a. *Die Lampe ist sehr alt. Die Lampe steht hinter dem grünen Sessel.*
   b. *Der Auktionär hat viele schöne Uhren. Der Auktionär hat ein Büro am Opernplatz.*
   c. *Die Sessel sind grün. Ich sitze sehr gerne in den Sesseln.*
   d. *Die Wohnung liegt sehr zentral. Ich möchte gerne in die Wohnung einziehen.*
   e. *Herr Hansen will im Winter Ski fahren. Herr Hansen hat kein Geld.*
   f. *Das Hotel liegt weit weg von den Sehenswürdigkeiten. Das Hotel ist billig.*

**2.** *Setzen Sie den richtigen Komparativ oder Superlativ ein.* (Fill in the correct comparative or superlative.)

*BEISPIEL: Kirsten ist 38 Jahre alt. Christian ist 42 Jahre alt.*
*Kirsten ist _____ als Christian. (jung)*
*Kirsten ist jünger als Christian.*

*Die Lampe ist 60 cm hoch. Sie ist 18 cm breit. Die Statue ist 1,45 m hoch. Sie ist 15 cm breit. Die Standuhr ist 2 m hoch.*

   a. *Die Lampe ist _____ als die Statue. (klein)*
   b. *Die Lampe ist _____ als die Statue. (breit)*
   c. *Die Standuhr ist _____ (groß).*

*Die Frau hat eine große Wohnung in München. Sie hat einen Sohn in Innsbruck. Er hat ein großes Haus und einen Garten mit vielen Blumen. Sie hat einen Balkon mit drei Geranien.*

   d. *Der Sohn hat ein _____ Haus als seine Mutter. (groß)*
   e. *Sie hat _____ Blumen als er. (wenig)*
   f. *Ihre Wohnung und ihr Balkon sind _____ als das Haus und der Garten in Innsbruck. (klein)*
   g. *Der Schloßgarten hat die _____ Blumen. (viel)*

**3.** *Setzen Sie den richtigen Komparativ oder Superlativ ein: gerne/lieber/besser/hässlicher/mehr/schneller/höchsten/am besten.*

   a. *Er hat _____ Zeit als früher.*
   b. *Sie geht _____ ins Theater.*
   c. *Markus mag Tennis _____ als Ski fahren.*
   d. *Die alten Möbel gefallen mir _____ als die modernen.*

e. *Ich finde die Ohrringe viel _____ als die anderen.*
f. *Der Ring gefällt mir _____.*
g. *Er ist _____ gefahren als angezeigt und bekam einen Strafzettel.* (traffic citation)
h. *Die _____ Berge der Welt sind im Himalaya Gebirge.*

4. **Benutzen Sie die passende Struktur:** *(genau) so . . . wie; viel . . . als; mehr . . . als; and weniger . . . als.* (Use the suitable structure: *[genau] so . . . wie; viel . . . als; mehr . . . als;* and *weniger . . . als.*)

   a. *Das Buch kostet 75 EUR. Die Uhr kostet auch 75 EUR*
      *Das Buch ist _____.*
   b. *Christian hat sehr viele Antiquitäten. Ich habe weniger.*
      *Christian hat _____ ich.*
   c. *Das antike Sofa ist teuer. Es kostet 10.000 EUR. Die Uhr kostet nur 350 EUR.*
      *Das antike Sofa kostet _____ die Uhr. Die Uhr kostet _____ das Sofa.*
   d. *Ich habe letzten Monat viel Geld verdient. Kirsten hat auch soviel Geld verdient.*
      *Kirsten hat _____ ich.*
   e. *Ich kann mich nicht entscheiden. Die Armbanduhr ist _____ teurer _____ die Kette, aber sie ist schöner.*

5. *Übersetzen Sie*

   a. She was at an antique dealer's yesterday.
   b. I have to go to work.
   c. We are here for the seventh time already.
   d. What did you (singular, informal) negotiate with him?
   e. You (plural, informal) have not called us since your vacation.

6. *Setzen Sie das richtige Demonstrativpronomen ein.* (Fill in the correct demonstrative pronoun.)

   a. *Das Geschirr ist aus dem 18. Jahrhundert. _____ kann ich nicht ersetzen.*
   b. *Der Stuhl gefällt mir. _____ werde ich kaufen.*
   c. *Die Bilder sind sehr schön. Haben Sie _____ neu gekauft?*
   d. *Kennst du den Händler aus Zürich? Nein, _____ kenne ich nicht.*
   e. *Welchem Herrn haben Sie die Uhr gezeigt? _____ in dem grünen Mantel, oder _____ in der Lederjacke?*

# LEKTION 5

ARBEITSSUCHE.   Job Search.

## A. DIALOG

*Susanne Keller hat sich um die ausgeschriebene Position als*
*Assistentin[1] der Hotelleitung des Hotels Stern\* in Hannover[2]*
*beworben.[3] Aufgrund[4] ihrer Bewerbung hat sie ein*
*Vorstellungsgespräch bekommen.*

HERR BERGER: Guten Tag, Frau Keller. Bitte nehmen Sie doch
    Platz.

FRAU KELLER: Danke.

HERR BERGER: Ihr Lebenslauf und Ihre Unterlagen sind ja
    wirklich sehr beeindruckend. Wenn ich mich recht erinnere,
    haben Sie zwei Jahre in Frankreich und ein Jahr in Tschechien
    verbracht.

FRAU KELLER: Ja, das ist richtig. In Paris habe ich im Hotel du
    Nord[†] an der Rezeption gearbeitet und später im Einkauf[5] für
    das Restaurant.

HERR BERGER: Dann sprechen Sie ja sicher sehr gut französisch.

FRAU KELLER: Ja, ich spreche fließend französisch, und ich
    spreche gut genug tschechisch, um mich in jeder Situation
    verständlich machen zu können.[‡]

HERR BERGER: Gut, solche Sprachkenntnisse sind sehr wichtig für
    uns. Sie haben also Hotelkauffrau[6] gelernt und sind dann aber
    gleich in die Gastronomie[7] gegangen.

FRAU KELLER: Ja, damals war es schwer, als Schulabgänger der
    Hotelfachschule[8] eine Anstellung zu finden.[¶]

HERR BERGER: Was haben Sie gemacht nachdem Sie in der
    Gastronomie waren?

FRAU KELLER: Ich habe drei Jahre lang in einem Dortmunder
    Hotel am Frühstücksbuffet und in der Rezeption gearbeitet.
    Während dieser Zeit habe ich in Abendkursen Französisch
    gelernt. Danach bin ich nach Paris gegangen.

---

   \* The hotel name is fictional. Any reference to a hotel of such a name is unintended and
purely coincidental.
   † The hotel name is fictional. Any reference to a hotel of such a name is unintended and
purely coincidental.
   ‡ *um mich verständlich machen zu können* is an infinitive construction with *zu* (see Lesson 11).
   ¶ *eine Anstellung zu finden* is an infinitive construction with *zu* (see Lesson 11).

HERR BERGER: In Ihrem Lebenslauf steht, dass[9] Sie einen Kongress im Hotel du Nord in Paris organisiert haben. Wieviele Teilnehmer waren bei dem Kongress?

FRAU KELLER: Wir hatten über 120 Kongressgäste allein[10] im Hotel. Zusätzlich fanden täglich mindestens 4 Seminare und Gesprächsrunden in den Versammlungsräumen des Hotels statt. Insgesamt waren bis zu 300 Kongressteilnehmer pro Tag im Hause.

HERR BERGER: Das war ja eine große Aufgabe für Sie.

FRAU KELLER: Tja, das kann man wohl sagen.[11] Aber es hat mir großen Spaß[12] gemacht. Als der Kongress beendet war, wurde* ich in die Leitung des Restaurants befördert.[13]

HERR BERGER: Und warum haben Sie diese Position verlassen?

FRAU KELLER: Ich bekam ein Angebot von einem großen deutschen Konzertveranstalter, für den ich als Organisatorin von Großveranstaltungen gearbeitet habe. So kam ich auch nach Prag.

HERR BERGER: Wie lange waren Sie dann in der Position?

FRAU KELLER: 8 Jahre.

HERR BERGER: Darf ich fragen, warum Sie wieder in ein Hotel möchten?

FRAU KELLER: Längerfristig sehe ich meine Karriere in der Hotel- und nicht in der Konzertbranche.

HERR BERGER: Was ist Ihr Ziel in einem Haus wie dem Hotel Stern?

FRAU KELLER: Ich möchte im Management eines Drei-Sterne-Hotels arbeiten, um die Attraktivität des Hauses eventuell zu verbessern.

HERR BERGER: Ist es im Moment nicht attraktiv?

FRAU KELLER: Doch, selbstverständlich, aber man könnte mit internationalen Tourneeveranstaltern zusammenarbeiten, die eine regelmäßige Anzahl von Hotelgästen garantieren können. Meine Kontakte könnten dabei sehr hilfreich sein.

HERR BERGER: Ja, das ist eine recht interessante Idee. Haben Sie irgendwelche Fragen?

FRAU KELLER: Ja. Suchen Sie eine Assistentin, die stellvertretend für die Hotelleitung arbeitet, oder jemanden, der eigenständig bestimmte Bereiche übernimmt?

---

* *wurde . . . befördert* is passive tense (see Lesson 6).

HERR BERGER: **Wir sind ein renommiertes[14] Haus mit über 100 Betten und möchten unser Führungsteam erweitern. Und dafür brauchen wir einen Mitarbeiter oder eine Mitarbeiterin, die das Hotelpersonal leitet.**

FRAU KELLER: **Das ist genau die Position, die ich suche.**

HERR BERGER: **Gut. Ich habe noch drei weitere Bewerbungen auf dem Tisch, die in Frage kommen. Sobald ich eine engere Auswahl getroffen habe, gebe ich Ihnen natürlich Bescheid.[15]**

FRAU KELLER: **Gut. Ich bedanke mich, Herr Berger.**

HERR BERGER: **Nichts zu danken.[16] Auf Wiedersehen.**

---

### TRANSLATION

Susanne Keller applied for the advertised position as Assistant Manager of the Hotel Stern in Hanover. Because of her application she got an interview.

MR. BERGER: Hello, Ms. Keller. Please have a seat.

MS. KELLER: Thanks.

MR. BERGER: Your résumé and papers are really very impressive. If I remember correctly, you spent two years in France and one year in the Czech Republic.

MS. KELLER: Yes, that's correct. In Paris I worked in the Hotel du Nord at the reception desk, and later in purchasing in the restaurant.

MR. BERGER: I'm sure you speak French very well.

MS. KELLER: Yes, I speak French fluently, and I speak Czech well enough to be able to make myself understood in every situation.

MR. BERGER: Good, these language skills are very important for us. You were trained in the hotel business but then you went straight into catering.

MS. KELLER: Yes. Back then it was hard for graduates from the hotel business school to find employment.

MR. BERGER: What did you do after you left the restaurant?

MS. KELLER: I worked in a Dortmund hotel at the breakfast buffet and at the reception for three years. During that time I also studied French in evening school. Afterward I went to Paris.

MR. BERGER: According to your résumé you organized a convention at the Hotel du Nord in Paris. How many participants were present at the convention?

MS. KELLER: We had 120 convention participants at the hotel alone. Additionally at least four seminars and panels took place in the conference rooms each day. Altogether up to 300 convention members gathered at the hotel daily.

MR. BERGER: That was quite a big responsibility for you.

MS. KELLER: Yes, that's for sure. But I enjoyed it very much. When the convention was over, I was promoted to the management of the restaurant.

MR. BERGER: Why did you leave that position?

MS. KELLER: I got an offer from a leading German concert promoter where I worked as an organizational coordinator of large size events. This is how I came to go to Prague.

MR. BERGER: For how long did you work in this position?

MS. KELLER: Eight years.

MR. BERGER: May I ask why you want to return to a hotel now?

MS. KELLER: In the long run I envision my career in a hotel and not in the concert business.

MR. BERGER: What is your goal in a hotel such as the Hotel Stern?

MS. KELLER: I would like to work in a three-star hotel to improve the attractiveness of the hotel.

MR. BERGER: Is it not attractive at the moment?

MS. KELLER: Yes, of course, but one could work with international tour promoters who can guarantee a regular number of hotel guests. My contacts could be very valuable.

MR. BERGER: Yes, that's a rather interesting idea. Do you have any questions?

MS. KELLER: Yes. Are you looking for an assistant who works as a representative of the management, or someone who takes charge independently in certain areas?

MR. BERGER: We are a renowned hotel with more than 100 beds and we'd like to expand our management team. Therefore we need an employee to supervise the staff.

MS. KELLER: That's exactly the position I'm looking for.

MR. BERGER: Fine. I have three more applications for consideration on my desk. As soon as I have short-listed the applicants, I'll get back to you.

MS. KELLER: Good. Thank you, Mr. Berger.

MR. BERGER: My pleasure. Good-bye.

# B. IN KÜRZE

1. As most German job titles have a male and a female form, advertisers are using rather unorthodox methods to remain politically correct in their use of language: you will often see spellings such as *AssistentIn* or *HoteldirektorIn, Assistent/in* or *Hoteldirektor/in,* and *Assistent(in)* or *Hoteldirektor(in).* All these forms are meant to signify that male and female applicants are equally welcome.

2. *Hannover,* founded in 1241, is the capital of *Niedersachsen* (Lower Saxony). Parts of its historic architecture have been preserved and restored. A favorite tourist attraction is the *Orangerie,* the gallery of the former castle in *Hannover-Herrenhausen.* More information on this city is available at www.Hannover.de.

3. *Sich bewerben* (to apply) is a reflexive verb and can be used with two prepositions: *um* and *bei.*

*Sie hat sich um die Stelle als Managerin beworben.*
She applied for the managerial position.

*Sie hat sich bei Schneider & Co. beworben.*
She applied with Schneider & Co.

4. *Aufgrund* (because of) always takes the genitive case.

5. *Der Einkauf* can refer to the purchasing department of a company, a retail store, or a restaurant, as well as purchases in general.

*Sie arbeitet im Einkauf des neuen Hotels.*
She works in the purchasing department of the new hotel.

*Meine Einkäufe gestern waren sehr billig.*
My purchases yesterday were very cheap.

The word appears in several compounds, such as *das Einkaufszentrum* (shopping center), and as a verb, *einkaufen (gehen)* (to go shopping). *Einkaufen* is a separable prefix verb.

6. *Die Kauffrau* (f), *der Kaufmann* (m) is an official title in German for individuals with a degree in commerce. Individuals usually concentrate on a particular field: *Einzelhandelskaufmann, -frau* (retail business man/woman). In some cases, German distinguishes between male and female job titles by adding *-mann* or *-frau.*

7. *Die Gastronomie* refers to the catering trade or the restaurant business as a whole.

8. *Die Hotelfachschule,* a vocational school for the hotel business, is a secondary school comparable to a business college.

9. *Dass* (that) introduces a subordinated clause modifying or defining the main clause. *Dass* and other subordinate conjunctions are discussed in Lesson 11.

10. *Allein* here is used as a stress marker much like "alone" in English. Please note the different word order: in German the stress marker appears before the noun it refers to.

*Allein im April hatten wir mehr als 50.000 EUR Umsatz.*
In April alone we had more than €50,000 in sales.

11. *Das kann man wohl sagen* (You're right about that/You can say that again/That's for sure) is an idiomatic expression used quite frequently. Another similar expression adds a little more colloquial color: *Das kannst du laut sagen* (lit.: You can say that aloud).

12. The letter *ß* is known as *sz* (pronounced: s-tset). It often replaces double *s* after long vowels or dipthongs: *der Fuß*, but *der Fluss; der Spaß*, but *das Fass*.

13. *Befördern* (to be promoted) is mostly used in the passive voice with *werden*.

*Ich bin befördert worden. Toll, nicht wahr?*
I just got promoted. Great, isn't it?

Both the noun *(die Beförderung)* and the verb *(befördern)* also appear in other contexts:

*Die öffentlichen Verkehrsmittel befördern 15 000 Reisende pro Monat.*
Public transportation transports 15,000 travelers per month.

*Ich habe ihn zur Tür hinausbefördert.*
I kicked him out.

14. *Renommiert* (renowned) is only used with establishments, such as hotels, schools, companies, and organizations. In reference to people use either of the following expressions:

*Er hat einen sehr guten Ruf.*
He enjoys an excellent reputation.

*Sie ist eine anerkannte Expertin auf dem Gebiet.*
She is a renowned expert in that field.

15. *Bescheid geben* (to let someone know, to get back to someone)

*Er gibt mir morgen Bescheid.*
He's going to let me know tomorrow.

*Bescheid wissen* (to know, to have been informed)

*Frag ihn, er weiß hier über alles Bescheid.*
Ask him, he knows everything (around here).

16. *Nichts zu danken* (lit.: [You have] Nothing to thank [me for]) is a common phrase best translated as "You're welcome." or "My pleasure."

# C. GRAMMATIK UND GEBRAUCH

## 1. *ZEITAUSDRÜCKE* (TIME EXPRESSIONS)

a. Subordinate Conjunctions and Prepositions

German has as many time expressions as English. Most of them are subordinate conjunctions just as "since," "when," and "as" are in English: the subclause they introduce cannot stand on its own. If the sentence starts with the main clause, the word order is regular:

Subject + verb + object, conjunction + subject + object + verb.

*Ich besuchte den Zoo, als ich in London war.*
I visited the zoo when I was in London.

If the sentence starts with the subordinated clause, the word order is as follows:

Conjunction + subject + (object or pronoun) + verb, verb + subject + object (+ verb).*

*Während ich auf Bernd warte, kocht Sybille das Essen.*
While I am waiting for Bernd, Sybille is cooking dinner.

*Während ich auf Bernd wartete, hat Sybille das Essen gekocht.*
While I was waiting for Bernd, Sybille was cooking dinner.

The following is a list of the most common temporal conjunctions. Some of them can also appear as prepositions.

*WÄHREND* (during/while)
*Er las ihren Lebenslauf, während sie wartete.*
He read her résumé while she waited.

---

* The verb is divided only if it consists of a conjugated auxiliary and a participle or infinitive. In the case of a single verb it remains in the first position. The verb is also split into stem and prefix in the case of separable verbs (see Lesson 10 for separable verbs).

As a preposition, *während* is always followed by the genitive.

*Während der Zeit lernte sie Französisch.*
    During that time she learned French.

*SOBALD* (as soon as)
*Sobald ich mit der Schule fertig bin, gehe ich arbeiten.*
    As soon as I have completed school, I will go and work.

*SOWIE* (as soon as)
*Sowie ich von ihr höre, rufe ich Sie an.*
    As soon as I hear from her, I will call you.

*SEIT/SEITDEM* (since)
*Seit ich hier arbeite, verdiene ich viel Geld.*
    Since I've been working here, I've been making a lot of money.

*Ich kann bei Musik besser lernen. Seitdem ich das weiß, mache ich große Fortschritte.*
    I can study better with music (playing). Since finding out about that,
    I'm making great progress.

Note that English requires the present perfect continuous form in
sentences with "since." German takes the simple present tense after
*seit* or *seitdem.* As a preposition, *seit* is always followed by dative (see
Lesson 4).

*Seit dem Vorstellungsgespräch hat sie jeden Tag auf einen Anruf gewartet.*
    Since her interview she has been waiting for a phone call every day.

*NACHDEM* (afterward)
*Nachdem er gegessen hatte, ging er ins Kino.*
    After he had eaten, he went to the movies.

It is common to find the past perfect in the subordinated clause
introduced by *nachdem,* followed by the simple past in the main clause.
As *nachdem* already refers to the time when an action has been
completed, it never takes the present or the future tense.

*Nachdem ich gegessen habe, gehe ich spazieren.*
    After I've eaten, I (will) go for a walk.

Although both *wenn* and *als* mean "when," they are not interchangeable. *Wenn* is used with the present and past tenses to describe recurrent events or habits. It can also describe singular acts in the present tense.

*Wenn Frau Keller morgen vom Hotel Stern zurückkommt, rufe ich dich an.*
When Ms. Keller comes back from Hotel Stern tomorrow, I'll call you.

*Wenn ich nach Frankreich fahre, trinke ich immer Wein.*
When(ever) I go to France, I always drink wine.

Note that *wenn* is also used to introduce conditional subclauses (see Lessons 3 and 16).
*Als,* on the other hand, is used with time expressions relating to a specific moment or action in the past that only occurred once. Since *als* always speaks of a singular event, it is always followed by the past or perfect tense.

*Als ich 1990 in Paris war, habe ich im Hotel du Nord übernachtet.*
When I was in Paris in 1990, I stayed at the Hotel du Nord.

BEVOR (before)
*Bevor er ins Bett ging, putzte er sich die Zähne.*
Before he went to bed, he brushed his teeth.

b.  Word order with time adverbs and time expressions

Time adverbs and time expressions are usually placed after the conjugated verb.

*Er geht abends schwimmen.*
He goes swimming in the evening.

Time adverbs can stand at the beginning of the sentence to stress the time factor. Note the inversion of verb and subject.

*Vorgestern hatten wir Schnee.*
We had snow the day before yesterday.

*Heute scheint die Sonne.*
Today the sun is out.

The most common are:

| | | | |
|---|---|---|---|
| *früher* | earlier | *später* | later |
| *heute* | today | *jetzt* | now |
| *gestern* | yesterday | *vorgestern* | the day before yesterday |
| *morgen* | tomorrow | *übermorgen* | the day after tomorrow |
| *im Moment* | at the moment | *zur Zeit (z.Zt.)* | at present |

## 2. *PERSONALPRONOMEN* (PERSONAL PRONOUNS)

Personal pronouns are used to determine the person speaking or spoken of. Depending on their function in the sentence, personal pronouns appear in the nominative (subject), accusative (direct object) or dative (indirect object).

| | | |
|---|---|---|
| NOMINATIVE | *Ich habe angerufen.* | I called. |
| ACCUSATIVE | *Sie hat mich gesehen.* | She saw me. |
| DATIVE | *Er hat mir geholfen.* | He helped me. |

| NOMINATIVE | ACCUSATIVE | DATIVE |
|---|---|---|
| ich *(I)* | mich *(me)* | mir *(me)* |
| du *(you)* | dich *(you)* | dir *(you)* |
| er *(he)* | ihn *(him)* | ihm *(him)* |
| sie *(she)* | sie *(her)* | ihr *(her)* |
| es *(it)* | es *(it)* | ihm *(it)* |
| wir *(we)* | uns *(us)* | uns *(us)* |
| ihr *(you)* | euch *(you)* | euch *(you)* |
| sie *(they)* | ihnen *(them)* | ihnen *(them)* |
| Sie *(you-formal)* | Sie *(you)* | Ihnen *(you)* |

If a sentence includes both indirect and direct object and both appear as nouns, the indirect object (dative object) precedes the direct object (accusative object).

*Ich habe der Frau den Lebenslauf per Post geschickt.*
I have sent the woman the résumé by mail.

When both indirect and direct objects are pronouns, the accusative precedes the dative.

*Ich habe es ihr per Post geschickt.*
I have sent it to her by mail.

When one object is a noun and the other a pronoun, the pronoun (accusative or dative) precedes the noun.

*Ich habe es dem Direktor per Post geschickt.*
I have sent it to the director by mail.

*Ich habe ihm das Paket per Post geschickt.*
I have sent him the package by mail.

## 3. *REFLEXIVE VERBEN* (REFLEXIVE VERBS)

As in English, some verbs relating to the self require reflexive pronouns.

*Wir freuen uns auf das Wochenende.*
We are looking forward to the weekend.

Note that the reflexive pronouns are identical to the accusative form of the personal pronouns except in the third person singular and plural and the formal *Sie*. The reflexive pronoun *sich* for the formal *Sie* is not capitalized.

*Sie haben sich bei uns beworben.*
You have applied with us.

| PERSONAL PRONOUN | REFLEXIVE PRONOUN |
|---|---|
| ich | mich *(myself)* |
| du | dich *(yourself)* |
| er | sich *(himself)* |
| sie | sich *(herself)* |
| es | sich *(itself)* |
| wir | uns *(ourselves)* |
| ihr | euch *(yourselves)* |
| sie | sich *(themselves, yourself)* |
| Sie | sich *(yourself)* |

*SICH UNTERHALTEN* (to talk)
*Wir haben uns gestern 3 Stunden lang unterhalten.*
We talked for three hours yesterday.

*SICH FREUEN* (to be glad)
*Ich freue mich. Ich habe Arbeit gefunden.*
I am glad I found work.

*SICH RASIEREN* (to shave)
*Er hat sich nachmittags rasiert.*
He shaved in the afternoon.

*SICH SONNEN* (to sunbathe)
*Wir lagen am Strand und haben uns gesonnt.*
We lay on the beach and sunbathed.

*SICH VERIRREN* (to get lost)
*Sie hat sich verirrt.*
She got lost.

*SICH ERINNERN* (to remember)
*Du erinnerst dich sicher an mich, ich habe dein Auto repariert.*
    Surely you remember me, I repaired your car.

*SICH ENTSCHULDIGEN* (to apologize)
*Ihr wollt euch bei uns entschuldigen? Das ist aber nett.*
    You want to apologize to us? That's nice.

    Reflexive verbs also appear in reciprocal action. The English "each other" or "one another" is the German *gegenseitig.* Compare:

*SICH ANSEHEN* (to look at, to view)
*Wir sahen uns die Bilder im Louvre an.*
    We looked at the pictures in the Louvre.

*Wir sahen uns (gegenseitig) an und fingen an zu lachen.*
    We looked at each other and started to laugh.

    Reflexive pronouns take the dative case when another object appears in the sentence. Most of these verbs relate to the body or to a piece of clothing. Compare:

*SICH KÄMMEN* (to comb)
*Ich kämme mich.*
    I'm combing myself.

*Ich kämme mir die Haare.*
    I'm combing my hair.

*SICH AUSZIEHEN* (to undress, to take off clothing)
*Du ziehst dich aus.*
    You are undressing.

*Du ziehst dir den Mantel aus.*
    You are taking off your coat.

    Note that one's own clothing or parts of the body usually don't take possessive pronouns* in German.

*Er wäscht sich die Hände.*
    He is washing his hands.

*Ich wasche mir die Haare.*
    I'm washing my hair.

    Certain reflexive verbs are always followed by the dative:

---

* Please refer to Lesson 8 for a complete discussion of possessive pronouns.

*SICH WÜNSCHEN* (to wish)
*Ich wünsche mir einen Fotoapparat zum Geburtstag.*
    I wish (to get)/have asked for/want a camera for my birthday.

*SICH KAUFEN* (to buy)
*Er hat sich ein neues Auto gekauft.*
    He bought (himself) a new car.

*SICH HELFEN* (to help oneself)
*Ich kann mir nicht helfen, ich liebe Schokolade.*
    I can't help it (myself); I love chocolate.

*SICH LEISTEN* (to afford)
*Das kannst du dir doch nicht leisten.*
    Come on, you can't afford it.

*SICH ANZIEHEN* (to dress oneself)
*Wir wollen uns 'was anderes anziehen.*
    We want to get changed.

*SICH KÄMMEN* (to comb)
*Kämm dir mal die Haare.*
    Comb your hair.

*SICH PUTZEN* (to clean oneself)
*Die Katze putzt sich den ganzen Tag.*
    The cat is cleaning itself all day.

*SICH LASSEN\** (to leave, to let)
*Lass dir Zeit, das muss heute nicht fertig werden.*
    Take your time; it doesn't have to be done today.

# D. REIN GESCHÄFTLICH

## 1. EDUCATION IN GERMANY

All public education in Germany is free. Most kindergartens, schools, and universities are public, although some specialized private schools exist. Pre-school children enter a *Kindergarten* (kindergarten) at three or four years of age. At age six all children have to be enrolled in the *Grundschule* (elementary school). *Grundschulen* run from the first to the fourth grade in most states (in some from first to sixth grade).

    The German school system offers three different types of schools

* *lassen* is discussed in detail in Lesson 17.

90

after the fourth (or sixth) grade. The *Hauptschule* (to ninth grade) prepares students for apprenticeships in trade and crafts; the *Realschule* (to tenth grade) prepares students for administrative careers; and the *Gymnasium* (to thirteenth grade) grants the *Abitur,* the diploma necessary to attend university.

While the grade point average at the end of the *Grundschule* determines which of the three schools the child would be most suitable for, no one is barred from attending the school of his/her choice. If the grade point average of a student changes for the better or the worse, a change of schools is recommended.

The so-called *zweite Bildungsweg* (second educational way) offers adults who did not stay in school long enough to get the *Abitur* but wish to go to university the opportunity to attend *die Abendschule* (special evening schools) to obtain the diploma.

Vocational training is greatly encouraged and very popular. The public school system and businesses and industry work together successfully to make a unique combination of on-the-job training and academic schooling possible. After having completed at least nine years of schooling, the student can choose to learn a craft. (S)he will work for three years as an *Auszubildender* (apprentice) in a business of his/her choice, while attending the appropriate *Berufsschule* (vocational school) twice a week. The time needed to attend school is granted by the employer. During this time an *Auszubildender* receives a salary, and at the end of the three years, the graduate will receive a *Gesellenbrief,* a diploma certifying that (s)he is qualified to work in the chosen field. After at least one more year of working as a *Geselle,* the student can return to school, study business administration, and apply to take the exam for the *Meisterbrief.* Only as a *Meister* (lit.: master) are you entitled to go into business by yourself.

Vocational schools for administrative or technical professions require a *Realschulabschluss.* Certain professional schools require the applicant to have completed the twelfth grade. These vocational schools are called *Fachhochschulen* (*Fach*—course, subject, major; *-hochschulen*—high schools), offering academic schooling with an emphasis on practical training.

All *Abiturienten* (graduates of the *Gymnasium*) who want to attend university have to apply for admission. Since in an average year more students apply than *Studienplätze* are available, a quota system called *Numerus Clausus,* which admits only students of a high grade point average, was introduced for all popular subjects such as medicine, law, and languages. Often it is hard even for those fulfilling the *Numerus Clausus* to find a *Studienplatz* in their subject or at the university of their choice. Therefore transfers from subject to subject and university to university are rather frequent.

Foreign students are readily accepted at German schools and universities. As the curriculum may vary significantly between countries, the school will conduct an evaluation test to place the student at the appropriate level within the German school system. Foreign college or university students can request an application from any German university. Admission requirements may vary, yet most universities require proof of sufficient knowledge of the German language. Many German universities offer exchange programs with American universities. Contact the *DAAD—Deutscher Akademischer Austauschdienst* (German Academic Exchange Service) for details.

## 2. EMPLOYMENT OPPORTUNITIES

Any citizen of any country that is not a member of the European Community who wishes to seek and accept permanent employment in Germany must register with the local municipal authorities and obtain *die Aufenthaltserlaubnis* (residence permit) and *die Arbeitserlaubnis* (work permit) from the local *Ausländeramt* (Alien Registration Office).* While Germany's strong economy offers employment opportunities in any given field, finding the right job may be difficult, with language problems and registration requirements complicating the job search. The local *Arbeitsamt* (employment office) may be able to assist you in your job search, as may any of the private employment agencies or headhunters. The classifieds in the Saturday edition of the local newspaper, as well as of a few larger national papers such as the *FAZ (Frankfurter Allgemeine Zeitung), Die Zeit,* and *Die Süddeutsche Zeitung,* are always worth a look.

## 3. EMPLOYMENT BENEFITS

Germans are very particular when it comes to legal matters. It is most unusual in Germany to start work of any kind without an employment contract signed by the prospective employee and countersigned by the employer. Although most employment contracts are standardized, they are open to negotiation. Payment as well as all employment benefits discussed with your prospective employer will be and should be part of this contract.

Most employees in Germany get at least eighteen days of *bezahlten Urlaub* (paid vacation) per year, the minimum as stipulated by law. Twelve days can be taken consecutively, and the rest upon negotiation with the employer. Paid vacation excludes the numerous *Feiertage* (public and religious holidays), raising the amount of paid time off to

---

* Employees of a foreign employer can work for such an employer in Germany up to two months without a work permit, as long as they do have a residence permit. The following employees also do not need a work permit to work in Germany because they represent a legal entity: a managing director *(Geschäftsführer)* of a limited liability company *(Gesellschaft mit beschränkter Haftung),* an executive officer *(Vorstandsmitglied)* of a stock corporation *(Aktiengesellschaft),* general partners of a general commercial partnership *(offene Handelsgesellschaft),* and certain members of other partnerships and managerial employees who have the general power of representation *(Prokura).*

much more than in the U.S.A. Because of either the *Tarifvertrag* (union agreement) or seniority with the company, most Germans have much more vacation than the required eighteen days: the average is around twenty-four days per year.

Most employees in both the private and the public sector receive *Urlaubsgeld* (an additional daily payment for vacation days), and a *13. Monatsgehalt* (thirteenth month's salary) as a Christmas bonus.

*Überstunden* (overtime) are compensated either by time off, as is common in administrative positions, or by overtime pay, as is common in production. Overtime is paid at an hourly rate plus 25 percent, on weekends plus 50 to 100 percent. The overtime rate is set in the union-negotiated *Tarifvertrag*.

Health insurance is mandatory in Germany. Each employee has to have his/her own insurance arranged, through either a private carrier or a public health insurance group. The employer and the employee split the costs 50%:50%. The payment is made directly by the employer, and the employee's share is deducted from the paycheck.

During pregnancy an employee is entitled to *Schwangerschaftsurlaub* (maternity leave) six weeks prior to and eight weeks after the birth of her child. During maternity leave the employee continues to receive her full salary. This period is extended by another eighteen months, which can be taken by either parent *(der Mutterschafts-* or *Vaterschaftsurlaub)*. During this period the parent receives *Erziehungsgeld* (child-raising expenses), the amount of which is proportional to prior earnings. After the eighteen months have expired, the employer has to guarantee the position for another eighteen months.

# 4. JOB APPLICATIONS

Your language skills will be an important factor in your job search. While most Germans speak English, proficiency in German will almost certainly be a requirement for any position in any company. Being able to respond to *die Stellenanzeige* (employment ad) or *die Stellenausschreibung* (job announcement) with the proper application materials in German is an absolute must.

## A CLASSIFIED EMPLOYMENT AD

Wir suchen eine(n) AssistentIn für unser Führungsteam im

### HOTEL STERN

Der/die passende KandidatIn sollte zwischen 30 und 40 Jahre alt sein, mind. 5 Jahre Hotelerfahrung, sowie hervorragende Sprachkenntnisse in mind. einer europäischen Sprache mitbringen. Bewerbungen mit Lebenslauf u. Lichtbild bitte an Herrn Hartmut Berger,

### Hotel Stern

Am Kleinen Stern, 33052 Hannover.
Wir bitten von tel. Anfragen abzusehen.

We are looking for an assistant for our management team at

### HOTEL STERN

The suitable candidate should be between thirty and forty, and have at least five years of hotel experience and excellent knowledge of at least one European language. Address applications with résumé and photo to Hartmut Berger,

### Hotel Stern

Am Kleinen Stern, 33052 Hannover.
No calls, please.

Note that the ad asks for a photo to be sent with the résumé. This is common practice throughout Europe and not considered discriminatory.

The application materials required may vary, yet *der Begleitbrief* (cover letter) and *der Lebenslauf* (résumé) are standard. While it was common in the past to submit a *handgeschriebenen Lebenslauf* (handwritten résumé in prose), a typewritten *tabellarischer Lebenslauf* (itemized résumé) is now common practice.

94

# A COVER LETTER

*Susanne Keller*
*Marienplatz 15*
*30518 Hannover*

*02.02.2004*

*Hotel Stern*
*z. Hd. v. Herrn Berger*
*Am Kleinen Stern 3*
*3052 Hannover*

*Sehr geehrter Herr Berger,*

*in Antwort auf Ihre Anzeige in der Hannoveranischen Post vom 27.01.2004, möchte ich mich hiermit um die ausgeschriebene Position bewerben.*

*Wie Sie aus beiliegendem Lebenslauf ersehen können, verfüge ich über mehrjährige Hotelerfahrung im Management, sowie über hervorragende Fremdsprachenkenntnisse.*

*Ich würde mich über die Gelegenheit eines persönlichen Gesprächs sehr freuen und hoffe, bald von Ihnen zu hören.*

*Hochachtungsvoll,*

*Susanne Keller*

*Anlage*

# TRANSLATION

February 2, 2004

Susanne Keller
Marienplatz 15
30518 Hanover

Hotel Stern
Attn.: Mr. Berger
Am Kleinen Stern 3
3052 Hannover

Dear Mr. Berger,

In reference to your advertisement in the *Hannoveranische Post* of January 27, 2004, I would like to apply for the position advertised. As you will see from the enclosed résumé, I have many years of managerial experience in the hotel business as well as excellent language skills.

I would greatly appreciate the opportunity to meet you personally and look forward to hearing from you soon.

Sincerely,

Susanne Keller

Enc.

# A RÉSUMÉ

*LEBENSLAUF*
Persönliche Daten
Name: *Susanne Keller*
Familienstand: ledig
*geb. 04.05.1966 in Augsburg*

Wohnort:

*Marienplatz 15
30518 Hannover
Tel. 89 54 32 6*

Schulausbildung
*1972–1978 Grundschule Zehlendorf, Berlin
1978–1983 Realschule Wilmersdorf, Berlin*

Berufsausbildung & Berufliche Tätigkeit

*1984–1987 Hotelfachschule Berlin und 6 Monate
    Praktikum im Hotel Am Flughafen
1991–1994 Sprachenschule für Erwachsene
    (Französisch)
1987–1989 Kellnerin/Buchhalterin im Restaurant
    Mövenpick am Großen See
1989–1992 Rezeption, Hotel am Markt,
    Dortmund
1992–1994 Einkauf für das Restaurant,
    Hotel du Nord, Paris
1994–2003 Organisation, Deutsche Konzert
    Agentur, Hamburg*

Zusätzliche Berufserfahrung:
*Organisatorin des deutschen Handelskongresses
    1992 im Hotel du Nord, Paris
Management des Restaurants, Hotel du Nord, Paris
Konzertveranstalterin in Prag (2001–2002)*

Besondere Fähigkeiten und Kenntnisse:

*Sehr gute Französischkenntnisse
Gute Tschechischkenntnisse
Weiterbildung in den Programmiersprachen
    Basic and Pascal*

## Annotation

*Lebenslauf* résumé
*Persönliche Daten* personal data

marital status: *ledig* single; *verheiratet*
married; *geschieden* divorced; *getrennt*
separated
*geb.* = abbreviation of *geboren* D.O.B.

*Wohnort* residence, *wohnhaft in*
residing at

*Schulausbildung* schooling, education

*Berufsausbildung* professional training,
*berufliche Tätigkeit* employment history
*Praktikum* practical training

*Sprachenschule* language school

*Kellnerin* waitress, *Buchhalterin*
accountant
*Rezeption* reception

*Einkauf* purchase

*zusätzliche Berufserfahrung* additional
professional experience

*Konzertveranstalterin* concert promoter

*Besondere Fähigkeiten und Kenntnisse*
special skills and experience
*Kenntnisse* here: command

*Weiterbildung* additional training

# ÜBUNGEN

**1.** *Übersetzen Sie und beantworten Sie die Fragen.*

    a. Why did Ms. Keller go to the Hotel Stern?
    b. What did she do in Dortmund?
    c. Where did she work in Paris?

**2.** *Setzen Sie das richtige Personalpronomen ein.* (Fill in the correct personal pronoun.)

*BEISPIEL: Er hat _____ (ich) gesehen, als ich nach Hause kam.*
      *Er hat mich gesehen, als ich nach Hause kam.*

    a. *Wir haben _____ (Sie) gesagt, dass der Zug spät ankommt.*
    b. *Er gab _____ (ich) ein Blatt Papier.*
    c. *Kann ich _____ (Sie) helfen?*
    d. *Du hast _____ (ich) ein Buch mitgebracht?*
    e. *Er hat _____ (sie) eine Tasse Kaffee gekocht.*

**3.** *Setzen Sie das richtige Reflexivpronomen ein.* (Fill in the correct reflexive pronoun.)

*BEISPIEL: Sie haben _____ beworben, Frau Berger.*
      *Sie haben sich beworben, Frau Berger.*

    a. *Nach dem Bad musst du _____ abtrocknen.*
    b. *Wir freuen _____, dass die Sonne schien.*
    c. *Bitte melden Sie _____ bei mir, wenn Sie wieder zurück sind.*
    d. *Als er _____ rasierte, hat er _____ geschnitten.*
    e. *Ihr habt _____ erst Montag gemeldet.*
    f. *Ich habe _____ die Hände gewaschen.*
    g. *Er hat _____ ausgezogen.*
    h. *Sie haben _____ geirrt, Frau Keller!*
    i. *Du musst _____ den Mantel ansehen.*

**4.** *Setzen Sie „wenn" oder „als" ein.* (Fill in *wenn* or *als*.)

*BEISPIEL: Ich sah den Rhein zum ersten Mal, _____ ich Basel besuchte.*
      *Ich sah den Rhein zum ersten Mal, als ich Basel besuchte.*

    a. *_____ das Telefon klingelt, stehe ich immer auf.*
    b. *_____ du das letzte Mal hier warst, hast du den Regenschirm vergessen.*
    c. *_____ ich noch in New York wohnte, bin ich oft im Central Park spazieren gegangen.*
    d. *_____ der Bus kam, war es 17 Uhr 33.*
    e. *_____ die Sonne untergegangen ist, muss ich draußen das Licht über der Garage anmachen.*

**5.** *Formulieren Sie Sätze mit den Konjunktionen in Klammern.* (Form sentences using the conjunctions in parentheses.)

BEISPIEL: *Ich wohne in Dresden. Ich gehe oft ins Museum. (seitdem)*
*Seitdem ich in Dresden wohne, gehe ich oft ins Museum.*

   a. *Er hat das Abendessen gekocht. Er geht ins Theater. (sobald)*
   b. *Ich warte auf meine Eltern. Ich lese ein Buch. (während)*
   c. *Wir haben drei Bewerber ausgewählt. Wir rufen Sie an. (sobald)*
   d. *Ich war schon im Kino. Der Film fing an. (bevor)*
   e. *Das Vorstellungsgespräch war beendet. Ich ging eine Tasse Tee trinken. (nachdem)*

# LESESTÜCK 1 (Reading Section 1)

*CAFÉ UND STAMMTISCH*

Während die Schweiz bekannt ist für ihre hervorragenden[1] Köche und deren vielseitige Delikatessen, so sind Deutschland und Österreich bekannt für Kaffee und Kuchen jeder Art. Man trifft sich an Wochenenden bei schönem Wetter im Café oder zu Hause auf der Terrasse[2] zu Kaffee und Kuchen. Dieser Tradition zuliebe gibt es unzählige[3] Straßencafés in jedem Ort, und Kaffeehäuser am See, an der Küste oder an Ausflugszielen[4]. Im Sommer herrscht[5] dort überall Hochbetrieb.[6]

Ein regelmäßiges[7] Treffen von älteren Damen wird oft als Kaffeeklatsch[8] oder Kaffeekränzchen[9] bezeichnet. Obwohl junge Leute oft über diese Tradition der älteren Generation schmunzeln,[10] treffen sie sich genauso gerne in Cafés, um sich im Kreise ihrer Freunde zu unterhalten.

Cafés wurden schon vor 100 Jahren zu beliebten Treffpunkten[11] der Künstler, Literaten und Studenten. Berühmte Cafés aus der Zeit der Jahrhundertwende und den 20er Jahren waren das Café Central und das Café Schwarzberg in Wien, sowie das Café Kranzler und Café Central in Berlin, das, wie auch das berühmte Romanische Café in Berlin, im Krieg zerstört[12] wurde. Die Wiener Kaffeehäuser sind noch erhalten,[13] und man kann sich dort bei Sachertorte und Kaffeehausmusik die Künstlerszene[14] der vergangenen Jahre gut vorstellen.

Diese Oasen der Gemütlichkeit[15] dienten besonders denen, die kein Geld hatten, da sie dort stundenlang bei einer Tasse Kaffee sitzen konnten, ohne zum Zahlen oder zum weiteren Verzehr[16] aufgefordert zu werden. Das ist auch heute noch so. Viele Cafés haben nach wie vor ihre Stammkunden,[17] die tagein tagaus für ihren Kaffee und eine kleine Mahlzeit dort einkehren. Manchmal hat der Stammkunde auch einen Stammtisch,[18] der für ihn durch ein »Reserviert" Zeichen freigehalten wird.

Eine ähnliche Stammtischtradition gibt es in Biergärten,[19] Kneipen[20] und Weinstuben.[21] Eine Gruppe von Gästen kann sich ihren Stammtisch für einen bestimmten Abend in der Woche, jeden Freitagabend z. B., reservieren lassen. Sie treffen sich dort regelmäßig, trinken Wein oder Bier, diskutieren die wichtigsten politischen Ereignisse, oder unterhalten sich über Sport. Manchmal spielen die Stammkunden auch Karten, wie Skat oder Rommee. In Weinstuben oder Kneipen ist der Stammtisch oft durch ein kleines Wappen[22] gekennzeichnet. Es ist ein ungeschriebenes Gesetz,[23] dass sich außer den Stammkunden niemand an diesen Tisch setzen darf, selbst dann nicht, wenn er frei ist.

# VOKABELN (VOCABULARY)

1. *hervorragend* — excellent, fine
2. *die Terrasse* — terrace, deck, patio
3. *unzählig* — innumerable, numerous
4. *das Ausflugsziel* — (weekend trip) resort, point of interest
5. *herrschen* — to rule
6. *der Hochbetrieb* — rush hour, busy season
7. *regelmäßig* — regular
8. *der Kaffeeklatsch* — coffee gossip
9. *das Kaffeekränzchen* — coffee circle
10. *schmunzeln* — to smirk, to smile
11. *der Treffpunkt* — meeting point, meeting place
12. *zerstören* — to destroy
13. *erhalten* — to preserve
14. *die Künstlerszene* — art scene
15. *die Gemütlichkeit* — comfort, coziness
16. *der Verzehr* — (food) consumption
17. *der Stammkunde* — regular, best (customer)
18. *der Stammtisch* — table for the regulars
19. *der Biergarten* — beer garden
20. *die Kneipe* — pub, bar
21. *die Weinstube* — wine bar, restaurant (in a wine region)
22. *das Wappen* — coat of arms
23. *das ungeschriebene Gesetz* — unwritten law

# LEKTION 6

VEREINTES BERLIN.   Unified Berlin.

## A. DIALOG

*Ein amerikanischer Architekturstudent besucht Berlin[1] und wird*
*von einer Bekannten durch die Stadt geführt.*

MARINA KRAUSE: Unser Besuch in der Akademie und der
   Kunstbibliothek[2] war für dich bestimmt interessant.

GARY RODRIGUEZ: Klar,[3] die alten Entwürfe von Mies van der
   Rohe, Gropius und Taut[4] sind faszinierend. Ich muss auch
   noch ins Bauhaus-Archiv.[5]

MARINA: Morgen sehen wir uns die Hufeisensiedlung[6] in Britz[7] an.

GARY: Die wurde 1925 gebaut, nicht wahr?

MARINA: Ja, genau. Gefällt dir diese Bauweise?

GARY: Nicht so sehr. Aber immer noch besser als diese anonymen
   Mietshäuser aus den 50er Jahren. Es gibt[8] in Berlin einfach
   zuviele Bauten aus der Zeit.

MARINA: Na ja, Berlin war nach dem Krieg total zerstört.

GARY: Das stimmt. Fahren wir jetzt zur Spreeinsel?[9]

MARINA: Ja.

GARY: Sind die langen, breiten Alleen Paradestraßen aus der
   Kaiserzeit?[10]

MARINA: Ja, die hier um den Großen Stern wurden z.T.[11] schon
   vom Großen Kurfürsten[12] für die Jagd angelegt.

GARY: In Berlin wurde gejagt?

MARINA: Natürlich, im 17. Jahrhundert wurden im Tiergarten[13]
   Wildschweine und Rehe gejagt. Darum heißt der Tiergarten
   auch „Tiergarten."

GARY: Das kann man sich gar nicht vorstellen.

MARINA: Heute ist das natürlich nur ein großer Park, die „grüne
   Lunge" der Stadt sozusagen.[14] Sieh mal, da vorne ist das
   Brandenburger Tor und dahinter fängt Unter den Linden[15] an.

GARY: Lass mich raten, das Brandenburger Tor wurde von
   Langhans[16] gebaut, stimmt's?

101

MARINA: Ja, stimmt. So, nun sind wir auf der Spreeinsel. Hier stand das alte Stadtschloss.[17] Es war völlig zerstört und wurde dann abgerissen. Dieses moderne Gebäude hier wurde zu DDR Zeiten gebaut. Das war der Palast der Republik.

GARY: Soll das Stadtschloss wieder aufgebaut werden?

MARINA: Es besteht schon Interesse daran, aber wie so oft fehlt im Moment noch das Geld.

GARY: Wie schade.

MARINA: Komm, ich will dir was zeigen. Wir gehen jetzt ins Nikolaiviertel.

GARY: Steht da nicht das älteste Gebäude Berlins?

MARINA: Richtig, die Nikolaikirche aus dem 13. Jahrhundert. Und der Gendarmenmarkt ist auch nicht weit.

GARY: Und da steht Schinkels[18] Schauspielhaus und der Französische und der Deutsche Dom.[19]

MARINA: Früher war der Gendarmenmarkt einfach ein Marktplatz.

GARY: Oh ja, ich habe mal ein Bild gesehen, da kamen die Kähne aus dem Spreewald[20] in die Stadt und die Leute verkauften Fische und Obst.

MARINA: Im Nikolaiviertel wurde der alte Stadtkern restauriert. So wurde aus einem alten Viertel wieder ein neues Wohnviertel im Zentrum der Stadt.

GARY: Ja, das ist ganz wichtig für die Infrastruktur.

MARINA: Diese alten Wohnviertel nennt man Kiez.[21] Kreuzberg und Prenzlauer Berg[22] sind die bekanntesten.

GARY: Aha.

MARINA: Hier, das wollte ich dir zeigen. Schau mal, da drüben. Ein Leierkastenmann![23]

---

## TRANSLATION

An American student of architecture is visiting Berlin and is shown through town by an acquaintance of his.

MARINA KRAUSE: I assume our visit at the academy and art library were of interest to you.

GARY RODRIGUEZ: Certainly, those old drawings by Mies van der Rohe, Gropius, and Taut are fascinating. I have to see the Bauhaus-Archive as well.

MARINA: Tomorrow we'll go and see the Horseshoe Development in Britz.

GARY: That was built in 1925, right?

MARINA: Correct. Do you like this style?

GARY: Not really. But they're still a lot better than those anonymous tenement buildings from the 1950s. There are simply too many buildings from that time in Berlin.

MARINA: Well, Berlin was completely destroyed after the war.

GARY: That's true. Are we going to the Spreeinsel now?

MARINA: Yes.

GARY: Are these long, wide boulevards from imperial days?

MARINA: Yes, some of these here around the Große Stern were already laid out by the Great Elector for his hunting trips.

GARY: Hunting in Berlin?

MARINA: Of course, during the seventeenth century wild boar and deer were hunted in the Tiergarten. That's why the Tiergarten is called "Tiergarten."

GARY: That's hard to imagine.

MARINA: These days it is just a large park, of course, a "green lung" for the city, so to speak. Look, the Brandenburg Gate is just ahead and Unter den Linden starts just beyond it.

GARY: Let me guess; the Brandenburg Gate was built by Langhans; am I right?

MARINA: Yes, that's right. So now we're on the Spreeinsel. This is where the old city castle was. It was totally destroyed and then torn down. This modern building right here was built during GDR times. It was the Palace of the Republic.

GARY: Are they planning to rebuild the city castle?

MARINA: They want to, but as usual there's no money at the moment.

GARY: That's too bad.

MARINA: Come, I want to show you something. We're now going into the Nikolai quarter.

GARY: Isn't that where the oldest building in Berlin is?

MARINA: Right, the Nikolai church from the thirteenth century. And the Gendarmenmarkt isn't far either.

GARY: That's where Schinkel's Theater and the French and German cathedrals are.

MARINA: In the old days the Gendarmenmarkt was just another marketplace.

GARY: Oh yes, I saw a picture of that once. Barges from the Spree forest came into the city and people were selling fish and fruit.

MARINA: In the Nikolai quarter the old city center was restored. Thus an old quarter was turned into a new residential area again right in the center of town.

GARY: That's really important for the infrastructure.

MARINA: These old residential districts are called Kiez. Kreuzberg and Prenzlauer Berg are the best known.

GARY: I see.

MARINA: Here, that's what I wanted to show you. Look, over there. An organ-grinder!

# B. IN KÜRZE

1. Berlin is the largest city in Germany with well over 3½ million inhabitants. Between 1945 and 1989 Berlin was divided into four sectors: the British, American, and French sectors were part of West Germany, and the Russian sector was the capital of East Germany. Between 1961 and 1989 East and West Berlin were divided by the wall. During its occupation and division, West Berlin was considered a "free" island in the midst of a socialist East Germany. After reunification, Berlin was re-elected as the capital of reunited Germany. Go to www.Berlin.de for comprehensive information on Germany's capital.

2. *Die Akademie,* or *die Akademie der Künste* (the Academy for the Arts), is a cultural exhibition center concentrating on twentieth-century art and architecture. *Die Kunstbibliothek* is part of the *Staatliche Museen Preußischer Kulturbesitz* (State Museums of Prussian Cultural Possessions), the large local group of art, historical, ceramics, and photo museums in Berlin.

3. *Klar* literally means "clear" and is used in informal conversation to express agreement. The expression is best translated as "of course," "obviously," or "naturally."

4. Mies van der Rohe (1886–1969) was a world-renowned architect and the last director of the *Bauhaus* group of designers, artists, and architects. The *Bauhaus,* which was formed by Walter Gropius (1883–1969), was dissolved when Hitler came to power. Most of the architects and designers fled Germany, and some of them, like Mies van der Rohe, resettled in the U.S.A. The Taut brothers, Bruno (1880–1938) and Max (1884–1967), were architects and became important modern urban designers. Both were forced to flee the Nazi regime.

5. *Das Bauhaus-Archiv* is a museum and archive in Berlin organizing exhibitions commemorating the numerous artists and designers of the *Bauhaus* from 1919 to 1933.

6. *Die Hufeisensiedlung* (the Horseshoe Development) by Bruno Taut and Martin Wagner is a public housing complex built between 1925 and 1931, exemplary for its modern definition of comfortable and space-efficient living for the working class.

7. *Britz* is a district in the south of Berlin.

8. *Es gibt* (there is, there are) is always singular as it can only be used with the impersonal *es* (it) or *das* (that). The past tense is *es gab* (there was, there were).

9. *Die Spree,* the river running through Berlin, forms an island in the center of town, *die Spreeinsel*. It is also often referred to as the *Museumsinsel* since it houses five historic museums and other historic buildings.

10. *Die Kaiserzeit* is the imperial time of Prussia after 1871. After the end of the Franco-Prussian War and the formation of a Greater Germany under Chancellor Otto von Bismarck, *Kaiser Wilhelm I* was declared Emperor of Germany in 1871. The *Kaiserzeit* officially ended in 1918, when *Kaiser Wilhelm II* abdicated.

11. *Z. T.* is the abbreviation of *zum Teil* (partly). Like *z. B.* (Lesson 3), *z.T.* is always pronounced fully and frequently abbreviated in writing.

12. *Der Große Kurfürst* was the title given to the Elector or the Electoral Prince *Friedrich Wilhelm,* who governed Berlin-Brandenburg during the seventeenth century. He was the great-grandfather of *Friedrich der Große* (Frederick the Great).

13. *Der Tiergarten* literally means "the animal garden" and is now a major park in the center of Berlin, subdivided by boulevards that meet like beams of a star in the center at *der Große Stern* (Great Star), a traffic circle with the *Siegessäule* (victory column) in the middle.

14. You will often hear Germans or Austrians refer to their city parks as *grüne Lungen* (green lungs), expressing the need for recreational areas for the urban population.

15. *Unter den Linden* (lit.: Under the Linden Trees) is a famous boulevard leading up to the former castle. Many historic buildings as well as fashionable stores and restaurants line the street. During the nineteenth century and early twentieth century it was famous as a popular promenade, a status it has reacquired after lying dormant between 1961 and 1989, when *Unter den Linden* was located in East Berlin.

16. The Brandenburg Gate was built in 1788–1791 by Carl Langhans d. Ä. (short for *der Ältere,* "the elder," 1732–1808) as a free reinterpretation of a gateway within the Acropolis of Athens.

17. *Das Stadtschloss* (city castle) was destroyed during WWII, and the remaining walls were torn down by the GDR to make room for new government buildings. It had been the primary castle for the imperial family during the eighteenth and nineteenth centuries. Other imperial castles are *Schloss Charlottenburg* in Berlin and *Sanssoucis* in Potsdam.

18. Karl Friedrich Schinkel (1781–1841), whose neoclassical design became a trademark for stately grandeur, was an architect of churches, as well as imperial and public buildings in Berlin.

19. *Der Französische Dom* (built between 1701 and 1705) and *der Deutsche Dom* (built between 1701 and 1708) are cathedrals that stand opposite and mirror each other in design and construction.

20. *Der Spreewald* (the Spree forest) is a densely forested area outside Berlin. It is a favorite tourist attraction for day trips and offers boat rides and festivities where locals display their costumes.

21. *Der Kiez* is a colloquial term for a deeply assimilated and traditional working-class district. The term derives from the Slavic languages, meaning *ärmliche Fischersiedlung* (poor fishermen settlement), and originated in Brandenburg and Mecklenburg.

22. *Kreuzberg* and *Prenzlauer Berg* are both districts within the city center of Berlin. *Kreuzberg,* a part of former West Berlin, has a large Turkish community. *Prenzlauer Berg* is a district in former East Berlin. Areas such as *Kreuzberg* and *Prenzlauer Berg* today are popular residential areas for students, artists, and those who desire the mix of old inner-city life and alternative life-style. *Kreuzberg* is named after the only natural hill in the city. Other hills are man-made from war debris.

23. *Der Leierkasten, die Drehorgel* is a barrel organ. *Der Leierkastenmann* is a traditional Berlin figure, dating back to the period of industrialization. As unemployment ran high among the working class in Berlin during these times, beggars would often wheel the *Leierkasten* through town and play popular tunes on the street or in tenement yards for pennies.

# C. GRAMMATIK UND GEBRAUCH

## 1. *DIE UNBESTIMMTEN PRONOMEN „JEMAND" UND „NIEMAND"* (THE INDEFINITE PRONOUNS *JEMAND* AND *NIEMAND*)

*Jemand* (someone, anyone) and *niemand* (no one, not anyone) belong to a group of indefinite pronouns, which describe objects or people that are not specifically mentioned or defined. They are used only in the singular and take case endings as nouns. In the dative and accusative, however, the endings can be omitted.

| | | |
|---|---|---|
| NOM. | *jemand* | *niemand* |
| ACC. | *jemand(en)* | *niemand(en)* |
| DAT. | *jemand(em)* | *niemand(em)* |
| GEN. | *jemandes* | *niemandes* |

*Jemand aus der Schule hat mir das Museum gezeigt.*
Someone from school has shown me the museum.

*Ich habe niemand(en) gehört.*
I didn't hear anyone.

*Er hat mit jemand(em) vom Archiv gesprochen.*
He spoke with someone from the archives.

*Sie hat ihr Studium selbst finanziert. Sie brauchte niemandes Hilfe.*
She financed her studies herself. She didn't need anyone's help.

If "anyone" is used in a positive statement or question, use *jemand*.

*Hat jemand den Architekten\* gesehen?*
Has anyone seen the architect?

While in English it is possible to use the pronoun *anyone* in a negative statement, it is not possible to do so with *jemand*. You have to use *niemand* in such cases.

*Ich habe niemand(en) gesehen.*
I didn't see anyone./I saw no one.

\* *der Architekt* is an *n*-noun. (See Lesson 3 for details.)

# 2. *DAS PASSIV* (THE PASSIVE VOICE)

The passive voice is formed with the auxiliary *werden* plus the past participle of the main verb.

ACTIVE
*Der Tourist fotografiert den Leierkastenmann.*
The tourist takes a picture of the organ-grinder.

PASSIVE
*Der Leierkastenmann wird (vom Touristen) fotografiert.*
The organ-grinder is being photographed (by the tourist).

The accusative object of the active sentence, *den Leierkastenmann,* becomes the subject of the passive sentence, *der Leierkastenmann.* The subject of the active sentence, *der Tourist,* becomes the agent of the passive sentence, *vom Touristen,* and may or may not be mentioned.

*Der Architekt baut das Haus.*
The architect is building the house.

*Das Haus wird (vom Architekten) gebaut.*
The house is being built (by the architect).

The auxiliary *werden* takes on other tenses. The main verb remains in the past participle in all tenses.

PAST TENSE
*Das Schloss wurde 1735 gebaut.*
The castle was built in 1735.

The present perfect is a compound tense, which in itself requires an auxiliary. *Werden* is conjugated with *sein* in compound tenses. *Werden* becomes *worden* and moves to the last position in the sentence, whereas the main verb remains in the past participle.

ACTIVE
*Marina hat uns zum Museum gefahren.*
Marina took us to the museum.

PASSIVE
*Wir sind zum Museum gefahren worden.*
We were driven to the museum.

Since the simple future uses *werden* as its auxiliary as well, *werden* is conjugated and the main verb remains as a part participle. The passive *werden* as an infinitive takes the last position in the sentence.

ACTIVE
*Er wird das Haus wahrscheinlich ändern.*
He will probably change the house.

PASSIVE
*Das Haus wird wahrscheinlich geändert werden.*
The house will probably be changed.

If the active has two verbs, modal and main, the modal verb takes the last position in the passive future.

ACTIVE
*Wir werden das Haus nicht zeigen können.*
We won't be able to show the house.

PASSIVE
*Das Haus wird nicht gezeigt werden können.*
It won't be possible to show the house.

## 3. *DEMONSTRATIVE ADJEKTIVE* (DEMONSTRATIVE ADJECTIVES)

The emphasis placed on a noun can be stressed with the demonstrative adjective. Demonstrative adjectives are often called *der-*words, as they take the same endings as the definite article* when showing gender, number, and case of the noun they refer to.

*Das Haus ist schön. Dieses Haus ist schöner.*
The house is beautiful. This house is more beautiful.

*Die Kirche ist nicht weit von hier.*
The church is not far from here.

*Diese Kirche ist von Schinkel, nicht wahr?*
This church is by Schinkel, right?

The difference between demonstrative pronoun and demonstrative adjective is that the demonstrative adjective always requires a noun, whereas the pronoun can stand by itself. When differentiating between two or more things, use the demonstrative adjective. The demonstrative pronoun usually only appears to relate to something previously mentioned.

*Die Kirche am Marktplatz ist von Schinkel.*
The church located at the marketplace is by Schinkel.

* For a chart of the article endings, please refer to the appendix.

*Die ist aber schön.*
  It's really beautiful.

DEMONSTRATIVE ADJECTIVE
*Hat er diese Kirche vor oder nach der anderen gebaut?*
  Did he build this church before or after the other (one)?

*Sind wir schon über die Schloßbrücke gefahren?*
  Have we already driven across the castle bridge?

DEMONSTRATIVE PRONOUN
*Was, die da vorne?*
  What, that one up ahead?

DEMONSTRATIVE ADJECTIVE
*Du meinst nicht diese Brücke, du meinst die beim Reichstag.*
  You don't mean this bridge; you mean the one near the Reichstag.

  Other demonstrative adjectives are *jede, -r, -s* (every, each); *manche, -r, -s* (some, several, many a); and *solche, -r, -s* (such, such a).

*Jedes Kind möchte Riesenrad fahren.*
  Every child wants to ride on the Ferris wheel.

*Solche schönen Rosen sind selten.*
  Such beautiful roses are rare.

*Manche Besucher verlaufen sich.*
  Some visitors get lost.

  The interrogative adjective *welche, -r, -s,* also takes the endings of the definite article.

*Ich finde diese Bilder sehr interessant.*
  I find these paintings/pictures very interesting.

*Welches finden Sie denn am interessantesten?*
  Which one do you find the most interesting?

*In welche Richtung muss ich gehen?*
  Which direction should I take?/In which direction do I have to go?

*Für welches Haus interessieren Sie sich?*
  Which house are you interested in?

  Note that if a preposition is involved in the verbal structure the preposition precedes *welche(-r/-s).*

# 4. DA-ZUSAMMENSETZUNGEN (DA-COMPOUNDS)

The dialogue mentions a few *da*-compounds: *dazu* (for that), *dahinter* and *dahinten* (back there, over there), *dafür* (for that), *dabei* (along), and *daran* (in/on that), consisting of *da,* referring to something previously mentioned, plus the proper preposition.

*Dahinten ist das Brandenburger Tor.*
Back there is the Brandenburg Gate.

*Es besteht schon Interesse daran.*
There is certainly some interest in it.

*R* is inserted between prepositions beginning with a vowel and *da* to facilitate pronunciation.

| | | |
|---|---|---|
| *da + an* | = | *daran* (in which, regarding, about) |
| *da + auf* | = | *darauf* (onto, on which) |
| *da + über* | = | *darüber* (over that, about that) |
| *da + unter* | = | *darunter* (beneath) |
| *da + in* | = | *darin* (therein, in which) |

*Weißt du, dass wir uns morgen treffen?*
Do you know that we're meeting tomorrow?

*Nein, davon weiß ich nichts.*
No, I don't know anything about that.

*Weißt du über die Hohenzollern Bescheid?*
Do you know (anything) about the Hohenzollern*?

*Nein, darüber weiß ich nichts.*
No, I know nothing about them.

*Ich möchte durch Europa reisen.*
I would like to travel through Europe.

*Dafür brauche ich viele Informationen.*
I need a lot of information for that.

---

* The *Hohenzollern* family was the Prussian imperial family. The name originated in Swabia in the eleventh century. The dynasty was later linked by inheritance to northern Brandenburg. By acquiring large territories such as Prussia, the house of *Hohenzollern* became as powerful as the *Habsburger.*

Some *da*-compounds actually function as both *da*-compound and separate conjunction:

*DABEI* (while doing something, in the course of, during)
DA-COMPOUND
*Wann bist du fertig mit dem Reisebericht?—Ich bin gerade dabei.*
When will you be done with the travel report?—I'm working on it right now.

*DABEI* (despite that, although)
CONJUNCTION
*Sie hat immer noch nicht alles gesehen. Dabei war sie schon dreimal in der Stadt.*
She still hasn't seen everything, although she's already been to the city three times.

## 5. WO-ZUSAMMENSETZUNGEN (WO-COMPOUNDS)

*Wo*-compounds are the interrogative counterpart to *da*-compounds.

*Er hat die Tür mit einem Schlüssel aufgemacht. Womit hat er die Tür aufgemacht?*
He opened the door with a key. What did he open the door with?

*Ich weiß nicht mehr, wofür ich das gekauft habe.*
I don't remember what I bought this for.

The most common *wo*-compounds are:

| | | | |
|---|---|---|---|
| *wofür* | what for | *wodurch* | through what |
| *womit* | what with | *worüber* | about what |
| *wovon* | what of | *worauf* | on what |
| *worin* | in what | *wozu* | to what, what for |

# D. REIN GESCHÄFTLICH

## 1. CHALLENGES OF A UNIFIED BERLIN

When the Berlin wall fell in 1989, a city that had been divided into two for decades was suddenly politically and economically reunited. After the initial euphoria, however, Berlin's inhabitants found themselves confronted with a variety of unique problems. The chasm between the eastern and the western parts turned out to be much greater than expected, and the city will be struggling to become one for years to come. Many wounds left by the wall are in plain sight: large areas such as the *Pots-*

*damer Platz* and the no man's land on the eastern side of the wall, which had been major streets and city squares in pre-war days, lay deserted during the division. Other wounds are hidden from the naked eye: in the eastern part of Berlin wages are lower and unemployment rates higher, health care facilities underdeveloped, housing sparse and in bad condition, transportation systems and infrastructure in need of improvement. The construction sector is and will be one of the major areas for foreign investment in eastern Germany as a whole and Berlin in particular, as the entire infrastructure—from roads, rails, and airports to power and sewage plants, government buildings, hospitals, and private housing— needs improvement. In past years the city organized several *Internationale Bauwettbewerbe* (international architectural contests) for redesigning the inner-city area of Berlin, and record numbers of architects and construction companies from around the globe contributed.

One of the biggest private sector construction projects in German history is the rebuilding of the *Potsdamer Platz*. Before World War II, *Potsdamer Platz* had been the busiest public square in Europe and the heart of Berlin, but lay bare while Berlin was divided due its proximity to the no-man's land. German and international companies have since undertaken the development of the area. Among the most notable developments are the *Sony Center* (developed by the Sony Corporation and designed by Helmut Jahn) and *Debis Stadt* (developed by Daimler-Chrysler and designed by Renzo Piano and Christoph Kohlbecker). Other sites at or near the *Potsdamer Platz* and other parts of the no man's land are still under construction, and most likely will be for some time.

When doing business in housing and housing renovation in Germany, bear in mind that local governments and city administrations tend to be far less lenient than their American counterparts in issuing building permits, as regulations for size, shape, foundation, and even style are strict. *Der Bauherr* (lit.: the building chief), i.e., the person, company, or institution who commissions the construction, has to contact *die Stadtverwaltung Abt.* \* *Bauwesen* (city administration, construction department) for *eine Baugenehmigung* (building permit), before any work at *die Baustelle* (construction site) can be done.

## 2. EXPRESSIONS OF LIKES AND DISLIKES

| | |
|---|---|
| *gefallen* | to like |
| *Das gefällt mir (sehr) gut.* | I (really) like that. |
| *Das gefällt mir nicht.* | I don't like it. |
| *Gefallen finden an* | to like, to be pleased |
| *Er hat Gefallen an Ihrem Vorschlag gefunden.* | He was quite pleased about your suggestion. |
| *An den Zeichnungen konnte ich einfach keinen Gefallen finden.* | I didn't seem to like the drawings at all. |

* *Abteilung* (department) is mostly used in its abbreviated form *Abt.* (dept.) in writing.

| | |
|---|---|
| *mögen* | to like |
| *Ich mag moderne Kunst.* | I like modern art. |
| *den Geschmack treffen* | to be to one's taste, liking |
| *Das ist sehr interessant, aber leider trifft das nicht meinen Geschmack.* | That's very interesting but unfortunately it's not to my liking. |
| *dem Geschmack entsprechen* | to be to one's liking |
| *Ihr Entwurf entspricht leider nicht unserem Geschmack.* | Your draft unfortunately is not to our liking. |
| *geschmackvoll\** | tasteful |
| *Sie haben Ihr Haus wirklich sehr geschmackvoll eingerichtet.* | You've furnished your house in the most tasteful way. |
| *geschmacklos* | tasteless |
| *Dieses Bild ist wirklich geschmacklos.* | This picture is really tasteless. |
| *zusagen* | to appeal |
| *Dieser Plan sagt mir nicht zu.* | This plan doesn't appeal to me. |

## ÜBUNGEN

**1.** *Setzen Sie das richtige Demonstrativpronomen ein.*

a. *Ich war schon mal in _____ Haus.*
b. _____ *Kirche wurde 1902 gebaut.*
c. *Er hat _____ Frau gestern gesehen.*
d. *Kennen Sie _____ Straße?*
e. *Wir waren letztes Jahr in _____ Ort.*
f. _____ *Bäume sind Linden.*
g. _____ *Schloss ist das älteste.*
h. _____ (some) *wohnen lieber in Altbauten.*
i. _____ (which) *Haus gefällt Ihnen am besten?*
j. *Er kennt hier _____ (each) Gebäude.*
k. _____ (such) *Straßen werden nicht mehr gebaut.*

**2.** *Setzen Sie die folgenden Sätze ins Passiv. Nennen Sie den Agenten nicht.*

a. *Er baute das Haus zwischen 1975 und 1977.*
b. *Der Architekt zeigte Marina und Gary das Haus.*
c. *Die Stadt restauriert die Kirchen aus dem Mittelalter.*
d. *Der Hausmeister schließt die Tür um 20 Uhr.*
e. *Wir verkauften das Haus in Berlin.*

\* The suffixes -*voll* (full) and -*los* (less) are added to nouns to form adjectives. The most common ones are *sinnvoll* (appropriate, makes sense) and *sinnlos* (senseless).

**3.** *Übersetzen Sie und benutzen Sie „jemand" und „niemand."*

    a. Today no one has visited the church.
    b. Someone who studies architecture wants to see the *Bauhaus-Archiv.*
    c. Nobody knew where the marketplace was.
    d. Did nobody call?
    e. Has someone seen the student?
    f. Hasn't anyone told you?

**4.** *Setzen Sie die folgenden Sätze in das Passiv in der Vergangenheit. Nennen Sie den Agenten.*

BEISPIEL: *Hier hat die Stadt München eine Brücke gebaut.*
             *Hier wurde von der Stadt München eine Brücke gebaut.*

    a. *Die Firma Schobel & Co. streicht die alten Häuser am Marktplatz.*
    b. *Schinkel baute das Alte Museum.*
    c. *Marina hat Gary durch Berlin geführt.*
    d. *Das Architektenbüro Schmitt gewann den Bauwettbewerb.*
    e. *Viele Touristen besuchten die Ausstellung.*
    f. *Wir haben viele Stadtpläne gekauft.*

**5.** *Formulieren Sie die Sätze neu und benutzen Sie „Es gibt" oder „Es gab."*

BEISPIEL: *Hier war ein berühmtes Theater.*
             *Es gab hier ein berühmtes Theater.*

    a. *Viele Bäume wachsen in Berlin.*
    b. *Im Tiergarten waren Wildschweine.*
    c. *Berlin hatte vor dem 2. Weltkrieg viele alte Gebäude.*
    d. *Berlin hat viele Museen.*
    e. *Hier war im letzten Jahrhundert ein Markt.*
    f. *Viele Architekten arbeiten in Berlin.*

**6.** *Antworten Sie mit da-Zusammensetzungen.*

BEISPIEL: *Ich bin am Alten Museum. Wo ist der Berliner Dom? (neben)*
             *Der Dom ist daneben.*

    a. *Wo ist die Kirche von Schinkel? (hinten)*
    b. *Wo steht der Leierkastenmann? (drüben)*
    c. *Wo hält der Bus? (vorne)*
    d. *Wo soll ich mich hinstellen, damit sie ein Foto machen können? (hinter)*

# LEKTION 7

UMZUG IN EIN NEUES BÜRO.    Moving Into New Offices.

## A. DIALOG

*Die Büroleiterin Gisela Schumann und ihr Mitarbeiter Jens Ahrendt treffen sich mit Herrn Wiekland von der Umzugsfirma in den neuen Büroräumen in Stuttgart.*[1]

GISELA SCHUMANN: Ah, Herr Wiekland, schön, dass Sie schon da sind.

HERR WIEKLAND: Guten Tag, Frau Schumann.

GISELA SCHUMANN: Na, dann wollen wir uns mal die Räume ansehen. Das ist übrigens[2] mein Assistent, Herr Ahrendt.

JENS AHRENDT: Tag. Sie haben sicher Maßband und sowas[3] dabei.

HERR WIEKLAND: Ja, natürlich. Ich habe auch Zettel[4] und Kuli[5] dabei, damit ich mir Notizen machen kann.

JENS AHRENDT: Prima![6]

GISELA SCHUMANN: Hier ist der Empfang. Die Räume hier rechts sind die Büros von Herrn Neumann und Frau Schalk. Aber fangen wir am besten mit Herrn Ahrendts und meinem an.

HERR WIEKLAND: Wie Sie wünschen.[7]

JENS AHRENDT: Wo stellen wir denn meine Regale auf?

GISELA SCHUMANN: Ich habe mir das so gedacht. Herr Wiekland, wenn Sie sich das notieren wollen—die Aktenschränke aus meinem Zimmer kommen hier links an die Wand. Vor das Fenster kommt der große Schreibtisch. Rechts steht dann ein Regal. Und stellen Sie den Kopierer am besten neben das Regal.

JENS AHRENDT: Einverstanden.[8] Dann habe ich auch noch Platz, um Bilder an die Wand zu hängen.

GISELA SCHUMANN: Ja, bestimmt. Herr Wiekland, stellen Sie bitte zwei der schwarzen Schreibtische in die Büros rechts vom Flur, und den dritten vorne in den Empfang. Je[9] ein Aktenschrank kommt in die Büros.

JENS AHRENDT: Das rote Regal gehört neben den Schreibtisch im Empfang. Das Faxgerät stellen Sie bitte vorerst[10] in das Regal.

116

GISELA SCHUMANN: **Richtig. Moment, was machen wir nur mit Neumanns monströsem Schrank?**

JENS AHRENDT: **Aus dem Fenster werfen.**

GISELA SCHUMANN: **Ach, komm! Ich weiß, wir stellen ihn hinter die Tür. Dort sieht ihn keiner.**

HERR WIEKLAND: **Der Kopierer, von dem Sie sprachen, kommt der auf einen extra Tisch?**

JENS AHRENDT: **Nein, stellen Sie den einfach auf den Boden. Ich habe einen neuen Tisch dafür bestellt.**

GISELA SCHUMANN: **Dieser Raum hier ist das Konferenzzimmer.**

JENS AHRENDT: **Stellen Sie bitte acht schwarze Stühle hinein. Der Glastisch kommt natürlich auch in dieses Zimmer.**

GISELA SCHUMANN: **Die Aktenablage aus Chrom kommt unter das Fenster in das vorletzte[11] Zimmer links. Stellen Sie bitte die Statue neben den Chromtisch und zwei Stühle vor den Tisch.**

JENS AHRENDT: **Werden die Computer eigentlich[12] auch von der Umzugsfirma transportiert?**

GISELA SCHUMANN: **Nein, die bringt Herr Neumann am Montag.**

JENS AHRENDT: **Was machen wir denn bloß mit Annettes Wandregal?**

GISELA SCHUMANN: **Herr Wiekland, messen Sie doch bitte mal die Wand in dem größeren der zwei vorderen Räume aus.**

JENS AHRENDT: **Soll ich Ihnen helfen?**

HERR WIEKLAND: **Ja, das wär' nett. Halten Sie doch mal bitte fest.**

*Herr Wiekland gibt Jens das Ende des Maßbands.*

HERR WIEKLAND: **Wie lang, sagten Sie, ist das Wandregal?**

GISELA SCHUMANN: **6 Meter. Soweit ich mich erinnere, gibt es in diesem Büro keine einzige Wand, die 6 Meter lang ist.**

HERR WIEKLAND: **Na, an diese Wand passt es jedenfalls nicht.**

JENS AHRENDT: **Ich glaube, die Wand im Flur zwischen dem Konferenzraum und deinem Zimmer ist lang genug.**

GISELA SCHUMANN: **Gut. Herr Wiekland, bitte stellen Sie das lange Wandregal einfach in den Flur.**

JENS AHRENDT: **Und die Telefonanschlüsse sind bereits alle da, stimmt's?[13]**

GISELA SCHUMANN: **Ja, in jedem Raum ist mindestens ein Anschluss.**

JENS AHRENDT: **Na, prima. Ach, bevor ich's vergesse. Herr Wiekland, wir haben doch so viele Lampen. Lassen Sie die doch einfach alle vorne im Empfang.**

GISELA SCHUMANN: **Ich glaube, das war's. Haben Sie noch irgendwelche Fragen, Herr Wiekland?**

HERR WIEKLAND: **Nein, es ist alles soweit klar.**

GISELA SCHUMANN: **Vielen Dank. Bis Montag dann. Aber wahrscheinlich werden wir noch vorher miteinander telefonieren.**

HERR WIEKLAND: **Ja, sicherlich. Wiedersehen.**

GISELA SCHUMANN: **Lass uns gehen. Hast du Hunger? Ich lad' dich ein.**

JENS AHRENDT: **Na prima, das hör' ich gern.**

---

TRANSLATION

The office manager Gisela Schumann and her co-worker Jens Ahrendt are meeting Mr. Wiekland from the moving company at the new offices in Stuttgart.

GISELA SCHUMANN: Ah, Mr. Wiekland, good, you're here already.

MR. WIEKLAND: Good afternoon, Ms. Schumann.

GISELA SCHUMANN: Well, then let's go ahead and look at the offices. By the way, this is my assistant, Mr. Ahrendt.

JENS AHRENDT: Hello. You probably brought a tape measure and things like that along.

MR. WIEKLAND: Yes, of course. And I also have pen and paper to take notes.

JENS AHRENDT: Great.

GISELA SCHUMANN: This is the reception area. The rooms on your right are the offices of Mr. Neumann and Ms. Schalk. But it'll be best to start with Mr. Ahrendt's and mine.

MR. WIEKLAND: As you wish.

JENS AHRENDT: Where are we going to put my shelves?

GISELA SCHUMANN: I thought we should do the following. Mr. Wiekland, if you would please write this down—the filing cabinets from my office go against the wall on your left. The large desk goes in front of the window. A shelf will stand on the right. And let's put the copy machine next to the shelf. That'll be best.

JENS AHRENDT: Fine by me. Then I'll still have some room to hang pictures on the wall.

GISELA SCHUMANN: Yes, certainly. Mr. Wiekland, please put two of the black desks in the offices to the right of the hallway, and the third in the reception area. One filing cabinet goes into each office.

JENS AHRENDT: The red shelves go next to the desk in the reception area. Please put the fax machine on the shelf for now.

GISELA SCHUMANN: Right. Wait a minute, what are we going to do with Neumann's monstrosity of a cupboard?

JENS AHRENDT: Throw it out of the window.

GISELA SCHUMANN: Oh, come on! I know, we'll put it behind the door. No one will see it there.

MR. WIEKLAND: The copy machine you were talking about, does that go on a separate table?

JENS AHRENDT: No, please just put it on the floor. I've ordered a new table.

GISELA SCHUMANN: This room is the conference room.

JENS AHRENDT: Please put eight black chairs in here. Of course the glass table goes into this room as well.

GISELA SCHUMANN: The chrome file cabinet goes underneath the window in the second to last room on your left. Please put the statue next to the chrome table and two chairs in front of the table.

JENS AHRENDT: Will the computers also be shipped by the moving company?

GISELA SCHUMANN: No, Herr Neumann will bring those on Monday.

JENS AHRENDT: What in the world are we going to do with Annette's wall unit?

GISELA SCHUMANN: Mr. Wiekland, please measure the wall in the larger of the two front rooms.

JENS AHRENDT: Do you want me to help you?

MR. WIEKLAND: Yes, that would be nice. Please hold on to that.

Mr. Wiekland hands the end of the tape measure to Jens.

MR. WIEKLAND: How long did you say the wall unit was?

GISELA SCHUMANN: Six meters. As far as I remember there is not a single wall in this office that's 6 meters long.

MR. WIEKLAND: Well, it certainly won't go on this wall.

JENS AHRENDT: I think the one in the hallway between the conference room and your office is long enough.

GISELA SCHUMANN: Okay. Mr. Wiekland, please put the wall unit in the hallway.

JENS AHRENDT: And we already have telephone connections everywhere, right?

GISELA SCHUMANN: Yes, at least one in each office.

JENS AHRENDT: Well, great. Oh, before I forget. Mr. Wiekland, you know we have so many lamps. Just leave all of them up front in the reception area.

GISELA SCHUMANN: I think that's it. Do you have any questions, Mr. Wiekland?

MR. WIEKLAND: No, so far everything looks fine.

GISELA SCHUMANN: Thank you very much. I'll see you on Monday. But we'll probably talk before then.

MR. WIEKLAND: Yes, definitely. Good-bye.

GISELA SCHUMANN: Let's go. Are you hungry? I'm buying.

JENS AHRENDT: Great, I like to hear that.

# B. IN KÜRZE

1. Stuttgart, the capital of *Baden-Württemberg,* located in the southwest of Germany, is famous for its automobile industry, most notably *Daimler-Chrysler* and *Porsche. Die Schwaben\** (Swabians), the inhabitants of *Württemberg,* are considered to be an especially frugal people with a strong work ethic and a never-ending love affair with cleanliness. For more information, go to www.Stuttgart.de.

2. *Übrigens* (by the way) is an adverb and therefore takes no endings. The adjective *übrig* (remaining) takes regular adjective endings.

*Die übrigen Stühle können Sie in dieses Zimmer stellen.*
You may put the remaining chairs into this room.

There are also a few verbs with *übrig: erübrigen* (to be unnecessary), *übrig haben* (to have left over).

*Du hast schon angerufen? Dann erübrigt sich mein Anruf.*
You already called? Then my call won't be necessary.

*Ich habe alles ins Zimmer gestellt und habe noch viel Platz übrig.*
I have put everything into the room and I still have lots of space left.

\* See *Lesestück* 4.

3. *Sowas* is short for *so etwas* (something like that, things like that).

4. *Der Zettel* is a colloquial term for piece of paper. Alternative terms are *das Blatt Papier* (sheet of paper) or *der Briefbogen* (sheet of formal writing paper/letterhead).

5. *Der Kuli* is short for *der Kugelschreiber* (ballpoint pen). Previously only used as a colloquialism, this short form has become accepted usage in standard German.

6. *Prima!* has become a widespread colloquialism. Other German terms for expressing enthusiastic approval are *Klasse!*, *Toll!* and *Super!*

7. *Ganz wie Sie möchten/wünschen.* (Just as you like it/Just as you wish) can be used as alternative expressions.

8. *Einverstanden* is used only as a past participle with the auxiliary *sein.*

*Bist du mit dem Vorschlag einverstanden?*
Do you agree with the suggestion?

In a formal context, the term *das Einverständnis geben* (to give one's consent) is used.

*Wir haben unser Einverständnis gegeben.*
We agreed to it.

9. *Je* stands for "each" and is a short form of *jeweils.*

*Je(weils) ein Aktenschrank gehört in jedes Büro.*
One filing cabinet belongs in each office.

*je* also appears in other contexts: *je . . . desto* (the . . . the)

*Je schneller wir umziehen, desto besser.*
The quicker we move, the better.

It can be used as an exclamation:

*Oh je! Ich habe meine Schlüssel vergessen.*
Oh, no! I forgot my keys.

In another usage, *je* is short for *jemals* (ever).

*Ohne je in dem neuen Büro gewesen zu sein, sagte sie, es gefällt ihr nicht.*
Without ever having been to the new office, she said she didn't like it.

10. *Vorerst* and *fürs Erste* (for the time being, for now) are temporal adverbs.

11. *Vorletzt-* (the one before last), *letzt-* (last) and *erst-* (first) take adjective endings.

*Am vorletzten Tag haben wir die Koffer gepackt.*
On the day before last we packed our suitcases (bags).

*Heute ist der letzte Tag im alten Büro.*
Today is the last day in the old office.

*Dies ist die erste Kiste.*
This is the first box.

12. *Eigentlich* is a flavoring adverb.

*Ich habe eigentlich keine Zeit, aber ich komme mit.*
I don't really have time but I'll go with you anyway.

*Du hast eigentlich recht.*
You are actually right.

*Eigentlich* also appears as an adjective.

*Der eigentliche Wert des Geldes ist viel niedriger.*
The actual value of money is much less.

13. *Stimmt's = stimmt es?* (right?) *stimmen* means to correspond, to be accurate, to be true.

# C. GRAMMATIK UND GEBRAUCH

## 1. *WECHSELPRÄPOSITIONEN* (TWO-WAY PREPOSITIONS)

Two-way prepositions take either the dative or the accusative case. When describing the location of an object or a person, the dative is used. The accusative is used when describing the movement of an object or a person. Two-way prepositions take the dative if the sentence answers the question *Wo* (where?) and the accusative if it answers the question *Wohin* (where to?).

| DATIVE | ACCUSATIVE |
|---|---|
| *Wo hängt das Bild?* | *Wohin ging das Kind?* |
| Where is the picture? | Where did the child go (to)? |
| | |
| *Das Bild hängt <u>über dem</u> Fernseher.* | *Das King ging <u>in die</u> Schule.* |
| The picture is hanging above the TV. | The child went to school. |
| | |
| *Wo ist mein Büro?* | *Wohin soll ich die Lampe stellen?* |
| Where is my office? | Where shall I put the lamp? |

*Dein Büro ist <u>neben der</u> Küche.*

Your office is next to the kitchen.

*Stellen Sie die Lampe <u>neben den</u> Schreibtisch.*

Put the lamp next to the desk.

    The two-way prepositions are:

*AN* (on)
*Das Bild hängt an der Wand.*
The picture hangs on the wall.

*Er hängt das Bild an die Wand.*
He hangs the picture on the wall.

*UNTER* (beneath, under)
*Das Buch liegt unter dem Tisch.*

The book lies under the table.

*Stellen Sie das Regal unter den Tisch.*
Put the shelf underneath the table.

*AUF* (on, on top of)
*Sie sitzt auf dem Stuhl.*
She sits on the chair.

*Setzen Sie sich auf den Stuhl.*
Please sit on the chair.

*ZWISCHEN* (between)
*Er steht zwischen dem Fenster und der Tür.*
He is standing between the window and the door.

*Stellen Sie den Stuhl zwischen das Fenster und die Tür.*
Put the chair between the window and the door.

*VOR* (in front of, before)
*Wir haben vor dem Haus geparkt.*
We parked in front of the building.

*Stellen Sie die Kiste vor die Tür.*
Place the box in front of the door.

    Other two-way prepositions include *in* (in, to), *neben* (next to), *über* (over, above), *hinter* (behind).

## 2. *TRANSITIVE UND INTRANSITIVE VERBEN* (TRANSITIVE AND INTRANSITIVE VERBS)

    German has several verbs of placement and position:

| | |
|---|---|
| *stellen/stehen* | to put/to stand (vertical position) |
| *sitzen/setzen* | to sit/to set (vertical position) |
| *liegen/legen* | to lie/to lay (horizontal position) |

These verbs can be distinguished as transitive and intransitive verbs. Transitive verbs can take a direct object; intransitive ones cannot.

| INTRANSITIVE VERBS | TRANSITIVE VERBS |
|---|---|
| *Der Stuhl steht in der Ecke.* | *Er stellt den Stuhl in die Ecke.* |
| The chair stands in the corner. | He puts the chair into the corner. |
| *Wo steht der Stuhl?* | *Wohin stellt er den Stuhl?* |
| Where is the chair? | Where did he put the chair? |
| *In der Ecke.* | *In die Ecke.* |
| In the corner. (dative case) | Into the corner. (accusative case) |

As intransitive verbs usually describe an object's location, they are followed by a preposition of place and the dative. When transitive verbs describe an object's movement, they are followed by a preposition of movement and the accusative.

| | |
|---|---|
| *Das Bild hängt an der Wand.* | *Jens hängt das Bild an die Wand.* |
| The picture is hanging on the wall. | Jens hangs the picture on the wall. |
| *Wo hängt das Bild?* | *Wohin hängt Jens das Bild?* |
| Where does the picture hang? | Where is Jens hanging the picture? |
| *An der Wand.* | *An die Wand.* |
| On the wall. (dative case) | On the wall. (accusative case) |

Depending upon the context, *hängen* (to hang) can be both transitive and intransitive.

Intransitive verbs take the strong verb conjugation; transitive verbs take the weak conjugation:

| *SITZEN/GESESSEN* | *SETZEN\*/GESETZT* |
|---|---|
| *Ich habe 4 Stunden im Auto gesessen.* | *Sie hat sich auf den Stuhl gesetzt.* |
| I sat in the car for 4 hours. | She sat down on the chair. |
| *HÄNGEN/GEHANGEN* | *HÄNGEN/GEHÄNGT* |
| *Das Bild hat an der Wand gehangen.* | *Er hat das Bild an die Wand gehängt.* |
| The picture hung on the wall. | He hung the picture on the wall. |
| *STEHEN/GESTANDEN* | *STELLEN/GESTELLT* |
| *Die Lampe hat in der Ecke gestanden.* | *Ich habe sie jetzt in den Empfang gestellt.* |
| The lamp always stood in the corner. | I've put it in the reception area now. |

---

\* *sich setzen* (to sit down) is always used as a reflexive verb.

| LIEGEN/GELEGEN | LEGEN*/GELEGT |
|---|---|
| *Wir haben bis 11 Uhr im Bett gelegen.* | *Er hat sich für eine halbe Stunde auf das Sofa gelegt.* |
| We lay in bed until 11 A.M. | He lay down on the sofa for half an hour. |

## 3. *DER IMPERATIV* (THE IMPERATIVE)

The imperative verb form is used as a request, command, or suggestion. An exclamation mark is added in German.

*Gib mal her!*
Give it to me./Show me.

*Bitte setzen Sie sich!*
Please, take a seat.

*Also los, gehen wir!*
All right, let's go.

*Lass uns gehen!*
Let's go.

*Mal* is added as a stress marker.

*Sag mal, wo hast du den Kuli hingelegt?*
Tell me, where did you put the pen?

*Sieh mal, der Umzugswagen ist hier!*
Look, the moving truck has arrived.

To soften the request, add *bitte*.

*Gehen Sie mal bitte zur Tür und sagen Sie ihnen, sie sollen warten!*
Please go to the door and tell them to wait.

a. *Sie*-Form

The polite imperative has the same form as the regular present tense conjugation. In the imperative subject and verb trade places. It is necessary to repeat the personal pronoun *Sie*.

*Sehen Sie sich das an, Herr Krüger!*
Look at that, Mr. Krüger.

*Entschuldigen Sie!*
Excuse me.

* *sich legen* (to lie down) is always used as a reflexive verb.

b. *Du*-Form

The imperative of the second person singular familiar (*du*) is formed with the stem of the verb. It is not necessary to repeat the pronoun.

*Sag doch mal was.*
Say something.

*Schreib(e) die Adresse auf das Paket!*
Write the address on the parcel.

Verbs such as *sprechen* and *sehen* that take vowel changes in the second and third person singular present, take the same vowel change in the imperative.

*Er spricht französisch.*
He speaks French.

*Sprich leise!*
Speak quietly.

*Sie sieht den Bus.*
She sees the bus.

*Sieh mal, der Bus kommt!*
Look, the bus is coming!

Verbs with vowel changes from *a* to *ä* in the second and third person singular present, such as *laufen* and *fahren,* do not add the *Umlaut* in the imperative.

*Du fährst zu schnell.*
You drive too fast.

*Fahr langsamer!*
Drive slower (Slow down).

Verbs with a stem ending in -*t, -d,* or -*ig* such as *bad-en* (to bathe), *wart-en* (to wait), and *entschuldig-en* (to apologize) always add an -*e* in the imperative.

*Bade nicht so lange!*
Don't bathe so long.

*Warte!*
Wait.

*Entschuldige dich bitte bei ihm!*
Please apologize to him.

c. *Ihr-* and *Wir-* Forms

The imperative addressing a group of people *(ihr)* not including the speaker takes the regular present tense form. The personal pronoun is not repeated.

*Geht bitte! Ihr seid schon spät dran.*
Please go. You are late already.

*Jürgen und Klaus, wartet auf mich!*
Jürgen and Klaus, wait for me.

When making suggestions to a group of people including the speaker, the imperative can be formed in two ways. First, similarly to the English "Let's," with the verb *lassen:*

*Lasst uns gehen, ich bin müde.*
Let's go; I'm tired.

*Lasst uns* (second person plural of *lassen*) is used if the group consists of the speaker and at least two more people. If the group consists of only two people including the speaker, the second person singular *Lass uns* is used.

*Lass uns essen gehen. Ich habe Hunger.*
Let's go and eat. I'm hungry.

The second possible way to address a group of people including the speaker is by simply using the first person plural form of the verb. Subject and verb trade places.

*Sehen wir uns das an.*
Let's look at it.

*Gehen wir, ich bin müde.*
Let's go, I'm tired.

d. *Sein*

The only irregular verb in the imperative is *sein* (to be).

*Sei bitte leise!*
Please be quiet.

*Seid nicht so unfreundlich!*
Don't be so unfriendly.

*Seien Sie bitte pünktlich!*
Please be on time.

e. Public Commands

Public commands and requests such as announcements on airports or train stations, as well as public signs, are expressed with *bitte* and the infinitive.

*Auf Gleis 12 bitte einsteigen.*
  On platform 12 all aboard, please.

*Bitte weitergehen. Hier gibt's nichts zu sehen.*
  Please move on. There's nothing to see here.

*Bitte nicht stören.*
  Please do not disturb.

# D. REIN GESCHÄFTLICH

## 1. BUSINESS LETTERS

### ADDRESSING A BUSINESS LETTER

*zu Händen von Herrn Schlüter*
  Attention: Mr. Schlüter

*z. Hd. von Frau Schneider*
  Attn.: Ms. Schneider

*Persönlich*
  Personal

*Vertraulich*
  Personal & Confidential

### BEGINNING A BUSINESS LETTER

*Wir danken Ihnen für Ihr Schreiben vom 05.02.*
  Thank you for your letter of February 5.

*Vielen Dank für Ihren Auftrag vom 10.12.*
  Thank you very much for your order of December 12.

*Bezüglich Ihrer Anfrage vom 14.05. können wir Ihnen folgendes Angebot machen.*
  In reference to your inquiry of May 14, we are able to offer the following.

128

*Unter Bezugnahme auf Ihre Anfrage vom 14.05, freuen wir uns, Ihnen folgendes anbieten zu können.*
In reference to your inquiry of May 14, we are pleased (to be able) to offer you the following.

## ENDING A BUSINESS LETTER

*Bitte finden Sie in der Anlage unseren Katalog und unsere Preisliste.*
Please find enclosed our catalog and price list.

*Wir bitten um Bestätigung Ihrer Zahlungs- und Lieferbedingungen.*
Please confirm your terms of payment and delivery.

*Wir bestätigen den Erhalt Ihres Schreibens/Ihres Angebots/Ihrer Anfrage vom . . .*
We acknowledge receipt of your letter/your offer/your request, inquiry of . . .

*Wir werden Ihnen die gewünschten Daten innerhalb der nächsten Tage zusenden.*
We will supply the information requested within the next few days.

*Wir bitten um umgehende Mitteilung/Bestätigung.*
Please reply/confirm A.S.A.P./at your earliest convenience.

*Wir bitten um sofortige Überweisung des ausstehenden Betrages.*
We request immediate payment of the outstanding balance.

*Sie erhalten bei sofortiger Zahlung 2% Skonto. Der volle Rechnungsbetrag ist innerhalb von 30 Tagen ab Rechnungsdatum fällig.*
You will receive a 2% discount on immediate payment. The full amount is due within 30 days from the date of invoice.

## CLOSING LINES OF A BUSINESS LETTER

*Wir danken für Ihren Auftrag.*
We thank you for your order.

*Vielen Dank im Voraus.*
Thank you in advance.

*Mit freundlichem Gruß,*
Sincerely,

# 2. MOVING AND PACKING—A SCENARIO

*Firma Eduard Schlüter GmbH bestellt die Spedition EURAPID TRANSPORT\**
*um ihren Umzug zu organisieren:*

*EURAPID—Umzugsexperten im süddeutschen Raum*

**EU*RAPID***
**Spedition**
München • Stuttgart • Nürnberg

Tel (0711) 24 70 83 19
Fax (0711) 24 70 67 81

Eduard Schlüter GmbH
Alter Schulweg 1
62390 Rüsselsheim

**AUFTRAGSBESTÄTIGUNG**

Stuttgart, den 05.02.2004

*Wir bestätigen Ihren Auftrag für den Umzug Ihrer Firma am Freitag, den*
*12.02.2004 von* **Alter Schulweg 1, 62390 Rüsselsheim,** *nach* **Grashofstraße**
**75, 70231 Stuttgart.** *Sie bestellten bei uns:*

*Verpackungsmaterial*
*50 Kartons*
*10 große Säcke Styropor*

*Wir bringen zusätzlich Decken zum Transport von:*

*Transportgut*

| | | | |
|---|---|---|---|
| *10 Schreibtische* | *6 Aktenschränke* | *Faxgerät* | *9 Monitore* |
| *15 Stühle* | *Warenmuster (ca. 150)* | *3 Computer* | *6 Sessel* |
| *8 Wandregale* | *Frankiermaschine* | *2 Drucker* | *3 Tische* |

*EURAPID stellt Ihnen am Montag, dem 08.02., die gewünschten 50 Kartons zur*
*Verfügung. Sollten Sie mehr Kartons benötigen, bestellen Sie diese bitte telefonisch vor*
*Dienstag, dem 09.02., 16 Uhr, bei Frau Lammers, Tel (0711) 24 70 83-103, zur*
*Lieferung von weiteren Kartons am Mittwoch, dem 10.02., ab 11 Uhr.*

*Abholung des Transportgutes:* **Freitag, der 12.02.2004 zwischen 8.00 und**
**14.00 Uhr**

*Lieferung am Bestimmungsort:* **Montag, der 15.02.2004 ab 10 Uhr.**

*Bitte überprüfen Sie den Lieferschein vor Unterschrift auf fehlende Gegenstände*
*aus dem Transport. Schäden, die durch das Transportunternehmen erfolgten, bitten*
*wir auf dem Lieferschein zu vermerken. Für unsachgemäß verpackte Kartons, die*
*unser Personal von Ihnen in Empfang nahm, und daraus entstandenen Sachschaden*
*übernehmen wir keine Haftung. Sämtliche nicht auf dem Lieferschein vermerkten*
*Schäden sind innerhalb von 5 Tagen schriftlich anzumelden.*

*Die Rechnung ist nach Erhalt sofort zahlbar.*

*Wir danken Ihnen für Ihren Auftrag.*

*Mit freundlichem Gruß*

\* Both companies are fictional.

130

Eduard Schlüter GmbH hires the commercial freight carrier EURAPID to handle their move.

EU*RAPID*—Moving experts in the Southern German region

**EU*RAPID***
**Moving Service**
Munich • Stuttgart • Nuremberg

Phone (0711) 24 70 83 19
Fax (0711) 24 70 67 81

Eduard Schlütter GmbH
Alter Schulweg 1
62390 Rüsselsheim

**ORDER CONFIRMATION**

Stuttgart, February 5, 2004

We confirm your order for the move of your company on Friday, February 12, 2004, from Alter Schulweg 1, 62390 Rüsselsheim, to Grashofstraße 75, 70231 Stuttgart. You ordered from us:

Packing material
50 cardboard boxes
10 large bags of styrofoam
We will additionally supply blankets for the transportation of:

Freight

| | | | |
|---|---|---|---|
| 10 desks | 6 filing cabinets | fax machine | 9 computer monitors |
| 15 chairs | samples (approx. 150) | 2 printers | 6 armchairs |
| 8 shelves | postage meter | 3 computers | 3 tables |

EURAPID will supply you with 50 cardboard boxes on Monday, February 8, as requested. Should you require more boxes, please call Ms. Lammers at (0711) 24 70 83-102, before 4 P.M. on Tuesday, February 9, for delivery of additional boxes on Wednesday, February 10, after 11 A.M.

Pickup on: **Friday, February 12, 2004, between 8 A.M. and 2 P.M.**

Delivery at destination: **Monday, February 15, 2004, after 10 A.M.**

Please check the delivery note for any missing items before signing. Any damage caused by the moving service or our personnel is to be noted on the delivery note. We are not liable for any damage or loss resulting from poorly packed boxes that our staff received from you. Please advise us in writing within 5 days of any damage incurred not noted on the delivery note.

The invoice is payable upon receipt.

Thank you for your order.

Sincerely,

# ÜBUNGEN

**1.** *Formulieren Sie die Sätze im Imperativ.*

BEISPIEL: *(zum Flughafen/fahren/um 13 Uhr/bitte) Sie*
*Fahren Sie bitte um 13 Uhr zum Flughafen!*

    a. *(einen Brief/schreiben/an Herrn Weilandt/in Hannover) du*
    b. *(sagen/ihm/Bescheid/um 18 Uhr) ihr*
    c. *(setzen/dich/auf die Bank/und/warten/auf mich/bis um 4) du*
    d. *(stellen/die Kisten/unter den Tisch) Sie*
    e. *(vergessen/nicht/den Hund) du*
    f. *(legen/die Bücher/auf den Tisch) ihr*

**2.** *Setzen Sie den Artikel im richtigen Fall ein.*

BEISPIEL: *Vier Kartons standen (in) _____ Raum.*
*Vier Kartons standen im Raum.*

    a. *Sie nahm die Ordner (aus) _____ Karton und stellte sie (auf)*
       *_____ Regal.*
    b. *(Auf) _____ Regal stand eine Vase. Sie fiel hinunter und rollte*
       *(unter) _____ Tisch.*
    c. *Wo hast du die Karte hingelegt? Sie liegt (in) _____ Küche. Wo?*
       *(Auf) _____ Kühlschrank.*
    d. *Stell den Fernseher (neben) _____ Lampe!*
    e. *(Neben) _____ Lampe steht schon das Regal.*

**3.** *Übersetzen Sie.*

    a. Please put the boxes in the office to your left. *(Sie)*
    b. Has he already hung the picture in the conference room?
    c. The TV stands in front of the window.
    d. Please take a seat, Herr Klimke.
    e. Jens is lying on the floor. He is tired.
    f. Lay the books on the desk. *(Sie)*
    g. The truck is standing in front of the house.
    h. Jens put the red car next to the truck.

# LEKTION 8
TOURISMUS.   Tourism.

## A. DIALOG

*Zwei Schweizer[1] Reiseveranstalter treffen sich in Luzern[2] bei einer Tourismusbörse.[3] Eine Vertreterin des Umweltschutzes spricht für die Bürgerinitiative, die in Mürach,\* einem Sommer-und Skiressort im Berner Oberland,[4] den Autoverkehr durch Volksabstimmung[5] abschaffen will.*

HERR SCHMID: Gruezi, Frau Vetterli.

FRAU VETTERLI: Ja, gruezi! Sie auch hier? Was für eine Überraschung!

HERR SCHMID: Na, so einen Vortrag kann man sich doch nicht entgehen lassen. Ich hoffe, Sie haben ein Billet.[6]

FRAU VETTERLI: Natürlich. Der Vortrag ist bis auf den letzten Platz ausverkauft.

HERR SCHMID: Der Umweltschutz und der Tourismus sind eben[7] heiße Themen.

FRAU VETTERLI: Was halten Sie denn von den Plänen?

HERR SCHMID: Ich bin ganz dafür.[8] Autofreier Urlaub ist sehr populär. Wir können in den Dörfern im Berner Oberland mit viel mehr Sommergästen rechnen.

FRAU VETTERLI: Das kann ich verstehen. Aber ich bin gegen den Vorschlag. Viele unserer Reisenden fahren mit dem Auto nach Mürrach.

HERR SCHMID: Ach, tatsächlich?

FRAU VETTERLI: Ja, wir buchen viele Urlauber aus Süddeutschland und Frankreich, die ohne Auto wahrscheinlich nicht kommen würden†.

HERR SCHMID: Man kann den Postbusverkehr[9] doch ohne Probleme erweitern. Vergessen Sie außerdem nicht die Bahn, die Pferdekutschen und die Schlitten im Winter.

FRAU VETTERLI: Viele Gäste wollen nicht an einen Ort gebunden sein. Im Skiurlaub wollen Urlauber doch unabhängig sein.

---

\* *Mürach* is a fictional location.
† *würde* is the subjunctive II of *werden* (see Lesson 16).

HERR SCHMID: **Die Skilifts und die Zahnradbahn sind doch erstklassig. Damit kann man alle Skigebiete erreichen. Und bei den Straßenverhältnissen im Winter will nicht jeder mit dem Auto unterwegs sein. Ich habe gehört, dass es in den letzten Jahren auch extrem viele Probleme mit dem Parkieren[10] in Mürach gegeben hat.**

FRAU VETTERLI: **Ja, aber wenn man den Autoverkehr verbietet, hindert man doch die ansässige Bevölkerung auch daran zur Arbeit zu kommen, wenn nächstes Jahr das neue Uhrenwerk[11] aufmacht. Nicht alle Ansässigen arbeiten für den Tourismus.**

HERR SCHMID: **Ach, Sondergenehmigungen gibt es doch immer.[12] Das Uhrenwerk wird schon dafür sorgen.[13]**

EIN GAST: **Ruhe.**

DIE REDNERIN: **Ich freue mich, dass Sie so zahlreich erschienen sind. Das beweist, dass die gesamte Serviceindustrie der Schweiz in ihrem ökologischen Denken an erster Stelle in der Welt steht.**

*Die Anwesenden lachen.*

DIE REDNERIN: **Ganz im Ernst, meine Damen und Herren, wir haben Luzern ganz bewusst für unsere heutige Diskussion gewählt, denn das einzigartige Verkehrshaus Luzern[14] hält uns sowohl die Vergangenheit des Transportwesens als auch die Zukunft vor Augen.**

FRAU VETTERLI: **Entschuldigen Sie die Unterbrechung. Vetterli ist mein Name. Glauben Sie nicht, dass ein Autoverbot in Mürrach den Zugang zu einem der wichtigsten Tourismusgebiete der Schweiz verhindert?**

DIE REDNERIN: **Ganz im Gegenteil, Frau Vetterli. Wir wollen den Aufenthalt unserer Gäste erleichtern\* und verschönern. Und zwar ohne Autoverkehr.**

HERR SCHMID: **Erwarten Sie etwa einen stärkeren Zustrom von Urlaubern?**

DIE REDNERIN: **Genau. Die Nachfrage nach autofreiem Urlaub ist immens. Umfragen haben ergeben, dass bis zu 800 Kurgäste[15] mehr pro Jahr nach Mürrach kämen, gäbe† es keinen Autoverkehr.**

---

\* *erleichtern* (to facilitate) is a verb formed from an adjective, *leicht* (easy). See Lesson 19 for a detailed discussion of such verbs.

† *kämen* and *gäbe* are subjunctive II of *kommen* and *geben*. The subjunctive II is used to express a hypothetical situation. See Lesson 16.

HERR SCHMID: **Wie wollen Sie die Beförderung der Urlauber organisieren?**

DIE REDNERIN: **Durch regelmäßigen Bahn- und Busverkehr von Bern und Luzern.**

FRAU VETTERLI: **Da das Thema pressiert,[16] möchte ich wissen, wann die Volksabstimmung stattfinden wird?**

DIE REDNERIN: **Der Termin für die kantonale[17] Abstimmung ist für den September geplant.**

HERR SCHMID: **Na, also. Hoppla, ich werde gebiept.[18] Ich gehe mal kurz telefonieren.**

FRAU VETTERLI: **Kein Problem. Ich sage Ihnen, was besprochen wurde.**

HERR SCHMID: **Danke, bis gleich. Salut,[19] Frau Vetterli.**

FRAU VETTERLI: **Ja, ja, salut.**

---

## TRANSLATION

Two Swiss tour operators meet at a tourism convention in Lucerne. A representative of the environmental protection agency will speak on a petition by a communal initiative for a public referendum to ban automobile traffic in Mürrach, a summer and ski resort on the Bernese plateau.

MR. SCHMID: Good day, Ms. Vetterli.

MS. VETTERLI: Well, good day. You're here, too? What a surprise.

MR. SCHMID: One can't miss such a lecture. I hope you have a ticket.

MS. VETTERLI: Of course. The lecture is sold out to the last seat.

MR. SCHMID: Environmental protection and tourism are hot subjects, after all.

MS. VETTERLI: What do you think about the plans?

MR. SCHMID: I'm all for them. Car-free vacation is very popular. We can expect far more summer vacationers in the villages on the Bernese plateau.

MS. VETTERLI: I can relate to that. But I'm against the proposal. Many of our travelers drive to Mürrach.

MR. SCHMID: Oh, really?

MS. VETTERLI: Yes, we book many vacationers from the South of Germany and France who probably wouldn't come without their car.

MR. SCHMID: One could expand the postal coach service without any problems. And don't forget the railroad, the horse carriages, and the sled during the winter.

MS. VETTERLI: Many guests don't want to be tied to one place. During their skiing vacation, vacationers want to be independent.

MR. SCHMID: The ski lifts and the cogwheel train are first-class, after all. You can get to all ski resorts with them. And with the road conditions during the winter months, not everyone wants to be traveling by car. I heard that Mürrach had lots of problems with parking in the last few years.

MS. VETTERLI: Yes, but if you no longer allow automobile traffic in Mürrach you'll also prevent the resident population from getting to work when the new watch manufacturer opens next year. Not all residents work in the tourist industry.

MR. SCHMID: There are always special permits. The watch manufacturer will see to it.

A GUEST: Quiet!

THE SPEAKER: I'm glad to see so many of you here. That proves that the entire service industry of Switzerland is number one in the world in their attitude toward ecology.

The audience laughs.

THE SPEAKER: But seriously, ladies and gentlemen, we deliberately chose Lucerne for the discussion today, as the unique transportation museum of Lucerne shows us both the past of public transportation as well as the future.

MS. VETTERLI: Pardon my interruption. Vetterli is my name. Don't you think banning all automobile traffic from Mürrach would cut off access to one of the most important tourist areas of Switzerland?

THE SPEAKER: Quite the contrary, Ms. Vetterli. We want to facilitate an easier and more enjoyable stay for our guests. And I mean without automobile traffic.

MR. SCHMID: Do you expect higher numbers of vacationers?

THE SPEAKER: Exactly. The demand for car-free vacation is immense. Opinion polls have shown that up to 800 more spa guests would come to Mürrach per year if there was no automobile traffic.

MR. SCHMID: How do you propose to transport the vacationers?

THE SPEAKER: With regular rail and bus connections from Berne and Lucerne.

MS. VETTERLI: Since the subject is urgent I'd like to know when the referendum will take place?

THE SPEAKER: The referendum in the canton has been planned for a September date.

MR. SCHMID: There we have it. Whoops! I'm being beeped. I'll go make a quick phone call.

MS. VETTERLI: No problem. I'll tell you what was discussed.

MR. SCHMID: Thanks, I'll be back. Good-bye, Ms. Vetterli.

MS. VETTERLI: Yes, yes, bye-bye.

# B. IN KÜRZE

1. Switzerland is one of the few countries that take an article in German: *die Schweiz.* The nationality is *der Schweizer* and *die Schweizerin.* The German dialects are called *Schweizerdeutsch* (in standard German) or *Schwyzerdütsch* (in Swiss German). Visit the official Switzerland website at www.Schweiz.ch.

2. *Luzern* (Lucerne) is the major gateway for excursions into the *Berner Oberland.* Lucerne lies on the *Vierwaldstättersee* (Lake Lucerne). A popular tourist spot is *Mt. Pilatus,* where the world's steepest cogwheel train takes visitors up to the peak to enjoy a panoramic view from the Black Forest to the surrounding Alpine mountain ranges.

3. While the term *die Börse* is usually restricted to the stock markets, it is also a common name throughout Germany, Austria, and Switzerland for convention or trade fairs such as the *Tourismusbörse.*

4. *Das Berner Oberland* (the Bernese plateau), a popular tourist spot in both summer and winter, is the region around Berne.

5. *Die Volksabstimmung* (public referendum) is a very important part of the Swiss democracy. Every Swiss citizen is entitled to bring a subject into public discussion and propose a referendum, on a cantonal (state or county) or federal level, provided (s)he collects a minimum of 100,000 signatures supporting this motion.

6. *Das Billet* is any kind of ticket from bus ticket to theater ticket. While this French word is commonly used in Switzerland and Austria, in Germany the words *der Fahrschein* (bus or train ticket), *die Eintrittskarte* (admission ticket), and *das Flugticket* (plane ticket) are more common.

7. *Eben* is a flavoring word. It means "just so," "exactly," "after all," or "precisely."

*Das ist eben so.*
    That's just the way it is.

*Eben* also appears as part of the expression *gerade eben* (just this second).

*Herr Schmid ist gerade eben gegangen.*
Herr Schmid left just this second.

8. *Dafür* (for) and *dagegen* (against) are *da*-compounds used with *sein* to express one's stand on a subject.

9. *Der Postbusverkehr* (the postal coach connection) is an important means of transportation in remote alpine areas. Often there is no other public transportation available.

10. *Das Parkieren* (parking) is the noun of the verb *parkieren* (to park), a Swiss German term for "to park." Standard German uses the verb *parken*. Compare the Swiss German *Du kannst hier parkieren* with the standard German *Du kannst hier parken*. *Einparken* is used to describe the actual maneuver of parking a car into a space. The driving instructor *(der Fahrlehrer)* might say:

*Vorsicht beim Einparken!*
Use caution when parking your vehicle.

11. As in English, several terms refer to production facilities: *das Werk* (plant, production facility), *die Fabrik* (factory), *der Hersteller* (producer, manufacturer), *der Fabrikant* (factory owner, manufacturer). Try not to confuse *das Uhrenwerk* (watch manufacturer) with *das Uhrwerk* (clockwork).

12. Note the word order. *Sondergenehmigungen* is emphasized by being in the first position of the sentence. Placing the object in the first position results in verb and subject *(es)* switching places.

13. *Für etwas sorgen* is a non-reflexive verb meaning "to ensure, to make sure, to take care of."

*Das Uhrenwerk wird dafür sorgen.*
The manufacturer will make sure.

*Die Familie sorgte für das Kind.*
The family cared for the child.

*Sorgen* also appears as a reflexive verb, followed by the preposition *um,* and means "to worry."

*Er sorgte sich um das Kind, das nicht nach Hause kam.*
He worried about the child who did not come home.

14. *Das Verkehrshaus Luzern* is the Swiss Transport Museum, which is privately owned and subsidized by its members. It houses a large and interesting exhibit on transportation.

138

15. *Die Kur* is a spa vacation. A location that offers spa facilities is called *der Kurort* (spa location) or *das Kurzentrum* (spa center). It is much more popular to go on a *Kur* in Germany, Austria, and Switzerland than in the U.S.A., as health insurance covers at least partial costs. There are a great number of spas throughout Germany, which offer special mineral water springs or mud packs and other healthy treats. Probably the most famous *Kurort* is *Baden-Baden* in *Baden-Württemberg*. The prefix *Bad* (bath) often is an indication whether a village or town is considered a *Kurort*.

16. *Pressieren* (to be urgent, to be pressing) is a Swiss or Austrian expression. In Germany an adjective construction with *wichtig* (important) or *dringend* (urgent) is more common.

*Da die Angelegenheit dringend ist, brauche ich heute noch eine Antwort.*
As the matter is urgent, I need an answer today.

17. *Der Kanton* (canton, state) is the Swiss equivalent of a region or state of the confederation. Switzerland has twenty-six *Kantone*.

18. *Gebiept werden* is the German adaptation of "being beeped," or in other words, "being paged."

19. *Adieu, tschüss,* and *ciao* are the Swiss equivalents to "bye." The three variations signify Switzerland's multilingualism: *adieu* is French, *tschüss* German, and *ciao* Italian. The more formal standard German *auf Wiedersehen* is also used in Switzerland; however, in the Swiss dialect it will sound more like *Aufwiderluege*. The Swiss write standard German, although their pronunciation may lead you to believe otherwise.

# C. GRAMMATIK UND GEBRAUCH

## 1. *AKKUSATIVPRÄPOSITIONEN* (ACCUSATIVE PREPOSITIONS)

German prepositions are divided into four groups: those that take the dative (Lesson 4), two-way prepositions (Lesson 7), those that take the accusative, and those that take the genitive (Lesson 13). Prepositions with the accusative are used to describe movement, means, and direction. Listed below are the most common ones.

*DURCH* (through)
*Wir sind durch den Wald gegangen.*
We walked through the forest.

*Ich habe durch die Nachrichten erfahren, dass die Straße gesperrt ist.*
I learned from the news that the road is blocked.

*OHNE* (without)
*Ich komme ohne das Auto nicht nach Mürrach.*
I can't get to Mürrach without the car.

*Ohne mich will sie nicht in Urlaub fahren.*
Without me she doesn't want to go on vacation.

*GEGEN* (against)
*Wir müssen etwas gegen die Umweltverschmutzung tun.*
We have to do something against pollution.

*Frau Vetterli ist gegen das Autoverbot.*
Frau Vetterli is against the ban on automobile traffic.

*FÜR* (for)
*Ich bin für den Plan.*
I am for the plan.

*Wieviel hast du für das Hotelzimmer bezahlt?*
How much did you pay for the hotel room?

*UM* (around)
*Wir gingen immer um die Informationszentrale herum und fanden die Tür nicht.*
We kept walking around the information center and couldn't find the door.

When describing a circling of an object, *um* often teams up with *herum*.

*UM* (at)
*Um 17:30 muss ich zum Reisebüro.*
At 5:30 I have to go to the travel agent.

## 2. *POSSESSIVPRONOMEN* (POSSESSIVE PRONOUNS)

Possessive pronouns indicate ownership.

| | | | |
|---|---|---|---|
| *mein* | my | *unser* | our |
| *dein* | your | *euer* | your |
| *sein* | his | *ihr* | their |
| *ihr* | her | *Ihr* | your |
| *sein* | its | | |

*Unser Haus ist in Bern.*
Our house is in Berne.

*Wo ist deine Wohnung?*
Where is your apartment?

140

Possessive pronouns take endings depending on gender, number, and case of the nouns they refer to.

|  | MY DOG<br>MASC.<br>SING. | OUR TRIP<br>FEM.<br>SING. | HER HOUSE<br>NEUTER<br>SING. |
|---|---|---|---|
| NOM. | mein Hund | unsere Reise | ihr Haus |
| ACC. | meinen Hund | unsere Reise | ihr Haus |
| DAT. | meinem Hund | unserer Reise | ihrem Haus |
| GEN. | meines Hundes | unserer Reise | ihres Hauses |

|  | MY DOGS<br>MASC.<br>PL. | OUR TRIPS<br>FEM.<br>PL. | HER HOUSES<br>NEUTER<br>PL. |
|---|---|---|---|
| NOM. | meine Hunde | unsere Reisen | ihre Häuser |
| ACC. | meine Hunde | unsere Reisen | ihre Häuser |
| DAT. | meinen Hunden | unseren Reisen | ihren Häusern |
| GEN. | meiner Hunde | unserer Reisen | ihre Häuser |

*Ich bin mit meinen Hunden spazieren gegangen.*
I went for a walk with my dogs.

*Ohne sein Auto fährt er nie in den Urlaub.*
He never goes on vacation without his car.

*Auf unseren Reisen habe ich immer zugenommen.*
I always put on weight on our trips.

*Sie hat in ihrem Haus alles geändert.*
She has changed everything in her house.

## 3. UNBESTIMMTE PRONOMEN (INDEFINITE PRONOUNS)*

Indefinite pronouns refer to indefinite rather than particular persons or objects. German uses a variety of indefinite pronouns such as *viele* (many), *alles* (everything), *alle* (all), *man*† (one), *irgendwer* (anyone, someone), *irgendwo* (anywhere, somewhere), *irgendwann* (sometime, anytime), *etwas* (something), and *nichts* (nothing).

* Other indefinite pronouns, *jemand/niemand, jeder, welcher,* etc., were discussed in Lesson 6.
† See also Lesson 17.

| | SOMEBODY | ONE | MANY | ALL | SOMETHING |
|------|-----------|-------|--------|--------|-----------|
| NOM. | *irgendwer* | *man* | *viele* | *alle* | *etwas* |
| ACC. | *irgendwen* | *einen* | *viele* | *alle* | |
| DAT. | *irgendwem* | *einem* | *vielen* | *allen* | |
| GEN. | | | *vieler* | *aller* | |

*Irgend-wer/-wann/-wo* are used only in positive statements.

*Irgendwer wird schon wissen, wo das Hotel ist.*
Someone will surely know where the hotel is.

*Irgendwo wird es ja ein Telefon geben.*
There's got to be a telephone somewhere.

*Er wird schon irgendwann kommen.*
He will get here sometime.

Negative statements use *niemand* for persons, *nirgendwo* for places, and *nichts* for objects or ideas.

*Niemand weiß, wo Sonja ihre Ski gelassen hat.*
No one knows where Sonja left her skis.

*Sie hat sie nirgendwo gefunden.*
She found them nowhere.

*Ich habe nichts davon gewusst.*
I knew nothing about it.

If you wish to make a general statement about many people, use *viele* (many) or *alle* (all).

*Viele Menschen fahren jedes Jahr in die Schweiz.*
Many people go to Switzerland every year.

*Alle Schweizer Bürger dürfen jetzt ab dem 18. Lebensjahr wählen.*
All Swiss citizens may now vote from 18 years up.

*Alle* and *viele* also appear as indefinite pronouns for a comprehensive number of objects.

*Es standen viele Blumen auf dem Tisch.*
There were many flowers on the table.

*Bitte stellen Sie alle Koffer an der Rezeption ab.*
Please place/leave all suitcases in the reception area.

For comprehensive statements about objects or ideas, without nouns, use *alles.*

*Wir haben alles eingepackt.*
We packed everything.

*Haben Sie alles verstanden?*
Did you understand everything?

*Man* is frequently used to make a general statement. It is far more common than its English equivalent "one."

*Man weiß nie, wann es schneit.*
One never knows when it will snow.

*Den Vortrag kann man sich nicht entgehen lassen.*
One can't miss the lecture.

*Man hat mir das Hotel gezeigt.*
(Some)one showed me the hotel.

*Etwas* (something) is used to express indefinite objects or ideas.

*Können Sie mir etwas empfehlen?*
Can you recommend something?

*Etwas* often takes the *irgend*-prefix.

*Ich muss irgendetwas für meine Mutter kaufen. Sie hat Geburtstag.*
I have to buy something for my mother; it's her birthday.

# D. REIN GESCHÄFTLICH

## 1. GENERAL INFORMATION ON SWITZERLAND

Switzerland has four official languages: German, French, Italian, and Romansh. In the Western area, around Geneva and up toward Neuchatel, people speak French, and in the South near Locarno and Lugano Italian. The majority of the Swiss population speaks German in any of the numerous Swiss dialects. Romansh, a mixture of Latin and Italian, is spoken by only 1 percent of the population in the canton *Graubünden* (Grisons). Although Romansh is estimated to be well over 1,000 years old, it only became the fourth national language accepted by the electorate in 1938.
Switzerland was founded as *die Helvetische Eidgenossenschaft* (the Helvetic Confederation) in 1291 by the three *Kantone* (cantons) *Schwyz,*

*Uri* and *Ob- und Nidwalden* which pledged alliance and support to each other against the neighboring Habsburg Empire. Over the centuries Switzerland added more cantons to its confederation, and currently consists of twenty-six of them. Switzerland gained its neutrality at the Congress of Vienna in 1815.

Although Switzerland's population is only about 7 million, the country ranks among the richest in the world. It is best known for its service, the high quality of its products, as well as its finance and banking industry. The land area of Switzerland is only half the size of Maine. More than half of the country is alpine, offering a stunning view of valleys, lakes, and snow-topped peaks. Berne is the capital of Switzerland and is famous for its *Bärengraben* (bear pit). Switzerland is not part of the European Union, and therefore uses its own currency, *der Schweizer Franken (SF)* consisting of 100 *Rappen,* instead of the euro.

## 2. THE SWISS ECONOMY

Switzerland has no *natürliche Rohstoffe* (natural resources), and less than 10 percent of its agricultural products are homegrown. Yet Switzerland continues to have a healthy *Handelsbilanz* (trade balance). Its large export/import industry is attractive to importers and foreign investment because of low import duties, first-rate financial services, and high-quality production. Except for agricultural products, Switzerland has virtually no import quotas.

The Swiss industry specializes in several areas: the chemical and pharmaceutical industries (predominantly in Basel); insurance companies, banks, and money markets (in all major cities); precision and technical instruments (mainly in Zurich); and clockmaking (Solothurn and Geneva). The famous *Swatch* watches are made in Bienne. Switzerland's first-rate hotel, restaurant, and service industry has set worldwide standards, and *Emmentaler, Appenzeller, Gruyère,* and other Swiss cheeses have found their way to worldwide menus, as have chocolate products from companies such as *Nestlé* in Vevey. Last but not least, one of Switzerland's major export items is the Swiss pocketknife.

Tourism is a major source of income for Switzerland. Vacationers stream into the country at any time of the year for almost any type of vacation. Switzerland has an abundance of lakes which are perfect for sailing, wind-surfing, and other water sports. During the winter months, famous ski resorts such as *Gstaad* and *St. Moritz* host large numbers of ski, snowboard, and other snow enthusiasts.

## 3. ENVIRONMENTAL AWARENESS IN THE EUROPEAN UNION

Environmental issues are truly "hot" all over Europe. Both industry and consumers are trying to find ways to encourage environmentally safe products and behavior. Recycling in businesses and individual households has become the rule in most European countries, and the use of public transportation instead of individual cars is being encouraged, partly by incredibly high gasoline taxes.

Any company that wishes to market its products in the European Union and/or Switzerland must be aware of the extensive environmental legislation, which prescribes high taxation for environmentally unsafe or wasteful business practices. These regulations are meant to give incentives to producers and consumers to act environmentally responsibly. The so-called Eco-label program, for example, requires that any product distributed in the European Union carry a label guaranteeing that the distributing company disposes of its packaging waste itself. This program assists consumers to make environmentally aware purchasing decisions and to reward producers of "greener" products. Individual efforts should not be underestimated, either: in a concerted effort to save plastic, cut down on waste, and recycle, it is customary in German, Austrian, and Swiss supermarkets to use one's own bags, as supermarkets charge money for plastic or paper bags.

## ÜBUNGEN

1. *Übersetzen Sie.*

    a. We drove through the city.
    b. At 8 P.M. we arrived in Lucerne.
    c. We couldn't find the hotel without the city map.
    d. We can stay here overnight for SF 120.
    e. We kept walking around the hotel looking for a restaurant.
    f. At 10 P.M. we went back to the hotel.
    g. I wanted to stay in Lucerne but my friend was against the idea.

2. *Setzen Sie das richtige Possessivpronomen ein.*

BEISPIEL: *Das ist _____ Auto.* (my)
           *Das ist mein Auto.*

    a. *Haben Sie _____ Schlüssel gesehen?* (his)
    b. *_____ Haus ist in Lausanne.* (our)
    c. *_____ Skier stehen in der Ecke.* (your formal)
    d. *Ich gebe _____ Katzen und _____ Hund immer zu den Nachbarn, wenn ich in Urlaub fahre.* (my)
    e. *Habt ihr _____ Geld wieder gefunden?* (your)
    f. *Sie hat _____ Pass vergessen.* (her)
    g. *Wie war _____ Reise?* (your familiar)

**3.** *Entscheiden Sie sich zwischen „irgendwo", „irgendwann", und „irgendwer".*

    a. *War _____ hier?*
    b. *Ja, ich habe den Zettel _____ hingelegt.*
    c. *Wenn du ihn _____ findest, sag mir Bescheid.*
    d. *_____ habe ich doch mal an das Hotel Interlaken geschrieben.*
    e. *_____ muss der Brief ja sein.*

**4.** *Übersetzen Sie die Sätze aus Übung 3.*

# LEKTION 9

DER DEUTSCHSPRACHIGE FILM.   The German Film.

---

## A. DIALOG

---

*Miriam Wallstätter, eine österreichische Regisseurin aus Wien,[1] unterhält sich mit einem Filmkritiker aus Hamburg[2] auf der Berlinale.*

DIRK CLAUSEN: **Na, Frau Wallstätter, was halten[3] Sie denn von der Konkurrenz? Was glauben Sie, wer gewinnt?**

MIRIAM WALLSTÄTTER: **Mir gefielen der portugiesische und der kanadische Beitrag am besten.**

HERR CLAUSEN: **Ich denke, der deutsche Film wird gewinnen.**

FRAU WALLSTÄTTER: **Na, ich weiß ja nicht. Das einzig Umwerfende daran ist der Schnitt. Alles andere hat es schon mal gegeben.**

HERR CLAUSEN: **Sie sind wie immer viel zu kritisch. Was gibt es denn Neues in Österreich?**

FRAU WALLSTÄTTER: **Wir waren natürlich auf der Viennale.[4] Wo waren Sie denn? Ich habe Sie dort gar nicht gesehen.**

HERR CLAUSEN: **Die Viennale hab' ich leider versäumt. Aber ich werde nach Venedig[5] kommen.**

FRAU WALLSTÄTTER: **Sagen Sie mal, wo ist denn eigentlich Ihr Kollege?**

HERR CLAUSEN: **Dieter Hellberg?**

FRAU WALLSTÄTTER: **Genau der.**

HERR CLAUSEN: **Der ist doch zum Filmemacher geworden. Hat sich das noch nicht bis Wien herumgesprochen?[6]**

FRAU WALLSTÄTTER: **Nein.**

HERR CLAUSEN: **Dieter hat sich beim Kurz- und Dokumentarfilm Förderprogramm beworben und eine Dokumentation in Südamerika gedreht. Jetzt hat er viel um die Ohren.[7]**

FRAU WALLSTÄTTER: **Nun habe ich einen meiner besten Kritiker verloren. Was hat er denn sonst noch vor?[8]**

HERR CLAUSEN: **Er macht gerade eine deutsch-französische Koproduktion über Obdachlosenheime fürs[9] Fernsehen.**

FRAU WALLSTÄTTER: Da fällt mir g'rad[10] was ein! Geht Ihnen das auch so?[11] Im Gespräch, oder beim Zuhören, hab' ich immer die besten Ideen.

HERR CLAUSEN: Nein. Bei mir passiert das immer vor der Schreibmaschine.

FRAU WALLSTÄTTER: Na, Sie sind aber altmodisch.[12] Arbeiten Sie nicht am Computer? Egal.[13] Passen Sie auf, Sie kennen doch den Kritiker vom *Stern*,[14] nicht wahr?

HERR CLAUSEN: Ja, ganz gut. Allerdings habe ich ihn schon lange nicht mehr gesehen.

FRAU WALLSTÄTTER: Hat der nicht das letzte Mal einen Beitrag über die Wiener Filmfestspiele geschrieben?

HERR CLAUSEN: Ja, natürlich.

FRAU WALLSTÄTTER: Sind Sie dann nicht dran,[15] was über das neue europäische Förderungsprojekt mit Miriam Wallstätter zu schreiben?

HERR CLAUSEN: Ach, sieh mal einer an.[16] Worum geht's denn?

FRAU WALLSTÄTTER: Es geht um einen politischen Spielfilm mit staatlichen Zuschüssen aus allen beteiligten Ländern. Mafia, Interpol, Plutonium Schmuggel, große Namen.[17] Ab nächste Woche sind wir am Drehort in Mailand.

HERR CLAUSEN: Ich habe davon gehört. Hat es da nicht Probleme mit den Produktionskosten gegeben?

FRAU WALLSTÄTTER: Ja, schon, aber die sind jetzt alle gelöst. Das Drehbuch ist einzigartig.

HERR CLAUSEN: Wer hat es denn geschrieben?

FRAU WALLSTÄTTER: Claudio Santini.

HERR CLAUSEN: Der letzte Film von ihm war doch ein totaler Flop.[18]

FRAU WALLSTÄTTER: Ja, aber auch nur in Deutschland. Sie sollten wirklich über uns schreiben.

HERR CLAUSEN: Ich denke eine Besprechung wird reichen.

FRAU WALLSTÄTTER: Nein, absolut nicht. Es ist doch wichtig, europäische Koproduktionen ins Gespräch zu bringen\*, um die Überschwemmung des europäischen Marktes mit amerikanischen Filmen einzudämmen.

---

\* *zu bringen* is an infinitive construction with *zu* (see Lesson 11).

HERR CLAUSEN: **Da haben Sie schon recht. Aber sie sollten das Interesse des europäischen Kinopublikums an Hollywoodfilmen nicht vergessen.**

FRAU WALLSTÄTTER: **Aber das ist doch längst nicht alles, was hierzulande[19] in den Kinos gezeigt wird.**

HERR CLAUSEN: **Natürlich nicht, aber eine Reportage vom Drehort ist deshalb doch nicht gefragt.**

FRAU WALLSTÄTTER: **Na, schön. Dann rufe ich eben Ihren Kollegen beim *Stern* an.**

HERR CLAUSEN: **Na, wenn das so ist,[20] dann werde ich wohl mal mit der Redaktionsleitung plaudern.[21]**

FRAU WALLSTÄTTER: **Na bitte. Wo ein Wille ist, ist auch ein Weg.**

---

### TRANSLATION

Miriam Wallstätter, an Austrian director from Vienna, is talking to a film critic from Hamburg at the Berlinale.

DIRK CLAUSEN: Well, Ms. Wallstätter, what do you think of the competition? Who do you think will win?

MIRIAM WALLSTÄTTER: I liked the Portuguese and the Canadian entries the best.

MR. CLAUSEN: I think the German film will win.

MS. WALLSTÄTTER: Well, I don't know about that. The only fabulous thing was the editing. Everything else has been done before.

MR. CLAUSEN: You're too critical, as usual. What's new in Austria?

MS. WALLSTÄTTER: We went to the Viennale, of course. Where were you? I didn't see you there.

MR. CLAUSEN: Unfortunately, I missed the Viennale. But I'll come to Venice.

MS. WALLSTÄTTER: Tell me, where is your colleague?

MR. CLAUSEN: Dieter Hellberg?

MS. WALLSTÄTTER: That's the one.

MR. CLAUSEN: He became a filmmaker. Didn't you hear that in Vienna yet?

MS. WALLSTÄTTER: No.

MR. CLAUSEN: Dieter applied for a scholarship with the short and documentary film program and made a documentary in South America. Now he's swamped with work.

MS. WALLSTÄTTER: I just lost my best critic. What else is he up to?

MR. CLAUSEN: He's doing a German-French co-production about homeless shelters for TV.

MS. WALLSTÄTTER: I just thought of something. Does that happen to you too? While talking or listening to someone, I always get the best ideas.

MR. CLAUSEN: No, that only happens to me in front of the typewriter.

MS. WALLSTÄTTER: Aren't you old-fashioned! Don't you work on the computer? Never mind. Listen up, you know the critic from the *Stern,* don't you?

MR. CLAUSEN: Yeah, quite well. But I haven't seen him in a long time.

MS. WALLSTÄTTER: Didn't he write a report on the Viennese Film Festival once?

MR. CLAUSEN: Yes, of course.

MS. WALLSTÄTTER: Isn't it your turn then to write something about a new subsidized European project with Miriam Wallstätter?

MR. CLAUSEN: Well, who would've thought! What's that all about?

MS. WALLSTÄTTER: It's a political feature film with state subsidies from all the countries involved. Mafia, Interpol, plutonium smuggling, big names. As of next week we are on location in Milan.

MR. CLAUSEN: I heard about it. Weren't there some problems with the production costs?

MS. WALLSTÄTTER: Yes, that's right. But they've been taken care of. The script is unique.

MR. CLAUSEN: Who wrote it?

MS. WALLSTÄTTER: Claudio Santini.

MR. CLAUSEN: His last film was a total flop.

MS. WALLSTÄTTER: Yes, but only in Germany. You really should write about us.

MR. CLAUSEN: I think a review will be enough.

MS. WALLSTÄTTER: No, absolutely not. It is particularly important to introduce and talk about European co-productions to halt the flood of American films onto the market.

MR. CLAUSEN: You are right there. But don't forget the public's interest in Hollywood films.

MS. WALLSTÄTTER: But that's far from all that's being shown in the movie theaters in this country.

MR. CLAUSEN: Of course not, but that doesn't warrant an on-location report.

MS. WALLSTÄTTER: Okay, fine. Then I'll just call your colleague at the *Stern*.

MR. CLAUSEN: Well, if that's the way it is, I'll talk it over with the editorial department.

MS. WALLSTÄTTER: There you go. Where there's a will, there's a way.

# B. IN KÜRZE

1. *Wien* (Vienna), on the banks of the river Danube *(die Donau)*, is the capital of Austria. Like Paris, and unlike other European cities, Vienna is divided into *Bezirke* (districts) by numbers, starting in the center: *der erste Bezirk* (the first district). Vienna is a busy yet extraordinarily beautiful European capital. It has a great number of internationally renowned museums, stately palaces, parks, and a famous opera. Tourists and residents go on weekend excursions to the *Wienerwald* (Viennese forest) or to the suburbs for *Heurigen* (new wine). Go to www.Wien.at for more information.

2. Hamburg, a *Hansestadt* (see Lesson 15), is on the estuary of the river *Elbe*. Its first appearance in historical records is as the fort *Hammaburg* in 825. Hamburg is the largest German seaport, whose shipbuilding industry enjoys international status. After World War II Hamburg took a key position in the service industry, as a center for banking, insurance, news media, and publishing. Hamburg's official website is www.Hamburg.de.

3. *Halten von* (to think of/about) is a very common colloquial term for expressing one's opinion.

*Was halten Sie von dem Gedanken?*
What do you think about that idea?

*Ich halte nichts davon.*
I think it's not worth anything.

Literally, *halten* means "to stop" or "to hold."

*Bitte halten Sie hier an.*
Please stop here.

*Er hält einen Blumenstrauß in der Hand.*
He's holding a bunch of flowers in his hand.

4. *Die Viennale* is a newly formed term, borrowing from the original Venice film festival *Biennale*. Other European film festivals have since borrowed the term as well: *die Berlinale (Berlin Film Festspiele)*. The official German term for the Viennese festival is *die Internationalen Film-Festwochen*.

5. When speaking of Venice in this context, they are referring to the *Biennale.*

6. The German expression contains a slight mockery, implying that this particular bit of news is not earth-shattering, as big news would make it to Vienna.

7. *Viel um die Ohren haben* is a colloquial expression for having a full schedule, being very busy, or being swamped with work. Literally translated it means "to have lots around the ears." Synonymous expressions are *vielbeschäftigt sein* (to be very occupied) and *viel zu tun haben* (to have much to do).

*Wie geht es dem Geschäft?*
How's business?

*Wir sind vielbeschäftigt.*
We are very busy.

*Hast du Mittwoch Zeit?*
Do you have time on Wednesday?

*Nein, Mittwoch habe ich viel zu tun.*
No, Wednesday, I've got lots to do.

8. *Etwas vorhaben* (to plan something) is a verb with separable prefix. The corresponding noun is *das Vorhaben* (the project, the venture).

*Ich habe vor, im Mai nach Cannes zu fliegen.*
I'm planning to fly to Cannes in May.

*Sein Vorhaben ist geplatzt.*
His plan fell through.

9. *Fürs* is the colloquial short form of *für das,* joined in speaking to facilitate pronunciation. *Fürs,* however, is not an accepted grammatical short form such as *vom (von dem)* and should not be used in formal written text.

10. The apostrophe in *g'rad* (just now) replaces the *e.* This short form of *gerade* is common in colloquial language but should not be used in formal writing. *E* endings in conjugated verbs are also frequently dropped and replaced by an apostrophe.

*Ich hab' keine Zeit.*
I have no time.

11. *Gehen* (to go) is used in many different set expressions:

*Wie geht's?*
How are you?

*Geht's voran?*
Are we making progress?

*Das geht mir genauso.*
It's the same with me.

12. *Altmodisch* (old-fashioned) is used in the same way as the English term. *Neumodisch* (fashionable, newfangled), however, is a somewhat derogatory term in German.

*Ich kann dieses ganze neumodische Gerede nicht ertragen.*
I can't bear all this newfangled, fashionable talk.

Use *modern* (fashionable, modern) as a complimentary term.

13. The use and meaning of *egal* (indifferent) vary according to context and whether it stands by itself or not. Standing alone, it means "Never mind." In a sentence it means:

*Es ist mir egal./Das ist egal.*
It makes no difference (to me).

14. *Der Stern* is a popular weekly news and culture magazine. It ranks among the most popular magazines in Germany. Others are *Der Spiegel, Focus, Brigitte,* and *Bunte.*

15. *D'ran sein* (to take one's turn) is made up of the *da*-compound *daran* and *sein.* The apostrophe here replaces the missing *a.*

16. *Sieh mal einer an!* or *Schau mal einer an!* is a fixed expression implying surprise. It is often meant ironically.

17. *Große Namen* (big names) implies people well-known in their field. In this context, it refers to well-known actors, directors, or producers.

18. *Floppen* is the German adaptation of "to flop." All English verbs that are adapted into German take weak verb endings in the past participle, *ge-flopp-t.* The noun *der Flop* is used to express a failure and is not limited to films. The equivalent German words are *der Reinfall* (failure) and *die Pleite* (loss, failure). *Die Pleite* is also used in business terminology to describe bankruptcy.

19. *Hierzulande* (in this country, in these parts) doesn't necessarily have to refer to a country as a whole (as opposed to another), but may also refer to parts of a country, or a city.

20. *Wenn das so ist* (if that's what it is) is an expression of concession. The stress lies on *so.*

21. *Plaudern* (to chat) is a colloquial alternative to *reden* (to talk).

# C. GRAMMATIK UND GEBRAUCH

## 1. *KONZESSIVE NEBENSÄTZE* (CONCESSIVE SUBCLAUSES)

Subordinating conjunctions introduce a dependent clause containing pertinent or additional information to the action of the main clause. When the information given in the subordinated clause is restricted to the outcome of the main clause, the conjunction expresses this restriction and is therefore called concessive.* A clause introduced by a subordinating conjunction is most often linked to a main clause, although it can sometimes stand on its own. Main clause and dependent clause are separated by a comma.

*Ich habe mich verspätet, obwohl ich früh aufstand.*
I was running late although I got up early.

Since the concessive statement made by the dependent clause is often of great importance to the action in the main clause, concessive clauses often stand at the beginning.

*Obwohl 1993 die Deutschen keinen Film auf den Festspielen gezeigt haben, waren viele deutsche Journalisten dort.*
Although the Germans did not show a film at the festival in 1993, many German journalists were there.

The major concessive conjunctions are:

*OBWOHL* (although)
*Obwohl viele gute europäische Filme in Amerika gezeigt werden, haben nur wenige großen Erfolg an den Kassen.*
Although many good European films are shown in the U.S.A., only a few are successful at the box office.

*OBGLEICH* (although)
*Obgleich der Regisseur viel Geld für die Produktion bekam, hatte er nach 3 Wochen kein Geld mehr.*
Although the director got a lot of money for production, after three weeks he had none left.

*Obwohl* and *obgleich* are identical.

---

* Other subordinated conjunctions are temporal (Lesson 5), conditional (Lessons 3 and 16), final (Lesson 11), or causal (Lesson 12).

*TROTZDEM* (in spite of, despite, still)
*Ich habe alle Filme auf den Festspielen gesehen. Trotzdem weiß ich nicht,*
*über welchen ich schreiben soll.*

> I saw all films at the festival. In spite of that/Still, I don't know which
> one to write about.

> *Trotzdem* is often used at the beginning of a new sentence that
> introduces the concession.

> Another frequently used concessive word is the adverb *allerdings*
> (however).

*Er ist sehr erfolgreich, hat allerdings keine Lust mehr, weiterzumachen.*

> He is very successful; however, he doesn't feel like continuing to work.

> *Trotzdem* (despite, still) may also appear as an adverb, as it often does
> when moving into a different position in the sentence.

*Ich weiß trotzdem nicht, wo das Kino ist.*

> Despite all that I (still) don't know where the movie theater is.

## 2. *WORTSTELLUNG ZUR BETONUNG* (WORD ORDER FOR EMPHASIS)

> As you know, the regular German word order is subject-verb-object. If
> you want to emphasize a part of the sentence in particular, you can do
> so simply by moving it to the beginning of the sentence. Note that the
> verb and subject always switch places.

*In Venedig war es ganz anders.*
In Venice it was very different.

> Virtually every part of the sentence can be moved to the beginning for
> emphasis.

*Ohne das Geld kann ich den Film nicht drehen.*
Without the money I can't shoot that film.

*Den Film kann ich ohne das Geld nicht drehen.*
That film I can't shoot without the money.

*Drehen kann ich den Film ohne das Geld nicht.*
Shoot that film without the money, I can't do (that).

# 3. *WORTBILDUNG* (WORD FORMATION)

### a. Verbal Nouns

Verbs such as *gehen* (to go), *schreiben* (to write), *laufen* (to run), *fahren* (to drive) can form nouns in conjunction with a preposition.

*Beim Autofahren esse ich immer Schokolade.*
While driving my car I always eat chocolate.

These prepositions are *bei* (during, while), *zu* (for), *vor* (before), *nach* (after), and *von* (from). They always require the dative. The new verbal noun is always neuter and is always preceded by a definite article in the dative which contracts with the preposition:
*bei + dem = beim, zu + dem = zum,* and *von + dem = vom.*

*Dirk Clausen erinnerte sich beim Schreiben an das Gespräch mit Miriam Wallstätter.*
While writing Dirk Clausen remembered the conversation with Miriam Wallstätter.

*Zum Fernsehen muss ich eine Brille tragen.*
I have to wear glasses for watching TV.

*Vor* and *nach* don't contract with the article.

*Nach dem Autofahren bin ich immer müde.*
After driving a car I'm always tired.

*Vor dem Einschlafen trinke ich immer ein Glas Milch.*
Before falling asleep I always drink a glass of milk.

If the verb has a separable prefix, the prefix becomes part of the noun.

*Dirk Clausen schlief beim Zuhören ein.*
Dirk Clausen fell asleep while listening.

### b. Adjectival Nouns

All adjectives can become nouns. If the adjectival noun is preceded by a definite article, the noun takes adjective endings according to case, number, and gender.

*Der Kranke saß auf dem Sofa.*
The sick (man) sat on the sofa.

*Die Neue macht ihre Arbeit sehr gut.*
The new (female employee) works very well.

*Die Alten sind weise.*
The old (people) are wise.

If the adjectival noun is preceded by an indefinite article, it adds the *-er* ending to the noun.

*Ein Reisender saß am Tisch.*
A traveler sat at the table.

*Ein Kranker sollte nicht reisen.*
A sick (person) should not travel.

The indefinite article in the masculine is used for a nondescript purpose. When speaking of a specific gender, the adjectival noun takes adjective endings.

*Eine Blinde saß am Tisch.*
A blind (woman) sat at the table.

If adjectival nouns are general and descriptive, they are neuter: *das Gute, das Böse, das Neue.*

*Gibt es etwas Neues?*
Did anything new happen?

*Das Gute daran ist, dass wir die Filme der Konkurrenz kennen.*
The good thing is that we know the competitors' films.

*Alles Gute zum Geburtstag.*
All the best on your birthday.

If they refer to a particular person or thing, their gender is defined by the gender of their reference point.

*Die Rothaarige ist älter als die Blonde.*
The redhead(ed woman) is older than the blond (woman).

*Der Kleine ist älter als der Große.*
The little (guy) is older than the tall (guy).


## 4. IDIOMATIC EXPRESSIONS

German has many idiomatic expressions using parts of the human body. Let's start with the ear:

SICH AUFS OHR LEGEN (to take a nap; lit: to lie on one ear)
*Er hat sich für eine halbe Stunde aufs Ohr gelegt.*
He is taking a nap for half an hour.

JEMAND ÜBERS OHR HAUEN (to trick, to con; lit.: to hit someone over the ear)
*Er hat mich bei diesem Kauf wirklich übers Ohr gehauen.*
He really conned me with this purchase.

*DIE OHREN STEIF HALTEN* (to keep one's chin up; lit.: to keep one's ears stiff)
*Halt die Ohren steif! Es wird schon wieder besser.*
Keep your chin up. It'll get better.

*VIEL UM DIE OHREN HABEN* (to be busy; lit.: to have much around the ears)
*Seit ich befördert wurde, habe ich sehr viel um die Ohren.*
Since I got promoted, I'm so busy.

*JEMANDEM IN DEN OHREN LIEGEN* (to pester someone; lit.: to lie in someone's ears)
*Er liegt mir schon seit Tagen mit seinem neuen Projekt in den Ohren.*
He's been pestering me with his new project for days now.

*ZU OHREN KOMMEN* (to come to one's attention; lit.: to come to one's ears)
*Es ist mir zu Ohren gekommen, dass Sie einen neuen Film drehen.*
It has come to my attention that you're working on a new film.

*AUF DEN OHREN SITZEN* (to be absent-minded; lit.: to be sitting on one's ears)
*Sag mal, du sitzt wohl auf den Ohren. Ich habe dich schon dreimal gerufen.*
Hey, are you deaf? I've called you three times already.

# D. REIN GESCHÄFTLICH

## 1. FILM HISTORY AND FESTIVALS

Germany's film tradition has produced great talent. Some of the great film stars from the age of silent movies fled Germany with the onset of the Nazi regime. The list of German and Austrian directors, cameramen, writers, and actors who resettled in Hollywood includes Fritz Lang, Joseph von Sternberg, Ernst Lubitsch, Marlene Dietrich, Billy Wilder, and many more.

German, Austrian, and Swiss talent continues to influence American filmmaking. Contemporaries include Rainer Werner Fassbinder, Wim Wenders, Wolfgang Petersen, Tom Tykwer, Franka Potente, Maximilian Schell, Armin Mueller-Stahl, and Klaus-Maria Brandauer.

While Switzerland shows foreign films in their original with subtitles, Germany and Austria dub all films in languages other than German. A considerable part of the film industry therefore is dedicated to *Synchronisation* (synchronization, dubbing). Munich and Berlin have large *Synchronstudios* (dubbing studios). Germany's major film studios are in Munich, *die Bavaria Filmstudios,* and Berlin, *die UFA Studios.* Although many German productions and TV shows are filmed there, these studios also appeal to and draw many international clients.

In order to keep the European film industry alive by counterbalancing the overwhelming influx of American movies on the European market, many European countries channel public and private funds into their film industries. Every major city has programs run and financed by the local government, and private film funding groups offer grants to aspiring film teams. In Germany *die Landesbildstellen* (regional administration for visual arts) and *die Pressestellen* (press and communications departments) of the *Bundesländer* are directly involved in sponsoring independent film projects by allocating substantial sums each year to its *Förderungsprogramme* (subsidized programs). For details on available state funds, contact the regional administrative offices.

## 2. VOCABULARY

| | |
|---|---|
| *der Regisseur* | director |
| *Regie führen* | to direct |
| *der/die Schauspieler/in* | actor/actress |
| *die Hauptrolle* | lead, main role |
| *der Hauptdarsteller* | lead, main character |
| *die Nebenrolle* | supporting role |
| *das Kino* | movie theater |
| *ins Kino gehen* | to go to the movies |
| *fernsehen* | to watch TV |
| *die Leinwand* | screen (movie theater) |
| *der Fernseher* | TV set |
| *das Drehbuch* | script |
| *der Drehbuchautor* | screenwriter |
| *das Video* | video (film) |
| *die Videocassette* | video tape |
| *der Videorecorder* | VCR |
| *die Fernbedienung* | remote control |
| *die Kamera* | camera |
| *die Besetzung, die Mitwirkenden* | cast |
| *der Kritiker* | critic, film reviewer |
| *die Kritik* | critique, review |
| *der/die Komparse* | extra |

## 3. EXPRESSING OPINIONS

*Sagen Sie mal, was halten Sie denn von . . . ?*
　　Tell me, what do you think about . . . ?

*Wie finden Sie . . . ?*
　　What do you think about . . . ?

*Was sagen Sie dazu?*
　　What's your opinion on this?

*Meiner Meinung nach . . .*
   In my opinion . . .

*Ich bin sehr beeindruckt.*
   I'm quite impressed.

*Nein, ganz im Gegenteil, ich finde . . .*
   No, quite the contrary, I think . . .

*Wenn man das so sieht, dann . . .*
   If you look at it that way, then . . .

*Na, da sind wir wohl geteilter Meinung.*
   Well, we have different opinions about it.

*Ich teile Ihre Meinung nicht.*
   I don't share your opinion.

*Ich bin anderer Meinung.*
   I have a different opinion./I see that differently.

*Ich bin anderer Ansicht.*
   I have a different opinion on that./I see that differently.

*Ich sehe das anders.*
   I see it differently.

*Ich gebe Ihnen recht.*
   You are right.

*Da kann ich Ihnen aus vollem Herzen zustimmen.*
   I can agree with you wholeheartedly.

*Da haben Sie wohl recht.*
   Well, you're right.

---

## ÜBUNGEN

**1.** *Beantworten Sie die Fragen zum Text.*

   a. *Woher kommt Miriam Wallstätter und was ist sie von Beruf?*
   b. *Wo haben Frau Wallstätter und Herr Clausen sich getroffen?*
   c. *Was ist Herr Clausen und wo lebt er?*
   d. *Wer ist Dieter Hellberg?*
   e. *Warum ist Dieter Hellberg nicht bei den Festspielen?*
   f. *Worum geht es in dem Film von Frau Wallstätter?*

**2.** *Formulieren Sie Sätze aus den folgenden Satzteilen.*

BEISPIEL: *(vor/aufstehen/ich/hören/die Nachrichten/immer)*
*Vor dem Aufstehen höre ich immer die Nachrichten.*

    a. *(bei/zuschauen/ich/einschlafen)* present perfect
    b. *(nach/spielen/die Kinder/gehen/nach Hause)*
    c. *(vor/essen/er/gehen/in den Garten)*
    d. *(von/laufen/du/werden/müde)*
    e. *(bei/telefonieren/sie/gehen/in die Küche)* past tense
    f. *(nach/schwimmen/wir/legen/uns/in die Sonne)*

**3.** *Übersetzen Sie Ihre Antworten aus Übung 2.*

**4.** *Verbinden Sie die folgenden Sätze.*

BEISPIEL: *Wir gehen heute abend ins Kino. Ich bin sehr müde. (obwohl)*
*Obwohl ich sehr müde bin, gehen wir heute abend ins Kino.*

    a. *Er hat dich zur Biennale eingeladen. Du kannst nicht hinfahren. (obwohl)*
    b. *Ich möchte gerne nach Cannes fahren. Ich habe kein Geld. (trotzdem)*
    c. *Der Regisseur hat gefeiert. Er hat keinen Preis gewonnen. (obgleich)*
    d. *Die Schauspielerin war sehr schön. Sie fand keine Rollen. (obwohl)*
    e. *Gerd ist schon seit 5 Tagen weg. Ich habe seinen Blumen immer noch kein Wasser gegeben. (obwohl)*
    f. *Wir haben unseren Stadtplan vergessen. Wir sind weiter durch Cannes gegangen und haben das Kino gesucht. (trotzdem)*

**5.** *Formulieren Sie die Sätze um.*

BEISPIEL: *Der blinde Mann ging über die Straße.*
*Der Blinde ging über die Straße.*

    a. *Die guten Dinge sind stärker als die bösen Dinge.*
    b. *Der schwarzhaarige Mann bekam die Rolle.*
    c. *Die schlechten Filme gewinnen selten.*
    d. *Die neuesten Nachrichten sind immer am interessantesten.*

# LEKTION 10

INVESTITIONEN UND INVESTMENT.    Investment.

## A. DIALOG

*Jeff Gersen ist ein Unternehmer[1] aus Arizona. Er besucht Frau Albert im Investmentbüro[2] Schneider & Wiltner in Duisburg.[3]*

FRAU ALBERT: An welcher Art von Investition sind Sie denn besonders interessiert?

HERR GERSEN: Ich dachte zunächst daran, mir einige Industrieprojekte im Osten Deutschlands anzusehen.[4] Aber ich möchte auch etwas über Pfandbriefe erfahren.

FRAU ALBERT: An Aktien sind Sie also nicht interessiert.

HERR GERSEN: Nicht in erster Linie. Wenn Sie allerdings etwas ganz Besonderes im Auge[5] haben, sagen Sie mir Bescheid.

FRAU ALBERT: Gut. An welchen Industriezweigen haben Sie besonderes Interesse?

HERR GERSEN: Ich war kürzlich in Halle und Cottbus[6] und habe mir dort ein Zementwerk und eine Kabelfabrik angesehen.

FRAU ALBERT: Sind Sie schon im Gespräch mit den Werken?

HERR GERSEN: Nein, ich möchte erst Hintergrundinformationen[7] sowie eine Marktanalyse und Kapitalangaben über die Firmen haben.

FRAU ALBERT: Wir werden uns selbstverständlich darum kümmern. Der Gedanke, Geld in die östlichen Bundesländer[8] zu investieren, ist mit Sicherheit nicht falsch.[9] An welche Summe dachten Sie?

HERR GERSEN: Ach, das hängt ganz vom Projekt ab.

FRAU ALBERT: Ich kann Ihnen auch die Deutsche Bundesbahn empfehlen. Deren Aktien sind im allgemeinen sehr stabil.

HERR GERSEN: Die Bundesbahn ist eine AG[10] geworden?

FRAU ALBERT: Ja. Die Bahn baut ihr Netz weiter aus und nimmt enorme Erneuerungen vor, vor allem in den östlichen Bundesländern.

HERR GERSEN: Was halten Sie denn von Immobilien?

FRAU ALBERT: **Wir gehen davon aus, dass der Immobilienmarkt langfristig stabil bleibt und die Preise bundesweit[11] steigen. Es ist eine gute Anlage.**

HERR GERSEN: **Lohnt[12] es sich denn für mich, mir ein paar Wohnungen oder Häuser anzusehen?**

FRAU ALBERT: **Ja, je schneller desto besser, denn die Grundstückspreise in den östlichen Bundesländern steigen voraussichtlich um weitere fünf bis zehn Prozent.**

HERR GERSEN: **Kann ich von Ihnen einige Angebote bekommen?**

FRAU ALBERT: **Selbstverständlich. Welche Städte interessieren Sie denn?**

HERR GERSEN: **Magdeburg und Dresden.[13]**

FRAU ALBERT: **An welche Adresse darf ich das Material schicken?**

HERR GERSEN: **Ich fliege zwar[14] morgen zurück, bin aber in einem Monat wieder in Deutschland. Trotzdem ist es das Beste, wenn Sie es mir nach Arizona schicken. Hier ist meine Karte.**

FRAU ALBERT: **Danke. Darf ich fragen, was Sie zu uns geführt hat?**

HERR GERSEN: **Ein Kollege von der Hoechst AG hat Sie mir empfohlen.**

FRAU ALBERT: **Das hört man gerne. Wir werden Sie also sowohl über Immobilienangebote wie auch Wertpapiere auf dem Laufenden[15] halten. Und wir werden uns sofort an die Marktanalyse der Werke in Halle und Cottbus machen.[16]**

HERR GERSEN: **Prima. Sie können mir jederzeit ein Fax an diese Nummer in Arizona schicken.**

FRAU ALBERT: **Das machen wir gerne.**

HERR GERSEN: **Vielen Dank. Ich freue mich auf eine gute Zusammenarbeit. Ach ja,[17] schicken Sie mir bitte jeden Monat Ihre Rechnung für die Beratungskosten.**

FRAU ALBERT: **Ja, natürlich. Und vielen Dank für Ihren Besuch. Sie werden in Kürze von uns hören.**

HERR GERSEN: **Gut. Auf Wiedersehen, Frau Albert.**

FRAU ALBERT: **Auf Wiedersehen. Und guten Flug!**

HERR GERSEN: **Danke.**

# TRANSLATION

Jeff Gersen is an entrepreneur from Arizona. He is visiting Ms. Albert at the offices of the investment consultants Schneider & Wiltner in Duisburg.

MS. ALBERT: What type of investment are you most interested in?

MR. GERSEN: I'm primarily thinking of looking at some industrial projects in eastern Germany. But I'm also curious about bonds.

MS. ALBERT: So you're not interested in stock?

MR. GERSEN: Not primarily. If you have something special in mind, however, let me know.

MS. ALBERT: Good. Which types of industry are of particular interest to you?

MR. GERSEN: I visited Halle and Cottbus recently and looked at a cement plant and a cable factory.

MS. ALBERT: Are you already negotiating with these plants?

MR. GERSEN: No, I'd like to get some background information first, as well as a market analysis and details about the companies' assets.

MS. ALBERT: We'll certainly take care of that. The idea of investing in the eastern states is certainly not bad. Which sum did you have in mind?

MR. GERSEN: Oh, that depends entirely on the project.

MS. ALBERT: I can also recommend the German Federal Railroad. Their stock is, generally speaking, very stable.

MR. GERSEN: The railroad has become a stock company?

MS. ALBERT: Yes. The railroad is continuing to expand and update their system enormously, especially in the eastern states.

MR. GERSEN: What do you think about real estate?

MS. ALBERT: We presume that the real estate market will have long-term stability and that prices will rise throughout the country. That's a good investment.

MR. GERSEN: Is it worthwhile for me to look at some apartments and houses?

MS. ALBERT: Yes, the sooner the better, since the real estate prices in the eastern states are likely to go up by another five to 10 percent before the end of the year.

MR. GERSEN: Can you show me what's on the market?

MS. ALBERT: Of course. Which cities are you interested in?

MR. GERSEN: Magdeburg and Dresden.

MS. ALBERT: Which address may I send the material to?

164

MR. GERSEN: I'm flying back tomorrow, but I'll be back in Germany in a month. It'll still be best if you send it to me in Arizona. Here's my card.

MS. ALBERT: Thanks. May I ask what brought you to us?

MR. GERSEN: A colleague at the Hoechst AG recommended you to me.

MS. ALBERT: That's nice to hear. We'll keep you posted about real estate offers as well as bonds. And we'll start working on the market analysis of the plants in Halle and Cottbus immediately.

MR. GERSEN: Great. You can send me a fax to that number in Arizona at any time.

MS. ALBERT: We'll be happy to assist you.

MR. GERSEN: Thank you very much. I look forward to working with you. Oh yeah, please send me the bill for the consultant fees every month.

MS. ALBERT: Yes, of course. And thank you for coming to see us. You'll hear from me shortly.

MR. GERSEN: Good. Good-bye, Ms. Albert.

MS. ALBERT: Good-bye, and have a good trip.

MR. GERSEN: Thanks.

# B. IN KÜRZE

1. *Der Unternehmer* (entrepreneur) is the common term for a private businessman. Owners of retail stores are referred to as *der Geschäftsinhaber* (business owner). Although the word *Unternehmer* literally translated means "undertaker," it does not share the English connotation at all.

2. *Die Investition* and *das Investment* both mean investment. The first is mostly used for the actual transfer of funds. The second, *das Investment,* which was taken from English, is mostly used in compound nouns such as *das Investmentbüro* (investment office) or *der Investmentfonds* (investment funds). Both terms are frequently used in German. The verb is *investieren* (to invest).

3. *Duisburg* is a city in *Nordrhein-Westfalen* (North Rhine-Westphalia) near Düsseldorf. The area is typically referred to as the *Ruhrgebiet,* the industrial area on the banks of the rivers Ruhr and Rhine. Check out www.Duisberg.de for more information.

4. *Anzusehen* is an infinitive construction with *zu* (see Lesson 11). Since the infinitive is a verb with a separable prefix, *zu* sits between prefix and stem. Verbs with separable prefix are dealt with in detail in the grammar section of this lesson.

5. *Etwas im Auge haben* is used literally (to have something in the eye) as well as figuratively (to have something in mind).

6. *Halle* is an industrial city in southern *Sachsen-Anhalt* (Saxony-Anhalt). *Cottbus* is a city in the southeast of Berlin in *Brandenburg*.

7. Unlike in English, *die Information* forms a plural in German: *die Informationen.*

8. The Federal Republic of Germany refers to its sixteen states as *Länder* (states) or *Bundesländer* (federal states). The five *östlichen Bundesländer* (eastern states), which joined the republic in 1990 when Germany was reunited, are *Mecklenburg-Vorpommern* (Mecklenburg-Western Pomerania), *Brandenburg, Sachsen-Anhalt, Thüringen* (Thuringia), and *Sachsen* (Saxony). The eleven *westlichen Bundesländer* (western states) are *Nordrhein-Westfalen* (North Rhine-Westphalia), *Baden-Württemberg, Bayern* (Bavaria), *Rheinland-Pfalz* (Rhineland-Palatinate), *Saarland, Hessen* (Hesse), *Niedersachsen* (Lower Saxony), and *Schleswig-Holstein. Hamburg, Bremen,* and *Berlin* have special *Land* status despite being cities. After reunification in 1990, the eastern states were often referred to as *die neuen Bundesländer.* You may still hear people speak of *neue Bundesländer,* but with time the term is going to disappear.

9. The expression is either used as a deliberate understatement, implying that the thought is actually very good and appropriate, or, if in comparison with something else, as a soft criticism.

10. *AG* is the abbreviation for *die Aktiengesellschaft* (public or stock corporation).

11. *Bundesweit* is used to express a trend throughout the Federal Republic of Germany, whereas *landesweit* (statewide) refers to trends throughout the state.

12. *Sich lohnen* (to be worthwhile, to be cost-effective, to be lucrative) is a reflexive verb.

13. *Magdeburg* is the capital of *Sachsen-Anhalt. Dresden* is the capital of *Sachsen.*

14. *Zwar* (however, although) is a concessive flavoring particle.

*Er hat zwar wenig Geld, aber er will mir helfen.*
He might not have much money, but he wants to help me.

*Ich fliege zwar morgen nach Hause, aber ich komme bald wieder.*
Although I am going back tomorrow, I will be back soon.

15. *Jemanden auf dem Laufenden halten* (to keep someone updated, to keep someone posted) is a very common fixed expression, used in formal and informal situations. *Laufend* (running), the present participle of *laufen* (to run), is used as a noun *(das Laufende)* in the dative *(dem Laufenden).*

16. *Sich machen an* (to start, to get going) is a reflexive expression.

17. *Ach ja* is a colloquial expression used in many different contexts. Inflection can change the meaning. As an exclamation it means:

*Ach ja, da fällt mir ein, du solltest deinen Bruder anrufen.*
Oh, I just remembered, you were supposed to call your brother.

*Ach ja! Das waren noch Zeiten!*
Ah, well! Those were the days.

As a question it means:

*Er sagt, er hat Geld gewonnen.*
He said he won some money.

*Ach ja? Das ist ja schwer zu glauben.*
Oh really? That's hard to believe.

# C. GRAMMATIK UND GEBRAUCH

## 1. *DER KOMPARATIV* (THE COMPARATIVE)

Comparing things or people of equal attributes requires the positive of the adjective and *so . . . wie* (as).*

*Meine Firma is so groß wie deine.*
My company is as big as yours.

Comparing things of different qualities requires the comparative of the adjective and *als* (than).

*Das Interesse an Auslandsinvestitionen ist dieses Jahr größer als letztes Jahr.*
The interest in foreign investment is greater this year than last year.

Another way to express comparisons requires the comparative of the adjective and *je . . . desto* (the . . . the).

*Je länger ich deutsch lerne, desto besser verstehe ich es.*
The longer I learn German, the better I understand it.

Note the different word order of subject and verb in the two parts of the sentence. *Je* plus adjective is followed by the subject; the verb takes the last position. *Desto* plus adjective is followed by the verb; subject and verb switch places.

*Je mehr ich erfahre, desto schneller kann ich mich entscheiden.*
The more I know, the quicker I can decide.

* See Lesson 4.

As in English, the verb *sein* can be omitted in this comparative structure.

*Je älter das Haus, desto besser.*
The older the house, the better.

Even the noun the comparison refers to can be omitted, if the context makes it clear what is being talked about.

*Schicken Sie mir bitte viel Material über Wertpapiere. Je mehr, desto besser.*
Please send me a lot of material about bonds. The more the better.

## 2. *AUFZÄHLUNGEN* (ENUMERATIONS)

a. Punctuation in Sentences with *und*

The most frequent way to list items in German is, as in English, by separating them with commas and using *und* between the last two items.

*Ich war in Magdeburg, Dresden, Halle und Cottbus.*
I was in Magdeburg, Dresden, Halle, and Cottbus.

Note that German does not add a comma before *und*.

b. *Sowohl . . . als auch* and *sowie*

If only two items appear in the sentence, the term *sowohl . . . als auch* (as well as) often replaces the simple *und* for emphasis.

*Sie schickt ihm sowohl Immobilienangebote als auch Angaben über die Firmen in Halle und Cottbus.*
She is sending him real estate offers as well as details about the companies in Halle and Cottbus.

The term *sowie* appears in a longer list of nouns to emphasize the importance of even the last item.

*Er hat mir drei Briefe, zwei Akten sowie fünf Faxe geschickt.*
He sent me three letters, two files, as well as five faxes.

c. *etc., u.s.w., o.ä., u.a.*

Like English, German has several set expressions such as *etc.* used in word lists. In writing, these words are used only in their abbreviations. *Etc.* (et cetera), a Latin expression, can be used in German just as it is used in English. The German equivalent of etc., however, is more common: *u.s.w. (und so weiter)* always appears at the end of a list too long to be continued.

*Du weißt, wir brauchen Unterlagen, Kapitalangaben, die*
*Vorstandsmitgliederliste, die Verkäufe des letzten Jahres u.s.w.*
You know we need documents, details on the company's assets, the list
of board members, last year's sales, etc.

*O.ä. (oder ähnliches)* appears at the end of a list of similar things. Note
that *ähnlich* (similar, alike) changes case endings according to gender
and number, when fully pronounced in conversation. In writing it
always remains in its abbreviated form.

*Konnen Sie nicht mal bei der Firma anrufen und nach einem Bericht o.ä.*
*fragen?*
*Können Sie nicht mal bei der Firma anrufen und nach einem Bericht oder*
*ähnlichem fragen?*
Can't you call the company and ask them for a report or something like
that?

*U.a. (unter anderem)* is often used when listing people or
organizations. It is comparable to the English "among others."

*Jeff Gersen, Markus Vollbrecht, Sabrina Müller-Stolz u.a. waren diese Woche*
*persönlich zu Gesprächen in unserem Büro.*
Jeff Gersen, Markus Vollbrecht, Sabrina Müller-Stolz, among others,
visited our offices for consultation this week.

## 3. *VERBEN MIT VORSILBEN* (PREFIX VERBS)

### a. Separable Prefixes

Most verbs with prepositions as prefixes are separable.

| | | | |
|---|---|---|---|
| *an-sehen* | to look at | *vor-nehmen* | to plan |
| *ab-hängen* | to depend on | *sich etwas vor-stellen* | to imagine something |
| *aus-gehen* | to go out, to assume | *sich vor-stellen* | to introduce oneself |

Often prefixes change the meaning of the base verb:

| | | | |
|---|---|---|---|
| *nehmen* | to take | *vor-nehmen* | to plan |
| *fangen* | to catch | *an-fangen* | to begin |
| *hängen* | to hang | *ab-hängen* | to depend |

The prefix is separated from the stem in present and past tenses and
takes the last position in the sentence.

*Ich hänge finanziell von meiner Familie ab.*
Financially I depend upon my family.

*Wir sahen uns die Stadt an.*
We looked at the city.

Separable prefix verbs form their past participle by adding *-ge-* between the prefix and the stem.

| INFINITIVE | PAST PARTICIPLE |
|---|---|
| *ansehen* (to look at) | *angesehen* |
| *vornehmen* (to plan) | *vorgenommen* |
| *anbieten* (to offer) | *angeboten* |

*Sie nimmt sich vor, in Urlaub zu fahren. Hast du dir auch schon was vorgenommen?*
She plans to go on vacation. Have you also made some plans?

Verbs that end in *-ieren* don't add *-ge-* to their past participles, even though they have preposition prefixes and are separable.

| *anmontieren* (to install) | *anmontiert* |
|---|---|
| *abmontieren* (to dismantle) | *abmontiert* |

*Er montiert den Spiegel an.*
He is installing the mirror.

*Hat er den Spiegel schon anmontiert?*
Has he installed the mirror yet?

### b. Inseparable Prefixes*

Some prefixes cannot be separated from the stem. These are *be-, emp-, ent-, er-, ge-, miss-, ver-,* and *zer-*. Inseparable prefix verbs don't use *-ge-* to form their past participles. The inseparable prefix significantly changes the meaning of the base verb.

| INFINITIVE | PAST PART. | INSEP. PREFIX | PAST PART. |
|---|---|---|---|
| *stellen* (to put) | *gestellt* | *bestellen* (to order) | *bestellt* |
| *fangen* (to catch) | *gefangen* | *empfangen* (to receive) | *empfangen* |
| *achten* (to respect) | *geachtet* | *missachten* (to disrespect) | *missachte* |
| *fallen* (to fall) | *gefallen* | *gefallen* (to like) | *gefallen* |
| *schreiben* (to write) | *geschrieben* | *beschreiben* (to describe) | *beschrieben* |
| *stehen* (to stand) | *gestanden* | *entstehen* (to form) | *entstanden* |

*Frau Albert hat Herrn Gersen die Fabrik in Cottbus beschrieben.*
Ms. Albert described the factory in Cottbus to Mr. Gersen.

*Sie hat einen Verkaufsbericht bestellt.*
She ordered a sales report.

---

* Other inseparable prefix verbs and their change of meaning will be dealt with in Lesson 14.

*Herrn Gersen gefällt die Firma*
Mr. Gersen likes the company.

c. Separable and Inseparable Prefixes

Certain prefixes, such as *über-, unter-,* and *durch,* can be both separable and inseparable. Separable prefixes can be distinguished from their inseparable counterpart in two ways: if the prefix is separable, the verb is stressed on the prefix, whereas if the prefix is inseparable, the verb is stressed on the stem; if the prefix is separable, the verb forms its past participle with *-ge-,* whereas if the prefix is inseparable, the verb's past participle will not take *-ge.*

| SEPARABLE PREFIX | INSEPARABLE PREFIX |
|---|---|
| (STRESS ON THE PREFIX) | (STRESS ON THE STEM) |
| *unterbringen* (to accommodate) | *unterschreiben* (to sign) |
| *untergebracht* | *unterschrieben* |
| *Wir bringen ihn im Hotel unter.* | *Er unterschreibt den Vertrag.* |
| We put him up in a hotel. | He signs the contract. |
| | |
| *durchatmen* (to breathe deeply) | *durchqueren* (to cut across) |
| *durchgeatmet* | *durchquert* |
| *Er hat tief durchgeatmet.* | *Sie hat den Wald durchquert.* |
| He breathed deeply. | She walked through the forest. |

## 4. IDIOMATIC EXPRESSIONS

These expressions play on the human eye.

ETWAS IM AUGE HABEN (to have something in mind)
*Ich habe ein Projekt in Halle im Auge und weiß noch nicht, was daraus wird.*
I have a project in Halle in mind and don't know what's to become of that.

ETWAS INS AUGE FASSEN (to focus on; lit.: to grip something in one's eye)
*Wir müssen die wichtigsten Probleme ins Auge fassen.*
We have to focus on the most important problems.

UNTER VIER AUGEN (face to face, in private; lit.: under four eyes)
*Wir sollten das später unter vier Augen besprechen.*
We should talk about this later in private.

VOR ALLER AUGEN (in public; lit.: in front of all eyes)
*So etwas kannst du doch nicht vor aller Augen machen!*
You can't do something like that in public.

*KEIN AUGE ZUTUN* (to not sleep a wink; lit.: to not close an eye)
*Gestern Nacht habe ich kein Auge zugetan.*
Last night I didn't sleep a wink.

*WIE DIE FAUST AUFS AUGE* (like a square peg in a round hole; lit.: like the fist on the eye)
*Das passt ja wieder einmal wie die Faust aufs Auge.*
Once again this fits like a square peg in a round hole.

# D. REIN GESCHÄFTLICH

## 1. DOING BUSINESS IN *DEN ÖSTLICHEN BUNDESLÄNDERN*

On October 3, 1990, German reunification spelled the end of the German Democratic Republic. With unification, the entire legal system of the Federal Republic of Germany took effect in the *östlichen Bundesländer,* and, with the exception of some transitional regulations, there are no differences in doing business between the eastern and western German states. The entire Federal Republic of Germany has a free market system similar to that of the U.S.A., and *die östlichen Bundesländer* are also part of the integrated market of the European Union that took effect in 1993.

Therefore every form of European business incorporation is allowed: a limited liability company—*GmbH,* a publicly held corporation—*AG,* a limited partnership—*KG,* a sole proprietorship, branch offices of foreign companies, or joint ventures.

Most aspects of doing business in eastern Germany are identical to those in western Germany and the European Union as a whole. However, a few advantages and disadvantages should be addressed. Many potential business locations in the eastern states suffer from prior environmental abuse, and sites should be studied to see whether or not they were subject to leakages or whether or not any substances have been dumped there.

A lack of managerial experience with the market economy among professionals trained before 1990, and philosophical and educational excess baggage of the entire population from forty-five years of communism among the labor force in general may create unforeseen difficulties.

As very little English is spoken in *den östlichen Bundesländern* because of the former GDR's focus on eastern Europe, be aware that your ability and willingness to speak and negotiate in German will be essential when doing business there. People in the eastern states are hungry to work hard and do and learn whatever is necessary to catch up with the western states.

The best prospects for investing in the eastern states are, among others, in the construction sector,* especially housing, health care facili-

* See Lesson 6.

ties, and business centers. The upgrading and modernization of medical facilities, science and research institutes, transportation systems, and environmental protection facilities will spur the need for modern testing and monitoring equipment. The service sector offers a variety of opportunities as well, as years of deliberate underinvestment have left most service industries such as tourism, including hotels and restaurants, wanting.

In general the eastern German market is open to American products, yet local practices may make entering this market difficult and may require the American company to demonstrate a significant competitive advantage for its product. Despite the fact that per capita incomes are lower and the unemployment rate higher, *die östlichen Bundesländer* are not a dumping ground for "cheap" goods and used equipment. If a product has no prospects in western Germany, it won't in eastern Germany, either.

For information on market trends, contact your local German Chamber of Commerce.

## 2. VOCABULARY

| | |
|---|---|
| *der Markt* | market |
| *die Maschine, die Ausrüstung* | equipment |
| *die Anleihe* | loan (mostly used for state loans) |
| *der Pfandbrief* | (mortgage) bond |
| *das Wertpapier* | bond, securities |
| *das Darlehen* | loan (from a bank) |
| *die Zinsen* | interest |
| *der Zinssatz* | interest rate |
| *die Aktie* | share, stock |
| *die Börse* | stock exchange, stock market |
| *der Makler* | broker |
| *der Börsenkurs* | stock exchange rates, trading index |
| *der Börsenmakler* | stockbroker |
| *der Immobilienmakler* | real estate agent |
| *die Immobilie, -n* | real estate |
| *steigen* | to increase, to rise |
| *fallen* | to decrease, to fall |
| *der Aktienindex* | share index |
| *die amtliche Notierung* | listed shares and stocks at closing |
| *die Hypothek* | mortgage |
| *die Rendite* | yield, (rate of) return |
| *die Renten* | fixed interest security |
| *der Dispositionskredit* | overdraft (interest rate) |
| *die Obligation* | bond |
| *die Dividende* | dividend |

173

| | |
|---|---|
| *die Bilanz* | balance (sheet) |
| *die Börsentendenz* | the trend of the stock market |
| *der Spekulant* | speculator |

# ÜBUNGEN

**1.** *Verbinden Sie die Sätze unter Verwendung der Ausdrücke in Klammern.*

*BEISPIEL: Schnell, es ist besser, dass wir ihn sofort anrufen. (je . . . desto)*
*Je schneller wir ihn anrufen, desto besser (ist es).*

   a. *Das Auto fährt langsam. Er kommt spät an. (je . . . desto)*
   b. *Ich habe Tee und Kaffee gekauft. (sowohl als auch)*
   c. *Er hat drei Autos und zwei Fahrräder. (sowie)*
   d. *Die Aktien sind teuer. Wenn Du lange wartest, werden sie noch*
      *teurer. (je . . . desto)*
   e. *Wenn ich von Ihnen höre, kann ich mich entscheiden. (sobald)*
   f. *Alte Ware, Verkauf schwierig. (je . . . desto)*

**2.** *Setzen Sie das Partizip der Vergangenheit ein.*

*BEISPIEL: Er hat den Vertrag _____ (durchlesen) und _____*
*(unterschreiben). Er hat den Vertrag durchgelesen und*
*unterschrieben.*

   a. *Wir sind gestern _____ (ankommen).*
   b. *Wir sind an der Börse _____ (aussteigen).*
   c. *Sie haben sich erst _____ (vorstellen).*
   d. *Habt ihr schon etwas _____ (unternehmen)?*
   e. *Nein, wir sind sofort _____ (einschlafen).*
   f. *Ich bin um 10 Uhr _____ (aufstehen).*

**3.** *Setzen Sie die Sätze aus Übung 2 in das Imperfekt.*

**4.** *Formulieren Sie Sätze im Präsens.*

*BEISPIEL: (er/sich vorstellen/eine Investition/in Ostdeutschland)*
*Er stellt sich eine Investition in Ostdeutschland vor.*

   a. *(es/abhängen/von/Investmentberater)*
   b. *(wir/vornehmen/viel/für das nächste Jahr)*
   c. *(Frau Keller/missachten/das Gesetz)*
   d. *(Bitte/Sie/anrufen/und/beschreiben/das Haus)*
   e. *(Sie/ausgehen/und/sich ansehen/die Altstadt)*
   f. *(Frau Albert/anbieten/Herr Gersen/Aktien)*

# ERSTE WIEDERHOLUNGSAUFGABE
## (First Review Quiz)

1. *Setzen Sie die richtigen Endungen ein.*

   a. *Er stellte die alt _____ Lampe in die Ecke.*
   b. *Sie setzte sich auf das schön _____, grün _____ Sofa und sah eine klein _____ Handtasche auf dem Boden liegen.*
   c. *Er trinkt gerne kalt _____ Wasser.*
   d. *Sie mag lieber heiß _____ Kaffee.*
   e. *Lieben Sie modern _____ oder antik _____ Möbel?*
   f. *Für die Umbauten brauchen Sie viel _____ klein _____ Nägel, einen groß _____ und einen klein _____ Hammer, verschieden _____ Schrauben und ein Maßband.*
   g. *Haben Sie meinen Bauplan gesehen? Er lag auf dem flach _____ Tisch.*
   h. *Das Haus der reich _____ Familie wird zum zwei _____ Male umgebaut.*

2. *Setzen Sie „haben" oder „sein" ein.*

   a. *Sie (pl.) _____ gestern angekommen und _____ sofort ausgepackt.*
   b. *Sie war müde und _____ sich hingelegt.*
   c. *Er _____ spazieren gegangen und _____ sich die Umgebung des Hotels angesehen.*
   d. *Als er zurückkam, _____ sie (pl.) sich umgezogen und _____ essen gegangen.*
   e. *_____ es euch in Innsbruck gefallen?*
   f. *Wir _____ viel unternommen.*
   g. *_____ ihr oft abends weggegangen?*
   h. *Wir _____ das Theater besucht und _____ viel spazieren gegangen.*

3. *Setzen Sie die unterstrichenen Satzteile ins Plural.*

   a. *Das Buch lag auf dem Tisch.*
   b. *Die Uhr ist zu teuer.*
   c. *Der Flug nach Mailand ist gestrichen worden.*
   d. *Ein Haus mit kleinen Fenstern gefällt mir nicht.*
   e. *Er hat unser Treffen abgesagt.*
   f. *Der Überweisungsauftrag wurde erst gestern abgegeben.*
   g. *Ich ziehe mich immer gut an, wenn ich zu einem Vorstellungsgespräch gehe.*

4. *Setzen Sie das richtige Modalverb ein: mögen/dürfen/sollen/wollen/können/müssen*

   a. *_____ Sie noch eine Tasse Kaffee?*
   b. *Nein, danke. Ich _____ zahlen.*

c. _____ ich mich zu Ihnen an den Tisch setzen?

d. *Ja, natürlich. Sie _____ den Tisch gleich für sich alleine haben, ich _____ leider gehen.*

e. *Oh, wie schade. _____ Sie nicht noch etwas bleiben?*

f. *Nein, das geht nicht. Ich _____ meinen Chef um 16:30 Uhr vom Bahnhof abholen und es ist schon 16:25.*

g. *Oh, da _____ Sie sich aber beeilen.*

**5.** *Setzen Sie das Folgende ins Futur.*

a. *Ich lerne Ski fahren.*

b. *Er hat bestimmt schon angerufen.*

c. *Wir sehen uns bald wieder.*

d. *Bis dahin ist alles fertig.*

e. *Er hat mehr Geld. (wahrscheinlich/im nächsten Jahr)*

f. *Sie bringt den Koffer vorbei.*

g. *Sie kommt nicht mehr. (wohl)*

**6.** *Setzen Sie den bestimmten Artikel ein.*

a. *Sie parkte ihr Auto vor _____ Universität.*

b. *Sie ging in _____ Bücherei und suchte nach _____ Buch, das sie für _____ Kurs brauchte.*

c. *Er legte die Papiere auf _____ Schreibtisch und setzte sich in _____ Sessel.*

d. *Morgens gehen wir auf _____ Markt, kaufen Brot und Gemüse ein und fahren mit _____ Straßenbahn wieder nach Hause.*

e. *Haben Sie _____ Brief an _____ Anwalt geschrieben?*

f. *Gehen Sie über _____ Brücke. Auf _____ linken Seite ist _____ Rathaus und hinter _____ Rathaus ist _____ Bushaltestelle.*

**7.** *Personal-, Possessiv-, oder Reflexivpronomen?*

a. *Ich habe _____ verlaufen. Können Sie _____ helfen?*

b. *Ich kenne _____ hier auch nicht gut aus. Warten _____, ich hole mal eben _____ Stadtplan aus dem Auto.*

c. *Das ist aber nett von _____. _____ Bekannter hat _____ Adresse gegeben, aber leider hat er _____ nicht gesagt, wie ich dorthin finde.*

**8.** *Formulieren Sie den Imperativ.*

BEISPIEL: *(die Lampe/in die Ecke)*
    *Stellen Sie die Lampe in die Ecke!*

a. *(Platz nehmen/bitte)*

b. *(die Bücher/auf den Tisch)*

c. *(die Bücher/in das Regal)*

d. *(den Fernseher/auf den Tisch)*

e. *(die Bilder/an die Wand)*

**9.** *Verbinden Sie die Sätze.*

a. *Er hat den Schreibtisch verkauft. Der Schreibtisch gefiel mir am besten.* (relative subclause)

b. *Wir waren im letzten Jahr segeln. Meine Tochter malt nur noch Segelboote. (seit)*

c. *Sie besuchten Rom. Sie lernten die Familie Rossa kennen. (als)*

d. *Du gehst zur Arbeit. Du musst die Tür abschließen. (wenn)*

e. *Anette und Jörg Schumann leben in Mannheim. Sie fahren jedes Jahr nach München und besuchen die Obermeiers.* (related subclause)

f. *Der Herr mit den braunen Haaren kommt aus Boston. Er hat gerade ein Konto eröffnet. Er arbeitet für die DUS Trading in Frankfurt.* (relative subclause plus *und*)

g. *Das Geld ist da. Ich gebe Ihnen Bescheid. (sobald)*

**10.** *Trennbare oder untrennbare Verben?*

a. *Bitte _____ Sie. (ablegen)*

b. *Er _____ den Brief. (unterschreiben)*

c. *Bei unserem Spaziergang _____ wir den Wald. (durchqueren)*

d. *Wir haben uns für das nächste Jahr viel _____. (vornehmen)*

e. *Seit fünf Jahren _____ die Firma stark von Exporten. (abhängen)*

f. *Wir _____ uns am Sonntag die Gemäldeausstellung. (ansehen)*

g. *Er _____ uns Herrn Neumeister. (vorstellen)*

# LESESTÜCK 2

*Nach dem 2. Weltkrieg wurde im Rahmen des Wiederaufbaus[1] Europas, wie auch der gegenseitigen Völkerverständigung[2] ein Programm von weltweiten Städtepartnerschaften geschaffen. Die Partnerschaften sollen einen regelmäßigen Kontakt zwischen den Städten aufbauen, um auf diesem Wege unsichtbare[3] Grenzen zwischen Menschen abzubauen.*

*Das war vor allem für das Nachkriegsdeutschland[4] von Bedeutung[5]. Die Erinnerung an die Jahre der Nazidiktatur haben in vielen Europäern ein Bild vom „hässlichen Deutschen" geschaffen. Aus diesem Grunde wurden auch die Goethe Institute weltweit eingerichtet, und die Aktion „Im Dialog mit Deutschen" von der Deutschen Zentrale für Tourismus organisiert, um Reisenden den Kontakt mit Deutschen und ihrer Kultur zu ermöglichen und zu verbessern.*

*Die seit den 1950er Jahren bestehenden partnerstädtischen Gemeinschaften zwischen deutschen und ausländischen Städten haben seit der Demokratisierung der ehemaligen Ostblockstaaten stark an Bedeutung gewonnen. Seit die Grenzen gefallen sind, können ein intensiver Gedankenaustausch[6], ein persönliches Kennenlernen[7] und Hilfeleistungen[8] stattfinden, die zuvor nur der Stadtverwaltung[9] oder kulturellen Botschaftern[10] vorbehalten waren.*

*Obwohl Großstädte, wie z.B. Berlin, das eine Städtepartnerschaft mit Los Angeles unterhält, oft mehr ins Licht der Öffentlichkeit[11] gelangen, sind es doch vor allem die kleineren Städte, die erstaunlich viel zur Verstärkung[12] der internationalen Verbindungen[13] beitragen.*

*Jede Stadt hat natürlich ihre eigenen Ziele, die oft jedoch nicht einfach zu verwirklichen[14] sind, da die Gelder[15] zur finanziellen Unterstützung von Austauschprojekten[16] oft nicht vorhanden sind. Trotz beispielweise Magdeburgs beeindruckender Liste von Partnerstädten, u.a. Nagasaki und Sarajevo, stehen in manchen Jahren einfach nicht die Gelder zur Verfügung[17], um die partnerstädtischen Aktivitäten auszubauen. So geht es dieser Stadt hauptsächlich darum, die bereits bestehenden Partnerschaften zu erhalten.*

*Rostock, eine traditionsreiche Hansestadt, hat intensive Kontakte mit Riga in Lettland, Szczecin in Polen, Turku in Finnland und Aarhus in Dänemark. In den letzten Jahren wurde regelmäßig ein Schüleraustausch zwischen Turku und Rostock organisiert. Die Schüler fuhren per Boot nach Turku, untersuchten gemeinsam das Wasser der Ostsee auf Schadstoffe[18] und Algengehalt[19], und lernten dabei Finnen kennen. Rostock stiftete Rollstühle[20] für Riga, sandte Weihnachtspakete dorthin, und lud Studenten ein, über Umweltprobleme[21] zu diskutieren. Und Rostock stiftete Szezcin zwei Müllfahrzeuge[22], die in der polnischen Stadt dringend benötigt wurden.*

*Die kleine Stadt Zwickau im westlichen Sachsen ist ein gutes Beispiel, wie die Hilfe aus ökonomisch stabileren Städten sinnvoll weitergegeben wird. Zwickau hatte im 15. und 16. Jahrhundert großen wirtschaftlichen Erfolg durch den Abbau[23] von Silber, und zu DDR-Zeiten wurde hier* der berühmte „Trabbi"[24] gebaut. Seit Jahren aber verringert sich die Bevölkerung Zwickaus, so dass wirtschaftliche Maßnahmen[25] für die Arbeitsplatzbeschaffung[26] von großer Bedeutung sind. Zwickau unterhält drei Partnerschaften mit Jablonec nad Nisou in Tschechien, Zaanstad in Holland, und Dortmund im westlichen Deutschland. Das fünfmal so große Dortmund unterstützt Zwickau mit Geldern, Materialien und Ausbildungsexperten, während Zwickau dafür die kleinere tschechische Stadt Jablonec nad Nisou mit Verwaltungshilfe[27] und Erfahrungsaustausch[28] beim Wechsel[29] zur Demokratie unterstützt.

Gerade im Hinblick auf die massiven Veränderungen, die die Demokratisierung der östlichen Länder Europas mit sich bringt, sind Hilfsmaßnahmen und Erfahrungsaustausch zwischen Partnerstädten kein Tropfen auf den heißen Stein[30], sondern ein wichtiger und reeller Erfolg.

## VOKABELN

| | | |
|---|---|---|
| 1. | *der Wiederaufbau* | rebuilding, restoration |
| 2. | *die Völkerverständigung* | cooperation, communication between nations |
| 3. | *unsichtbar* | invisible |
| 4. | *das Nachkriegsdeutschland* | postwar Germany |
| 5. | *die Bedeutung* | meaning |
| 6. | *der Gedankenaustausch* | exchange of ideas |
| 7. | *das Kennenlernen* | meeting people, get-together, getting to know one another |
| 8. | *die Hilfeleistung* | aid |
| 9. | *die Stadtverwaltung* | city administration |
| 10. | *der Botschafter* | ambassador |
| 11. | *die Öffentlichkeit* | public, public knowledge |
| 12. | *die Verstärkung* | (mil.) support; backup; intensification; reinforcement |
| 13. | *die Verbindung* | connection |
| 14. | *verwirklichen* | to realize |
| 15. | *die Gelder* | funds (mostly public) |
| 16. | *das Austauschprojekt* | exchange program |
| 17. | *zur Verfügung stehen* | to be available |
| 18. | *der Schadstoff* | harmful substance |
| 19. | *der Algengehalt* | algae concentration |
| 20. | *der Rollstuhl, ¨-e* | wheelchair |
| 21. | *das Umweltproblem* | environmental problem |
| 22. | *das Müllfahrzeug* | garbage truck |
| 23. | *der Abbau* | mining |
| 24. | *der „Trabbi"* | nickname for the East German car model *Trabant* manufactured from 1949 to 1989 |

| | | |
|---|---|---|
| 25. | *die Maßnahme* | measure |
| 26. | *die Arbeitsplatzschaffung* | creation of jobs |
| 27. | *die Verwaltungshilfe* | administrative assistance |
| 28. | *der Erfahrungsaustausch* | exchange of experience |
| 29. | *der Wechsel* | change |
| 30. | *ein Tropfen auf den heißen Stein* | proverb; lit.: a drop on a hot stone; no matter how well intended the help is, it is too small even to be noticeable |

# LEKTION 11

DAS DEUTSCHE FERNSEHEN.   German Television.

## A. DIALOG

*Adrian McCormick kam im Rahmen des CDS International[1]
Austauschprogramms nach Deutschland und ist für ein Jahr beim
ZDF[2] in Mainz[3] angestellt. Adrian soll in der Produktionsabteilung
und Programmgestaltung mitwirken.*

HERR McCORMICK: **Woran arbeiten Sie denn im Moment?**

FRAU KROHN: **Wir entwickeln gerade ein neues Programm für das
Frühstücksfernsehen.**

HERR RIEMERS: **Im Herbst, wenn Sie in der Produktionsabteilung
sind, werden Sie an dem Programm mitarbeiten, das Sie mit
Frau Krohn entwickeln.**

FRAU KROHN: **Haben Sie in den USA schon an
Frühstücksprogrammen gearbeitet? Ich weiß, dass es davon ja
eine ganze Menge im amerikanischen Fernsehen gibt.**

HERR McCORMICK: **Ja, aber wir haben auch viel mehr
Sendeanstalten.**

HERR RIEMERS: **Das sind bei uns ja auch mehr geworden. Früher
waren es nur drei Programme. Eines davon sendete nur
abends bzw.[4] nachmittags.**

FRAU KROHN: **Es gibt jetzt soviel mehr Sender. Natürlich immer
noch die zwei öffentlich-rechtlichen, ARD und ZDF, und jetzt
auch noch zahlreiche private. Die Konkurrenz wird für uns
immer härter.**

HERR RIEMERS: **Sie haben ja gestern in der Vorführung gesehen,
dass das Programm des ZDF sehr viel lebhafter und
abwechslungsreicher geworden ist.**

HERR McCORMICK: **Das ist richtig. Sie zeigen auch erstaunlich
viele Serien aus den USA.**

FRAU KROHN: **Die erfolgreichsten werden eingekauft. Aber wir
entwickeln auch unsere eigenen. „Derrick" beispielsweise ist
eine der erfolgreichsten deutschen Krimiserien.[5] Und „Tatort"
von unseren Kollegen bei der ARD ist ja auch nicht schlecht.**

HERR RIEMERS: Das Problem ist, dass in dem Wettstreit der Sendeanstalten untereinander, schnell ein Überangebot[6] von Programmen entsteht, die sich alle sehr ähnlich sind. Das wollen wir natürlich vermeiden.

HERR McCORMICK: Gibt es denn keine Sender, die sich spezialisieren, wie ESPN oder CNN zum Beispiel?

FRAU KROHN: Nein, nicht so wie in den USA. Das müssen Sie so sehen: das deutsche Publikum will eine bestimmte Mischung aus Uunterhaltung, Information und Nervenkitzel.[7] Natürlich gibt es unter den privaten Kabelsendern einen Sportsender, und wir haben seit Jahren MTV und CNN. Aber deswegen zeigen alle anderen Sender weiterhin ihre eigenen Sport- und Nachrichtensendungen.

HERR RIEMERS: Die Veränderungen, die es in den letzten 10 Jahren beim deutschen Fernsehen gab, sind viel einschneidender[8] als beim amerikanischen. Vor nicht allzu[9] langer Zeit konnte sich in Deutschland kein Mensch vorstellen, dass wir mal ein so reiches Angebot an Sendern haben würden.

FRAU KROHN: Für Amerikaner war es selbstverständlich, dass die Sendungen mit Werbung unterbrochen wurden. Das gab es bis vor kurzem in Deutschland überhaupt nicht.

HERR RIEMERS: Uns geht es darum, nicht dem Trend der Privaten einfach hinterherzulaufen, sondern stattdessen dem Publikum zu zeigen, dass die öffentlich-rechtlichen Sender nach wie vor qualitatives[10] Fernsehen bringen.

FRAU KROHN: Wir wollen ein wirklich neues, originelles[11] Frühstücksfernsehen entwickeln.

HERR RIEMERS: Die Sendung soll sich auch soweit von den anderen Programmen unterscheiden, dass sie auch die Zuschauer anspricht, die Frühstücksfernsehen bisher abgelehnt haben.

HERR McCORMICK: Sind das denn nicht einfach Menschen, die morgens nicht fernsehen wollen?

HERR RIEMERS: Möglicherweise schon. Aber es geht uns darum, eine anspruchsvollere und informative Sendung zu schaffen. Eine Frühstückssendung mit Niveau sozusagen. Ich freue mich, dass wir daran zusammen arbeiten können.

FRAU KROHN: Kommen Sie, ich zeige Ihnen heute noch ein Band von Moderatoren,[12] damit Sie sich noch ein besseres Bild[13] vom deutschen Publikumsgeschmack machen können.

---

# TRANSLATION

Adrian McCormick came to Germany as part of the CDS International exchange program and will be employed at the ZDF in Mainz for one year. Adrian is scheduled to work in production and program development.

MR. McCORMICK: What are you working on at the moment?

MS. KROHN: We're currently developing a new show for breakfast TV.

MR. RIEMERS: In the fall, when you're in production, you'll be working on the program you developed with Ms. Krohn.

MS. KROHN: Did you already work on breakfast shows in the U.S.? I know that you have quite a number of them on American TV.

MR. McCORMICK: Yes, but we also have more TV stations.

MR. RIEMERS: Well, we've got more now too. Years ago there were only three stations. One of them only broadcast during the evening and in the afternoon.

MS. KROHN: There are so many more now. Of course, we still have the two public stations, ARD and ZDF, and now in addition numerous private stations. Our competition is getting tougher all the time.

MR. RIEMERS: You could tell from the demonstration yesterday that our programming has become much more lively and diverse.

MR. McCORMICK: That's right. You're broadcasting an amazing number of series from the U.S.A.

MS. KROHN: The most successful ones are bought. But we're also developing our own. "Derrick" for instance is one of the most popular German crime shows. And "Tatort" from our colleagues of the ARD isn't bad either.

MR. RIEMERS: The problem is that because of the competition between stations it easily happens that too many similar programs are created. Of course, we want to avoid this.

MR. McCORMICK: Are there no stations that specialize like ESPN and CNN?

MS. KROHN: No, not like in the U.S. You have to look at it this way: the German audience wants a certain mix of entertainment, information, and thrill. Of course there is a sports channel among the cable stations and we've had MTV and CNN for years, but the public stations nonetheless continue to show their own sports and news programs.

MR. RIEMERS: The changes that occurred in German TV over the past 10 years are much more radical than in the U.S.A. Not so long ago no one in Germany could imagine that we would have such a wide array of stations.

MS. KROHN: For Americans it was second nature to have the programming interrupted by commercials. Until just recently, we didn't have that kind of thing here at all.

MR. RIEMERS: We intend not to simply copy the trend of the private cable stations, but instead to show the audience that the public stations still show quality television.

MS. KROHN: In other words, we want to develop a truly new and ingenious breakfast show.

MR. RIEMERS: The program is supposed to be different from other shows by appealing even to the viewers who've rejected breakfast TV so far.

MR. McCORMICK: Aren't those simply people who don't want to watch TV in the morning?

MR. RIEMERS: Maybe. But we intend to create a more sophisticated and informative show. A breakfast program with a high standard, so to speak. I'm glad that we can work together on this.

MS. KROHN: Come, I'll show you the anchors' tape now, so that you can get an even better idea of the tastes of German viewers.

# B. IN KÜRZE

1. CDS International stands for Carl Duisberg Society, an American non-profit organization founded in 1968 to organize international fellowships, professional exchange programs, and internships around the globe. It is linked to the *Carl Duisberg Gesellschaft (CDG),* founded in Germany in 1949 to foster international exchange.

2. *Das ZDF* is short for *das Zweite Deutsche Fernsehen* (Second German Television). The "first" station is *die ARD,* short for *Allgemeine Rundfunkanstalten Deutschlands* (General Radio and Television Stations of Germany). These are the two original *öffentlich-rechtlich* (public) TV stations. The ZDF broadcasts nationally; the ARD runs eleven regional programs in addition to its national programming.

3. *Mainz* is on the Rhine river in *Rheinland-Pfalz.* It hosts the headquarters of the *ZDF.* To learn about the history and culture of the city, please go to www.Mainz.de.

4. *Bzw.* is short for *beziehungsweise* (respectively). It always appears abbreviated in writing.

5. *Der Krimi* is the colloquial term for *Kriminalgeschichte* (crime story).

6. *Das Überangebot* (surplus offer) is used in both colloquial and economic language. An *Überangebot* creates a saturated market.

7. *Der Nervenkitzel* is an idiomatic term which, literally translated, means "nerve tickle." It is often used in entertainment to describe *die Spannung* (thrill or suspense). The word only appears as a noun. The adjective *kitzlig* (ticklish) describes the sensitivity to touch. The corresponding adjective to *Nervenkitzel* is *spannend* (suspenseful, thrilling).

8. *Einschneidend* (radical, drastic) is a derivative of *schneiden* (to cut). While German also uses *drastisch* (drastic) and *radikal* (radical), *einschneidend* is more effective because of its visual connotation (severing, penetrating).

9. *Allzu* stresses *zu* (too) in negative descriptions with *nicht.*

*Wenn es nicht allzu viel kostet, nehme ich es.*
If it doesn't cost too much, I'll take it.

*zu,* on the other hand, is used just like its English equivalent "too."

*Was? Eine halbe Stunde muss ich warten, das ist mir zu lang.*
What? Half an hour I have to wait? That's too long.

10. The adjective *qualitativ* (with regard to quality) appears frequently in German texts and conversation. Its partner word is *quantitativ* (with regard to quantity). *hoch-/minderwertig* (high value or inferior value) is often added.

*Wir wollen qualitativ hochwertiges Fernsehen anbieten.*
We want to offer high-quality TV.

11. *Originell* (funny, innovative, unusual, ingenious) is quite different from *original* (original).

12. *Der Moderator* (anchor, showmaster) and *die Moderation* (presentation) are false friends, as they don't share the meaning of the English "moderation."

13. *Sich ein Bild machen können* (to be able to get a clear idea/picture of something) is an idiomatic expression always used reflexively. It often appears with the comparative *besser:*

*Er soll sich ein besseres Bild vom deutschen Publikum machen können.*
We want him to get a better idea of German viewers.

# C. GRAMMATIK UND GEBRAUCH

## 1. *NEBENSÄTZE MIT „DASS"* (*DASS*-SUBCLAUSES)

As in English, expressions of hope, belief, expectation, and wishes are followed by *dass* (that). Unlike in English, it is not possible to drop *dass.*

*Ich hoffe, dass ich an dem Austauschprogramm teilnehmen kann.*
I hope (that) I can participate in the exchange program.

*Wir erwarten, dass sie schon nächste Woche konkrete Pläne entwickelt haben.*
We expect (that) you will have developed precise plans by next week.

*Sie verspricht, dass sie am Montag pünktlich kommt.*
She promises (that) she will be on time on Monday.

Subclauses with *dass* always have a subject, which can, but doesn't have to, be identical with the subject in the introductory main clause.

*Ich denke, dass ich morgen zu Hause bleibe.*
I think I will stay at home tomorrow.

*Meine Eltern erwarten, dass ich erfolgreich bin.*
My parents expect me to be successful.

The verb in the *dass*-subclause takes the last position.

## 2. „DASS" ODER „DAS"? (*DASS* OR *DAS?*)

Although they are pronounced identically, *dass* and *das* are spelled differently, and they have very different meanings. *Das* is the definite article for singular neuter nouns, and their relative pronoun, referring either to the subject (nominative) or the object (accusative or dative) of the preceding main clause.

*Das Theaterstück, das gestern abend im 2. lief, wurde 1988 schon mal gezeigt.*
The play that was broadcast last night on Channel 2 was already shown in 1988.

*Das Programm, das Sie heute nachmittag gesehen haben, ist das gleiche, das jetzt verändert werden soll.*
The program that you watched this afternoon is the same that is to be changed now.

*Dass* introduces a subordinate clause different from a relative clause. It doesn't refer to a subject or object, but adds to the information of the entire sentence.

*Ich weiß, dass Sie das nicht wissen können.*
I know that you can't know that.

*Er befürchtet, dass es zu spät ist.*
He fears that it's too late.

Both *das*- and *dass*- sentences require a comma.

## 3. INFINITIVE MIT „ZU" (INFINITIVES WITH ZU)

While *dass* sentences require a subject, infinitive constructions with *zu* never have a subject, but relate to the subject and action of the introductory main clause.

*Er plant Samstag zum Fernsehstudio zu fahren.*
He is planning to drive to the TV studio on Saturday.

In these infinitive constructions, *zu* always precedes the infinitive.

*Hast du Zeit heute mit mir zu arbeiten?*
Do you have time to work with me today?

If the infinitive is a separable verb, *zu* stands between prefix and stem.

*Wir erwarten schon vor 23 Uhr anzukommen.*
We expect to arrive even before 11 P.M.

If the subclause has more than one verb, an auxiliary or modal verb and the main verb, *zu* always stands between the main verb and the auxiliary or modal in the last position.

*Sie war überrascht schon im Mai nach Schweden reisen zu können.*
She was surprised to be able to travel to Sweden as early as May.

*Wir waren glücklich soviel Geld verdient zu haben.*
We were glad to have earned so much money.

## 4. INFINITIVE MIT „UM ... ZU" (INFINITIVES WITH UM ... ZU)

*Um ... zu* plus infinitive is comparable to the English "in order to."

*Adrian McCormick ging nach Mainz, um etwas über das deutsche Fernsehen zu lernen.*
Adrian McCormick went to Mainz in order to learn something about German TV.

Just like infinitives with *zu*, the *um ... zu* construction demands that main and subclause share the same subject.

*Das Frühstücksfernsehen soll neu gestaltet werden um mehr Zuschauer zu gewinnen.*
Breakfast TV is to be redesigned in order to win more viewers.

In order to ask for the purpose of an action, use *warum* (why) or *wozu* (what for).

*Wir brauchen viel Zeit um die neue Sendung zu gestalten.*
We need a lot of time to create the new show.

*Warum brauchen Sie viel Zeit? Um die neue Sendung zu gestalten.*
Why do you need a lot of time? To create the new show.

*Wozu brauchen Sie das Programmheft? Um die Programme zu vergleichen.*
What do you need the program booklet for? To compare the programs.

## 5. *ANDERE INFINITIVE MIT „ZU"* (OTHER INFINITIVES WITH *ZU*)

Sentences with *ohne . . . zu* plus infinitive (without) or *anstatt . . . zu* plus infinitive (instead of) also never have their own subject.

*Er schlief ein ohne den Fernseher auszumachen.*
He fell asleep without switching off the TV.

*Sie blieb einfach weg anstatt anzurufen.*
She just stayed away instead of calling.

Note that if the main clause follows the *zu* construction, subject and verb switch places.

*Anstatt zu warten geht sie immer einkaufen, wenn die Läden voll sind.*
She always goes shopping when the stores are packed instead of waiting.

## 6. *FINALSÄTZE* (FINAL SUBCLAUSES)

Like *um . . . zu* plus infinitive, subclauses with *damit* or *so dass* express the purpose of an action. Unlike *um . . . zu,* subclauses with *damit* and *so dass* require their own subject. Compare:

*Ich zeige Herrn McCormick die beliebteste Fernsehshow des letzten Jahres, damit er sich ein Bild vom deutschen Zuschauergeschmack machen kann.*
I'll show Mr. McCormick last year's favorite TV show so that he can get an idea of German viewer taste.

*Ich zeige ihm die beliebteste Fernsehshow um ihm einen Eindruck vom deutschen Zuschauergeschmack zu geben.*
I'll show him the favorite TV show in order to give him an idea of German viewer taste.

*Sie müssen mit der Programmgestaltung bis August fertig sein, damit wir am 1. Oktober in die Produktion gehen können.*
You have to complete the program development by August so that we can start production on October 1.

*Ich zeige Ihnen jetzt die beliebteste Fernsehshow des letzten Jahres, so dass Sie sich ein Bild vom deutschen Zuschauergeschmack machen können.*
I'll show you the favorite TV show of last year so that you can get an idea of German viewer taste.

As with *um . . . zu,* the appropriate question words are *warum* and *wozu.* Please note that the answer requires a subject.

*Unser Reporter benutzt eine Videokamera, damit er flexibel ist.*
Our reporter uses a video camera in order to be flexible.

*Wozu benutzt der Reporter diese Kamera? Damit er flexibel ist.*
What does the reporter use this camera for? To be flexible.

# D. REIN GESCHÄFTLICH

## 1. TV IN GERMANY, SWITZERLAND, AND AUSTRIA

*Die öffentlich-rechtlichen Sender* (public television stations) *ARD* and *ZDF* are funded by viewer fees. Everyone who owns and operates a TV set or radio is required to pay *Fernseh- und Rundfunkgebühren* (TV and radio fees). These fees make it possible to broadcast virtually commercial-free. Commercials interrupt programs only once.

The *Bundesländer* have their own local TV and radio stations. Some of these local TV stations are *öffentlich-rechtliche Sender* operated by the *ARD: WDR, Westdeutscher Rundfunk,* located in Cologne; *BR, Bayerischer Rundfunk,* from Munich; *NDR, Norddeutscher Rundfunk;* and many more. Two stations in Berlin still carry names that are reminiscent of the city's recent divided past: *SFB, Sender Freies Berlin* (Radio Free Berlin), and *RIAS, Radio im Amerikanischen Sektor* (Radio in the American Sector).

German television takes part in *Eurovision,* the simultaneous broadcast of certain major features such as live coverage of sports events. The European media collaboration also includes the numerous *Koproduktionen* (co-productions) ranging from crime-search programs broadcast in Germany, Switzerland, and Austria, to TV series made in, by, and for several European countries.

The major private stations include *VOX, Pro 7, Sat 1,* and *Sat 2* as well as *3 Sat.* New private stations are constantly put into operation, often owned and operated by print media conglomerates, film studios, or other private corporations. The rapid development in cable hook-up will guarantee that every household in Germany will soon have access to cable television offering more than 30 channels.

The competition between the *öffentlich-rechtlichen* and the *privaten Sendeanstalten* is fierce, especially in view of the commercial appeal of private cable stations. *ARD* and *ZDF,* which have always competed against each other, are now faced with strong competition from outside. In an attempt to maintain their powerful hold on the German television audience, *ARD* and *ZDF,* are working together more closely than ever before.

Switzerland's major TV stations are *DRS, Deutsch und Rätoromanische Schweiz* (German and Rhaeto-Romansh Switzerland), and *Splus.* There are also *TSR* (Television Swiss Roman) and *TSI* (Television Svizzera Italiana). *DRS, TSR,* and *TSI* are owned and operated by *SRG, Schweizer Radio & Fernsehgesellschaft* (Swiss Radio and Television Company). Switzerland also receives *ARD* and *ZDF, Südwest 3,* and *Bayern 3* (from Southern Germany), as well as the Austrian channel *ORF, Österreichischer Rundfunk* (Austrian TV & Radio). Several cable channels exist. Because of Switzerland's multilingual population, and the proximity to France and Italy, *France TF, Television Française 1, 2,* and *3* as well as the Italian station *RAI, Radio Televisione Italiana 1,* are rather popular.

The major Austrian TV stations are *ORF 1* and *ORF 2 (Österreichischer Rundfunk 1* and *2).* Austria also receives the German stations and is hooked up to international and European cable stations.

## 2. VOCABULARY

| | |
|---|---|
| *der Zuschauer* | viewer |
| *die Einschaltquote* | rate of viewers |
| *einschalten* | switch on (TV) |
| *die Sendeanstalt* | TV station |
| *der Live Bericht* | live report |
| *aufzeichnen* | to record |
| *die Aufzeichnung* | (pre)recording |
| *die Reportage* | report |
| *der Reporter* | reporter |
| *die Werbung* | commercial break (TV) |
| *der Sender* | station |
| *die Programmvorschau* | preview, upcoming programs |
| *die Nachrichten* | news |
| *der Spielfilm* | feature film |
| *die Kindersendung* | children's program |
| *die Serie* | (mini) series |
| *die Fernsehsendung* | TV series, program |
| *die Sendung* | series, program |

190

| | |
|---|---|
| *das Fernsehspiel* | theater (for TV) |
| *die Show* | show, entertainment |
| *die Musiksendung* | music program |
| *die Sportsendung* | sports broadcast |
| *die „Sportschau"* | weekly sports program, originated by the *ARD*, running for decades on Saturday evenings; because of its incredible popularity its name has been adopted for all and any type of sports program |

# ÜBUNGEN

**1.** *„dass" oder „das"*

BEISPIEL: *Es ist schön, _____ ich Deutschland besuchen kann. (dass)*
*Die Sendung läuft doch immer im ZDF, _____ weißt du doch. (das)*

   a. *Das war das letzte Mal, _____ ich mir diese Sendung angesehen habe.*

   b. *Er hat gemerkt, _____ Ursula schon zu Hause war.*

   c. *Adrian wusste nicht, _____ viele Programme aus den USA gekauft werden.*

   d. *Er ist in Italien? _____ habe ich nicht gewusst.*

   e. *Das Fernsehgerät, _____ in der Ecke steht, ist alt.*

   f. *Sie erwarten, _____ ich Sie morgen anrufe.*

   g. *_____ Sie Programmdirektor beim ZDF sind, ist mir neu.*

   h. *Das Sportprogramm, _____ abends zwischen 19:30 und 20 Uhr lief, gibt es nicht mehr.*

**2.** *Beantworten Sie die Fragen zum Text. Benutzen Sie „damit" oder „zu" oder „um . . . zu".*

BEISPIEL: *Warum ist Adrian McCormick nach Deutschland gekommen?*
*Adrian McCormick ist nach Deutschland gekommen, um im Rahmen des Austauschprogramms beim ZDF zu arbeiten.*

   a. *Wozu zeigt Herr Riemers Adrian das Moderatenband?*

   b. *Warum ist Adrian McCormick in Mainz?*

   c. *Warum freut sich Herr Riemers?*

   d. *Wozu gibt es Austauschprogramme für Geschäftsleute?*

**3.** *Verbinden Sie die Sätze mit „um . . . zu", „anstatt . . . zu", or „ohne . . . zu".*

BEISPIEL: *Er hat mich durch Mainz gefahren. Er zeigte mir die Stadt.*
*Er hat mich durch Mainz gefahren, um mir die Stadt zu zeigen.*

a. *Sie schaltete das Licht an. Sie machte den Fernseher aus.*
b. *Werbung wird gezeigt. Die Sendungen werden nicht unterbrochen.*
c. *Wir wollen deutsch lernen. Wir fliegen nach Hannover.*
d. *Er ging schlafen. Er schloss die Tür nicht ab.*
e. *Adrian ist nach Mainz gekommen. Er arbeitet beim ZDF.*
f. *Wir sahen uns Schlösser an. Wir haben geschlafen.*
g. *Sie ändern das Fernsehprogramm. Sie senden immer wieder dasselbe.*

**4.** *Übersetzen Sie.*

a. He decided to go to Innsbruck as part of the exchange program.
b. We look forward to seeing you in Freiburg. (formal you)
c. I'm planning to become program director at the ARD.
d. They decided to change the breakfast program.
e. We expect to be able to change our program by January.
f. They hope to have the program ready by April.

**5.** *Formulieren Sie die Sätze neu und benutzen Sie „immer", „immer wieder", „schon immer", „immer noch", „immer noch nicht".*

BEISPIEL: *Jeden Dienstag sehen wir uns die Talkshow an.*
*Am Dienstag sehen wir uns immer die Talkshow an.*

a. *Ich habe den Film schon ganz oft gesehen.*
b. *Ich weiß schon seit vielen Jahren, dass ich beim Fernsehen arbeiten will.*
c. *Was? Er hat nicht angerufen? Ich warte schon seit Wochen.*
d. *Sie fahren jedes Jahr nach Dänemark.*
e. *Ich habe seit vielen Jahren das gleiche Auto.*
f. *Ihr Fernseher ist nicht repariert. Er ist seit 3 Wochen kaputt.*

# LEKTION 12

FIRMENEXPANSION. Expansion.

## A. DIALOG

*Sylvia Stettner ist Innenausstatterin. Sie war auf der Internationalen Bau- und Einrichtungsmesse im Wiener Messezentrum Prater[1] und hat mehrere Aufträge bekommen, davon zwei in Deutschland, einen in Stuttgart und einen anderen in Kiel.[2]*

SYLVIA STETTNER: Was meinst du, liege ich richtig[3] in der Annahme, dass wir in zwei Monaten anfangen und zum September fertig sind?

WOLFGANG MIERBACH: Von welchem Auftrag sprichst du?

SYLVIA STETTNER: Von dem Kunstzentrum in Kiel.

WOLFGANG MIERBACH: Ja, sicherlich.

SYLVIA STETTNER: Den Stuttgarter Auftrag kann ich noch gar nicht abschätzen.

WOLFGANG MIERBACH: Hast Du denn überhaupt schon eine feste Zusage aus Stuttgart?

SYLVIA STETTNER: Ja, ich hab' sogar eine Unterschrift. Und wir haben schon so einiges fixiert,[4] was den Stil und die Farben angeht.[5]

WOLFGANG MIERBACH: Was ist denn das für ein Gebäude?

SYLVIA STETTNER: Ein Bürohaus mit Arztpraxen, Rechtsanwälten, ein Architekt und eine Grafikzentrale—sowas halt.[6]

WOLFGANG MIERBACH: Soll ich nach Kiel fahren, oder fährst du selber[7] hin?

SYLVIA STETTNER: Ich finde, du solltest nach Kiel fahren.

WOLFGANG MIERBACH: Einverstanden. Und wer fährt nach Stuttgart?

SYLVIA STETTNER: Wir werden sehen. So, wie sieht's aus mit dem Kieler Projekt?

WOLFGANG MIERBACH: Nun, wir brauchen die Bestätigung des Kostenvoranschlages aus Kiel. Ich warte auf deren Rückruf.

SYLVIA STETTNER: Frag auch, ob sie uns Arbeitsräume zur Verfügung stellen[8] und ob sie dich unterbringen können.

WOLFGANG MIERBACH: Ich halte es für ratsam, schon ein paar Tage vorher hinzufahren, um Kontakte zu knüpfen.[9]

SYLVIA STETTNER: Gute Idee. D.h.[10] also, du brauchst ein Auto, damit du beweglich bist.

WOLFGANG MIERBACH: Wer weiß, vielleicht kannst du ja schon bald eine deutsche Zweigstelle aufmachen, „Exclusiv Design Vienna".

SYLVIA STETTNER: Immer mit der Ruhe.[11] Ich freue mich wahnsinnig[12] über[13] diese Aufträge. Aber für eine zweite Filiale ist es noch zu früh.

WOLFGANG MIERBACH: Wer weiß . . .

SYLVIA STETTNER: Bleib mal schön auf dem Teppich. Ich habe dem Kunstzentrum in Kiel angeboten, etwas in Richtung Hundertwasser[14] zu machen.

WOLFGANG MIERBACH: Warum?

SYLVIA STETTNER: Weil die Deutschen ganz verrückt sind nach Hundertwasser, und weil ihnen meine Entwürfe gut gefallen haben.

WOLFGANG MIERBACH: Wie wäre es denn mit einem Spiegelglastreppenaufgang, damit schön viel[15] Licht von den Dachfenstern in die Ausstellungshalle dringt.

SYLVIA STETTNER: Eine großartige Idee! Als erstes muss ich mich um die Gewerbeanmeldung in Kiel kümmern, damit wir so schnell wie möglich ein Bankkonto in Deutschland eröffnen können. Dann muss ich dir nicht immer Geld schicken, solange du in Kiel bist.

WOLFGANG MIERBACH: Bekommen wir etwa keinen Vorschuss?

SYLVIA STETTNER: Doch natürlich. Damit kannst du dann Einkäufe machen und die Handwerker anheuern.[16]

*Das Telefon klingelt.*

WOLFGANG MIERBACH: Das ist bestimmt der Anruf aus Kiel. Exclusiv Design, Mierbach am Apparat. Grüß Gott.

---

Sylvia Stettner is an interior designer. She went to the International Fair for Building and Interior Design at the Viennese Fair Center Prater, and got several new contracts, two of which are in Germany, one in Stuttgart, and another in Kiel.

SYLVIA STETTNER: What do you think, am I right in assuming that we can start in two months and will be ready by September?

WOLFGANG MIERBACH: Which contract are you talking about?

SYLVIA STETTNER: About the art center in Kiel.

WOLFGANG MIERBACH: Yes, sure.

SYLVIA STETTNER: I can't really assess the job in Stuttgart yet.

WOLFGANG MIERBACH: Did Stuttgart even confirm yet?

SYLVIA STETTNER: Yes, I even have a signature. And we already decided upon several things concerning style and color scheme.

WOLFGANG MIERBACH: What type of building is it?

SYLVIA STETTNER: An office building with doctors' practices, lawyers, an architect, and a graphic design center—that kind of thing.

WOLFGANG MIERBACH: Should I go to Kiel or are you going there yourself?

SYLVIA STETTNER: I think you should go to Kiel.

WOLFGANG MIERBACH: Agreed. And who's going to Stuttgart?

SYLVIA STETTNER: We'll see. So, where are we with the Kiel project?

WOLFGANG MIERBACH: Well, we need confirmation from Kiel on our estimate. I'm waiting for them to return my call.

SYLVIA STETTNER: Also, ask them whether they can give us some work space and whether they can put you up.

WOLFGANG MIERBACH: I think it would be a good idea if I went up there a few days earlier to make some contacts.

SYLVIA STETTNER: Good idea. That means you'll need a car so you'll be mobile.

WOLFGANG MIERBACH: Who knows, maybe you can even open a German branch soon, "Exclusiv Design Vienna."

SYLVIA STETTNER: Hold your horses. I'm extremely excited about these contracts. But it is far too early for a second branch.

WOLFGANG MIERBACH: Who knows . . .

SYLVIA STETTNER: Let's stick to reality, shall we? I offered the art
   center in Kiel to do something along the lines of Hundertwasser.

WOLFGANG MIERBACH: Why?

SYLVIA STETTNER: Because the Germans are crazy about
   Hundertwasser and because they liked my drafts.

WOLFGANG MIERBACH: How about a mirror glass staircase, so that
   plenty of light can come in through the skylights down to the
   exhibition hall?

SYLVIA STETTNER: A grand idea. First, I'll have to look into getting a
   business license for Kiel, so that we can open a bank account in
   Germany as soon as possible. Then I won't have to keep sending you
   money while you're in Kiel.

WOLFGANG MIERBACH: Aren't we getting an advance?

SYLVIA STETTNER: Of course we are. You'll use that for shopping and
   hiring the workmen.

The telephone rings.

WOLFGANG MIERBACH: I'm sure that's the call from Kiel. Exclusiv
   Design, Mierbach speaking. Good afternoon.

# B. IN KÜRZE

1. The Vienna fairgrounds are *das Wiener Messezentrum Prater. Der
   Prater* is an amusement park, famous for a recreational park area
   and the largest cabin Ferris wheel in the world. The fairgrounds
   are a modern complex hosting many international trade fairs. *Die
   Wiener Messen & Kongress GmbH* also organizes fairs and exhibitions in Salzburg and St. Pölten, Prague, Budapest, and Bucharest.

2. *Kiel,* the capital of the *Bundesland Schleswig-Holstein,* is in the
   north of Germany on the Baltic Sea. Check out www.Kiel.de for
   information on the city's rich background.

3. *Richtig/falsch liegen* (to be right or wrong; lit: to lie right or false) is
   a common idiomatic expression.

*Da liegst du total falsch.*
   You're (totally) wrong there.

*Ich liege doch richtig in dem Glauben, dass Sie heute geöffnet haben.*
   I'm correct in thinking that you're open today, right?

4. *Fixieren* (to confirm, to decide) is an Austrian expression. Standard
   German would use the term *schriftlich festhalten* (to put into writing) or *bestätigen* (to confirm) or *reservieren* (to reserve).

5. *Was . . . angeht* (as far as . . . is concerned, regarding) is a fixed expression that could be replaced by *was . . . betrifft.*

*Was das Geld angeht, werden wir ein Bankkonto in Deutschland einrichten.*
As far as money is concerned, we'll open a bank account in Germany.

*Was den Kieler Auftrag betrifft, habe ich gestern die schriftliche Bestätigung des Kostenvoranschlages per Fax erhalten.*
Regarding the Kiel project, I received the written confirmation of the estimate by fax yesterday.

Note that the word order changes (subject and verb invert) in the clause following the comma.

6. *Halt,* which tends to be more common in the south, and *eben,* which is more common in the north, are used synonymously when they are used as stress markers.

*Er hat eben recht.*
He's right, after all.

*Sie ist halt früher gekommen.*
Well, she did arrive earlier.

7. *Selbst* (self) and *selber* are synonymous. Both never take endings and follow either the subject or the verb in simple tenses. In compound tenses *selbst* stands between the auxiliary and the main verb:

*Er hat alles selbst gebaut.*
He built everything himself.

If *selbst* precedes the noun it means "even" and cannot be replaced by *selber:*

*Selbst meine Konkurrenz war beeindruckt.*
Even my competitors were impressed.

8. Compare: *jemandem etwas zur Verfügung stellen* (to offer) and *zur Verfügung stehen* (to be available).

*Ich stelle Ihnen gerne mein Büro zur Verfügung.*
I'll be happy to offer you my office for your use.

*Mein Auto steht Ihnen jederzeit zur Verfügung.*
My car is available to you at any time.

9. *Kontakte knüpfen* (to set up contacts, to form friendships, to get acquainted) is an idiomatic expression. *Knüpfen* literally means "to knot."

10. *D.h.* is an abbreviation of *das heißt* (that means, that is). It often appears abbreviated in writing and is always fully pronounced in conversation.

11. Less colorful synonyms for *immer mit der Ruhe* (hold your horses; don't panic) are:

*Nun mal langsam.*
Let's take it slow.

*Eins nach dem anderen.*
One thing at a time.

12. *Wahnsinnig* (crazy, insane) appears in several literal expressions as an adjective—*wahnsinnig werden* (to become/go crazy, to go mad):

*Bei diesem Lärm werde ich wahnsinnig.*
I'm losing my mind in this noise.

and as an adverb—*jemanden wahnsinnig machen* (to make someone go insane, to drive someone mad):

*Sie macht mich wahnsinnig mit ihrem Gesang.*
She's driving me mad with her singing.

13. *Sich freuen* can appear with two different prepositions, *auf* and *über*.

*Sie freut sich sehr über die neuen Aufträge.*
She is very happy about the new contracts.

*Wolfgang freut sich auf den Aufenthalt in Kiel.*
Wolfgang looks forward to his stay in Kiel.

14. Friedensreich Hundertwasser (1928–2000; born as Friedrich Stowasser) was an Austrian contemporary artist known for his colorful, vivid paintings. Vienna has two famous Hundertwasser sites, the *Hundertwasser-Haus* and the *KunstHaus Wien*. Both are unique and unconventional buildings, with colorful tiles, colorful window frames, and no symmetrical forms.

15. *Schön viel* is a colloquialism meaning "a good amount, an abundance" and should not be translated literally as "pretty much." *Schön* can generally be used as a stress marker:

*Sie möchte schön viele Blumen und Bäume ums Haus.*
She wants an abundance of flowers and trees surrounding the house.

*Wir haben schön sauber gemacht.*
We really cleaned the place (to a shine).

16. *Anheuern* (to hire) originated in the merchant and navy ship trade. Sailors or seamen would go to the harbor or port and wait to be hired on board. Nowadays this term is used colloquially for hiring for a limited time rather than permanently. *Beschäftigen* and *beauftragen* can be used in similar contexts:

*Wir haben ein paar Leute mit den Bauarbeiten beschäftigt.*
We hired a couple of people for the building work.

*Wir haben einige Bauleute beauftragt.*
We ordered some builders to work for us.

# C. GRAMMATIK UND GEBRAUCH

## 1. *KAUSALE NEBENSÄTZE* (SUBCLAUSES OF CAUSALITY)

The reason for a particular action in the main clause is often given in a subclause, introduced by a subordinating conjunction such as *weil* (because), *da* (because, since, as), or *zumal* (especially because, since). The verb in the subclause takes the last position, and the subclause is separated from the main clause by a comma.

*Wir sind nach Kiel gefahren, weil wir uns das Projekt ansehen mussten.*
We drove to Kiel because we had to take a look at the project.

*Da unser Auto alt ist, fahren wir lieber mit dem Bus.*
As our car is old, we prefer to take the bus.

*Ich kann diesen Monat wirklich nicht verreisen, zumal ich auch gar kein Geld habe.*
I really can't go away this month, expecially since I don't have any money.

While *weil* and *da* are often interchangeable, subclauses introduced by *da* can precede the main clause, whereas those with *weil* should always follow the main clause.

*Da heute schönes Wetter ist, gehen wir nachmittags in den Park.*
Since the weather is nice today, we're going to the park in the afternoon.

*Sylvia Stettners Telefonrechnung ist viel höher, weil sie jetzt jeden Tag mit Deutschland telefoniert.*
Sylvia Stettner's telephone bill is much higher as she makes phone calls to Germany every day now.

*Da die Firma neue Kunden hat, müssen die Dekorateure hart arbeiten.*
As the company has new clients, the designers have to work hard.

Note that when the subclause precedes the main clause, subject and verb in the main clause switch places.

   *Zumal* is used to introduce an additional cause or reason that has not been mentioned previously, or that takes precedence over other reasons. Subclauses with *zumal* always follow the main clause.

*Du hast wirklich zuviel Arbeit, zumal du jetzt auch noch zur Messe fährst.*
   You really have too much work, especially since you're now also going to the trade fair.

Subclauses introduced by *zumal* often add the adverbial construction *auch* or *auch noch* (in addition, also) as a stress marker.

## 2. *ANDERE KAUSALE KONJUNKTIONEN* (OTHER CAUSAL CONJUNCTIONS)

Although sentences introduced by *darum* (that's why), *deswegen* (for that reason), and *deshalb* (for that reason, that's why) can stand by themselves, they depend upon the preceding clause, which explains the cause of the action. *Darum* replies to *warum* (why), *deswegen* replies to *weswegen* (why), and *deshalb* replies to *weshalb* (why).

*Warum hat Frau Stettner ein Büro in Kiel aufgemacht?*
*Sie hat einen großen Auftrag in Kiel bekommen. Darum hat sie ein Büro aufgemacht.*
   Why did Ms. Stettner open an office in Kiel?
   She got a large contract in Kiel. That's why she opened an office.

*Weswegen bist du nach Stuttgart gefahren?*
*Wir haben einen Auftrag bekommen. Deswegen bin ich nach Stuttgart gefahren.*
   Why did you go to Stuttgart?
   We got a contract. That's why I went to Stuttgart.

## 3. *INDIREKTE FRAGEWÖRTER* (INDIRECT QUESTION WORDS)

Question words, such as *wer* (who), *wo* (where), *wie* (how), *wieviel* (how much), *was* (what), *weswegen* (for what reason, why), *weshalb* (why), and *warum* (why), often appear as conjunctions to introduce a subordinate clause.

*Herr Mierbach weiß nicht, wann er nach Kiel fährt.*
   Mr. Mierbach doesn't know when he is going to Kiel.

*Frau Stettner weiß, warum sie soviele neue Aufträge bekam.*
   Ms. Stettner knows why she got so many new contracts.

*Er weiß nicht, wo er Arbeit finden soll.*
He doesn't know where to find work.

*Ich habe nicht verstanden, was er gesagt hat.*
I didn't understand what he said.

These question words are also used in indirect speech.*

DIRECT SPEECH
*Herr Mierbach: „Warum fahren wir nicht nächste Woche nach Kiel?"*
Mr. Mierbach: "Why don't we go to Kiel next week?"

INDIRECT SPEECH
*Herr Mierbach fragt, warum wir nicht nächste Woche nach Kiel fahren.*
Mr. Mierbach asks why we don't go to Kiel next week.

Questions without a question word use the conjunction *ob* (whether, if) to introduce the subclause. Compare the use of *ob* with the English "if"/"whether."

*Können Sie uns irgendwo in Kiel unterbringen?*
Can you put us up somewhere in Kiel?

*Wir werden sie fragen, ob sie uns unterbringen können.*
We will ask them whether they can put us up.

*Ich habe Herrn Mierbach gefragt, ob er mich anrufen kann.*
I asked Mr. Mierbach if he could call me.

# D. REIN GESCHÄFTLICH

## 1. GENERAL INFORMATION ON AUSTRIA AND VIENNA

*Österreich* (Austria) has been a neutral state since 1955, when it regained its sovereignty after World War II. In a referendum in 1994, the population (8 million) overwhelmingly voted to become a member of the European Union.

*Wien* (Vienna), the capital of the *Republik Österreich* (Republic of Austria), has always been a gateway to the East. Its close proximity to Prague, Budapest, and Bratislava has not only deepened its citizens' understanding and involvement in East-West relations, but also created a city deeply rooted in tradition and diplomacy. Vienna is, with New York, Geneva, and Paris, one of the major UN locations in the world.

Its strategically important and central location was first discovered by the Romans, who set up camp, named it Vindobona, and stayed for

* See Lesson 13.

three centuries. Austria's most famous and best-remembered period was under the Habsburg family, which came to power in 1278 and formed *das Habsburger Reich* (the Austro-Hungarian Empire). The monuments of the Empress Maria-Theresa, the Emperor Franz Joseph, and the much loved Queen (and later Empress) Elizabeth, lovingly called *Sissi,* still remind the visitor of Vienna's grandiose past and the Austrians' love for their imperial family.

Vienna played a major role in the history of music and coffee. During multiple, unsuccessful attempts by the Turks to conquer Vienna, the invaders, as legend has it, forgot a couple of bags of coffee beans outside the city. The bags and their contents were duly inspected by the curious Viennese and quickly turned into one of their most beloved drinks. Viennese coffeehouses are a charming reminder of a past when the city's musical and literary talent gathered around *Melange* (coffee with steamed milk), *Einspänner* (mocha in a glass with whipped cream), and *kleiner Brauner* (black coffee with cream on the side).

Music without Vienna, and Vienna without music, is unimaginable. *Wolfgang Amadeus Mozart,* the *Strauss* family, who invented the waltz, *Gustav Mahler, Johannes Brahms,* and *Ludwig von Beethoven* have left their grandiose mark on musical history as well as on Vienna.

## 2. STARTING A BUSINESS IN GERMANY

Everyone is required to report the establishment of an enterprise at the local *Ordnungsamt* (licensing office) to receive a *Gewerbeschein* (business certificate). The *Handelsregister* (commercial register) lists all corporations, commercial partnerships, and sole proprietorships. Registration at this public register includes the company's name, the name of the managing director, and the name of any employee with the power of attorney for procurement, the *Prokurist.* Every new firm name must be distinct from all other firm names registered in the *Handelsregister.*

The easiest way to start a business is to form a *GbR, eine Gesellschaft bürgerlichen Rechts* (company under civil law). No minimum investment or start-up capital is required. The owners are personally liable for any debt or punitive damages with their private and company assets. The application for a *GbR* is available from the *Amt für Finanzen und Wirtschaft* (state authority for finances and economy).

Another alternative is to form a *GmbH, eine Gesellschaft mit beschränkter Haftung* (company with limited liability). This requires minimum start-up capital of 50,000 DM, 50% of which has to be deposited into a company bank account at the time of founding; the other 50% can be shown as assets, in the form of business equipment.

Other types of companies are *KG, Kommanditgesellschaft* (a limited partnership of one or more general partners); *AG, Aktiengesellschaft* (a public or stock corporation); and *OHG, Offene Handelsgesellschaft* (general partnership).

# ÜBUNGEN

**1.** *Beantworten Sie die Fragen zum Text.*

   a. *Warum muss sie ihre Firma in Deutschland anmelden?*
   b. *Warum will Frau Stettner ein Bankkonto in Deutschland aufmachen?*
   c. *Warum bleibt Frau Stettner in Wien?*

**2.** *Formulieren Sie Fragen.*

BEISPIEL: *Das Papier ist aus. Deshalb kommt das Fax nicht an.*
          *Weshalb kommt das Fax nicht an?*

   a. *Ich war schon oft in Wien, aber darum fahre ich immer wieder hin.*
   b. *Der Stil ist sehr modern, und das Haus ist alt. Deswegen möchte ich lieber was anderes.* (use *Sie*)
   c. *Es ist heiß in der Messehalle. Deshalb habe ich Kopfschmerzen. (du)*
   d. *Wir kennen da oben ja keinen Menschen. Deswegen brauchen wir unbedingt Kontakte in Kiel.*
   e. *Da wir keinen Menschen in Kiel kennen, müssen wir dort hinfahren.*

**3.** *Formulieren Sie die Fragen um. Benutzen Sie „wissen Sie" und indirekte Fragewörter.*

BEISPIEL: *Kennt Frau Stettner den Kieler Kunden gut?*
          *Wissen Sie, ob Frau Stettner den Kieler Kunden gut kennt?*

   a. *Fährt Herr Mierbach jetzt jede Woche einmal nach Wien?*
   b. *Findet die Bau- und Design Messe einmal pro Jahr statt?*
   c. *Wann ist der Brief angekommen?*
   d. *Hat der Arzt den Kostenvoranschlag schon zurückgeschickt?*
   e. *Ich habe das Fax auf den Tisch gelegt. Ich finde es nicht mehr.*
   f. *Ist der Vertrag datiert und unterschrieben?*
   g. *Sylvia hat Geld abgehoben. Die Summe weiß ich nicht.*

**4.** *Übersetzen Sie.*

   a. Ms. Stettner drives to Stuttgart because she has a client in Stuttgart.
   b. Since the building in Stuttgart isn't ready, I don't have to work on the design just yet. *(noch nicht)*
   c. Did he tell you why he thinks so?
   d. What did you say? (formal)
   e. Mr. Mierbach, do you know whether Ms. Stettner is at home?
   f. I cannot take a rental car, especially since I forgot my credit card.

**5.** „Da", „weil" oder „deswegen/deshalb"?

    a. _____ wir morgen schon in Wien sind, muss ich heute abend noch den Stadtführer lesen.

    b. Ich bin eingeschlafen. _____ weiß ich das Ende vom Film nicht.

    c. Er ist nach New York zurückgekehrt, _____ er sein Studium beenden will.

    d. _____ wir neue Aufträge haben, müssen wir länger arbeiten.

    e. Frau Stettner hat sehr viel um die Ohren. _____ geht sie vor 22 Uhr nicht nach Hause.

# LEKTION 13

BEIM RECHTSANWALT.  At the Lawyer's Office.

## A. DIALOG

*Nach einem leichten Verkehrsunfall, bei dem nur Sachschaden[1]*
*verursacht wurde, spricht Frau Schröder mit ihrem Rechtsanwalt.*

RA[2] HUBERT: Tag, Frau Schröder. Bitte setzen Sie sich doch. Ich
habe heute die Gegendarstellung des Unfalls vom Kläger
bekommen.

FRAU SCHRÖDER: Und?

RA HUBERT: Tja, er behauptet, Sie hätten das Vorfahrtsrecht[3]
nicht beachtet.

FRAU SCHRÖDER: Wer mit über 60 in einer 30 km/h[4] Zone[5] um
die Ecken schleudert, braucht[6] sich doch wohl nicht zu
wundern . . .

RA HUBERT: Haben wir denn dafür Zeugen?

FRAU SCHRÖDER: Der Mann am Kiosk hat mir bestätigt, dass der
Fahrer des BMW mit mindestens 60 um die Ecke gefahren
sein muss. Er sagt, er sei richtig erschrocken, weil die Reifen
so gequietscht haben.

RA HUBERT: Sie sind also die Marburger Straße entlang gefahren,
die schon vor dem Unfallort, Marburger Ecke Stoltzstraße, ein
30 km/h Gebiet ist.

FRAU SCHRÖDER: Ja, der BMW kam von rechts aus der
Stoltzstraße, und da war es schon zu spät.

RA HUBERT: Sie haben also vor der Kreuzung nicht gehalten.

FRAU SCHRÖDER: Das braucht man doch nicht. Ich bin langsam
gefahren, um zu sehen, ob ein Wagen aus der Stoltzstraße
kommt.

RA HUBERT: Und Sie haben den BMW nicht gesehen?

FRAU SCHRÖDER: Nein.

RA HUBERT: Hmm. Sie sagen, Sie hätten den Wagen nicht
gesehen, haben allerdings nicht angehalten, sondern sind mit,
sagen wir, 20 km/h quasi über die Kreuzung gerollt. Richtig?

FRAU SCHRÖDER: Ja.

RA HUBERT: **Dann müsste ja der Fahrer des BMW blitzschnell auf die Kreuzung zugeschossen sein, so dass der Zusammenstoß überhaupt noch stattfinden konnte. Der BMW war doch schon in der Kurve, als Ihr Wagen auf seinen hinteren Kotflügel stieß. Es muss also mehrere Sekunden gegeben haben, in denen Sie den BMW direkt vor Augen hatten.**

FRAU SCHRÖDER: **Ich schwöre, ich habe den BMW vorher nicht gesehen. Die Ecke Marburger und Stoltzstraße ist mit Büschen bepflanzt. Die müssten\* dringend mal geschnitten werden.**

RA HUBERT: **Na, wenn Sie nicht sehen konnten, ob da ein anderer Verkehrsteilnehmer[7] aus der Seitenstraße kommt, hätten Sie aber anhalten müssen.**

FRAU SCHRÖDER: **Ja schon. Aber ist es denn nicht genauso verkehrswidrig[8] mit überhöhter Geschwindigkeit zu fahren?**

RA HUBERT: **Natürlich. Das Problem ist nur, dass mein Kollege schreibt, sein Mandant sei nicht schneller als 40 gefahren.**

FRAU SCHRÖDER: **Das ist nicht wahr. Das wird der Gutachter sicherlich bestätigen. Ganz abgesehen davon habe ich doch auch noch die Aussage von dem Kioskverkäufer.**

RA HUBERT: **Der andere Zeuge, der am Fußgängerübergang stand, hat zwar auch die quietschenden Reifen gehört, aber er behauptet, Sie hätten eindeutig die Vorfahrt missachtet.**

FRAU SCHRÖDER: **Aber, Herr Rechtsanwalt,[9] bei 40 quietschen doch nicht die Reifen!**

RA HUBERT: **Das mag sein, aber das ändert nichts an der Tatsache, dass Sie gegen die Straßenverkehrsordnung[10] verstoßen und somit vermutlich den Unfall verschuldet haben.**

FRAU SCHRÖDER: **Die Vorfahrt beachten ist wohl oberstes Gebot[11] auf deutschen Straßen.**

---

TRANSLATION

After a light traffic accident which caused only material damage, Ms. Schröder consults her lawyer.

LAWYER HUBERT: Hello, Ms. Schröder. Please take a seat. I received the counterclaim on the accident from the plaintiff today.

MS. SCHRÖDER: And?

---

\* *müssten* is the subjunctive II of the modal auxiliary *müssen*. The statement implies a contrary-to-fact condition. Contrary-to-fact statements are discussed in Lesson 16.

LAWYER HUBERT: Well, he claims that you ignored the right of way.

MS. SCHRÖDER: Whoever skids around the corner at 60 in a 30 km/h zone shouldn't be surprised . . .

LAWYER HUBERT: Do we have witnesses for that?

MS. SCHRÖDER: The man at the kiosk confirmed that the driver of the BMW must have been doing at least 60 around that corner. He says he was alarmed, because the tires were screeching.

LAWYER HUBERT: So you were driving along Marburger Straße, which is already a 30 km/h zone before the site of the accident at Marburger and Stoltzstraße.

MS. SCHRÖDER: Yes, the BMW came from the right out of Stoltzstraße and then it was already too late.

LAWYER HUBERT: So you didn't stop before the intersection.

MS. SCHRÖDER: You don't have to. I was going slowly to see whether a car was coming from the Stoltzstraße.

LAWYER HUBERT: And you didn't see the BMW?

MS. SCHRÖDER: No.

LAWYER HUBERT: Hmm. You say you didn't see the car, yet you didn't stop and instead, as it were, you rolled across the intersection at, say, 20 km/h. Correct?

MS. SCHRÖDER: Yes.

LAWYER HUBERT: Then the driver of the BMW had to have shot into the intersection in a flash for the accident to have happened. The BMW was already at the corner when your car hit its rear fender. There must have been several seconds during which you must have had the BMW right in front of your eyes.

MS. SCHRÖDER: I swear I didn't see the BMW beforehand. There are bushes and plants on the corner of Marburger and Stoltzstraße. They really should be trimmed.

LAWYER HUBERT: Well, if you couldn't see whether another car was coming out of the side street, you should've stopped.

MS. SCHRÖDER: Yes, okay. But isn't it just as illegal to speed?

LAWYER HUBERT: Of course. The problem is that my colleague writes that his client was doing no more than 40.

MS. SCHRÖDER: That's not true. The expert will definitely confirm that. Besides, I also have the statement of the kiosk salesperson.

LAWYER HUBERT: The other witness who was at the crosswalk also heard the screeching tires, but he claims that you clearly ignored the right of way.

MS. SCHRÖDER: But, Mr. Hubert, tires don't screech at 40!

LAWYER HUBERT: That may be so, but it doesn't change the fact that you violated traffic regulations and thus probably caused the accident.

MS. SCHRÖDER: The right of way obviously rules supreme on German streets.

# B. IN KÜRZE

1. *Sachschaden* (material damage) has a more serious counterpart: *Personenschaden* (personal injury).

2. *RA* is short for *Rechtsanwalt* (lawyer). This abbreviation is used in written correspondence with a lawyer, especially in the address: *Herrn RA Jürgen Hubert.*

3. *Das Vorfahrtsrecht* (right of way), also just called *die Vorfahrt,* is different in Germany: if no yield or right of way signs are posted, the traffic coming from the right always has the right of way, even if the side street to the right is much smaller. This rule applies in most residential areas. Go to www.ADAC.de (German Automobile Club) for more traffic rules.

4. Germany uses the metric system: *30 km/h* is approximately 20 miles an hour. To convert from mile/h to km/h multiply by 1.6. *Km/h* stands for *Stundenkilometer* (kilometer per hour).

5. *30 km/h Zone* is a reduced-speed area, set into effect in most residential areas and in the vicinity of schools and kindergartens. Some *30 km/h Zonen* have speed bumps. The speed limit in these areas is strictly enforced.

6. *Brauchen* (to need) can act as a main verb.

*Ich brauche ein Auto.*
I need a car.

It can also replace the modal auxiliary *müssen* (to have to, must), in the negative. Here it takes an infinitive with *zu.*

*Man braucht doch hier nicht anzuhalten.*
You don't have to stop here.

7. *Der Verkehrsteilnehmer* (traffic participant) is a common term in Germany for everyone participating in traffic (pedestrians, bicyclists, cars, buses, trucks).

8. The suffix *-widrig* always implies that a violation has occurred: *gesetz(es)widrig* (illegal, in violation of the law), *verkehrswidrig* (against traffic regulations).

9. A lawyer in court, and sometimes in consultation, is formally addressed as *Herr Rechtsanwalt.* Similar ways to address individuals with a title would be *Herr/Frau Doktor,* or *Herr Professor* (see Lesson 1). These forms of address have become uncommon in regular conversation.

10. *Die Straßenverkehrsordnung* (street traffic order) contains all official terms of German traffic regulations. You will receive a *Strafzettel* (traffic citation) if you violate the *Straßenverkehrsordnung.*

11. *Das Gebot* (order, command, rule) is rather common in figurative expressions.

*die 10 Gebote*
the Ten Commandments

*Das Gebot der Vernunft hindert mich daran, ihn zu verklagen.*
Reason prevents me from taking him to court.

*Wir können nichts machen. Das Gebot der Stunde heißt abwarten.*
We can do nothing. The only thing to do is to wait.

# C. GRAMMATIK UND GEBRAUCH

## 1. *INDIREKTE REDE* (INDIRECT SPEECH)

Indirect speech (also known as reported speech or indirect discourse) reports what someone has said without giving a direct quote.

*Marlies Schröder: „Ich habe den BMW nicht gesehen."*
Marlies Schröder: "I didn't see the BMW."

*Marlies Schröder sagt, sie habe den BMW nicht gesehen.*
Marlies Schröder says she didn't see the BMW.

Note that the pronoun changes as the point of view shifts. The introductory phrase and indirect speech are always separated by a comma. The conjunction *dass* is often used to link the introductory phrase with the indirect speech. If *dass* is used, the sentence reporting indirect speech becomes a subordinate clause, and the verb moves to the end. Compare:

*Mein Kollege schreibt, dass sein Mandant nicht mehr als 40 km/h gefahren sei.*
My colleague writes that his client was not driving faster than 40 km/h.

*Mein Kollege schreibt auch, ein Fußgänger an der Kreuzung könne dies bezeugen.*
My colleague also writes, a pedestrian at the intersection would be able to confirm that.

When reporting a question, you must repeat the question word.

*Er fragte: „Warum haben Sie nicht angehalten?"*
He asked: "Why didn't you stop?"

*Er fragte, warum sie nicht angehalten habe.*
He asked why she didn't stop.

If the question reported has no question word, *ob* is used.

*Marlies fragte den Mann: „Können Sie für mich als Zeuge aussagen?"*
Marlies asked the man: "Could you act as my witness?"

*Marlies fragte den Mann, ob er für sie als Zeuge aussagen könne.*
Marlies asked the man whether he could act as her witness.

## 2. *DER KONJUNKTIV IN INDIREKTER REDE* (THE SUBJUNCTIVE IN INDIRECT SPEECH)

Although indirect speech requires the subjunctive I, it is generally accepted to use the indicative in conversation. In writing, however, the subjunctive should be used. Compare:

*Er sagte: „Ich komme morgen."*
He said: "I'll come tomorrow."

*Er sagt, er kommt morgen.* (indicative)
*Er sagte, er komme morgen.* (subjunctive I)
He said he'd come tomorrow.

The endings of the subjunctive I in the present tense— *-e, -(e)st, -e, -en, -(e)t,* and *-en*—are added to the present tense stem of the verb. Except for the third person singular, the forms of the subjunctive I are almost identical to the indicative forms.

*KOMMEN*

| |
|---|
| *ich komme* |
| *du komm(e)st* |
| *er komme* |
| *wir kommen* |
| *ihr komm(e)t* |
| *sie kommen* |

*GEHEN*

| |
|---|
| *ich gehe* |
| *du geh(e)st* |
| *er gehe* |
| *wir gehen* |
| *ihr geh(e)t* |
| *sie gehen* |

If you wish to distance yourself from the message you're reporting, indicating that you doubt the truth of the reported statement, you must use the subjunctive. As the subjunctive I is almost identical to the indicative, the subjunctive II* is often used to make the distinction between direct and indirect speech clear. Compare:

*Der Anwalt sagte, der Bericht des Gutachters komme morgen.* (subjunctive I)
The lawyer said the expert's report will come tomorrow.

*Der Anwalt sagte, der Bericht des Gutachters käme morgen.* (subjunctive II)
The lawyer said the expert's report would come tomorrow.

The endings of the subjunctive II— *-e, -(e)st, -e, -en, -(e)t, -en*—are added to the past tense stem of the verb. Many strong verbs, such as *kommen,* take an umlaut, and some, such as *gehen,* undergo a vowel change.

*KOMMEN*

*GEHEN*

| | |
|---|---|
| *ich käme* | *ich ginge* |
| *du käm(e)st* | *du ging(e)st* |
| *sie käme* | *sie ginge* |
| *wir kämen* | *wir gingen* |
| *ihr käm(e)t* | *ihr ging(e)t* |
| *sie kämen* | *sie gingen* |

To report events in the past, the subjunctive forms compound tenses with *haben* or *sein* plus the past participle. The subjunctive I and II of *haben* and *sein* are used frequently. As the subjunctive I of *haben* is hard to distinguish from the indicative, the subjunctive II is mostly used instead (*hätte*).

| | INDICATIVE | | SUBJUNCTIVE I | | SUBJUNCTIVE II | |
|---|---|---|---|---|---|---|
| INFINITIVE | *HABEN* | *SEIN* | *HABEN* | *SEIN* | *HABEN* | *SEIN* |
| *ich* | *habe* | *bin* | *habe* | *sei* | *hätte* | *wäre* |
| *du* | *hast* | *bist* | *habest* | *sei(e)st* | *hättest* | *wär(e)st* |
| *er/sie/es* | *hat* | *ist* | *habe* | *sei* | *hätte* | *wäre* |
| *wir* | *haben* | *sind* | *haben* | *seien* | *hätten* | *wären* |
| *ihr* | *habt* | *seid* | *hab(e)t* | *sei(e)t* | *hättet* | *wär(e)t* |
| *sie* | *haben* | *sind* | *haben* | *seien* | *hätten* | *wären* |
| *Sie* | *haben* | *sind* | *haben* | *seien* | *hätten* | *wären* |

* This is discussed in detail in Lesson 16.

*Der BMW Fahrer sagte, ein Fußgänger habe/hätte an der Ecke gestanden.*
The BMW driver said the pedestrian (had) stood on the corner.

*Marlies Schröder sagte, sie sei/wäre langsam gefahren.*
Marlies Schröder said she drove/had driven slowly.

*Der Anwalt sagte, dass seine Mandantin den BMW nicht gesehen habe/hätte.*
The lawyer said that his client did not see/had not seen the BMW.

## 3. *GENITIVPRÄPOSITIONEN* (GENITIVE PREPOSITIONS)

Just as there are prepositions with dative (Lesson 4), prepositions with accusative (Lesson 8), and two-way prepositions (Lesson 7), there are prepositions that always take the genitive.* Here is a list of the most common ones:

*BINNEN/INNERHALB* (within)
*Der Brief des Gutachters sollte innerhalb einer Woche hier eintreffen.*
The expert's letter should arrive here within one week.

*Binnen eines Monats will er sein Haus verkaufen.*
He wants to sell his house within one month.

Although the two prepositions are interchangeable, if used as a temporal preposition, *innerhalb* is a little more common. *Innerhalb* can also be used as a preposition of place. *Binnen,* however, cannot.

*Innerhalb der 30 km/h Zone dürfen nur Krankenwagen und die Polizei schneller als 30 fahren.*
Within the 30 km/h zone, only ambulances and the police can drive faster than 30.

*AUßERHALB* (outside, beyond)
*Außerhalb des Landes sollten Sie Ihren Pass dabei haben.*
Outside of the country you should carry your passport with you.

*LAUT* (according to)
*Laut Straßenverkehrsordnung § 42 Absatz 2 haben Sie die Geschwindigkeitsbegrenzung überschritten.*
According to traffic regulation § 42 No. 2 you exceeded the speed limit.

Note that the noun following *laut* often stands without article. In written text, *laut* is often abbreviated into *lt.*

*ANHAND* (by use of)
*Er hat mir anhand des Gesetzbuches bewiesen, dass ich recht habe.*
By use of the law book he proved to me that I was right.

* For a review of the genitive endings of nouns, please see the appendix.

*ENTLANG* (along, alongside)
*Sie fuhr entlang der Autobahn.*
She drove alongside the highway.

*JENSEITS* (beyond)
*Jenseits der Grenze können Sie zollfrei einkaufen.*
Beyond the border you can shop duty-free.

*INMITTEN* (in the midst of, in the middle of)
*Inmitten der Kreuzung saß ein kleiner Junge.*
A young boy sat in the middle of the intersection.

*WÄHREND\** (during)
*Während des Treffens mit dem Anwalt kam ein Anruf.*
During the meeting with the lawyer a call came in.

*WEGEN†* (because of, due to)
*Wir sind wegen des schlechten Wetters nicht gefahren.*
We didn't go because of the bad weather.

*TROTZ* (in spite of, despite)
*Trotz des Regens sind wir spazieren gegangen.*
Despite the rain we went for a walk.

*(AN)STATT* (instead of)
*(An)statt des Gutachtens bekam sie einen Brief vom Gericht.*
She received a letter from the court instead of the evaluation.

## 4. *ZUSAMMENGESETZTE SUBSTANTIVE* (COMPOUND NOUNS)

If a possessive connection exists between two nouns, the possession is expressed either by using the genitive case, *das Büro des Anwalts,* or by forming a compound noun, *das Anwaltsbüro.* Compound nouns describing a possessive connection often add an *-s-* between the two nouns. As with all compound nouns, the last noun dictates the gender.

| | |
|---|---|
| *der Anwalt + die Kanzlei* | = *die Anwaltskanzlei* (law office) |
| *die Straße + der Verkehr +* | = *die Straßenverkehrsordnung* (traffic |
|    *die Ordnung* |    regulation) |
| *der Verkehr + der Unfalll* | = *der Verkehrsunfall* (traffic accident) |
| *die Vorfahrt + das Recht* | = *das Vorfahrtsrecht* (right of way) |

---

\* Compare the use of *während* as a genitive preposition with *während* as a temporal conjunction (Lesson 5).

† It is generally accepted to use the dative after *trotz, während,* and *wegen* in conversation, but you should always use the genitive in writing.

| | |
|---|---|
| *der Verkehr + der Teilnehmer* | = *der Verkehrsteilnehmer* (road user, traffic participant) |
| *der Schaden + der Ersatz* | = *der Schadensersatz* (compensation) |
| *der Verband + der Kasten* | = *der Verbandskasten* (first-aid kit) |
| *das Gericht + das Gebäude* | = *das Gerichtsgebäude* (courthouse) |
| *der Unfall + der Wagen* | = *der Unfallwagen* (damaged vehicle) |
| *die Polizei + das Auto* | = *das Polizeiauto* (police car) |
| *der Zeuge + die Aussage* | = *die Zeugenaussage* (witness's statement) |

## 5. DIE VORSILBE „UN" (THE PREFIX UN)

The prefix *un-* expresses the opposite. It can be attached to nouns and adjectives.

| | |
|---|---|
| *gewiss* (certain, definite) | *ungewiss* (uncertain) |
| *das Wissen* (knowledge) | *das Unwissen* (lack of knowledge) |
| *die Schuld* (guilt) | *die Unschuld* (innocence) |
| *schuldig* (guilty) | *unschuldig* (innocent, not guilty) |
| *vorsichtig* (careful) | *unvorsichtig* (careless) |
| *der Sinn* (sense, mind) | *der Unsinn* (nonsense) |

*Es ist unvorsichtig, das Auto nicht abzuschließen.*
    It's careless not to lock the car.

*Wie das Gerichtsverfahren ausgeht, ist ungewiss.*
    How the court case will end is uncertain.

*Sie sagte, sie sei unschuldig.*
    She said she was not guilty.

Some words take on a completely different meaning with the prefix *un-*.

| | |
|---|---|
| *der Fall* (fall) | *der Unfall* (accident) |
| *der Rat* (advice) | *der Unrat* (garbage, waste) |
| *sicher* (sure, secure) | *unsicher* (self-conscious, insecure, nervous) |

*Er ist sehr unsicher beim Autofahren.*
    He is very nervous driving a car.

*Bist du dir sicher, dass wir hier richtig sind?*
    Are you sure we came to the right place?

While *gegen* (against) is used to describe an adverse reaction (against, anti-), *wider* (against, contrary to) is used in certain fixed expressions to describe a change of position or perspective. Note that fixed expressions with *wider* mostly appear in elevated language. The most common of these expressions is *wider Erwarten*.

*Das Autoverbot wurde wider Erwarten abgelehnt.*
The car stop was rejected, contrary to expectation.

*Wider* forms compound verbs and nouns.

*WIDERSTEHEN* (to resist)　　　　　*DER WIDERSTAND* (resistance)
*Können Sie diesem Angebot widerstehen?*
Can you resist such an offer?

*Während des Krieges gab es eine Widerstandsbewegung.*
During the war there was a resistance movement.

*WIDERSPRECHEN* (to contradict)　　*DER WIDERSPRUCH* (contradiction)
*Das widerspricht meinen Prinzipien.*
That's against my principles.

*Der Rechtsanwalt hat ihr widersprochen.*
The lawyer contradicted her.

*WIDERRUFEN* (to withdraw, to cancel) *DER WIDERRUF* (denial, cancellation)
*Ich möchte diese Aussage widerrufen.*
I'd like to withdraw that statement.

*Der Richter war sehr erstaunt über den Widerruf seiner Aussage.*
The judge was very surprised that he denied his statement.

*Wieder* (again) expresses repetition.

*WIEDERSEHEN* (to see again)　　　*DAS WIEDERSEHEN* (reunion)
*Ich hoffe, wir sehen uns bald wieder.*
I hope we see each other again soon.

*Ich freue mich auf unser Wiedersehen.*
I look forward to when we meet again.

*WIEDERHOLEN* (to repeat)　　　*DIE WIEDERHOLUNG* (repetition, rerun)
*Wiederholen Sie das bitte!*
Please repeat.

*Ich habe die Wiederholung im Fernsehen gesehen.*
I saw the rerun on TV.

# D. REIN GESCHÄFTLICH

## 1. THE GERMAN LAW AND THE JUDICIAL SYSTEM

The German legal system is based on *das Grundgesetz* (basic law), which guarantees human rights, individual rights within society, and the rights of the individual versus the state. *Das Grundgesetz* was drawn up in 1949 and became the constitution of the Federal Republic of Germany.

The highest court in Germany is *das Bundesverfassungsgericht* (Federal Constitutional Court) in Karlsruhe, Baden-Württemberg, which handles all constitutional complaints that have exhausted all other legal channels. The courts are otherwise subdivided into *das Arbeitsgericht* (Court of Labor), *das Sozialgericht* (Social Court), *das Finanzgericht* (Finance Court), and *das Verwaltungsgericht* (Administrative Court). Each is headed by a federal court in its division.

Civil law and criminal law in Germany are divided into *das Zivilrecht* and *das Strafrecht.* Civil and criminal lawsuits are brought to justice at *das Amtsgericht* (Local Court), *Bezirksgericht* (Regional Court), or *Landesgericht* (Higher Regional Court or State Court). All these are headed by the *Bundesgerichtshof* (Federal Court of Justice).

*Der Richter* (the judge) is independent and subject only to the law. There are no *Geschworene* comparable to American jurors. The German *Schöffengericht* (jury system) is only in effect for capital crimes. Jury selection is made at the *Amtsgericht* from candidate lists compiled from the electorate. Being a *Schöffe* is an honorary post for four years. A trial for a capital crime is supervised by the *Richter* and the *Schöffen* who sit on either side of the *Richter.* The makeup of the bench varies, depending on the court division and the crime: some benches consist of three *Richter* and two *Schöffen,* whereas less severe cases may only have one *Richter* and four *Schöffen.*

All legal professionals, including those in commerce and legal advisers, have to go through the same course of university studies and professional training. No separate law schools exist in Germany. Instead, a future lawyer studies *Jura* (law studies) at the university. After four to six years of course work are completed, law students take *das erste Staatsexamen* (first state law examination). Before applying for *das zweite Staatsexamen* (second state law examination) any legal professional has to complete two and a half years of practical training, either in the courts, with public authorities, or in an attorney's office.

A person apprehended in suspicion of a crime can be held for only one day. Arraignment has to take place the following day, when either *der Haftbefehl* (warrant for arrest) is issued or the suspect is released. Under the German criminal law everyone has the right to an attorney. *Die Todesstrafe* (capital punishment) was abolished in Germany in 1949.

# 2. VOCABULARY

| | |
|---|---|
| *der Mandant* | (legal) client |
| *die Klage* | lawsuit |
| *der Kläger* | (civil law) plaintiff |
| *der Angeklagte* | (civil law) defendant |
| *der Verteidiger* | defense counsel |
| *der Staatsanwalt* | public prosecutor |
| *der Jurist* | legal professional, lawyer |
| *der Zeuge* | witness |
| *der Kronzeuge* | main witness (for the prosecution) |
| *der Richter* | judge |
| *der Schöffe* | juror |
| *klagen* | to file a complaint, to file a lawsuit |
| *vor Gericht gehen* | to go to court |
| *verklagen* | to sue (someone) |
| *der Rechtsweg* | legal steps |
| *rechtlich gegen jemanden vorgehen* | to take legal steps against someone |
| *die erste Instanz* | court case, first trial |
| *in die zweite Instanz gehen* | to appeal |
| *der (Rechts) Anwalt* | lawyer, attorney |
| *die Anwaltskanzlei, das Anwaltsbüro* | law offices |
| *der Eid* | oath |
| *unter Eid stehen* | to be under oath |
| *vereidigt werden* | to be sworn in, to be put under oath |
| *aussagen* | to testify |
| *die Aussage* | testimony |
| *die falsche Aussage* | false statement, perjury |
| *falsch aussagen* | to make a false statement, to lie (before the court), to commit perjury |
| | |
| *der Haftbefehl* | warrant for someone's arrest |
| *vorladen* | to subpoena |
| *die Vorladung* | subpoena |
| *eine Vorladung bekommen* | to receive a subpoena |
| *die Gerichtsverhandlung, das Gerichtsverfahren* | trial |
| | |
| *der Schaden* | damage, punitive damages |
| *der Sachschaden* | material damage |
| *der Personenschaden* | personal injury |
| *der Schadensersatz* | compensation (for damages) |
| *das Verhör* | questioning (by police) |
| *der Strafzettel* | traffic violation, citation |
| *der Verstoß, die Ordnungswidrigkeit* | violation |

217

| | |
|---|---|
| *die Parkuhr* | parking meter |
| *das Halteverbot* | no-stopping zone |
| *das Aktenzeichen* | case number |
| *das Verwarnungsgeld* | fine |
| *der PKW, der Personenkraftwagen* | automobile, (private) vehicle, car |

*Hohes Gericht!*
Honorable Judge/Honorable Court.

*Sie haben das Recht, einen Anwalt hinzuzuziehen.*
You have the right to obtain legal counsel/advice.

*Sie haben das Recht, die Aussage zu verweigern.*
You have the right to remain silent.

## 3. APOLOGIES AND DEFENSE

*Das tut mir leid. Das habe ich nicht gesehen.*
I am sorry/I apologize; I didn't see it.

*Es tut mir leid.*
I'm sorry.

*Ich bitte um Verzeihung.*
Please forgive me.

*Das habe ich nicht gewollt/beabsichtigt.*
That's not what I intended.

*Es war nicht meine Absicht, Sie zu verletzen.*
It was not my intention/I didn't mean to hurt you.

*Das ist mir aber peinlich.*
I'm embarrassed.

*Entschuldigen Sie bitte. Ich habe mich geirrt/getäuscht.*
Please accept my apologies. It was an oversight on my part./I was wrong.

*Das ist meine Schuld.*
It's my fault.

*Ich konnte nichts anderes tun.*
I couldn't do anything else.

*Ich wusste nicht, was ich tun sollte.*
I didn't know what to do.

*Ich musste mich verteidigen.*
I had to defend myself.

*Es war Selbstverteidigung.*
It was self-defense.

218

*Es gab keine andere Möglichkeit.*
There was no alternative./I had no choice.

*Ich bitte um Verständnis für meine Situation.*
Please understand my position.

*Was hätten Sie denn an meiner Stelle getan?*
What would you have done in my place?

*Zu meiner Verteidigung möchte ich folgendes anmerken.*
In my defense I'd like to add the following.

---

# ÜBUNGEN

**1.** *Übersetzen Sie die folgenden Fragen zum Text und antworten Sie auf Deutsch.*

BEISPIEL: Where does the lawyer work?
*Wo arbeitet der Rechtsanwalt?*
*Der Rechtsanwalt arbeitet in einer Anwaltskanzlei.*

   a. Where was the accident?
   b. Who are the witnesses?
   c. What does the driver of the BMW claim?
   d. Why is Marlies Schröder probably at fault in the accident?

**2.** *Bilden Sie Sätze mit dem Genitiv.*

BEISPIEL: *(das Auto/der Mann/sein/grün/neu)*
*Das Auto des Mannes ist grün und neu.*

   a. *(das Büro/der Anwalt/liegen/außerhalb/die Stadt)*
   b. *(die Gegendarstellung/der Mandant/sein/falsch)*
   c. *(der Kotflügel/das Auto/sein/kaputt)*
   d. *(Frau Schröder/das Auto/sein/neu)*
   e. *(außerhalb/die Innenstadt/sein/die Anwälte/billiger)*
   f. *(binnen/ein Monat/werden/die Bäume/schneiden)*

**3.** *Formulieren Sie den folgenden Text in der indirekten Rede.*

BEISPIEL: *Frau Schröder fragte Herrn Hubert: „Wissen Sie, wie hoch der Schaden ist?"*
*Frau Schröder fragte Herrn Hubert, ob er wisse, wie hoch der Schaden sei.*

   a. *Er sagte: „Ich weiß, dass der BMW Fahrer schneller als 40 gefahren ist."*
   b. *Wir fragten: „Können Sie uns den Weg zeigen?"* (use *er* for *Sie*)
   c. *Herr Hubert sagte: „Der Bericht des Gutachters ist noch nicht da."*
      (use *dass*)

d. *Der Mann am Kiosk sagte: „Ich habe mich richtig erschrocken."* (present tense, use *dass*)
e. *Frau Schröder sagte: „Ich habe noch nie einen Unfall gehabt."*
f. *Herr Hubert sagte: „Die Gegendarstellung war richtig."* (use *dass*)

**4.** *Formulieren Sie das Gegenteil.*

   a. *Der Angeklagte ist <u>schuldig</u>.*
   b. *Ich bin mir <u>sicher</u>.*
   c. *Der Zeuge hatte gelogen und wurde immer <u>sicherer</u>.*
   d. *Das Ende des Gerichtsverfahrens ist <u>gewiss</u>.*
   e. *Er zeigte sein <u>Wissen</u>, indem er alles falsch beantwortete.*

**5.** *Bilden Sie zusammengesetze Substantive und übersetzen Sie.*

| | |
|---|---|
| a. *das Gericht* | 1. *die Ordnung* |
| b. *der Zeuge* | 2. *das Gericht* |
| c. *der Verkehr* | 3. *der Hof* |
| d. *das Recht* | 4. *die Aussage* |
| e. *die Zeitung* | 5. *der Weg* |
| f. *der Anwalt* | 6. *der Bericht* |
| g. *die Verfassung* | 7. *die Kanzlei* |

# LEKTION 14

DIE PRESSE.   The Press.

## A. DIALOG

*Björn Heidemann und Anita Schiller arbeiten kurz vor Redaktionsschluss einer Göttinger[1] Zeitung an zwei kürzlich eingetroffenen Berichten.*

BJÖRN: **Na, Anita, alles klar?[2]**

ANITA: **Nichts ist klar. Ich bin müde, der Artikel ist langweilig, und ich finde einfach keine passende Schlagzeile.**

BJÖRN: **10 Minuten hast du noch.**

ANITA: **Ach, hör bloß auf.[3] Willst du mich ärgern?**

BJÖRN: **Nein, ganz im Gegenteil. Kann ich dir helfen? Ich bin mit meinem Artikel fertig. Worum geht's denn?**

ANITA: **Der sechste Einbruch bei einem leitenden Angestellten der Gö-Bau KG.[4]**

BJÖRN: **Immer bei demselben?**

ANITA: **Nein, immer bei einem anderen Angestellten.**

BJÖRN: **Das hört sich ja stark nach Spionage an.**

ANITA: **Wie meinst du das denn?**

BJÖRN: **Na, das sieht doch so aus, als ob da jemand bei der Gö-Bau was herausfinden will.**

ANITA: **Ja, ich habe mir auch schon überlegt, was die Einbrecher dort wohl[5] suchen. Leider stehlen sie immer nur Wertsachen und keine Papiere.**

BJÖRN: **Na, da liegt doch der Hase im Pfeffer.[6] Ich bin mir sicher, die Gö-Bau gibt der Polizei gar nicht an, dass Papiere gestohlen worden sind, weil sie keine Schlagzeilen über Industriespionage lesen wollen.**

ANITA: **Meinst du?**

BJÖRN: **Ist doch durchaus im Bereich des Möglichen.[7]**

ANITA: **Wieviele Minuten habe ich noch?**

BJÖRN: **Sieben. Was für eine Schlagzeile hast du denn bis jetzt?**

ANITA: **Einbruch beim Gö-Bau Prokuristen.[8]**

BJÖRN: Das ist ja wirklich zum Gähnen.

ANITA: Fällt dir vielleicht was Besseres ein?

BJÖRN: Wie wär's mit: Mysteriöse Einbruchserie bei Gö-Bau setzt sich fort.

ANITA: Am liebsten würde ich schreiben: Was hat Gö-Bau in den Privathäusern zu verbergen?

BJÖRN: Damit hast du den Nagel auf den Kopf getroffen, aber das geht leider nicht. Pure Vermutung ohne Fakten. Was hältst du von: Mysteriöse Einbrecher suchen die Gö-Bau zum sechsten Mal heim.

ANITA: Gö-Bau Einbrüche gehen weiter.

BJÖRN: Nein, wie wär's mit: Was suchen Einbrecher bei Führungskräften der Gö-Bau? Das impliziert eine Intrige, aber verstößt nicht gegen journalistische Objektivität.

ANITA: Ist zwar ein bisschen lang, aber immerhin.[9]

BJÖRN: Ach ja, ich könnte mir den ganzen Tag lang Schlagzeilen ausdenken.

ANITA: Schon wieder ein Anfall von Größenwahn![10] So berauschend[11] sind deine Einfälle auch wieder nicht, mein Lieber!

BJÖRN: Soll ich dir mal meinen Artikel vorlesen?

ANITA: Hast du den schon abgegeben? Da kommt schon der Chef.[12]

HARTMUT BERGER: Na, was ist? Fertig?

BJÖRN: Ja, die fleißigsten Göttinger Journalisten warten schon auf Sie. Hier, unsere heutigen Beiträge.

HERR BERGER: Prima. Na, dann machen Sie mal Feierabend[13] für heute. Bis morgen.

ANITA: Tschüss.[14]

BJÖRN: Sag mal, sollten wir nicht mal bei der Polizei nachforschen, was da eigentlich bei der Gö-Bau los ist?[15]

ANITA: Das macht schon der Jens.

BJÖRN: Das wage ich zu bezweifeln.[16] Sonst würde er doch nicht so einen langweiligen Bericht abliefern.

ANITA: Doch, doch, er ist ganz mit Nachforschungen beschäftigt. Darum schreibe ich den Bericht für ihn. Normalerweise macht er sowas doch selber.

BJÖRN: Ach, sieh mal einer an. Kollege Schiller und Kollege Altdorf spielen Detektiv.

ANITA: **Na und? Das ist völlig normale Journalistenarbeit. Was willst du eigentlich? Das betrifft dich doch überhaupt nicht.**

BJÖRN: **Pure Neugier, Anita, nichts als pure Neugier. Der wichtigste Instinkt eines Journalisten.**

ANITA: **Wie spät ist es eigentlich?**

BJÖRN: **Kurz nach 6.**

ANITA: **So ein Mist, jetzt habe ich meinen Bus verpasst.**

BJÖRN: **Komm, ich fahr dich nach Hause. Liegt sowieso[17] auf meinem Weg.**

---

## TRANSLATION

Just before copy deadline at a Göttingen newspaper, Björn Heidemann and Anita Schiller are working on two reports that recently arrived.

BJÖRN: Anita, everything okay?

ANITA: Nothing's okay. I'm tired, the article is boring, and I simply can't find a suitable headline.

BJÖRN: You still have ten minutes.

ANITA: Ugh, don't start. Are you trying to annoy me?

BJÖRN: No, on the contrary. Can I help you? I'm done with my article. What's yours about?

ANITA: Sixth burglary at the house of a leading employee of the Gö-Bau KG.

BJÖRN: Always the same?

ANITA: No, always a different employee.

BJÖRN: Sounds very much like espionage to me.

ANITA: What do you mean?

BJÖRN: Well, looks like someone wants to find out something about the Gö-Bau.

ANITA: I've also been trying to figure out what the burglars could be looking for. Unfortunately they only steal valuables and no papers.

BJÖRN: Well, that's exactly the crux of the matter. I'm sure the Gö-Bau never tells the police about the stolen papers, because they don't want to read headlines about industrial espionage.

ANITA: Do you think so?

BJÖRN: Well, it's certainly possible.

ANITA: How many more minutes do I have?

BJÖRN: Seven. What kind of headline do you have so far?

ANITA: Burglary at the head accountant's of the Gö-Bau.

BJÖRN: That really makes me yawn.

ANITA: Well, can you think of anything better?

BJÖRN: How about: Mysterious series of break-ins at Gö-Bau continues.

ANITA: I'd really love to write: What is Gö-Bau hiding at their private residences?

BJÖRN: That hits the nail on the head; unfortunately you can't write that. Pure assumption, no facts. What do you think of: Mysterious burglars hit home for sixth time at Gö-Bau.

ANITA: Gö-Bau burglaries continue.

BJÖRN: No, how about: What are the burglars at Gö-Bau's executive homes looking for? That implies an intrigue and won't violate journalistic objectivity.

ANITA: It's a bit long, but still.

BJÖRN: Oh well, I could invent headlines all day long.

ANITA: Yet another case of delusions of grandeur! Your ideas aren't that fabulous, my dear!

BJÖRN: Shall I read my article to you?

ANITA: Did you already submit it? The boss is approaching.

HARTMUT BERGER: Well, what's up? Are you done?

BJÖRN: Yes, the hardest-working journalists in Göttingen have been waiting for you. Here are today's pieces.

MR. BERGER: Great. Well, let's call it a day. See you tomorrow.

ANITA: Bye.

BJÖRN: Tell me, shouldn't we go and investigate with the police as to what's going on with Gö-Bau?

ANITA: Jens is doing that already.

BJÖRN: I have my doubts. If he were, he would hardly deliver such a boring article.

ANITA: Yes, he's quite busy investigating. That's exactly why I'm writing the article for him. Usually he does stuff like that himself.

BJÖRN: Well, what do you know! A little detective game is going on between colleague Schiller and colleague Altdorf.

ANITA: So what? That's regular journalistic work. What are you after anyway? It has nothing to do with you at all.

BJÖRN: Pure curiosity, Anita, nothing but pure curiosity. The most important instinct of any journalist.

ANITA: What time is it?

BJÖRN: Just after 6.

ANITA: What a drag! Now I missed the bus.

BJÖRN: Come, I'll drive you home. It's on my way, anyway.

# B. IN KÜRZE

1. *Göttingen* is a city in the southern part of *Niedersachsen* (Lower Saxony), which has become well known for its university, the Max-Planck-Institute for brain research, and the Karl-Bonhoeffer-Institute for biophysical chemistry. Göttingen's industry includes microscopic instrument production, pharmaceutical companies, printers, and publishers. Please refer to the city's website at www.Göttingen.de.

2. *Alles klar* (lit.: all clear) is a colloquial expression that can be used as a question or as a response. It can also be used as the English "I see" or "I understand."

*Alles klar?*     Everything okay?     *Alles klar.*     Yes, everything's okay.

3. *Hör bloß auf* is an idiomatic expression that translates best into "Don't start" or "Don't remind me." *Aufhören* means "to stop" and *bloß* means "merely," if used as an adverb, and is very similar in meaning to *nur* (only). *Bloß* as an adjective means "naked" or "exposed."

*Er braucht bloß zur Polizei zu gehen.*
All he needs to do is go to the police.

*Er stand mit bloßem Oberkörper vor dem Fenster.*
He stood at the window bare-chested.

4. *KG* is short for *die Kommanditgesellschaft* (limited partnership).

5. *Wohl* is an adverb that appears in many different contexts.

*Was können die Einbrecher wohl gesucht haben?*
What could the burglars possibly have been looking for?

*Sehr wohl.*
Very well.

*Ich fühle mich sehr wohl in der neuen Wohnung.*
I am very comfortable in the new apartment.

225

*Das mag wohl sein.*
That may well be.

*Er wird wohl Dokumente gesucht haben.*
Surely he was looking for documents.

6. *Da liegt doch der Hase im Pfeffer* (lit.: That's where the hare lies in the pepper) is an idiomatic expression comparable to "That's the crux of the matter." The expression originates from the myth that pepper chases away hares and rabbits. Therefore, if the hare is lying *in* the pepper, something must be seriously wrong.

7. *Im Bereich des Möglichen liegen* (to be within the realm of possibility) has a very similar synonym: *im Bereich der Möglichkeit.*

8. *Der Prokurist* is the head accountant of a company. The word derives from the Latin term *procura,* which is the individual with the power of attorney to sign documents or arrange payments.

9. *Zwar . . . aber immerhin* is a conjunctional construction that's best translated as ". . . but at least."

*Ich habe zwar kein Auto mehr, aber immerhin spare ich Geld.*
I don't have a car anymore, but at least I'm saving money.

10. *Der Größenwahn* (delusions of grandeur) also forms an adjective in German: *größenwahnsinnig.*

11. *Berauschend* (thrilling, fabulous) is a present participle* formed from the verb *berauschen.* Although its literal meaning is "intoxicating," it is mainly used figuratively:

*Das war ein berauschendes Fest.*
That was a fabulous/thrilling party.

*Das ist ja nicht gerade berauschend.*
It didn't exactly blow my mind.

12. *Der Chef* is always "the boss," and never "the chef." The chef in the kitchen is *der Chefkoch.*

13. *Der Feierabend* is the common term for the end of a workday. The verb is *Feierabend haben* (to be off work) or *Feierabend machen* (to leave work).

14. *Tschüss* (good-bye, bye) is a colloquial term most common among young people and friends.

15. *Los sein* (lit.: to be loose) is a colloquialism.

*Weißt du, was da los ist?*
Do you know what's going on there?

* Present participles are discussed in Lesson 20.

*Was ist los?*
    What's going on?

16. *Etwas bezweifeln* (to doubt something) is often linked with *wagen* (to dare) as a polite expression of doubt. *Wagen* (to dare to do something) takes *zu* plus infinitive.

*Ich wage das zu bezweifeln.*
    I have my doubts about that.

*Bezweifeln* can also stand by itself and is always followed by a *dass* subclause:

*Sie bezweifelte, dass die Einbrecher nur Wertsachen suchten.*
    She doubted that the burglars were only looking for valuables.

*Zweifeln* (to doubt) is always followed by the preposition *an*.

*Er zweifelte an ihrer Unschuld.*
    He doubted her innocence.

17. *Sowieso* (anyway) and *so oder so* (anyway, either way you look at it) are interchangeable.

*Ich brauche mir das nicht überlegen, ich habe sowieso kein Geld.*
    I don't need to think about it; I don't have any money anyway.

*Es macht so oder so keinen Sinn.*
    It doesn't make sense, either way you look at it.

# C. GRAMMATIK UND GEBRAUCH

## 1. *WEITERE VERBEN MIT VORSILBEN* (MORE PREFIX VERBS)

As mentioned before, prefixes, whether separable or inseparable, change the meaning of a verb. Compare:

*Martin und Lisa treffen sich jeden Tag.*
    Martin and Lisa meet every day.

*Herr Berger trifft um 18.25 Uhr ein.*
    Mr. Berger arrives at 6:25 P.M.

*Das betrifft mich nicht.*
    That doesn't concern me.

In previous chapters we were dealing with separable prefixes such as *an-*, *aus-*, *vor-*, and *mit-*. New separable prefixes are *ein-*, *ab-*, and *zu-*. Inseparable prefixes are *be-*, *ver-*, and *zer-*.

| *BRECHEN* (to break) | SEPARABLE: | INSEPARABLE: |
|---|---|---|
| | *einbrechen* (to break in), *zusammenbrechen* (to break down, to collapse), *ausbrechen* (to break out, to escape) | *verbrechen* (to commit a crime), *(sich) erbrechen* (to vomit) |

*Gestern abend brachen drei Personen in das Haus des Gö-Bau Prokuristen ein.*
  Last night three burglars entered the house of the Gö-Bau head accountant.

*Wir haben nichts verbrochen.*
  We didn't do anything (illegal).

*Er war sehr krank und hat sich erbrochen.*
  He was very sick and vomited.

*Sie war so erschöpft, dass sie total zusammengebrochen ist.*
  She was so exhausted that she totally collapsed/had a breakdown.

*Im 14. Jahrhundert brach die Pest aus.*
  In the fourteenth century the bubonic plague broke out.

| *STOßEN* (to push) | SEPARABLE: | INSEPARABLE: |
|---|---|---|
| | *zustoßen* (to meet up with, to be afflicted), *anstoßen* (to toast, to drink to someone) | *verstoßen* (to break a law or a rule) |

*Ich hörte, bei Webers wurde eingebrochen. Ist ihnen etwas zugestoßen?*
  I hear that the Webers were burglarized. Were they injured at all?

*Wir wollten auf dich anstoßen. Hier, nimm ein Glas Sekt.*
  We wanted to drink to you./Let's have a toast. Here, take a glass of champagne.

*Sie haben gegen das Gesetz verstoßen.*
  You broke the law.

*DENKEN* (to think)    SEPARABLE: *ausdenken* (to dream up, to think of), *umdenken* (to change plans, to rethink)    INSEPARABLE: *(nicht) verdenken* (not to blame someone), *bedenken* (to think about something carefully)

*Er muss sich etwas ausdenken, aber ihm fällt nichts ein.*
He must think of something, but nothing comes to mind.

*Ihr müsst umdenken, diese Schlagzeile geht so nicht.*
You have to reconsider; this headline won't work.

*Sie ist nach Hamburg zum Stern gegangen. Das kann man ihr nicht verdenken.*
She went to the Stern in Hamburg. You can't blame her for that.

*Bitte bedenken Sie, dass unsere Zeitung recht klein ist.*
Please remember that our paper is relatively small.

*LESEN* (to read)    SEPARABLE: *vorlesen* (to read out loud, to read to someone)    INSEPARABLE: *verlesen* (to slip up in reading)

*Bitte lesen Sie mir Ihren Artikel vor.*
Please read your article to me.

*War das falsch? Dann muss ich mich wohl verlesen haben.*
Was that wrong? Then I must've slipped up while reading.

*GEBEN* (to give)    SEPARABLE: *abgeben* (to hand in, to submit), *zugeben* (to admit)    INSEPARABLE: *vergeben* (to forgive someone, to give away, to hand out)

*Ich gab meine Arbeit am Montag ab.*
I handed in my work on Monday.

*Ich gebe zu, dass ich noch nie in Göttingen war.*
I admit that I've never been to Göttingen.

*Er vergibt Aktien zu Weihnachten.*
He hands out shares at Christmas.

*Gott vergibt die Sünden.*
God forgives the sins.

*FALLEN* (to fall)    SEPARABLE: *einfallen* (to have an idea, to remember), *ausfallen* (to be canceled)    INSEPARABLE: *zerfallen* (to decay, to rot), *verfallen* (to become void, to expire)

*Es fiel Sylvia ein, dass sie ihren Chef anrufen wollte.*
Sylvia remembered that she had wanted to call her boss.

*Die Redaktionssitzung fällt aus.*
The editorial meeting is canceled.

*Das Holz ist ganz zerfallen.*
The wood has rotted.

*Mein Abonnement verfällt im April 2005.*
My subscription expires in April 2005.

While the number of prefix verbs may look overwhelming, it is best to learn them one by one. As a general guideline, the *zer-* prefix usually implies some destructive action as in *zerreißen* (to tear apart), *zerstören* (to destroy), and *zerbrechen* (to break apart). The prefix *be-* usually implies some internal, personal action as in *bemerken* (to notice), *besprechen* (to discuss in detail). The prefix *ab-* usually implies a negative action or a separating action as in *absagen* (to cancel), *abbrechen* (to break off), *abhaken* (to cross off).

Some prefix verbs change meaning when used reflexively: *versprechen* (to promise) and *sich versprechen* (to mispronounce, to make a slip of the tongue).

*Er hat mir den Bericht versprochen.*
He promised me that article.

*Ich habe mich wohl versprochen, denn er sagte, ein Herr Heidemann arbeite hier nicht.*
I must have mispronounced something, because he said Mr. Heidemann didn't work there.

BUT: *sich etwas versprechen* (to expect)

*Was versprichst du dir davon?*
What do you expect to gain from that?

## 2. *SUBSTANTIVBILDUNG* (THE FORMATION OF NOUNS)

Weak verbs form nouns either by taking the same form as the infinitive

| *leben* | *das Leben* (life) |
| *schreiben* | *das Schreiben* (letter, writing) |

or by forming a noun from the stem of the infinitive:

| *schlafen* | *der Schlaf* (sleep) |
| *arbeiten* | *die Arbeit* (work) |
| *suchen* | *die Suche* (search) |

230

Strong verbs form nouns from the infinitive with vowel and/or consonant changes:

| | |
|---|---|
| *annehmen* | *die Annahme* (supposition, acceptance) |
| *geben* | *die Gabe* (gift) |
| *einbrechen* | *der Einbruch* (burglary) |
| *sehen* | *die Sicht* (view) |
| *gehen* | *der Gang* (walk) |
| *fahren* | *die Fahrt* (drive, trip) |

Some verbs form nouns with the *ge-* prefix:

| | |
|---|---|
| *sprechen* | *das Gespräch* (talk) |
| *backen* | *das Gebäck* (cookies, small bakery items) |
| *denken* | *der Gedanke* (thought) |

Although most adjectives form the noun by adding *-keit* or *-heit* (see Lesson 15), there are several common nouns from adjectives that are exceptions:

| | |
|---|---|
| *kalt* | *die Kälte* (cold) |
| *heiß* | *die Hitze* (heat) |
| *alt* | *das Alter* (age) |
| *warm* | *die Wärme* (warmth) |
| *fern* | *die Ferne* (distance) |
| *weit* | *die Weite* (width) |

## 3. IDIOMATIC EXPRESSIONS

Human body parts feature in several idiomatic expressions.

*SICH EIN BEIN AUSREIßEN* (to overexert oneself; lit.: to pull out a leg)
*Sie hat sich ein Bein ausgerissen für diese Firma.*
She worked so hard for that company.

*HALS- UND BEINBRUCH* (to wish someone well; lit.: break one's neck and leg)
*Sie investieren in Eiskrem? Na, dann wünsche ich Ihnen Hals- und Beinbruch.*
You're investing in ice cream? Well, good luck to you.

*JEMANDEM EIN BEIN STELLEN* (to trip someone up; lit.: to put a leg in front of someone)
*Immer, wenn mir was gelingt, kommt sie dazwischen und stellt mir ein Bein.*
Every time I manage to get something done, she gets involved and trips me up/ruins it.

*JEMANDEM BEINE MACHEN* (to scare away; lit.: to make someone legs)
*Meinen Bericht willst du kopieren? Ich mach' dir gleich Beine, mein Lieber.*
> You want to copy my report? Let's hope you can run fast (before I catch you).

*AUF DEN ARM NEHMEN* (to pull someone's leg; lit.: to take someone into one's arm)
*Sag mal, du willst mich wohl auf den Arm nehmen!*
> Hey, you're pulling my leg.

*JEMANDEM UNTER DIE ARME GREIFEN* (to help someone out; lit.: to hold someone under their arms)
*Kannst du mir mal unter die Arme greifen, Papa? Ich brauche etwas Geld.*
> Can you help me out, Dad? I need some money.

*JEMANDEM IN DIE ARME LAUFEN* (to run into someone; lit.: to run into someone's arms)
*Ich wollte Horst nie mehr wiedersehen, aber ich bin ihm gestern direkt in die Arme gelaufen.*
> I never wanted to see Horst again, but I ran directly into him yesterday.

*DEN KOPF VOLL HABEN* (to be busy; lit.: to have one's head full)
*Er kann im Moment nicht an Urlaub denken; er hat den Kopf voll.*
> He can't think about his vacation at the moment; he is very busy.

*SICH DEN KOPF ZERBRECHEN* (to worry; lit.: to break one's head)
*Nun zerbrech' dir mal nicht den Kopf deswegen. Es ist alles nicht so schlimm.*
> Don't worry yourself (to death). Nothing's that bad.

*SEINEN KOPF DURCHSETZEN* (to have it one's way; lit.: to push one's head through)
*Immer muss er seinen Kopf durchsetzen.*
> He always has to have it his way.

*SICH AUS DEM KOPF SCHLAGEN* (to banish something from one's mind)
*Eine Gehaltserhöhung schlagen Sie sich lieber aus dem Kopf.*
> You better banish the raise from your mind.

# D. REIN GESCHÄFTLICH

## 1. THE PRESS

The Germans, Austrians, and Swiss are avid newspaper readers. Most households subscribe to a daily newspaper. Every city has one major local paper, and some metropolitan areas such as Berlin, Munich, Stuttgart, Frankfurt, and Hamburg even have two or three. The tabloids such as *BILD* (national), *Berliner Zeitung* (Berlin), and the *Morgenpost* (Hamburg, Berlin) are the most popular ones with more than one million circulation.

The most respected German newspapers are *die Frankfurter Allgemeine Zeitung*, or short *FAZ* (Frankfurt), *die Süddeutsche Zeitung* (Munich), *der Tagesspiegel* (Berlin), and the weekly *Die Zeit* (Hamburg). Popular weekly magazines are *Der Spiegel*, focusing on political, social, and economic news, and *Der Stern*, a color magazine focusing on culture, entertainment, and politics. *Der Stern* is also well respected for its photojournalism. Other popular color magazines include *FOCUS, Brigitte, BUNTE,* and *Freundin. Das Capital* focuses on financial reporting. The most well-known Swiss paper is *Die Neue Zürcher Zeitung* (Zurich). Austrian papers are *Die Kronenzeitung, Der Standard,* and *Der Wiener Kurier* (Vienna).

Freedom of the press is part of the law, and therefore any form of censorship is illegal. German newspapers tend to have far less advertising than their American counterparts.

Prospective journalists study *Journalismus* (journalism) or *Kommunikationswissenschaft* (communication science) at the university. During or after their course of study, students complete a two-year *Volontariat* (practical training) at a newspaper, magazine, or media firm.

The most important press agencies are the *dpa,* short for *Deutsche Presse Agentur* (German press agency), based in Hamburg; the *ADN,* short for *Allgemeiner Deutscher Nachrichtendienst* (general German news service), based in Berlin; and the *ddp,* short for *Deutscher Depeschen Dienst* (German cable message service), based in Bonn. All of these press agencies can be accessed on the Internet, as can most large newspapers and magazines.

## 2. VOCABULARY

| | |
|---|---|
| *die Schlagzeile* | headline |
| *die Rubrik* | section (of a newspaper) |
| *die Redaktion* | editorial (department) |
| *der Leitartikel* | editorial (in a newspaper) |
| *das Impressum* | imprint; details of publication, address, etc. |
| *der Kommentar* | commentary |
| *die Spalte* | column |
| *die Boulevardpresse* | popular press, tabloid press |
| *abonnieren* | to subscribe |
| *das Abonnement* | subscription |
| *der Beitrag* | contribution, report |
| *die Zeitungsente* | false news report |

# 3. A (FICTIONAL) NEWSPAPER ARTICLE

## WAS SUCHEN EINBRECHER BEI FÜHRUNGSSPITZE[1] DER GÖ-BAU?

*Göttingen, 15.10.2003.—Wie uns aus polizeilichen Berichten bekannt wurde, ist in der vergangenen Nacht ein weiterer Einbruch bei einem leitenden Angestellten der Gö-Bau verübt worden. Die Einbrecher drangen gegen Mitternacht in das Haus des Prokuristen ein und entwendeten[2] Eigentum im Werte von ca. 17.500 EUR. Die Polizei, die sofort alarmiert wurde, konnte nur noch den Sachschaden aufnehmen.[3] Bisher fehlt jede Spur[4] der Täter.[5] Es wird von polizeilicher Seite angenommen, dass dies der sechste einer seit vier Monaten andauernden Einbruchsserie ist, die sich auf Angestellte der hiesigen Gö-Bau KG, die z.Zt. mit dem Bau der Entlastungsstraße[6] im Norden der Stadt beeschäftigt ist, konzentriert. Bei jedem der sechs Einbrüche wurden ausschließlich Wertgegenstände[7] entwendet. Die Geschäftsleitung der Gö-Bau bestätigte, dass keinerlei[8] Dokumente oder betriebseigene[9] Unterlagen entwendet wurden, und somit ein Motiv für die Einbruchserie immer noch unklar ist. Von polizeilicher Seite wurde bestätigt, dass alle Privathäuser der Gö-Bau Führungsspitze fortan von einer Wach- und Schließgesellschaft[10] überwacht werden.*

## VOKABELN

| | |
|---|---|
| (1) *die Führungsspitze* | top management |
| (2) *entwenden* | to steal, to remove (illegitimately) |
| (3) *aufnehmen* | to take down (on paper), to record |
| (4) *die Spur* | trace |
| (5) *der Täter* | criminal, suspect |
| (6) *die Entlastungsstraße* | a city freeway circumventing the inner city |
| (7) *der Wertgegenstand* | valuable (item) |
| (8) *keinerlei* | none (whatsoever) |
| (9) *betriebseigen* | owned or originated by the company |
| (10) *die Wach- und Schließgesellschaft* | security (company) |

## ÜBUNGEN

**1.** *Beantworten Sie die Fragen zum Text.*

    a. *Bei wievielen Angestellten wurde eingebrochen?*
    b. *Was wurde entwendet?*
    c. *Warum schreibt Anita die Zeitungsberichte für Jens?*
    d. *Warum glaubt Björn, dass die Einbrecher spionieren?*

**2.** *Setzen Sie die folgenden Verben in ihrer korrekten Form ein: eintreffen, absagen, versprechen, bemerken, aussagen, zerreißen.*

    a. *Er nahm den Artikel und _____ ihn.*
    b. *Sie hat mir _____, am Samstag um 17 Uhr hier zu sein, und dann hat sie plötzlich kurz nach 16 Uhr _____.*
    c. *Der Zeuge _____ vor Gericht _____, dass der Einbrecher eine schwarze Jacke trug.*
    d. *Wir _____ um 18.40 zu Hause _____ und _____ sofort, dass Einbrecher im Haus waren.*

**3.** *Übersetzen Sie*

    a. Don't start.
    b. What's going on?
    c. He's not old enough, anyway.
    d. We left the office at 1 A.M.
    e. At 11:45 P.M. the last piece of news arrived.
    f. The boss wished us a nice evening.
    g. I'd like to research the burglary at the police station.
    h. Are you done?

**4.** *Finden Sie die richtige Alternative.*

    a. *Da liegt doch der Hase im Pfeffer.*
    b. *Wie geht es voran?*
    c. *Nicht gerade berauschend!*
    d. *Erklär das mal genauer.*
    e. *Sie wird ja wohl zu Hause sein.*
    f. *Ich habe sowieso keine Zeit.*
    g. *Alles klar?*
    h. *So geht es aber nicht.*

    1. *Wie meinst du das?*
    2. *Das kannst du so nicht machen.*
    3. *Ich vermute, sie ist zu Hause.*
    4. *Da stimmt doch was nicht.*
    5. *Alles in Ordnung?*
    6. *Macht ihr Fortschritte?*
    7. *Ich habe so oder so keine Zeit.*
    8. *Ich bin nicht beeindruckt.*

# LEKTION 15

BESUCH EINER HANSESTADT.    Visiting a Hanseatic City.

---

## A. DIALOG

---

*Brigitte Lüdicke und Hans Bornheim sind Mitglieder einer Gesellschaft für Kulturgeschichte. Zum diesjährigen Treffen besuchen sie Lübeck.[1]*

FRAU LÜDICKE: Am besten gibst du mir auf unserem Spaziergang durch die Altstadt eine Kostprobe von deinem Vortrag.

HERR BORNHEIM: Zuerst gehen wir zu Niederegger[2] Marzipan essen.

FRAU LÜDICKE: Das habe ich befürchtet. Keine fünf Minuten in der neuen Stadt, und schon sind alle meine guten Vorsätze dahin.

HERR BORNHEIM: Die Spezialitäten einer Stadt sind ein Teil ihrer Geschichte, liebe Brigitte.

FRAU LÜDICKE: Womit wir beim Thema sind. Lübeck ist doch eine der ältesten Hansestädte,[3] nicht wahr?

HERR BORNHEIM: Ja, nicht nur das, sie war auch der Sitz der Hanse[4] und somit der größte Umschlagplatz[5] für die Ostsee und alle angrenzenden Länder.

FRAU LÜDICKE: Und wann genau war das?

HERR BORNHEIM: Du willst mich wohl prüfen.

FRAU LÜDICKE: Na, klar.

HERR BORNHEIM: Also gut, Lübeck wurde, nach totaler Zerstörung im Jahre 1138, 1159 neu gegründet und war bald danach neben Köln[6] die größte deutsche Stadt.

FRAU LÜDICKE: Wie, größer als die heutigen deutschen Städte?

HERR BORNHEIM: Ja, die waren damals fast alle noch nicht einmal gegründet. Es gibt zwar noch ältere Städte in Deutschland, aber durch den Handel wurde Lübeck damals zu einer richtigen Metropole.

FRAU LÜDICKE: Schön sind sie ja wirklich, diese alten Häuser mit den Speicherkammern unter den Giebeln. Womit wurde denn entlang der Trave[7] gehandelt?

HERR BORNHEIM: Mit allem, was du dir vorstellen kannst. Weizen, jede Art von Getreide, Fische natürlich, Gewürze, Tee, Wein und Salz, das über die alte Salzstraße[8] aus Lüneburg kam.

FRAU LÜDICKE: Die Hanse war also[9] ein Handelsverbund.[10]

HERR BORNHEIM: Genau. Nach und nach[11] kamen immer mehr Städte hinzu, die sich durch das Handelsabkommen gegenseitig den Wohlstand garantierten, gleichzeitig aber auch ein Abkommen hatten, sich nie gegenseitig anzugreifen und sich in Kriegszeiten zu beschützen.

FRAU LÜDICKE: Welche Städte gehörten noch dazu?

HERR BORNHEIM: Hamburg und Bremen natürlich, die sich wie auch Lübeck weiterhin[12] Freie Hansestädte nennen. Die Hanse reichte bis nach Nowgorod. Stralsund, Rostock,[13] Stettin, Kolberg und Danzig[14] gehörten auch dazu. Riga und Tallin[15] natürlich ebenfalls.

FRAU LÜDICKE: Und bis wann gab es die Hanse?

HERR BORNHEIM: Bis in die Mitte des 17. Jahrhunderts. Aber die Glanzzeit war im 14. und 15. Jahrhundert. Die damaligen Lübecker Kaufleute waren so einflussreich, dass die Dänen um Erlaubnis bitten mussten, wenn sie einen neuen König ernennen wollten.

FRAU LÜDICKE: Dann war Lübeck ja weit über[16] seine Grenzen hinaus bekannt.

HERR BORNHEIM: Oh ja, bis nach Rom und London.

FRAU LÜDICKE: Hier entlang des Ufers haben also die Schiffe geankert, und die Waren sind mit Seilen in die Speicher gezogen worden, richtig?

HERR BORNHEIM: Ja, und der Kaufmann saß unten im Kontor,[17] hat alles mitgezählt und vermutlich den Lieferschein unterschrieben und Münzen gezählt.

FRAU LÜDICKE: Wenn du dir den Mercedes und die Ampeln wegdenkst,[18] kann man sich das ganz gut vorstellen.

HERR BORNHEIM: Viele Leute sehen Lübeck natürlich auch als die Stadt der Buddenbrooks, nach Thomas Manns berühmtem Roman.[19]

FRAU LÜDICKE: Sag mal, die Mann Familie war doch auch eine wohlhabende Lübecker Kaufmannsfamilie. Weiß man eigentlich, ob das seine Familie war, die er in „ Die Buddenbrooks" beschrieb?

HERR BORNHEIM: **Na, ich würde sagen mit Abstrichen[20] ja. Der schriftstellerischen Freiheit sind keine Grenzen gesetzt.**

FRAU LÜDICKE: **Er ist doch ganz schön ins Gerede gekommen, weil viele Lübecker Hanseaten sich mächtig auf den Schlips[21] getreten fühlten.**

HERR BORNHEIM: **Ja, klar. In den Charakteren im Roman erkannten sich einige vermeintlich hochangesehene Lübecker wieder, und die waren natürlich empört über seine Darstellung. Kritik aus den eigenen Rängen ist immer am schwersten zu verkraften.**

FRAU LÜDICKE: **Vor allem, wenn man so ein stolzer Hanseat ist.**

HERR BORNHEIM: **Du weißt ja, dass die Leute im hohen Norden oft als stocksteif[22] beschrieben werden . . .**

FRAU LÜDICKE: **Das brauchst du mir nicht zu sagen! Die Familie meines Mannes ist doch aus Lüneburg.**

HERR BORNHEIM: **Na, wie wär's jetzt mit einem Marzipanschwein?[23]**

FRAU LÜDICKE: **Auf jeden Fall, und eine Tasse Kaffee.**

---

## TRANSLATION

Brigitte Lüdicke and Hans Bornheim are members of a society for cultural history. This year they are visiting Lübeck for their annual meeting.

MS. LÜDICKE: The best thing'll be if you give me a taste of your speech while we take a walk through the old town.

MR. BORNHEIM: First we'll go to Niederegger to eat marzipan.

MS. LÜDICKE: I was afraid of that. We've been in a new city hardly five minutes and all my resolutions have gone to pot.

MR. BORNHEIM: The specialties of a city are part of its history, dear Brigitte.

MS. LÜDICKE: Which brings us back to the subject. Lübeck is one of the oldest Hanseatic cities, right?

MR. BORNHEIM: Yes, not only that, it was also the center of the Hanseatic League, and therefore the biggest commercial hub for the Baltic Sea and all bordering countries.

MS. LÜDICKE: And when exactly was that?

MR. BORNHEIM: You're quizzing me, aren't you?

MS. LÜDICKE: Of course.

MR. BORNHEIM: Okay, Lübeck, after being totally destroyed in 1138, was newly founded in 1159 and soon after became the biggest city in Germany besides Cologne.

MS. LÜDICKE: What, bigger than today's German cities?

MR. BORNHEIM: Yes, most of those weren't even founded at that time. There are older German cities than Lübeck, but because of its trade Lübeck became a real metropolis.

MS. LÜDICKE: They are certainly beautiful, these old houses with the storage lofts under the gabled roofs. What were they trading along the Trave?

MR. BORNHEIM: Everything you can imagine. Wheat, every kind of grain, fish of course, spices, tea, wine, and salt, which came via the old salt road from Lüneburg.

MS. LÜDICKE: So the Hanseatic League was really a trade federation.

MR. BORNHEIM: That's it. Gradually more and more cities joined the League, which guaranteed wealth to each other while joining in a mutual non-aggression and protection pact in war times.

MS. LÜDICKE: What other cities belonged to it?

MR. BORNHEIM: Hamburg and Bremen, of course, which, just like Lübeck, continue to call themselves Free Hanseatic Cities. It stretched all the way to Nowgorod. Stralsund, Rostock, Szczecin, Kolberg, and Gdansk belonged to it, too. And of course Riga and Tallinn.

MS. LÜDICKE: And until when did the Hanseatic League exist?

MR. BORNHEIM: Until the mid-seventeenth century. But it had its best days in the fourteenth and fifteenth centuries. The former Lübeck tradespeople were so influential that the Danes had to ask permission before electing a new king.

MS. LÜDICKE: Then Lübeck was well known far beyond its borders.

MR. BORNHEIM: Oh yes, all the way to Rome and London.

MS. LÜDICKE: Here along the banks the ships lay anchored and the goods were hoisted up into the storage lofts with rope, right?

MR. BORNHEIM: And the tradesman sat downstairs in the office, checking everything that came in, probably signed the delivery note and counted the coins.

MS. LÜDICKE: If you ignore the Mercedes and the traffic lights, it's easy to imagine.

MR. BORNHEIM: Many people see Lübeck of course as the city of the Buddenbrooks, made famous by Thomas Mann's novel.

MS. LÜDICKE: Tell me, the Mann family was also a wealthy Lübeck trade family, right? Does one know whether he described his own family in *Die Buddenbrooks?*

MR. BORNHEIM: Well, I'd say to some extent. Artistic freedom knows no restrictions.

MS. LÜDICKE: Wasn't he bad-mouthed quite a bit because some Lübeck Hanseats were offended?

MR. BORNHEIM: Yes, of course. Some allegedly well-respected Lübeck citizens recognized themselves in some of the novel's characters, and they weren't pleased about the characterization. Critique from one's own ranks is always hard to swallow.

MS. LÜDICKE: Especially if you're a proud Hanseat.

MR. BORNHEIM: As you know, people in the north are often described as very stiff.

MS. LÜDICKE: Tell me about it! My husband's family is from Lüneburg.

MR. BORNHEIM: Well, how about a marzipan pig(let) now?

MS. LÜDICKE: Definitely, and a cup of coffee.

# B. IN KÜRZE

1. *Lübeck,* originally *Liubice* (the Lovely), is in the *Bundesland Schleswig-Holstein,* on the Baltic Sea. For more information, go to www.Lübeck.de.

2. *Niederegger* is the name of the world-renowned marzipan manufacturer which, even after centuries, has its headquarters in the center of Lübeck.

3. The title *die Hansestadt* (city of the Hanseatic League) is still used by Lübeck, Hamburg, and Bremen. Their long-standing tradition of trade and pride in their liberal history is preserved in family chronicles and museums.

4. *Die Hanse* (the Hanseatic League) was the name of the trade league. At the peak of the *Hanse* some 100 cities were either part of the league or associated with it.

5. *Der Umschlagplatz* (trade center; also processing center) refers to a place of transfer of goods. If you want to be more specific as to the means of transportation, use *der Umschlagbahnhof* (transfer rail station of commercial goods) or *der Umschlaghafen* (port of transfer).
   Note that *der Umschlag* (envelope) and *umschlagen* (to roll up) have different meanings in different contexts.

6. *Köln* (Cologne) is one of the oldest settlements, dating back to Roman times. In the Middle Ages, *Köln* and *Lübeck* are both said to have had more than 25,000 inhabitants, thus making them the largest German cities at the time. One of the most important export items in modern *Köln* is *Kölnisch Wasser* (Eau de Cologne = water from Cologne, 70% alcohol). The inventor allegedly is the Italian Giovanni Paolo Feminis, who lived in Cologne when he first produced the perfume.

7. *Die Trave* is one of the two rivers running through Lübeck. The other is the *Wakenitz*. Both flow into the Baltic Sea.

8. *Die Alte Salzstraße* is an old country road that became a significant trade route as early as the Middle Ages for the salt from Lüneburg, which was sent to Lübeck to be shipped overseas. The *Salzstraße* still exists, leading through old villages with thatched-roof farmhouses.

9. *Also* (therefore) should not be confused with the English "also" *(auch)*.

10. *Der Verbund* (union, federation) is a federation of cities, states, or groups, whereas *der Verband* (association) usually refers to a group of people such as a club *(der Verein)*. *Verband* also means bandage or (wound) dressing.

11. *Nach und nach* (gradually) describes progress over time.

12. *Weiterhin* (furthermore, continuously, still) is an adverb used to describe a continuous action. A related verb is *weitermachen* (to continue).

*Wenn ihr so weitermacht, werdet ihr Geld verlieren.*
If you go on like that, you'll lose money.

13. *Stralsund* and *Rostock* are cities to the east of *Lübeck* on the Baltic Sea.

14. *Stettin* (Szczecin), *Kolberg* (Kolobrzeg), and *Danzig* (Gdansk) are Polish cities. Their German names are used in this chapter as you will frequently hear them used in Germany, although the cities have not belonged to Germany since the end of WWII.

15. *Riga* is the capital of the Baltic state Latvia. *Tallin* (Tallinn) is the capital of the Baltic state Estonia.

16. *Weit über seine Grenzen* (far beyond its borders) uses the adverbial construction *weit über/unter* (far above/below or under). Other common expressions using this structure are:

*Er lebt weit über seine Verhältnisse.*
He lives far beyond his means.

*Meine Note lag weit unter dem Durchschnitt.*
My grade was far below average.

17. *Das Kontor* is an antiquated term for an office in a warehouse or storage facility.

18. *Wegdenken* is hard to translate as its English equivalent, to unthink, is rarely used. The prefix *weg* means "away" or "gone." *Wegdenken* is a separable prefix verb.

*Wenn du dir die Beule wegdenkst, sieht das Auto doch noch prima aus.*
If you disregard the dent, the car looks great.

19. Thomas Mann (1875–1955), one of the most influential and distinguished German writers, won the Nobel Prize for Literature in 1929. *Die Buddenbrooks* (1909), which is about the rise and fall of a Lübeck trade family during the nineteenth century, is one of his most famous novels. During the Nazi regime he had to emigrate to Switzerland and later to California. He returned to Switzerland in the early fifties.

20. *Mit Abstrichen* (lit.: with mark-downs, cutbacks) is an idiomatic expression. *Abstriche machen* is used to express acceptance without full compliance, or despite some flaws.

*Der Umzug hat uns viel Geld gekostet. Jetzt müssen wir anderswo Abstriche machen.*
The move cost us a lot of money. We have to cut back somewhere else.

*Ich finde seine Arbeit mit Abstrichen ganz gut.*
If I'm not too critical, I like his work quite a bit.

21. *Auf den Schlips treten* (to offend; lit.: to step on someone's tails) is an old idiomatic expression. Please see the *Idiomatic Expressions* in this lesson.

22. *Stocksteif* (very stiff) is frequently used to describe a reserved, rigid, and often humorless mentality and composure. People from northern Germany, and in particular the *Hanseatic* cities, are rumored to be *stocksteif,* while people from the south are supposed to be cheerful, fun-loving folk. Like all prejudice, it is largely unfounded, presumptuous, and easily proved wrong.

23. *Das Marzipanschwein* is a pig or piglet made of marzipan. Niederegger has become famous all over Germany for designing fruit, vegetables, and animals out of marzipan. The pig is a *Glücksbringer* (good luck charm) in Germany, and you will often find little pigs decorating flowers or greeting cards.

# C. GRAMMATIK UND GEBRAUCH

## 1. *DAS IMPERFEKT* (THE SIMPLE PAST)

As discussed before, the present perfect tense is commonly used in conversation to refer to events in the past.

*Letztes Jahr haben wir in der Stadtmitte gewohnt.*
Last year we lived downtown.

*Wir sind letztes Jahr nach Italien gefahren.*
We went to Italy last year.

The simple past is used mostly in written texts or in historical narration to refer to past events (narrative past):

*Hier stand 1736 die Stadtmauer. Sie wurde 1737 abgerissen und durch den Graben ersetzt.*
This is where the city fortification stood in 1736. It was torn down in 1737 and replaced by the ditch.

As in English, the simple past is also the common tense for formal or literal writing:

*Frau Goldbreck saß an ihrem Schreibtisch und sah aus dem Fenster auf die Straße hinunter. Vor ihrem Haus hielt eine Kutsche. Bald darauf klingelte es.*
Ms. Goldbreck sat at her desk and looked out of the window into the street below. A horse carriage stopped in front of the house. Soon afterward the doorbell rang.

Please note that *haben* and *sein* form exceptions as they are mostly used in the simple past tense, even in conversation.

*Wo warst du? Ich habe auf dich gewartet.*
Where were you/have you been? I've been waiting for you.

While English uses "would" plus infinitive to describe a repetitive course of action in the distant past, German uses either the simple past or the present perfect:

*Der Kaufmann saß in seinem Kontor, zählte Münzen und sah zu, wie die Waren geliefert wurden.*
The trader would sit in his office, count the coins, and watch the goods arrive.

243

*Hier hat der Seemann gestanden und gewartet. Während er hier gewartet hat, ist er sicher auch auf und ab gegangen.*
Here the sailor would stand and wait. While he was waiting, he probably paced up and down.

To relate a more lively and immediate account of a specific event in the distant past, use the present perfect. Often adverbs of time and place are used to locate the event clearly.

*Am 17.03.1764 ist hier der Seemann Johannes Wachter ertrunken.*
On March 17, 1764, the seaman Johannes Wachter drowned at this spot.

*Hier hat Napoleon ein Lager errichtet und an Josephine geschrieben.*
This is where Napoleon set up camp and wrote to Josephine.

## 2. *DAS PLUSQUAMPERFEKT* (THE PAST PERFECT)

The past perfect is formed with the past tense of the auxiliary verb *haben* or *sein* plus the past participle of the main verb. It relates events in the past that began and ended before another event in the past set in.

*Wir hatten Hamburg besucht bevor wir nach Lübeck fuhren.*
We had visited Hamburg before we went to Lübeck.

*Sie war immer mit dem Auto nach Lübeck gefahren, bevor sie von den billigen Bahnpreisen hörte.*
She had always driven by car to Lübeck before she heard of the cheap train ticket prices.

When relating two events in the past, of which one preceded the other, use a combination of simple past and past perfect.

*Schon bevor die Hanse 1630 endete, hatten viele ehemalige Hansestädte neue Abkommen mit anderen Ländern und Städten abgeschlossen.*
Even before the Hanseatic League ended in 1630, several former Hanseatic cities had already entered into agreements with other countries and cities.

*Es hatte viele Jahre gedauert, bis der Bau der Stadtmauer vollendet war.*
It had taken many years until the construction of the city fortification was completed.

*Wir hatten uns schon schlafen gelegt, als das Telefon klingelte.*
We had already gone to sleep when the phone rang.

# 3. ADJEKTIVE MIT „-IGE" ENDUNGEN (ADJECTIVES WITH -IGE ENDINGS)

*Damals* is a temporal adverb.

*Vor dem 1. Weltkrieg stand hier das alte Rathaus. Damals gab es auch noch die alte Kettenbrücke.*
Before WWI the old town hall stood right here. Back then the old chain bridge still existed too.

To form an adjective, *damals* drops the final *-s* and adds *-ig* plus adjective ending depending on gender, case, and number:

*Das damalige Rathaus war aus dem Mittelalter.*
The former town hall was from the Middle Ages.

*Die damaligen Schiffe waren alle aus Holz.*
Ships back then were made of wood.

Other temporal adverbs, such as *vorher* (previous), *heute* (today, present), *jetzt* (now, present), *einst* (once), and *ehemals* (former, previous), also form adjectives in this way.

*Die vorherige Ansage war falsch.*
The previous announcement was wrong.

*Voriges Jahr waren wir in Dänemark.*
Last year we were in Denmark.

*Der ehemalige Bürgermeister Lübecks wohnt jetzt in Bad Schwartau.*
Lübeck's former mayor now lives in Bad Schwartau.

*Der jetzige Bürgermeister lebt in der Nähe des Holstentores.*
The current mayor lives near the Holstentor.

*Im einstigen Fürstentum mussten die Bürger Steuern an den Fürsten zahlen.*
In the former principality, citizens had to pay taxes to the prince.

*In der heutigen Zeit ist alles anders.*
In the present age, everything is different.

# 4. SUBSTANTIVE MIT „-EI", „-UNG", „-HEIT", „-KEIT", UND „-SCHAFT" (NOUNS WITH -EI, -UNG, -HEIT, -KEIT, AND -SCHAFT)

Some verbs form nouns with the suffix *-ung:*

| | |
|---|---|
| *bearbeiten* | *die Bearbeitung* (processing, review) |
| *beschreiben* | *die Beschreibung* (description) |
| *darstellen* | *die Darstellung* (characterization) |
| *vermitteln* | *die Vermittlung* (arranging, mediation) |
| *anmelden* | *die Anmeldung* (registration) |
| *melden* | *die Meldung* (message, news item) |

Adjectives form nouns with the suffixes *-heit* and *-keit.*

| | |
|---|---|
| *wahr* | *die Wahrheit* (truth) |
| *krank* | *die Krankheit* (sickness, illness, disease) |
| *schön* | *die Schönheit* (beauty) |
| *freundlich* | *die Freundlichkeit* (friendliness) |
| *wahrscheinlich* | *die Wahrscheinlichkeit* (probability) |

Nouns with the suffixes *-ei, -ung, -heit, -keit,* and *-schaft* are always feminine.

*-UNG*
*die Darstellung* (characterization)
*die Beschreibung* (description)
*die Gründung* (formation)
*die Verantwortung* (responsibility)

*-KEIT*
*die Unabhängigkeit* (independence)
*die Einsamkeit* (loneliness)
*die Sauberkeit* (cleanliness)
*die Dankbarkeit* (thankfulness)

*-HEIT*
*die Einheit* (unity)
*die Eigenheit* (peculiarity)
*die Schönheit* (beauty)
*die Dummheit* (stupidity, silliness)

*-SCHAFT*
*die Eigenschaft* (trait)
*die Landwirtschaft* (agriculture)
*die Gesellschaft* (society)
*die Wirtschaft* (economy)

*-EI*
*die Bäckerei* (bakery)
*die Metzgerei* (meat store, butcher)

# 5. IDIOMATIC EXPRESSIONS

German has many idiomatic expressions that use clothing symbolically. The expression *auf den Schlips treten* (to offend; lit.: to step on someone's tails), for example, emerged when *Schlips* (in northern dialect) still meant "jacket tails" rather than the modern "tie."

*Die Bürger fühlten sich auf den Schlips getreten.*
The citizens felt offended.

The expression *den Mantel nach dem Wind hängen* (to follow the trend; lit.: to hang one's coat in the wind) is mostly used in a political context and always has a derogatory connotation.

*Du kennst ihn doch, der hat keine Meinung. Der hängt seinen Mantel nur nach dem Wind.*
You know him. He has no opinion. He's always been a yes-man.

Other expressions are:

*DIE HOSEN ANHABEN* (to be dominant; lit.: to wear the pants)
*In der Familie hat sie die Hosen an.*
In that family she's the dominant partner.

*JEMANDEM ETWAS IN DIE SCHUHE SCHIEBEN* (to blame someone; lit.: to shove something into someone else's shoes)
*Den Fehler wollte er mir in die Schuhe schieben.*
He wanted to blame me for it.

*IN JEMANDES SCHUHEN STECKEN* (to be in someone else's place; lit.: to stand in someone else's shoes)
*In deinen Schuhen möchte ich nicht stecken.*
I wouldn't like to be in your place/position.

*DEN GÜRTEL ENGER SCHNALLEN* (to make sacrifices; lit.: to pull the belt tighter)
*In dieser wirtschaftlichen Lage müssen wir alle den Gürtel etwas enger schnallen.*
In this economic state we all have to make sacrifices.

*SICH AUF DEN HOSENBODEN SETZEN* (to get cracking; lit.: to sit down on the bottom of your pants)
*Du musst dich halt auf den Hosenboden setzen, wenn du heute noch fertig werden willst.*
Well, you just have to get cracking, if you want to be finished today.

*DER HUT HOCHGEHEN* (to be enraged/furious; lit.: hat-raising, the hat lifts off)
*Als er das hörte, ist ihm der Hut hochgegangen.*
When he heard that, he was furious.

*JACKE WIE HOSE SEIN* (to be the same, either way you slice it; lit.: like jackets like pants)
*Ob wir zuerst nach Lüneburg und dann nach Lübeck fahren, ist Jacke wie Hose. Wir müssen auf jeden Fall über Hamburg.*
Whether we go to Lüneburg or to Lübeck first makes no difference. Either way we have to go via Hamburg.

# D. REIN GESCHÄFTLICH

## 1. SHIPPING AND MOVING

Lübeck and Kiel are the major German seaports on the Baltic Sea. Most sea cargo shipped from the United States, however, enters Germany through *der Hafen* (the ports) of Hamburg, Bremen, or Bremerhaven. Bremen, Bremerhaven, Cuxhaven, Emden, Hamburg, and Kiel have free port facilities where foreign goods may enter and be stored without customs inspection or declaration. Eastern Germany does not have container ports and relies heavily on the western ports.

Many industrial raw materials are unloaded at Dutch or Belgian ports and transported by *Lastkahn* (barge) directly to the manufacturing areas along the Rhine and its tributaries. Germany's inland waterway system is the busiest in Europe. The system is centered along the Rhine river, has over sixty inland harbors, and is about 4,500 kilometers long. The Rhine river is also a major freight route between Switzerland, Germany, and the Netherlands.

The container ports of Hamburg, Bremen, and Bremerhaven are linked by daily rail service with primary container terminals in Frankfurt, Hanover, Bochum, Cologne, Düsseldorf, Mannheim, Ludwigsburg (near Stuttgart), Nuremberg, and Munich. In addition, container cars can be transported to a number of secondary terminals throughout the country. The *DB,* short for *Deutsche Bundesbahn* (German rail system) with a network of about 30,000 kilometers of track (and increasing as the dilapidated rail tracks in the eastern states are being improved) also links these inland terminals with those of the adjacent European countries.

Domestic air freight, while extensively used by American exporters, is limited by the relatively short distances between major cities and the rapid service provided by surface carriers. Most commercial shipping within Europe is done on surface roads. The German highway and municipal road network is extensive (over 173,600 highway kilometers and an additional 320,000 kilometers of municipal roads) and in excellent condition. All major *Autobahnen* are well serviced with *die Tankstelle* (gas stations) and *die Raststätte* (rest areas). Trucks are subject to a *Straßen-*

*benutzungsgebühr* (toll), which is an attempt to reduce heavy freight traffic and pollution while keeping the major transport routes open and unclogged. Alpine passes and tunnels in Austria and Switzerland require a toll. Some alpine passes are closed during the winter months.

## 2. A HISTORICAL SURVEY OF CRAFTSMANSHIP

Germany's refined apprenticeship system* for those who wish to learn a particular *Handwerk* (craft) has a long-standing tradition. Up until the beginning of the twentieth century part of this tradition required that *der Lehrling, der Auszubildende,* or *der Azubi* (all words for apprentice) go on *Wanderschaft* (travels) after having received the *Gesellenbrief,* a certificate of completed studies and apprenticeship, turning a *Lehrling* into a *Geselle.* The tradition originated in rural areas where young men would learn a craft with a local craftsman and then embark on a three-year and one-day stretch wandering the countryside (on foot!) in search of work. They were welcome all over the country as they were considered hardworking, honest folk who sought to carve an existence for themselves.

Tradition dictated certain outfits for *Wandergesellen* (journeymen) such as black corduroy suits with two zippers, enamel or horn buttons on the jackets, a hat, and a carved walking stick. The suits were sewn with pockets in both jackets and pants to store tools such as hammers and pliers. Legend has it that these young men tied their possessions into a checkered cloth which would dangle from their walking stick. A variety of German folk songs are dedicated to these *Wanderburschen* (walking boys), the most famous being *Das Wandern ist des Müllers Lust* ("Walking Is the Miller's Joy"). The trials and tribulations of *Wanderschaft* are further immortalized in Johann Wolfgang von Goethe's novel *Wilhelm Meisters Wanderjahre.*

---

## ÜBUNGEN

**1.** *Setzen Sie die folgenden Sätze in das Perfekt, Imperfekt, oder Plusquamperfekt.*

   a. *Die Kaufleute setzen die Preise fest.*
   b. *Obwohl wir schon lange unseren Besuch geplant haben, müssen wir absagen.*
   c. *Das Rathaus wird umgebaut. Darum sind der Bürgermeister und die Stadtverwaltung in ein anderes Haus gezogen.*
   d. *Er soll zuerst nach Kiel und dann nach Magdeburg fahren, obwohl er gar nicht soviel Zeit hat.*
   e. *Sind Sie in Schwerin?*

\* See Lesson 5.

f. *Ich weiß nicht, wie weit die Stadt entfernt ist.*
g. *Sie haben uns vorher Bescheid gesagt. Darum bleiben wir hier.*

**2.** *Bilden Sie ganze Sätze.*

BEISPIEL: *(einst/es/geben/hier/viele/Heringe)*
*Einst gab es hier viele Heringe.*

a. *(früher/haben/die Schiffe/hier/anhalten/um/Waren/liefern)*
b. *(jetzt/das/geben/es/nicht/mehr)*
c. *(wir/sein/1950/umziehen/von/Friedrichshafen/nach/Helmstedt)*
d. *(die Hansestadt/werden/gründen/1143)*
e. *(die/heute/Stadt/werden/gründen/1158)*
f. *(da/die Stadt/oft/werden/zerstören/müssen/sie/neu/gründen/werden)*
g. *(damals/sie/sein/eine/größten/Städte/Deutschland)*

**3.** *Übersetzen Sie.*

a. Several years ago I visited the trade museum in Bremen.
b. We had lost him but then we found him.
c. The tradespeople visited the former factory.
d. In the beginning it was difficult, but now it is easy.
e. The tradespeople came to Lübeck from all over for the Hanse meetings.

**4.** *Bilden Sie Substantive.*

a. *schnell*
b. *leicht*
c. *freundlich*
d. *sauber*
e. *krank*
f. *gründen*
g. *beobachten*
h. *richtig*
i. *beschreiben*

# LESESTÜCK 3

DER EURO STREIFT DIE PARITÄT ZUM DOLLAR*

*WASHINGTON, 1. November — Der Euro ist am Freitag zum ersten Mal seit dem Sommer über die Parität[1] zum Dollar gestiegen. Währungshändler[2] begründeten den Kurssprung[3] mit den sich eintrübenden[4] Konjunkturaussichten[5] in den Vereinigten Staaten. Die Nachricht über einen Anstieg der Arbeitslosenquote[6] in Amerika habe† das Bild von der Wirtschaftsschwäche[7] abgerundet, das sich durch die verschiedene Konjunkturdaten[8], vor allem das gesunkene[9] Verbrauchervertrauen[10] schon zuvor angedeutet habe. Die Akteure[11] an den Finanzmärkten[12] fühlten sich dadurch in ihrer Einschätzung[13] bestärkt, dass die amerikanische Notenbank[14] in der kommenden Woche zum ersten Mal in diesem Jahr die Zinsen senken wird.*

*Die Lage[15] am Arbeitsmarkt[16] hat einen großen Einfluss auf die Zinspolitik[17] der Fed, weil sie Rückschlüsse[18] auf das Verhalten[19] der Verbraucher[20] und damit auf die private Nachfrage[21] zulässt, die für die Wirtschaftsentwicklung[22] von Bedeutung[23] ist.*

## VOKABELN

| | |
|---|---|
| 1. *die Parität* | parity, par of exchange |
| 2. *der Währungshändler* | currency dealer |
| 3. *der Kurssprung* | sudden rise in exchange rate |
| 4. *sich eintrüben* | to cloud over (use here is reflexive) |
| 5. *die Konjunkturaussicht* | economic trend |
| 6. *die Arbeitslosenquote* | unemployment rate |
| 7. *die Wirtschaftsschwäche* | weak economy, downturn of the economy |
| 8. *die Konjunkturdaten* | economic data |
| 9. *sinken* | to sink, to reduce |
| 10. *das Verbrauchervertrauen* | consumer confidence |
| 11. *der Akteur* | participant |
| 12. *der Finanzmarkt* | financial market |
| 13. *die Einschätzung* | to assess |
| 14. *die Notenbank* | Federal Reserve, issuing bank (general) |

---

* Excerpts from an article entitled *DER EURO STREIFT DIE PARITÄT ZUM DOLLAR* by Claus Tigges, which appeared in the online version of the *Frankfurter Allgemeine Zeitung*, November 2, 2002.

† Note the style of the article, in particular the use of the subjunctive and the frequent multiple subordinate clauses.

| 15. | *die Lage* | situation, condition |
|---|---|---|
| 16. | *der Arbeitsmarkt* | employment market |
| 17. | *die Zinspolitik* | interest policies |
| 18. | *der Rückschluss* | conclusion |
| 19. | *das Verhalten* | behavior |
| 20. | *der Verbraucher* | consumer |
| 21. | *die Nachfrage* | demand |
| 22. | *die Wirtschaftsentwicklung* | economic development, economic trend |
| 23. | *die Bedeutung* | significance |

# LEKTION 16

EIN NEUES COMPUTERPROGRAMM.  A New Computer Program.

## A. DIALOG

*Zwei Angestellte eines Heidelberger[1] Marktforschungsinstituts, Markus Vollstätter und Beate Bäcker, nehmen an einer Schulung für ein neues Computersoftwareprogramm teil.*

HERR WALLNER: Da Sie jetzt gelernt haben, Dateien einzurichten und das Programm schon recht gut im Griff haben,[2] würde ich vorschlagen, dass wir jetzt zu einem konkreten Beispiel übergehen.

BEATE BÄCKER: Was mich ganz besonders interessieren würde, wären statistische Abbildungen.

MARKUS VOLLSTÄTTER: Können wir vielleicht eine demografische Abbildung[3] herstellen?

HERR WALLNER: Gut, sagen wir mal, Sie sollen die Aufteilung von Angestellten, Arbeitern, Freiberuflichen und Geschäftsinhabern in der werktätigen[4] Bevölkerung Deutschlands aufzeichnen.

FRAU BÄCKER: Am besten macht man das wohl mit einer Torte.[5]

HERR WALLNER: Genau, Kreisdarstellung. Richten Sie sich eine neue Datei ein, und klicken Sie mit der Maus in die obere Randleiste, so dass Sie den Werkzeugkasten auf dem Bildschirm[6] sehen.

FRAU BÄCKER: Ich habe den Kreis und die Linien für die Kreisabschnitte gezogen. Wie rechne ich jetzt die prozentuale Verteilung aus?

HERR WALLNER: Das macht der Computer für Sie.

FRAU BÄCKER: Ich habe ein Problem. Die Farben sehen nicht so aus, wie ich sie gerne hätte.

HERR WALLNER: Das liegt daran,[7] dass Sie an Ihrem Computer nicht alle Farbnuancen zur Verfügung haben. Wenn Sie Ihre Farbskala auf 48 erweitern, dann müsste das klappen.[8]

HERR VOLLSTÄTTER: Mein Kreis ist zu groß. Ich habe keinen Platz für die Legende.

HERR WALLNER: Hätten Sie Platz, wenn der Kreis kleiner wäre?

253

HERR VOLLSTÄTTER: Ja, klar. Darauf[9] hätte ich selbst kommen können.

HERR WALLNER: Wie sieht es denn bei Ihnen aus,[10] Frau Bäcker?

FRAU BÄCKER: Bunt auf jeden Fall. Ich habe mit den Farbskalen gespielt. Jetzt ist es allerdings etwas unübersichtlich.[11]

HERR VOLLSTÄTTER: Oh je, meine Legende ist über den Rand hinausgeschossen.

HERR WALLNER: Demnach haben Sie den Seitenrand nicht eingegeben. Bitte immer daran denken: wenn Sie das Format der Datei von horizontal auf vertikal oder umgekehrt[12] ändern, müssen Sie die Seitenränder neu eingeben.

HERR VOLLSTÄTTER: Ah, da liegt der Fehler.

FRAU BÄCKER: Ich glaube, mir gefällt mein altes Softwareprogramm besser.

HERR WALLNER: Na, na! Nicht gleich das Handtuch werfen![13] So, Frau Bäcker, nun richten Sie sich mal eine neue Datei ein und kopieren Ihre Kreise als Säulendarstellungen.

FRAU BÄCKER: In der neuen Datei muss ich ja wohl eine 100% Randskala einrichten, um die proportional richtige Angabe zu übertragen.

HERR WALLNER: So ist es, Sie haben den Nagel auf den Kopf getroffen.[14]

HERR VOLLSTÄTTER: Können wir dann vielleicht erst mal eine Pause machen?

---

TRANSLATION

Two employees of a Heidelberg market research institute, Markus Vollstätter and Beate Bäcker, are taking part in a training program for new computer software.

MR. WALLNER: Since you have now learned how to open new files and you have a feel for the program, I'd suggest that we go on to a concrete example.

MS. BÄCKER: What I would be most interested in are statistical charts.

MR. VOLLSTÄTTER: Perhaps we can create a demographic chart?

MR. WALLNER: Fine, let's say you were to show the percentage of employees, workers, freelancers, and entrepreneurs in the working population in Germany.

MS. BÄCKER: The best way to show that would probably be with a pie chart.

MR. WALLNER: That's it, circle graphic. Open up a new file and click with the mouse into the upper menu bar so that you'll see the toolbox on your monitor.

MS. BÄCKER: I've drawn a circle and lines for circle sections. How do I calculate the percentage now?

MR. WALLNER: The computer will do that for you.

MS. BÄCKER: I have a problem. The colors don't look the way I'd like them to.

MR. WALLNER: That's because you don't have all the color nuances available in your computer. If you expand the color chart to 48, it should work.

MR. VOLLSTÄTTER: My circle is too big. I have no room for the legend.

MR. WALLNER: Would you have room if the circle were smaller?

MR. VOLLSTÄTTER: Yes, of course. I could've thought of that myself.

MR. WALLNER: How is it coming along, Ms. Bäcker?

MS. BÄCKER: Colorful, that's for sure. I played around with the color chart. Now it's a little unorganized.

MR. VOLLSTÄTTER: Oops, the legend shot way over the margin.

MR. WALLNER: That means you didn't enter the margin. Please always remember if you change the format of your file from horizontal to vertical or vice versa, you have to enter the margins again.

MR. VOLLSTÄTTER: Oh, that's what's wrong.

MS. BÄCKER: I think I like my old software program better.

MR. WALLNER: Well, well, let's not give up that quickly! Ms. Bäcker, why don't you create a new file and copy-transfer your circles into column charts.

MS. BÄCKER: I'll have to draw a 100% scale in the new file in order to copy the data in the right proportion.

MR. WALLNER: That's it; you got it.

MR. VOLLSTÄTTER: Maybe we could take a break first?

# B. IN KÜRZE

1. *Heidelberg,* which lies on the banks of the *Neckar* river in the northern part of *Baden-Württemberg,* is a favorite destination for tourists because of its picturesque panorama with an old town, a castle, numerous bridges over the *Neckar,* and a lively university quarter.

2. *Im Griff haben* (to get a hold on, to grasp a situation) is derived from *greifen* (to grip; lit.: to grasp) and *begreifen* (to understand, to comprehend; fig.: to grasp).

3. *Die Abbildung* (illustration) refers to photos, prints, charts, or illustrations in books, catalogs, and any other written documentation. In an index or table of contents it is frequently abbreviated as *Abb.* (ill.).

4. The adjective *werktätig* (working) can also build a noun: *der Werktätige, die Werktätigen.* This term refers to the entire work force, i.e., anybody who is gainfully employed. A synonym is *berufstätig* (employed). Its corresponding nouns are *die Berufstätigen* (the work force) and *die Berufstätigkeit* (employment).

5. *Die Torte* (pie, cake) here is used as a colloquial term for a pie chart with sections resembling slices of a cake. *Torte* is German for a layered, round cake or a (large) fruit tart.

6. *Der Bildschirm* (monitor, screen) is used in German to describe the computer monitor and the TV screen. *Der Monitor* (monitor, screen) is predominantly used in computer language and in the film and TV industries.

7. *Das liegt daran, dass/Es liegt daran, dass* (that's because) is used only with the impersonal *das* or *es.* The expression is always followed by a dependent clause with *dass.*

8. *Klappen* is an idiomatic term referring to the outcome of a project:

*Hat es geklappt?*
Did it work?

*Bis jetzt hat alles geklappt.*
All smooth sailing so far.

*Heute klappt aber gar nichts.*
Today nothing works./It's not my day today.

9. *Darauf kommen* (to occur to somebody, to realize) is an idiomatic expression.

*Bist du auch schon darauf gekommen, dass diese Idee nicht gut war?*
Has it (finally) occurred to you that this idea wasn't so great?

*Wie kommst du denn darauf?*
What made you think of that?

10. *Aussehen* (to appear, to look) only takes on a figurative meaning in conjunction with the impersonal *es*.

*Sie sah sehr gut aus in dem schwarzen Mantel.*
She looked good in that black coat.

*Wie sieht's denn aus?*
How is it coming along?

11. Compare *unübersichtlich* (unorganized, confusing; lit.: unoverseeable) with *unübersehbar* (immense, uncalculable; lit.: unoverseeable):

*Auf dieser unübersichtlichen Karte findet man nichts.*
You can't find anything on this confusing map.

*Der Schaden nach dem katastrophalen Sturm war unübersehbar.*
The damage from the catastrophic storm was uncalculable.

12. *Umgekehrt* (lit.: turned upside down) is the German equivalent to vice versa. The corresponding verb is *umkehren* (to turn around, to go back).

13. *Das Handtuch werfen* (to give up) literally means "to throw in the towel" and originates in the sport of boxing, where the coach throws a towel into the ring to signal surrender. Another idiomatic expression signaling resignation is *die Flinte ins Korn werfen* (to throw the shotgun into the grain field).

*Nur weil du verloren hast, brauchst du nicht gleich die Flinte ins Korn zu werfen.*
Just because you lost, doesn't mean you have to give up.

14. *Den Nagel auf den Kopf treffen* (lit.: to hit the nail [right] on the head) is a rather frequent idiomatic expression for getting something exactly right.

# C. GRAMMATIK UND GEBRAUCH

## 1. *KONDITIONALSÄTZE* (CONDITIONAL SENTENCES)

As in English, German conditional sentences consist of an if-clause *(wenn-Satz)* stating the condition and a main clause stating the conclusion. In German, the *wenn-Satz* is a subordinate clause. Thus the conjugated verb is in the last position.

*Sie kauft einen neuen Computer, wenn sie genug Geld hat.*
She'll buy a new computer if/when she has enough money.

If the conditional sentence starts with the *wenn-Satz,* the main sentence begins with the verb.

*Wenn sie genug Geld hat, kauft sie einen neuen Computer.*
When/if she has enough money, she'll buy a new computer.

If the conditional clause starts the sentence, the conditional *wenn* can be omitted.

*Hat sie mehr Geld, kauft sie einen neuen Computer.*
(If) she has more money, she'll buy a new computer.

The condition stated in the *wenn-Satz* may or may not be contrary to fact. Use the indicative if it is not contrary to fact.

*Wenn man das Format ändert, muss man den Werkzeugkasten benutzen.*
If you change the format, you have to use the toolbox.

In all other cases, use the subjunctive II.

## 2. *KONJUNKTIV II IN KONDITIONALSÄTZEN* (THE SUBJUNCTIVE II\* IN CONDITIONAL CLAUSES)

The *wenn-Satz* may state a condition that is contrary to fact.

*Sie würde einen Computer kaufen, wenn sie mehr Geld hätte.*
She would buy a computer if she had more money.

*Ich wünschte, er würde anrufen.*
I wish he would call.

*Er hatte kein Geld und kannte niemanden. Er wünschte, es wäre anders.*
He had no money and knew no one. He wished it were different.

If the conditional starts with a *wenn-Satz,* the main sentence begins with the finite verb.

*Wenn sie mehr Geld hätte, würde sie einen Computer kaufen.*
If she had more money, she would buy a computer.

Again, *wenn* can be omitted.

*Hätte sie mehr Geld, würde sie einen Computer kaufen.*
Had she more money, she would buy a computer.

---

\* Refer to Lesson 13 for an explanation of the structure of subjunctive II.

If the condition stated is in the present, use the present subjunctive II. If the condition is in the past, use the past subjunctive II. Compare:

*Wenn er mehr Zeit hätte, würde er die Schulung nicht verpassen.*
If he had more time, he would not miss the training.

*Wenn er mehr Zeit gehabt hätte, hätte er die Schulung nicht verpasst.*
If he had had more time, he wouldn't have missed the training.

As many of the subjunctive II forms are outdated, *würde* (subjunctive II of *werden*) plus infinitive is used in colloquial conversation. In writing, however, it is common to stick with the subjunctive. Compare:

*Er sagte, er ginge heute abend zur Schulung.*
*Er sagte, er würde heute abend zur Schulung gehen.*
He said he would go to the training tonight.

Note that the *würde* plus infinitive construction is never used in the *wenn-Satz*.

## 3. *DER KONJUNKTIV VON HILFS- UND MODALVERBEN* (THE SUBJUNCTIVE OF AUXILIARY AND MODAL VERBS)

*Würde* is <u>never</u> used to replace the subjunctive II of *sein, haben,* or modal verbs.

*Er sagte, ich müsste nicht kommen.*
He said I didn't need to/have to come.

*Wenn ich das gewusst hätte, wäre ich nicht gekommen.*
If I had known that, I wouldn't have come.

*Wenn ich nur wüsste, wo sie ist, könnte ich zu ihr fahren.*
If (only) I knew where she is, I could drive to her.

*Mein Arzt hat gesagt, ich dürfte keinen Kaffee mehr trinken.*
My doctor said I should not drink any more coffee.

With modal verbs, a double infinitive construction is often necessary.

*Er sagte, wir hätten unseren Anwalt anrufen sollen.*
He said we should have called our lawyer.

*Wenn Sie rechtzeitig angerufen hätten, hätte ich das Treffen absagen können.*
If you had called in time, I could have canceled the meeting.

*Sie müssten das Programm längst gelernt haben.*
You should have learned the program by now.

## 4. *DER KONJUNKTIV IN HÖFLICHEN FRAGEN* (THE SUBJUNCTIVE IN POLITE REQUESTS)

To make questions or requests more polite, use either *würde* plus infinitive or—if appropriate—the subjunctive II of the modals. Compare:

*Zeigen Sie mir bitte, wo die Schule ist.*
Please show me where the school is.

*Könnten Sie mir zeigen, wo die Schule ist?*
Could you show me where the school is?

*Würden Sie mir zeigen, wo die Schule ist?*
Would you show me where the school is?

To make questions with *wollen* (to want) more polite, use *möchten* (subjunctive of *mögen**). Compare:

*Wollen Sie noch eine Tasse Tee?*
Do you want another cup of tea?

*Möchten Sie noch eine Tasse Tee?*
Would you like another cup of tea?

Another possibility is to use the following set phrases:

*Seien Sie so nett und wiederholen das bitte.*
Please be so kind as to repeat that.

*Wären Sie so freundlich, mir dabei zu helfen?*
Would you be so kind as to help me with that?

## 5. *KONSEKUTIVE NEBENSÄTZE* (CONSECUTIVE CLAUSES)

Consecutive conjunctions introduce conclusions or results of the previous action.

*so dass* (so that) and *damit* (so, so that)

*Sagen Sie mir bitte rechtzeitig Bescheid, so dass ich den Kurs nicht verpasse.*
Please let me know in time so that I won't miss the course.

*Drucken Sie die Dateien bitte aus, damit wir sie vergleichen können.*
Please print out your files so that we can compare them.

* See Lesson 3.

*So dass* is often split up, *so* joining the main clause and *dass* remaining at the beginning of the subordinated clause.

*Zeichnen Sie das Haus so, dass man das Dach von oben sehen kann.*
Draw the house in such a way that you can see the roof from above.

*Wenn Sie die Datei so eingerichtet hätten, dass die Legende am Rand liegt, könnten Sie die Abbildung nach unten vergrößern.*
If you had organized the file in such a way that the legend was positioned in the margin, you would be able to enlarge the illustration at the bottom.

While *so dass* and *damit* introduce subordinate clauses, *folglich* (subsequently, therefore, thus), *deshalb* (therefore, thus), and *demnach* (therefore) introduce main clauses.

*Ich habe vergessen, die Datei zu speichern. Folglich ging die letzte Version verloren.*
I forgot to save the file. Therefore I lost the last version.

*Ich habe alles vergessen, was ich letztes Jahr gelernt habe. Deshalb muss ich den Kurs dieses Jahr nochmal machen.*
I forgot everything I learned last year. That's why/Therefore I have to take the course again this year.

*Hier steht, man soll den Test zuerst eingeben. Demnach haben wir wohl einen Fehler gemacht.*
Here it says one should do the test first. Therefore we must have made a mistake.

# D. REIN GESCHÄFTLICH

## 1. TELECOMMUNICATION

Communications is an integral part of the national infrastructure, and the industry continues to have above-average growth potential. The industry is composed of many independent companies such as *die Deutsche Telekom, Telefunken, Blaupunkt,* and *Siemens,* which are on the forefront of the latest developments in telecommunications.

As everywhere, the internet is fast becoming a major source of information and communication in Germany, Austria, and Switzerland. Most German Internet addresses end in *.de,* most Austrian Internet addresses end in *.at,* and most Swiss Internet addresses end in *.ch.* The largest German internet provider is *die Deutsche Telekom;* therefore many German e-mail addresses end in *@t-online.de.* Many German private households have turned to American internet providers like AOL as well.

Several trade fairs cater to telecommunications and computer technology: the *CeBIT* in Hanover, the *Internationale Funkausstellung* in

Berlin, *Computer* in Lausanne, *Logic/Tele Net Com* and *Fera* in Zurich, *Micro-Comp* in Lucerne, *Telecom* in Geneva, and *IFABO* in Vienna.

However, telecommunication devices and computers overall are still far more expensive in Europe than in the U.S.A. or Southeast Asia.

## 2. VOCABULARY

Most Germans understand and frequently use English words when discussing computers. Words such as "software," "hardware," and "layout" have been adopted into everyday use. However, there are some German words you should know.

| | |
|---|---|
| *die Festplatte* | hard drive |
| *der Netzanschluß* | power outlet, plug |
| *der Speicher* | memory |
| *der Bildschirm/Monitor* | monitor, screen |
| *die Kapazität* | capacity, memory |
| *das Laufwerk* | drive |
| *die Datenverarbeitung* | data processing |
| *EDV (Elektronische Datenverarbeitung)* | electronic data processing |
| *die Diskette* | floppy disk |
| *der Arbeitsspeicher* | on-screen memory |
| *die Tastatur* | keyboard |
| *Menüleiste, Programmleiste* | menu bar |
| *die Datei* | file |
| *der Befehl* | command |
| *der Werkzeugkasten* | toolbox |
| *die Maus* | mouse |
| *die Einteilung* | sectioning, allocation, positioning |
| *einfügen* | to insert, paste |
| *bearbeiten* | to change, to process |
| *ausschneiden* | to cut |
| *die Zwischenablage* | temporary memory |
| *die Ansicht* | view |
| *kopieren* | to copy |
| *die Hilfe* | help |
| *Format* | format |
| *das Druckbild* | print preview |
| *ersetzen* | to replace |
| *Schrift* | font |
| *die Standardschrift* | standard font |
| *der Seitenumbruch* | page break |
| *drucken* | to print |

| | |
|---|---|
| *das Fenster* | window |
| *die Tabelle* | table |
| *das Inhaltsverzeichnis* | index, table of contents |
| *die Fußnote* | footnote |
| *numerieren* | to number |
| *öffnen* | to open |
| *schließen* | to close |
| *Kopfzeile* | header |
| *Fußzeile* | footer |
| *Seite einrichten* | page setup |
| *speichern* | to save |
| *eingeben* | to enter |
| *beenden* | to shut down |

Much of the terminology used around the Internet is borrowed from English as well. Here are the most important terms.

| | |
|---|---|
| *online* | online |
| *das Internet* | Internet |
| *die Web-Seite* | web page |
| *die Homepage* | homepage |
| *die Internetadresse* | URL |
| *die E-Mail* | e-mail |
| *die E-Mail Adresse* | e-mail address |
| *die Links* | links |
| *der Chat-Room* | chat room |
| *das Internet-Café* | Internet Café |
| *eine E-Mail schicken* | to send an e-mail |
| *E-Mail abfragen* | to check e-mail |
| *E-Mail beantworten* | to reply to e-mail |
| *E-Mail weiterleiten* | to forward e-mail |
| *löschen* | to delete |
| *herunterladen* | to download |
| *suchen* | to search |
| *anmelden* | to log on |
| *abmelden* | to log off |

# ÜBUNGEN

1. *Übersetzen Sie*

    a. You (familiar) should have learned it by now.
    b. I wish I had known that yesterday.

c. If only I had a car, I would drive to Augsburg.
d. If we had bought the program last year, we would not have made that mistake.
e. Could you tell me where the bus stop is?
f. If only I knew where he is.
g. If only I had known where he had been.

2. *Setzen Sie die unterstrichenen Satzteile in den Konjunktiv.*

   a. *Sie kommt früher, wenn sie weiß, wann die Schulung beginnt.*
   b. *Wenn er um 18 Uhr nach Hause gegangen ist, muss er längst zu Hause sein.*
   c. *Wenn die Firma kein Telefon hat, gibt es keine Aufträge.*
   d. *Herr Krüger sagte: „Sie ist nicht in der Schule gewesen."*
   e. *Ich wusste, er wird nicht mehr nach Regensburg kommen.*
   f. *Wenn ich Geld habe, kaufe ich mir sofort ein Haus.*

3. *Formulieren Sie die Sätze um.*

   BEISPIEL: *Der Zug ist verspätet.*
   *Wenn der Zug nur pünktlich käme.*

   a. *Sie haben keine Zeit. Wenn Sie doch _____.*
   b. *Es ist erst 16 Uhr. Ich wünschte, es _____. (später)*
   c. *Wir haben das Auto nicht gekauft. Ich wünschte, wir _____.*
   d. *Du bist nicht zum Zahnarzt gegangen. Wenn du doch nur _____.*
   e. *Es wird nicht klappen. Ich wünschte, es _____.*
   f. *Ihr habt nichts gelernt. Wenn ihr doch nur _____. (etwas)*
   g. *Leider regnet es. Ich wünschte, es _____.*

4. *Verbinden Sie die Sätze. Benutzen Sie die Konjunktion in Klammern.*

   a. *Er hat einen Preis gewonnen. Er kann seine Schulden bezahlen. (folglich)*
   b. *Sie hat die statistischen Angaben verändert. Jetzt kann man die Angaben viel besser verstehen. (so . . . dass)*
   c. *Sie hat 100% im Test bekommen. Sie hat alles richtig gemacht. (demnach)*
   d. *Ich weiß, was wir machen müssen. Wir müssen noch rechtzeitig ankommen. (damit)*
   e. *Ihr verdient viel mehr Geld als wir. Ihr habt recht gehabt mit eurer Idee. (demzufolge)*
   f. *Gib ihm alle Unterlagen. Er kann sonst die Arbeit nicht fertigstellen. (damit)*
   g. *Mir hat es sehr gut in Prag gefallen. Ich fahre nächstes Jahr wieder hin. (deshalb)*

# LEKTION 17

WERBUNG. Advertisement.

## A. DIALOG

*Margot Walther, Stefan Meier und Sabine Ranke von der Agentur*
*Walther & Schirmer besprechen das Konzept für eine neue*
*Werbekampagne. Ihr Kunde ist das große Sport- und*
*Freizeitmodehaus[1] AktivChic\* in Aachen.[2]*

FRAU WALTHER: **Also, wie gesagt, der Kunde will sowohl eine
Anzeigenkampagne, einen Werbespot[3] fürs Fernsehen und
einen fürs Radio, als auch Flugblätter. Und das Ganze mit
Schwerpunkt auf Radfahr-, Bergsteiger- und Segelkleidung.[4]**

HERR MEIER: **Man könnte die Flugblätter zum einen[5] als
Wurfsendung[6] rausgehen lassen, und zum anderen per Hand
in der Einkaufspassage,[7] vor Schulen und Sportzentren
verteilen.**

FRAU WALTHER: **Hört sich gut an. Sabine, lass mal deine
Entwürfe sehen.**

FRAU RANKE: **Ich habe drei verschiedene für jede Kategorie,
wobei eine jeweils[8] Jugendliche anspricht. Wir sollten die
Farbgestaltung der Anzeigen unbedingt mit der der Werbespots
koordinieren: Segeln in aqua, Bergsteigen in orangerot und
Radsport in grün und lila auf schwarz.**

FRAU WALTHER: **Wie sieht's denn mit Slogans aus?**

HERR MEIER: **Ich finde, wir sollten vor allem die Qualität der
Kleidung hervorheben. Die Bergsteigerkluft[9] ist komplett
reißfest und wasserdicht.**

FRAU RANKE: **Die Radfahrer- und Segelkleidung auch.**

FRAU WALTHER: **Na, also, da haben wir's doch.**

FRAU RANKE: **Hier ist mein Vorschlag fürs Radio: Mann und Frau
unterhalten sich. Geräuschkulisse: rollende Steine, Fußtritte
auf Kiesel. Dann irgendsowas wie: „ Gisela, achte auf die
Distel!" und plötzlich: ritsch-ratsch![10] „Mensch, mit der Jacke
von AktivChic wäre das nicht passiert!"**

---

\* This is a fictional company.

HERR MEIER: **Klasse, können wir so auch gleich filmen: Steinbruch reicht aus als Bergkulisse, ein paar verstreute Disteln. Und der Segelspot sieht so aus: Wassergeplätscher, Haifischflosse gleitet durchs Wasser. Musik im Hintergrund: „ Und der Haifisch, der hat Zähne."[11] Und dann der Kommentar: „ Meine Segeljacke schafft der Haifisch nicht!"**

FRAU WALTHER: **Nicht schlecht fürs Fernsehen, aber im Radio lässt sich der Hai wohl kaum zeigen, mein Lieber!**

FRAU RANKE: **Können wir jetzt vielleicht mal wieder auf die Slogans kommen? Ich soll nächsten Monat schon erste Anzeigen in den Tageszeitungen und Sportzeitschriften haben.**

FRAU WALTHER: **Fallen Sie aus der Rolle,[12] tragen Sie AktivChic.**

HERR MEIER: **Das Beste seit Seide, AktivChic für Sommer und Winter.**

FRAU RANKE: **1 A-achener[13] Qualität.**

FRAU WALTHER: **Okay, Spaß beiseite! Jetzt lasst uns mal angestrengt nachdenken. Die Leute wollen gut aussehen, bequeme Kleidung tragen und weder frieren noch schwitzen . . . Das müsste sich doch in 3 Worte fassen lassen.**

HERR MEIER: **Sicher ans Ziel! Bei allen drei Sportarten geht es um Transport, Fortbewegung und ein Ziel erreichen.**

FRAU WALTHER: **Ich glaube, heute wird das nichts mehr. Machen wir Schluss für heute! Neue Entwürfe und Slogans bis morgen um 15 Uhr. Dieser Kunde darf uns nicht verloren gehen, also lasst euch was einfallen.**

HERR MEIER: **In Promokleidung[14] lässt sich besser denken!**

FRAU RANKE: **Stefan, du blindes Huhn. Seit drei Tagen steht doch eine riesige Kiste mit AktivChic Kleidung in deinem Büro.**

FRAU WALTHER: **Moment mal! Unser blindes Huhn hat gerade den genialen Slogan erfunden: „ In AktivChic lässt sich jeder Berg erklimmen."**

HERR MEIER: **Ja, natürlich. „ In AktivChic lässt sich besser segeln." „ In AktivChic lässt sich radeln wie der Wind." Ich bin ein Genie!**

FRAU RANKE: **Ab und zu findet auch ein blindes Huhn mal ein Korn.[15]**

---

TRANSLATION

Margot Walther, Stefan Meier, and Sabine Ranke of the Walther & Schirmer agency are discussing the concept for a new ad campaign. Their client is the large sports and leisure wear fashion house AktivChic in Aachen.

MS. WALTHER: So, as I said, the client wants an ad campaign, a TV commercial, and an ad for the radio, as well as flyers. And the whole thing of course should concentrate on clothing for cycling, mountain climbing, and sailing.

MR. MEIER: The flyers could go out as bulk mail and also be distributed in the shopping area, in front of schools and sport centers.

MS. WALTHER: Sounds good. Sabine, let's see your drafts.

MS. RANKE: I have three for each category, of which one in each is targeted to teenagers. We should definitely coordinate the color design of the ads with that of the commercials. Sailing in aqua, mountain climbing in orange-red, and cycling in green with purple on black.

MS. WALTHER: What about the slogans?

MR. MEIER: I think we should mainly emphasize the quality of the clothing. The mountain climbing gear is absolutely tear- and waterproof.

MS. RANKE: The cycling and sailing wear as well.

MS. WALTHER: Well, there we are, then.

MS. RANKE: Here is my suggestion for the radio: man and woman talking. Background sound: rolling rocks, footsteps on gravel. Then something like "Gisela, watch out for the thistle," and suddenly, rip, "Oh dear, this wouldn't have happened with the wind jacket from AktivChic."

MR. MEIER: Great, we can film that too: a quarry will suffice for mountain scenery, a couple of scattered thistles. And the commercial for sailing: soft sound of water splashing, shark fin cuts through the water. Music in the background. "And the shark he has his teeth (and there they are for all to see)." And then the commentary: "The shark can't handle my sailing jacket."

MS. WALTHER: Not bad for TV, but you'll have trouble showing a shark on radio, my dear.

MS. RANKE: Maybe we could get back to the slogans now? I'm supposed to have first ads in the daily papers and sports magazines next month.

MS. WALTHER: Dare to be different; wear AktivChic.

MR. MEIER: The best thing since silk, AktivChic for summer and winter.

MS. RANKE: First-class Aachen quality.

MS. WALTHER: Okay, okay. Joking apart. Let's concentrate now. People want to look good, wear comfortable clothing, and neither freeze nor sweat . . . We should be able to put that into three words.

MR. MEIER: Get there safe! All three types of sports deal with transport, motion, and reaching a destination.

MS. WALTHER: I don't think we'll get anywhere today. Let's call it a day. New drafts and slogans by 3 P.M. tomorrow. We can't afford to lose this client. So you better come up with something.

MR. MEIER: Promotional clothes help the thinking process.

MS. RANKE: Stefan, you really are blind. A huge box of AktivChic clothes has been sitting in your office for three days.

MS. WALTHER: Wait a second. I think our blind man just invented the perfect slogan: "AktivChic helps you climb every mountain."

MR. MEIER: Yes, of course. "AktivChic guarantees easy sailing." "AktivChic will help you ride like the wind." I'm a genius.

MS. RANKE: Sometimes even a blind man can see.

# B. IN KÜRZE

1. *Die Freizeit* (spare time) is revered by Europeans, and many people engage in various kinds of activities. Sports, camping, fishing, and gardening are among the most popular spare time activities, as are cultural pursuits, bar-hopping, and playing cards. *Die Freizeitgestaltung* (organization of spare time) has become a serious business, as Germans have a lot of spare time available.

2. *Aachen* is a small German town close to the Dutch, Belgian, and French borders. It is most famous for its Gothic cathedral and its chocolate-covered gingerbread *(Aachener Printen)*. Aachen's website is at www.Aachen.de.

3. *Der Werbespot* is the commercial in both TV and radio. Commercial breaks in general are called *die Werbung* (advertising).

4. Although soccer beats all other sports in numbers of enthusiastic fans and amateur players, *Radfahren, Bergsteigen und Segeln* are next to *Wandern* (hiking) and *Windsurfen* (wind surfing) probably the most popular and rigorous sports activities in Germany, Austria, and Switzerland. The bicycle is also a favored means of transportation, increasingly so in urban areas, as Germans are very *umweltbewußt* (ecologically aware) and have adopted the bike as a perfect way to cut down on traffic jams, pollution, and noise. Cyclists' lives are made easier by a well-developed network of bicycle paths.

5. Don't mix up *zum einen und zum anderen* (while . . . also) with *einerseits und andererseits* (on the one hand and on the other hand).

*Zum einen sollten wir Werbung machen und zum anderen unsere Preise senken.*
While we should advertise, we should also lower our prices.

*Einerseits ist Werbung wichtig, andererseits ist sie im Moment zu teuer.*
On the one hand advertising is important; on the other hand it's too expensive right now.

6. *Die Wurfsendung* (bulk mail; lit.: throw mail) is what Americans generally refer to as "junk mail." In Germany *Wurfsendungen* are not distributed by the mailman, but by private carriers who are employed for that purpose only. By posting *Keine Werbung* on your mailbox, you avoid receiving *Wurfsendungen*.

7. *Die Einkaufspassage* (shopping mall) is a small indoor shopping mall on the ground floor level in the center of cities and towns. There is no real equivalent to the suburban American mall, as Europe has more *Kaufhäuser* (department stores) and *Fußgängerzonen* (pedestrian shopping streets barring all automobile traffic) than *Einkaufspassagen* (shopping malls).

8. *Jeweils* (in each case, respectively, at times) is an adverb.

*Verteilen sie jeweils 100 Flugblätter in den Aachener Schulen.*
Distribute 100 flyers respectively in all Aachen schools.

9. *Die Kluft* is a particular kind of dress or uniform such as garb or gear. *Die Kluft* also refers to a cleft or a symbolic gap.

10. *Ritsch-ratsch* is the sound of paper or fabric being torn. Its English equivalent would be "rip."

11. *Und der Haifisch, der hat Zähne* (And the shark he has his teeth) is a line from *Mackie Messer* (Mac the Knife), a song by Kurt Weill, which became famous as part of the *Dreigroschenoper* (Threepenny Opera) by Bertholt Brecht.

12. *Aus der Rolle fallen* is borrowed from theatrical language and literally translated means "to fall out of your role."

*Er fällt immer aus der Rolle.*
He always does his own thing.

13. *1 A* (pronounced *Eins A*) describes excellence. It is used here as a joke on advertising slogans in a combination with the city name, Aachen. The number 1 also stands for excellence in the German school system. Grades are 1 (excellent), 2 (good), 3 (fair), 4 (marginal pass). Fail grades are 5 (failed) and 6 (not acceptable).

14. The English term "promotional" is often used in the short form *Promo* as a colloquialism.

15. *Ein blindes Huhn findet auch mal ein Korn* (lit.: a blind hen sometimes also finds a grain) is a proverb meaning "A blind man sometimes can see." German has many other idiomatic expressions that incorporate animals.

# C. GRAMMATIK UND GEBRAUCH

## 1. *DER GEBRAUCH VON „LASSEN"* (THE USAGE OF *LASSEN*)

*Lassen* (to let) is used in several ways:

TO LEAVE
*Ich lasse meinen Hund immer zu Hause.*
    I always leave my dog at home.

*Lass mich in Ruhe!*
    Leave me alone.

TO LET
*Lass mal sehen!*
    Let me look at it.

*Ich lasse dich Sabines Entwürfe später sehen.*
    I'll let you see Sabine's drafts later.

TO GET/TO HAVE
*Ich lasse meinen Wagen reparieren.*
    I'm having/getting my car repaired.

*Lässt du deine Haare auch immer von ihm schneiden?*
    Do you have him cut your hair too?

TO ALLOW
*Ich lasse dich nicht gehen. Du bist krank und solltest zu Hause bleiben.*
    I won't let you go. You're sick and should stay at home.

*Lassen Sie es mich versuchen!*
    Allow me (to try it myself)!

SICH LASSEN (reflexive) (alternative to the passive voice)
*In Promokleidung lässt sich besser denken!*
    It's easier to think in promotional clothes.

*Es lässt sich besser so machen.*
    It can be done better this way.

In idiomatic expressions:

ES KANN SICH SEHEN LASSEN (to look [really] good, to be impressive)
*Diese Anzeige kann sich sehen lassen.*
    This ad looks really good.

SICH NICHTS SAGEN LASSEN (to let nobody interfere)
*Er lässt sich nichts sagen.*
    He won't listen./He won't let anyone tell him what to do.

*ES NICHT LASSEN KÖNNEN* (to be indulgent, unable to refrain)
*Du kannst es nicht lassen.*
> You just don't stop, do you?

*LASSEN VON* (to renounce, to let be)
*Sie muss endlich von der Sache lassen.*
> She should finally let it be.

## 2. *ABHÄNGIGE INFINITIVE* (DEPENDENT INFINITIVES)

*Lassen* (to let) is one of several German verbs that require an infinitive construction. The others are *sehen* (to see), *hören* (to hear), and *helfen* (to help).

*Ich höre ihn jeden Morgen singen.*
> I hear him sing every morning.

*Lass mich mal sehen.*
> Let me see.

*Er hilft mir einkaufen.*
> He helps me shopping.

*Ich sehe Frau Walther kommen.*
> I can see Frau Walther approaching.

Just like modals, in compound tenses a double infinitive becomes necessary.

*Er hat sich bei den Entwürfen helfen lassen.*
> He has had others help him with the drafts.

## 3. *NEBENSÄTZE* (MULTIPLE SUBORDINATED SUBCLAUSES)

Multiple subordinated clauses often appear in one sentence. To facilitate an easier comprehension of such long sentences, find the main clause, read it first, then add the subordinated clauses one by one.

| FIRST SUBORDINATED | MAIN | SECOND SUBORDINATED | MAIN |
|---|---|---|---|
| *Anstatt uns nur auf die Mode zu konzentrieren,* | *sollten wir,* | *um auch die Kleidung langfristig attraktiv zu machen,* | *den Sicherheitsaspekt hervorheben.* |
| Instead of concentrating on fashion | we should | in order to make the clothing attractive in the long run | stress the safety aspect. |

| MAIN | INSERTION | RELATIVE CLAUSE | MAIN |
|---|---|---|---|
| *Man könnte die Radfahran- zeigen,* | *ganz abgesehen von den Segelan- zeigen,* | *die in Reise- prospekte und Segelmagazine gehören,* | *vor allem in Familien- zeitschriften setzen.* |
| One could place the cycling ads | quite apart from the sailing ads, | which belong in travel bro- chures and sail- ing magazines | predominantly in family magazines. |

German has many ways of adding vital information to a sentence by inserting the clause, between commas, before the end of the sentence. Insertions do not have a verb and therefore are not considered subordinated sentences.

Students get disoriented by long German sentences, especially when they contain a compound verb. It may seem as if you were expected to compute an abundance of information about something without knowing the main verb until the very end of the sentence. It is actually much simpler to understand, especially when listening to native speakers, as they tend to pause and use inflection to facilitate the understanding of a sentence with numerous insertions.

## 4. IDIOMATIC EXPRESSIONS

There are several idiomatic expressions using animals in German:

*EINEN AFFEN AN JEMANDEN GEFRESSEN HABEN* (to be crazy about someone; lit.: to have eaten an ape)
*Sylvia hat wirklich einen Affen an ihrem neuen Freund gefressen.*
   Sylvia is totally crazy about her new boyfriend.

*SCHWEIN HABEN* (to be lucky; lit.: to have a pig)
*Mein Auto wurde geklaut, aber nichts wurde gestohlen. Da hast du aber Schwein gehabt!*
   My car was stolen, but they didn't take anything. That was lucky.

*EINEN KATER HABEN* (to have a hangover; lit.: to have a tomcat)
*Wir waren auf einer Party und heute morgen bin ich mit einem Kater aufgewacht.*
   We went to a party and this morning I woke up with a hangover.

*EIN HÜHNCHEN RUPFEN MIT JEMANDEM* (to pick a bone with someone; lit.: to pluck a chicken with someone)
*Mit dir habe ich noch ein Hühnchen zu rupfen. Du hast mir nicht die Wahrheit gesagt.*
   I have to pick a bone with you. You didn't tell me the truth.

*BEKANNT WIE EIN BUNTER HUND* (to be notorious; lit.: as famous as a colored dog)
*Diese Familie ist bekannt wie ein bunter Hund. Lass dir bloß nichts erzählen!*
This family is notorious. Don't let anyone tell you any different.

*DA STEHEN WIE DER OCHS VORM TOR* (to be dumbfounded; lit.: to stand like the ox in front of the gate)
*Als wir ihr das sagten, stand sie da wie der Ochs vorm Tor.*
When we told her, she was dumbfounded.

Here is a selection of common German onomatopoeias:

| | |
|---|---|
| *ritsch-ratsch* | rip (paper, fabric) |
| *klingeling* | ring-ring, dingaling (bicycle, doorbell) |
| *miau* | meow (cat) |
| *wauwau* | arf, woof-woof (dog) |
| *muh* | moo (cow) |
| *kikeriki* | cock-a-doodle-doo (rooster) |
| *schnurren* | to purr (cat) |
| *bellen* | to bark (dog) |

# D. REIN GESCHÄFTLICH

## 1. FACTS AND TRENDS IN ADVERTISING

German advertising resembles its American counterpart in most aspects. It should be noted, however, that the use of comparisons and superlatives in advertising is strictly regulated, and that *die Vergleichswerbung* (open comparison of two competitors) is illegal in both commercial and political advertising.

Advertising is common on the radio, on private and public TV, in movie theaters, and in newspapers and magazines. Although cigarette commercials have been banned from television, they may still appear anywhere else.

Newspapers and periodicals rank high in importance in terms of annual advertising expenditures, as daily newspaper circulation averages 25 million copies, and the corresponding number for periodicals is 275 million copies.

Public television stations, which began showing advertisements in 1956, are operated by regional authorities, with only a limited number of time spots allotted to advertising. Private satellite or cable stations are largely financed by advertising and come closer to the American commercial system.*

* See Lesson 11.

Radio advertising, like TV commercials, is subject to state controls and reaches a large audience. Cinema advertising in the form of slides or motion-picture shorts still offers an effective and significant medium, although its growth has been affected by the impact of television and home-video equipment.

*Litfaßsäulen* (advertising pillars), round street columns specifically designed for bill posting, are still rather common carriers of advertising in Europe. *Litfaßsäulen* take their name from their inventor, Ernst Litfaß (1816–1874), and were first used in 1854 in Berlin as bulletin boards for public notices and news items. *Litfaßsäulen* continue to be popular displays for theater schedules, announcements of concerts and sports events, as well as print advertising.

Advertising agencies are called *Werbeagenturen*. Public personalities and entertainers have a *Publizist* (publicist), *Presseagenten* (press agents), and/or *freie Promoter* (independent promotional personnel). The *Werbeagenturen* often list market research among their services, while others offer this service in cooperation with specialized research institutes. Agencies generally provide counsel, creative art and copy work, and translations as well as media selection and placement services.

Most people heading for a career in advertising will study either *Medienkommunikation* (media communication/media science), *Fotojournalismus* (photo journalism), or *Grafik* (graphic design).

## 2. VOCABULARY

| | |
|---|---|
| *die Anzeigenabteilung* | advertising department |
| *eine Anzeige aufgeben* | to place an ad |
| *die Anzeigenannahme* | classifieds department |
| *das Budget* | budget |
| *das Layout* | layout |
| *der Entwurf* | draft |
| *eine Anzeige buchen* | to book an ad (in advance) |
| *unlauterer Wettbewerb* | unfair competition |
| *die Falschwerbung* | false advertising |

## 3. SOME GERMAN ADVERTISING CLASSICS

*Meister Proper putzt so sauber, dass man sich drin spiegeln kann.*
Meister Proper cleans so clean that you can see your own reflection.

This is the slogan for an all-purpose cleaner. *Proper* is a synonym for *sauber* and means "very clean." Mr. Clean, a similar product, exists in the United States.

*Asbach Uralt ist der Geist des Weines.*
*Asbach Uralt* is the spirit/essence of the wine.

The term *Asbach Uralt* has been adopted into colloquial language for something that's been around forever, as *uralt* translates into "ancient."

*Dasch wäscht so weiß, weißer geht's nicht.*
*Dasch* washes so white that whiter is impossible.

The slogan for this laundry detergent plays on words as the comparative of "white"—whiter—does not exist.

*Mami, Mami, er hat überhaupt nicht gebohrt.*
Mom, Mom, he didn't drill at all (to fill cavities).

This slogan for toothpaste became a phrase used whenever referring to an unpleasant experience.

---

# ÜBUNGEN

1. *Übersetzen Sie.*

   a. Would you say that the ad campaign was successful?
   b. It can be done quite easily.
   c. You should have called him before.
   d. You would have to call the paper and change the ad.
   e. He was supposed to deliver the text yesterday afternoon.

2. *Formulieren Sie die Sätze um und benutzen Sie „lassen".*

   a. *Die Anzeigen wurden gestern von ihm gebucht.*
   b. *Das kann man so nicht sagen.*
   c. *Der Marketingchef wurde mit dem Auto zum Flughafen gefahren.*
   d. *Wir wollen morgen weiter machen.* (use the imperative)
   e. *Man kann ihm nichts sagen.*
   f. *Das ist leicht zu machen.*

3. *Setzen Sie das richtige Verb ein: sehen/hören/helfen/lassen.*

   a. *Ich _____ die Anzeigen machen.*
   b. *Sie _____ das Telefon klingeln.*
   c. *Wir _____ ihr umziehen.*
   d. *Wir _____ unsere Fotos beim Schnellservice entwickeln.*
   e. *_____ Sie von sich hören!*
   f. *Ich _____ Frau Ranke an ihrem Tisch sitzen.*

# LEKTION 18

DER KUNDENDIENST.    Customer Service.

## A. DIALOG

*Jens-Martin Köhler geht zum Kundendienst eines Kaufhauses. Eine Angestellte, Anke Kreibach, bedient ihn.*

FRAU KREIBACH: **Kann ich Ihnen helfen?**

HERR KÖHLER: **Ich habe hier vor einer Woche dieses Diktiergerät gekauft, und es funktioniert nicht.[1]**

FRAU KREIBACH: **Wieso, was stimmt denn damit nicht.[2]**

HERR KÖHLER: **Es nimmt nicht mehr auf.**

FRAU KREIBACH: **Lassen Sie mich mal hinein schauen.**

*Sie öffnet das Gerät.*

FRAU KREIBACH: **Tja,[3] kein Wunder, dass der nicht aufnimmt. Die Aufnahmevorrichtung ist lose. Tja, leider kann ich da gar nichts machen. Sie müssten das Gerät ans Werk schicken, damit die das nachsehen.[4]**

HERR KÖHLER: **Nein, das geht nicht.[5] Ich bin geschäftlich in der Stadt und brauche ständig ein Diktiergerät. Ich möchte es umtauschen.**

FRAU KREIBACH: **Das kann ich leider nicht machen. Wenn das Gerät beim Gebrauch beschädigt worden ist, haftet[6] das Werk leider nicht. Schauen Sie, wenn Sie das Gerät ans Werk zurückschicken, und es sollte sich herausstellen, dass dieses Gerät tatsächlich fehlerhaft[7] ist, dann bekommen Sie doch Ihr Geld zurück. Diese Dinger[8] sind ja nicht so teuer, dass man sich nicht mal ein neues kaufen könnte.**

HERR KÖHLER: **Also, hören Sie mal! Ich kann mir doch nicht laufend[9] neue Diktiergeräte kaufen.**

FRAU KREIBACH: **Ist es denn nicht möglich, dass mit dem Gerät vielleicht etwas unbehutsam umgegangen[10] worden ist?**

HERR KÖHLER: **Was unterstellen[11] Sie mir denn da? Jahrelang[12] benutze ich diese Dinger schon, und jetzt behaupten Sie, ich kann damit nicht umgehen. Also entweder bekomme ich jetzt mein Geld zurück oder ein neues Gerät, oder ich wende mich gleich mal an Ihren Vorgesetzten.**

FRAU KREIBACH: **Das wird nicht nötig sein, ich leite diese Abteilung.**

HERR KÖHLER: **Na, dann habe ich wohl Pech gehabt. Kann man denn nicht mal eine Ausnahme machen? Ich meine, das Gerät könnte doch auch bei Ihnen im Lager kaputt gegangen sein.**

FRAU KREIBACH: **Das einzige, was wir machen können, ist, das Gerät ans Werk zurückzuschicken.**

HERR KÖHLER: **Wie lange dauert das denn, bis das Werk Bescheid gibt?**

FRAU KREIBACH: **Etwa 4 bis 8 Wochen.**

HERR KÖHLER: **Tja, da kann man wohl wirklich nichts machen. Was sein muss, muss sein.**[13]

---

## TRANSLATION

Jens-Martin Köhler goes to the customer service of a department store. An employee, Anke Kreibach, serves him.

MS. KREIBACH: Can I help you?

MR. KÖHLER: I bought this microcassette recorder here a week ago and it doesn't work.

MS. KREIBACH: Why, what's wrong with it?

MR. KÖHLER: It doesn't record anymore.

MS. KREIBACH: Let me take a look at it.

She opens the device.

MS. KREIBACH: Well, no wonder it won't record. The recording mechanism has come loose. Well, unfortunately I can't do anything about that. You'll have to send the machine to the manufacturer so that they can take a look at it.

MR. KÖHLER: No, that's impossible. I'm in town on business and I need a recorder constantly. I want to exchange it.

MS. KREIBACH: I can't do that, unfortunately. If the device was damaged while in use by the customer, the manufacturer is not liable. Look, if you send the device back to the manufacturer and it should be determined that this device was indeed faulty, then you'll get your money back. These things aren't that expensive that you couldn't buy yourself a new one from time to time.

MR. KÖHLER: Well, listen, I can't keep buying new recorders all the time.

MS. KREIBACH: Is there a chance that maybe the device was handled in a somewhat careless manner?

MR. KÖHLER: What are you insinuating? I have been using these things for years and now you claim I don't know how to handle them. Well, either I get my money back right now or a new machine, or I'll go straight to your supervisor.

MS. KREIBACH: That won't be necessary. I'm in charge of this department.

MR. KÖHLER: Well, I guess that means I'm out of luck. Wouldn't it be possible to make an exception in this case? I mean that device could have been damaged in your warehouse.

MS. KREIBACH: The only thing we can do is return the machine to the manufacturer.

MR. KÖHLER: How long will it take until I hear from the manufacturer?

MS. KREIBACH: About four to eight weeks.

MR. KÖHLER: Oh well, it looks like nothing really can be done. What's got to be done, has got to be done.

# B. IN KÜRZE

1. *Nicht funktionieren* (not working) is the most common expression to describe a malfunctioning machine.

*Die Fernbedienung funktioniert nicht. Du musst sie umtauschen.*
The remote control doesn't work. You have to exchange it.

Other expressions of malfunction are:

*Der Fernseher geht nicht.*
The TV won't work.

*Mein Auto läuft nicht.*
My car has broken down.

*Wie spät ist es? Meine Uhr geht nicht richtig.*
What time is it? My watch is not accurate.

*Die Wanduhr ist stehen geblieben.*
The wall clock has stopped.

2. *Stimmen* has different meanings according to context.

*Das stimmt.*
I agree./That's right.

*Ich stimme dafür.*
I vote for it./I'm for it.

*Mit ihm stimmt etwas nicht.*
There's something wrong with him.

*Da stimmt doch etwas nicht.*
There's something wrong with that.

    3.  *Tja* (oh well) is a common concessive expression.

    4.  *Nachsehen* is a separable prefix verb with several meanings.

*Ich muss das Datum im Lexikon nachsehen.*
I have to look up the date in the encyclopedia.

*Kannst du mal nachsehen, wer an der Tür ist?*
Can you check who's at the door?

    5.  Here *nicht gehen* takes on a different meaning from above.

*Das geht nicht.*
I can't do that./That won't be possible.

*So geht das aber nicht.*
That's not how it's supposed to be.

    6.  *Haften* (to be liable) is used in business and legal contexts. The noun is *die Haftung* (liability).

*Das Werk haftet nicht bei unsachgemäßer Benutzung.*
The manufacturer does not accept liability in case of misuse.

*Wir übernehmen keine Haftung.*
We do not accept liability.

*Eltern haften für ihre Kinder.*
Parents will be held liable for damages caused by their children.

    7.  *Laufend* (constantly, continuously) is a present participle formed from the verb *laufen* (to go, to run).

*Das Auto stand mit laufendem Motor auf dem Parkplatz.*
The car stood with its engine running on the parking lot.

It also takes on different meanings:

*Ich will ihn nicht laufend anrufen.*
I don't want to keep calling him.

The expression *am laufenden Meter* usually conveys irritation.

*Er will nicht am laufenden Meter neue Batterien kaufen müssen.*
He doesn't want to continue having to buy batteries over and over again.

8. *Fehlerhaft* (faulty) describes an object with defects. You will often see substandard goods offered as *fehlerhafte Ware* at very low cost.

9. *Diese Dinger* (these things, this stuff) is a colloquialism. Note that the regular plural of *das Ding* (thing) would be *die Dinge*. *Dinger* is a more derogatory expression. A synonym is *das Zeug*.

10. Note that the expression *umgehen mit* (to be able to handle) requires an article in the singular but not in the plural.

*Er kann mit der Maschine umgehen.*
He can handle the machine well.

*Wir gehen gut mit Hunden um.*
We treat dogs well.

11. *Unterstellen* is used as both a separable and an inseparable verb: *unterstellen* (to put, place underneath)

*Stell die Kiste unter den Ladentisch.*
Put the box under the counter.

   *sich unterstellen* (to seek cover)

*Es fing an zu regnen. Wir haben uns unter einen Baum gestellt.*
It started to rain. We sought cover under a tree.

   *unterstellen* (to insinuate)

*Was unterstellst du mir denn da?*
What are you insinuating?

12. *-lang* is a common suffix: it frequently appears with *Woche* (week) and *Jahr* (year), *Sekunde* (second), *Minute* (minute), and *Stunde* (hour). When forming the adverb, all nouns take the plural form: *sekundenlang, wochenlang, monatelang.*

13. *Was sein muss, muss sein* is a proverb: "What's got to be done, has got to be done."

# C. GRAMMATIK UND GEBRAUCH

## 1. DIE VORSILBEN „HER-" UND „HIN-"
(THE PREFIXES *HER-* AND *HIN-*)

Some prepositions build compounds with the prefixes *her-* and *hin-*.

| | | |
|---|---|---|
| *hinaus* | *heraus* | out |
| *hinein* | *herein* | in |
| *hinauf* | *herauf* | up |
| *hinunter* | *herunter* | down |
| *hinüber* | *herüber* | across, over |

These prefixes describe the direction of the action, showing whether something is moving toward *(her)* or away from the speaker *(hin)*.

*Kommen Sie herein.*
Please come in.

The speaker is in the room the addressee is supposed to enter.

*Gehen Sie ruhig hinein.*
Go inside (You won't disturb him/her).

The speaker is not in the room the addressee is supposed to enter.

*Er kommt gerade in den Garten heraus.*
He is just coming/stepping out into the garden.

The speaker is in the garden.

*Ich gehe mal schnell in den Garten hinaus.*
I'll just quickly go into the garden.

The speaker is not in the garden.

In colloquial usage both prefixes are often shortened to *'r.* Compare:

*Komm doch mal bitte herauf.*
*Komm doch mal bitte 'rauf.*
Please come upstairs.

*Ich komme schon hinunter.*
*Ich komme schon 'runter.*
I'm coming downstairs.

*Wir wollten heute hinausfahren.*
*Wir wollten heute 'rausfahren.*
We wanted to drive out (to the country) today.

*Als wir aus dem Kino herauskamen, schien die Sonne.*
*Als wir aus dem Kino 'rauskamen, schien die Sonne.*
When we came out of the movie theater, the sun was shining.

*Er ist hinuntergegangen, um nachzusehen.*
*Er ist 'runtergegangen, um nachzusehen.*
He went downstairs to take a look.

To decide which prefix to use, ask yourself which question word would be appropriate: *wohin* (where to) or *woher* (where from).

*Wir sind 'rausgekommen und sahen, dass das Auto weg war.*
We went outside and saw that the car was gone.

*Woher kamt ihr denn?*
Where did you come from?

*Wir kamen aus dem Haus meiner Freunde heraus.*
We came out of my friends' house.

*Wir wollten 'rausfahren, und nun müssen wir zu Hause bleiben.*
We wanted to go driving, and now we have to stay at home.

*Wohin wolltet ihr denn?*
Where did you want to go?

*Wir wollten aufs Land hinaus.*
We wanted to go into the country(side).

## 2. ZWEITEILIGE KONJUNKTIONEN (COMPOUND CONJUNCTIONS)

The expression *nicht nur . . . sondern auch* (not only . . . but also) was briefly discussed in Lesson 2. Other such compound conjunctions include *entweder . . . oder* (either . . . or) and *weder . . . noch* (neither . . . nor).

*Entweder bekomme ich jetzt mein Geld zurück oder ich gehe mich beschweren.*
Either I'll get my money back now or I'll go and complain.

Note that subject and verb switch places after *entweder,* but keep their normal position, the subject followed by the conjugated verb, in the clause preceded by *oder.* The conjunction can also precede the object, rather than take the first position in either part of the sentence.

*Ich bekomme jetzt entweder mein Geld oder einen neuen Apparat.*
I'll get either my money or a new machine now.

*Sie brauchen weder das eine noch das andere tun.*
You needn't do one nor the other.

*Er möchte weder nach Bremen noch nach Koblenz fahren, sondern zu Hause bleiben.*
He wants to go neither to Bremen nor to Koblenz, but instead to stay at home.

*Sie hat mir nicht nur ein Telegramm geschickt, sondern mich auch angerufen.*
She not only sent me a telegram but also called me.

*Sondern* and *auch* are usually separated by subject or pronoun of the second clause which moves between them, unless no subject or pronoun is present. If *nicht nur* starts the sentence, subject and verb switch places.

*Nicht nur bin ich gestern im Kaufhaus gewesen, sondern auch im Kino.*
Not only did I go to the department store but also to the movies.

## 3. *WORTBILDUNG* (WORD FORMATION)

Verbs that end in *-ieren* form nouns with *-ion* suffixes:

| | | |
|---|---|---|
| *reklamieren* | *die Reklamation* | return, complaint |
| *diskutieren* | *die Diskussion* | discussion |
| *informieren* | *die Information* | information |

Exceptions are:

| | | |
|---|---|---|
| *respektieren* | *der Respekt* | respect |
| *arrangieren* | *das Arrangement* | arrangement |
| *reservieren* | *die Reservierung* | reservation |

# D. REIN GESCHÄFTLICH

## 1. A WORD ON CUSTOMER SERVICE

They say in Germany *Der Kunde ist König* (the customer is always right); nonetheless, customer service is not quite as elaborate as it is in the U.S.A. Service in restaurants, stores, supermarkets, and service stations tends to be less attentive to the individual than the American equivalent. Often there is no hostess in restaurants, you are expected to pack your own bags in supermarkets, and most gas stations offer only self-service lines. In general, you may not be automatically helped in a store. Yet if you politely ask for help, you will find that people are friendly and most willing to assist you.

If you are not satisfied with a product you bought or a service that was performed, turn to the *Kundendienst* (customer service department). If it is still under *Garantie* (warranty) you are allowed to return a defective machine or appliance to the store to be repaired or to be replaced by a new one. You can also return it to the manufacturer, referred to as *die Reklamation.*

Returning something for an *Umtausch* (exchange) or a *Gutschein* (voucher) may be subject to limitations. Often sales items cannot be exchanged. A complaint about the quality of the service is called *die Beschwerde.* The corresponding verb is reflexive: *sich beschweren* (to complain). If you return food or drinks in a restaurant, use the term *zurückgehen lassen.*

## 2. A USER'S MANUAL

Always check *die Gebrauchsanweisung* or *die Bedieungsanleitung* (owner's manual) before operating an instrument. Here is a sample:

*Diese Bedienungsanleitung befasst sich mit den Grundfunktionen ihres Aufnahmegerätes. Die Aufbewahrung, Handhabung sowie die Aufnahme, das Überspielen, und die Abspielfunktion werden in folgenden Kapiteln erklärt. Sehen Sie sich zuerst die Abbildung der Tastenfunktionen auf Seite 4 an. Zur weiteren Bedienung des Gerätes brauchen sie entweder einen Netzanschluss oder 2 AA Batterien.*

*Am Ende der Bedienungsanleitung befindet sich eine Problemaufstellung. Bei Störungen oder Problemen mit dem Gerät überprüfen Sie bitte, ob Sie den Fehler dort aufgeführt finden. Sollten Sie die Störung nicht beheben können, bringen Sie Ihr Gerät zum nächstliegenden Kundendienst oder Händler. Öffnen Sie das Gerät nicht selbstständig, da wir für gewaltsame Beschädigungen oder unsachgemäße Bedienung des Gerätes keine Haftung übernehmen.*

## TRANSLATION

This instruction manual covers the basic functions of your recording device. Storage and handling as well as recording, rerecording, and playback are explained in the following chapters. First, please turn to page 4 for a chart of the key functions. To operate the recorder you will need an adapter or 2 AA batteries.

Toward the end of the manual you will find a troubleshooting guide. In case of problems in the operation of your recorder, please check first to see whether the problem is listed there. Should you be unable to solve the problem, please take the recorder to the nearest customer service or dealership. Do not open the device yourself as we are not liable for any damages incurred by force or inappropriate handling and operation of the device.

## 3. COMPLAINTS

*Ich möchte mich beschweren.*
I'd like to complain.

*Ich möchte eine Beschwerde einreichen.*
I'd like to file/submit a complaint.

*Ich muss das leider reklamieren.*
Unfortunately, I have to return this.

*Können Sie mir einen Ersatz anbieten?*
Can you offer me a substitute/an adequate replacement?

*Ich möchte mein Geld/meine Anzahlung zurück bekommen.*
I would like to have my money/my deposit back.

*Ich habe den Beleg dabei./Ich lege den Beleg bei.*
I have the receipt (on me)./I'm enclosing the receipt.

*Ich bitte um volle Rückerstattung meiner Kosten.*
I request a full refund of my cost/expenses.

*Ich bin leider nicht mit dem Produkt/mit Ihrem Service zufrieden.*
Unfortunately, I'm not satisfied with the product/with your service.

---

# ÜBUNGEN

1. *Beantworten Sie die Fragen zum Text.*

   a. *Warum brachte Herr Köhler das Diktiergerät zum Kundendienst?*
   b. *Was funktioniert nicht mehr?*
   c. *Warum wollte Herr Köhler kein neues Gerät kaufen?*
   d. *Warum muss das Gerät zum Hersteller geschickt werden?*
   e. *Wann wird Herr Köhler vom Hersteller hören?*

2. *Übersetzen Sie.*

   a. I'd like to file a complaint.
   b. She wants to exchange the VCR.
   c. Can you repair my car?
   d. My car is being repaired.
   e. I'd like to return the soup. It is cold.
   f. We want to exchange these tickets.

3. *Wählen Sie die richtige Vorsilbe.*

   a. *Wir gingen ins Haus _____ ein.*
   b. *Gerade in dem Moment kam Herr Wilke _____ aus.*
   c. *Er ging die Treppe _____ unter.*

d. *Wir riefen ihm nach und sagten, er solle doch wieder _____ aufkommen.*

e. *Er hörte uns nicht, so gingen wir _____ ein, und warteten.*

f. *Sein Kollege machte die Tür auf, und bat uns, _____ einzukommen.*

g. *Der Kollege sagte, Herr Wilke käme gleich, er höre ihn schon die Treppe _____ aufkommen.*

**4.** *Verbinden Sie die Sätze und mit „weder . . . noch," „entweder . . . oder," or „nicht nur . . . sondern auch."*

a. *(das Gerät/kaputt gehen/sein/Sie/haben/beschädigen/es)*

b. *(ich/haben/Sie/anrufen/Ihnen/schreiben)*

c. *(das Gerät/sein/kaputt/die Batterien/sein/verbraucht)*

d. *(ich/jemand anders/haben/benutzen/es)*

e. *(Sie/geben/mir/ein/besser/Gerät/ich/sich beschweren)*

f. *(wir/sein/fahren/nach Mannheim/nach Ludwigshafen)*

**5.** *Beenden Sie die Sätze.*

a. *Ich weiß, warum das Gerät _____ (werden, müssen, reparieren).*

b. *Er sagt, er habe den Recorder nicht _____ (fallen, lassen).*

c. *Der Hersteller berichtet, das Gerät _____ (können, nicht mehr, werden, reparieren).*

d. *Frau Kreibach sagte zu ihrem Kollegen, dem anderen Kunden _____ (helfen, müssen, werden).*

e. *Der Kollege fragte, ob er der Frau _____ (helfen, können).*

# LEKTION 19

WEINPROBE.　Wine Tasting.

## A. DIALOG

*Claudia Zöllner und Eric McCarthy fahren von Graz[1] in Richtung slowenische Grenze entlang der österreichischen Weinstraße.[2] Sie wollen zur Weinprobe[3] auf das Weingut Meibel.\**

HERR McCARTHY: Es ist schön, mal von diesem ewigen Zollpapierkrieg[4] wegzukommen, um sich die schöne Landschaft anzusehen. Außerdem kann ich so meine Weinkenntnisse erweitern.

FRAU ZÖLLNER: Das ist wohl wahr. Waren Sie nicht das letzte Mal in Frankreich?

HERR McCARTHY: Oh ja, bei meinen Weinbauern an der Côte du Rhône bin ich sehr beliebt. Ich fahre oft zur Weinlese[5] hin.

FRAU ZÖLLNER: Na, ich bin gespannt auf Herrn Meibel. Ich hoffe, ich kann etwas für mein Restaurant bestellen.

HERR McCARTHY: Beziehen Sie Ihren Wein denn nicht vom Großhandel?

FRAU ZÖLLNER: Doch, aber ich möchte auch was Besonderes anbieten. Wir bekommen in Salzburg[6] so viele Gäste durch die Salzburger Festspiele und die Mozarttouristen. Da will man schon konkurrenzfähig sein. Ach, quatsch! Um ehrlich zu sein, ich will, dass der Besitzer vom Café über mein schönes Restaurant grün vor Neid wird.

HERR McCARTHY: Fahren Sie mal langsam. Das da vorne müsste Meibels Gut sein.

FRAU ZÖLLNER: Sie haben recht. Fast hätte ich die Abfahrt verpasst.

HERR McCARTHY: Na, dann auf ins Vergnügen.

*Im Weingut.*

HERR MEIBEL: Willkommen. Sie sind genau zur rechten Zeit gekommen. Das ist schön. So können Sie ein, zwei Tropfen[7] in Ruhe genießen.

---

\* This is a fictional vineyard.

FRAU ZÖLLNER: Grüß Gott, Herr Meibel. Das hört sich ja an, als seien Sie heute schon voll beschäftigt gewesen.

HERR MEIBEL: Ja, freilich.[8] Gleich um 10 Uhr früh kam eine ganze Reisegruppe, dann ein paar einzelne Touristen. Und dann kamen noch zwei weitere Busse. Aber ich beklage mich nicht.

HERR McCARTHY: McCarthy.[9] Grüß Gott, Herr Meibel. Ich bin ganz begeistert von Ihren Weinbergen. Bauen Sie hauptsächlich weiß oder rot an?

HERR MEIBEL: Beides. Aber ich habe wohl 60 bis 70% Weißwein. Kommen Sie herein! Dort, durch die Holztür bitte. Hier drinnen ist es angenehm kühl.

FRAU ZÖLLNER: Mein Bekannter, der Sie empfohlen hat, sagte, Sie seien bekannt für Ihren hervorragenden Chardonnay.[10]

HERR MEIBEL: Ja, der 94er ist wunderbar. Ein ganz besonders edles Bouquet, blumig. Hier, bitte schön. Zum Wohle.[11]

*Herr McCarthy und Frau Zöllner probieren. Herr Meibel stellt einen Teller mit Brot und Käse hinzu.*

HERR McCARTHY: Ja, der Wein ist gut. Auf den können Sie wirklich stolz sein. Leicht, aber schön abgerundet. Ein wunderbarer Nachgeschmack.

*Frau Zöllner hält das Glas hoch.*

FRAU ZÖLLNER: Und mit der Farbe können Sie auch sehr zufrieden sein.

HERR MEIBEL: Danke, danke. Wir haben wirklich gute Jahrgänge. Die diesjährige Lese ist auch erstklassig. Hier habe ich jetzt einen Riesling. Wenn Sie die alten Gläser dort hinstellen möchten? Danke.

HERR McCARTHY: Wer macht Ihre Exporte, Herr Meibel?

HERR MEIBEL: Firma Groß in Graz. Aber ich bin dort nicht exklusiv vertreten. Über meine österreichischen Einkäufer habe ich auch Direktabnehmer im Ausland bekommen.

FRAU ZÖLLNER: Hmm, der Riesling ist sehr gut. Den nehme ich auf jeden Fall.

*Sie nimmt ein Stück Brot.*

FRAU ZÖLLNER: Geben Sie mir noch etwas von dem Riesling, bitte. Halt, welches ist denn jetzt mein Glas?

HERR McCARTHY: Das hier ist meins.

HERR MEIBEL: Wären Sie auch an Rotwein interessiert?

HERR McCARTHY: **Auf jeden Fall.**

HERR MEIBEL: **Hier ist ein blauer Portugieser.**[12] **Und ich habe noch einen roten Landwein, auf den ich sehr stolz bin. Mein eigener Rebstock, sozusagen. Sehr schön, trocken, abgerundet, samtig könnte man fast sagen. Meibels Rote Lese . . . zum Wohle!**

FRAU ZÖLLNER: **Hmmm, der schmeckt mir sehr gut.**

HERR McCARTHY: **Ab welcher Menge können wir uns denn mal über gute Exportpreise unterhalten?**

HERR MEIBEL: **Na, ich würde sagen, ab 300 Flaschen mache ich Ihnen einen guten Preis.**

HERR McCARTHY: **300, das ist ja gar nichts.**

HERR MEIBEL: **Sie müssen ja schließlich den Transport und den Zoll bezahlen.**

HERR McCARTHY: **Und können Sie mir jederzeit ein Zertifikat über die Herstellung liefern, das garantiert, dass das Weingesetz**[13] **beachtet wurde?**

HERR MEIBEL: **Na, selbstverständlich, bei mir ist noch nie gepanscht**[14] **worden.**

HERR McCARTHY: **Frau Zöllner, was haben Sie denn? Sie sind plötzlich blass geworden.**

FRAU ZÖLLNER: **Ich glaube, der Riesling hat mir zu gut geschmeckt. Wenn ich so weiter mache, bin ich blau, und dann müssen wir hier übernachten, Herr McCarthy.**

HERR MEIBEL: **Na, das ist doch eine hervorragende Idee. Dann können wir uns Zeit lassen, Sie können noch ein paar Spätlesen**[15] **probieren, und ich zeige Ihnen ein paar besondere Jahrgänge.**

HERR McCARTHY: **Und Sie versprechen uns, dass wir morgen früh keinen Kater haben!**

HERR MEIBEL: **Nein, niemals. Außerdem gehen wir nachher gut essen.**

---

## TRANSLATION

Claudia Zöllner and Eric McCarthy are driving from Graz toward the Slovenian border along the Austrian wine road. They want to go to Meibel's vineyard for a wine tasting.

MR. McCARTHY: It's nice to get away once in a while from that continuous red tape of customs forms to look at the beautiful countryside. And on top of that I'm able to expand my knowledge of wine.

MS. ZÖLLNER: Too true. Didn't you go to France last time?

MR. McCARTHY: Oh yes, my wine growers at the Côte du Rhône love me. I often go there during the gathering season.

MS. ZÖLLNER: Well, I'm curious about Mr. Meibel. I hope I can order something for my restaurant.

MR. McCARTHY: Don't you get your wine wholesale?

MS. ZÖLLNER: Of course, but I'd really like to offer something special. We're having so many visitors in Salzburg, with the Salzburg Festival and the Mozart tourists. You have to be competitive. Oh, never mind. To be honest, I want the owner of the café to turn green with envy over my beautiful restaurant.

MR. McCARTHY: Slow down a bit. That one up here should be Meibel's vineyard.

MS. ZÖLLNER: You're right. I almost missed the turn-off.

MR. McCARTHY: Well, here comes the fun part.

In the vineyard.

MR. MEIBEL: Welcome. You're coming at exactly the right time. That's great. That way you can enjoy a drop or two in peace and quiet.

MS. ZÖLLNER: Hello there, Mr. Meibel. It sounds as if you were busy today.

MR. MEIBEL: Yes, of course, right at 10 in the morning a whole travel group stopped by, then a few individual tourists. And then two more buses. But I won't complain.

MR. McCARTHY: (My name is) McCarthy. Good afternoon, Mr. Meibel. Your vineyard is fabulous. Do you mostly grow white or red?

MR. MEIBEL: Both. But I probably grow about 60% to 70% white. Please come! There through the wooden door, please. It's nice and cool inside.

MS. ZÖLLNER: My acquaintance, who recommended you, said you were well known for your excellent Chardonnay.

MR. MEIBEL: Yes, the '94 vintage is wonderful. An especially elegant bouquet, flowery. There you are, to your health.

Mr. McCarthy and Ms. Zöllner try the wine. Mr. Meibel offers a plate with bread and cheese.

MR. McCARTHY: Yes, this wine is good. You can truly be proud of that. It's light but satisfying in a nice way. And an exceptional aftertaste.

Ms. Zöllner raises the glass to the light.

MS. ZÖLLNER: And you should be content with that color, too.

MR. MEIBEL: Thank you, thank you. We really have had some good vintage years. This year's gathering is also first rate. Here we have a Riesling. If you don't mind, place the used glasses over there? Thank you.

MR. McCARTHY: Who does your exports, Mr. Meibel?

MR. MEIBEL: The Groß company in Graz. But I'm not exclusively with them. Some of my Austrian clients have also set me up directly with customers abroad.

MS. ZÖLLNER: The Riesling is very good. I'll definitely take that one.

She takes a piece of bread.

MS. ZÖLLNER: Please give me a little bit more of the Riesling. Wait, which one is my glass?

MR. McCARTHY: This one is mine.

MR. MEIBEL: Would you be interested in red wine too?

MR. McCARTHY: Definitely.

MR. MEIBEL: Here's a blue Portuguese. And I also have a red table wine that I'm particularly proud of. My own grapevine so to speak. Very nice, dry, very satisfying, velvety, one could almost say. Meibel's Red Harvest. . . . Cheers!

MS. ZÖLLNER: Hmmm, it really tastes good.

MR. McCARTHY: What kind of quantity would be acceptable to start talking about reasonable export prices?

MR. MEIBEL: Well, I'd say from about 300 bottles up I'll give you a good price.

MR. McCARTHY: Three hundred, that's nothing.

MR. MEIBEL: After all, you'll have to pay transportation and customs.

MR. McCARTHY: And will you be able to supply me with a certificate of production that guarantees full compliance with the wine regulations?

MR. MEIBEL: Of course, we have never done any diluting here.

MR. McCARTHY: Ms. Zöllner, what's the matter? You turned pale all of a sudden.

MS. ZÖLLNER: I think I liked the Riesling too much. If I go on like this, I'll be drunk and then we'll have to stay overnight, Mr. McCarthy.

MR. MEIBEL: Well, that's a great idea. Then we can take our time, you may try some special reserves, and I'll show you some exceptional vintages.

MR. McCARTHY: And you promise that we won't have a hangover tomorrow morning.

MR. MEIBEL: No, never. In any case, we'll go and eat a nice dinner later on.

# B. IN KÜRZE

1. *Graz,* in southern Austria, is the second-largest city after Vienna. It is famous for its clock tower high above the city, which used to be part of its fortification. More at www.Graz.de.

2. *Die Weinstraße* (wine road) in Austria is located to the south and southeast of Graz spanning from *Deutschlandsberg, Kietzeck, Leibnitz,* and *Silberberg* to *Schloßberg* near the Slovenian border. Austria has 56,000 vineyards and grows 200 different grapes, of which only 28 are approved for high-quality wines. The major wine regions are along the Danube river, around Vienna, Lower Austria, and the Burgenland. The Austrian harvest is 86% white and 14% red. Primary Austrian wines are *Grüner Veltliner, Müller-Thurgau, Weißer Burgunder,* and *Traminer* (white), as well as *Blauer Portugieser, Blauer Burgunder,* and *Blaufränkischer* (red). German wine-growing regions are in the south and southwest of the country around the rivers *Rhein, Mosel, Saar, Neckar, Main,* and *Nahe.* Major wine grapes are *Müller-Thurgau, Riesling, Silvaner* (all white), as well as *Spätburgunder* and *Portugieser* (red).

3. *Die Weinprobe* (wine tasting) can be arranged at every vineyard. Call ahead of time to make reservations. Unlike famous American vineyards, European vineyards do not automatically cater to visitors by offering year-round tours. Check the local tourist office for information about particular vineyards.

4. *Der Papierkrieg* (paper war) is the equivalent of "red tape." You will also hear people refer to "red tape" as *die Bürokratie* (bureaucracy).

5. *Die Weinlese* (grape gathering, vintage) is the official term for the fall season of harvesting. In German wine-producing areas, the *Weinlese* will be officially started by an announcement from the mayor of the town and the local *Winzer Genossenschaft* (wine growers' committee). Immediately prior to and during the *Weinlese* the vineyards are closed, and everyone except the cutters and gatherers is denied access.

6. *Salzburg* has become a favorite tourist spot. Mozart lived and worked there before permanently relocating to Vienna as a young adult. Salzburg is extremely picturesque against the backdrop of Alpine mountain ranges, the castle overlooking the city, and an array of ancient cobblestone *Gassen* (alleys). It also hosts the classical music festival, the *Salzburger Festspiele,* from July through August. More at www.Salzburg.at.

7. *Der Tropfen* (drop) is used in wine circles, colloquially, and in advertising as a synonym for wine. *Ein guter/edler Tropfen* (a good/special drop) is an exceptionally good bottle of wine.

8. *Freilich* (of course, naturally) is a common expression in southern Germany, Austria, and Switzerland.

9. Remember that people will often introduce themselves simply by stating their last name.

10. *Chardonnay* is particular to Austria, just as it is to California, Australia, and South Africa. The white grape comes from Chardonnay (France) in the Burgundy region.

11. *Zum Wohle!* (To your health!) is considered the appropriate toast when drinking wine. It is considered informal or even unsophisticated to say *Prost* or *Prosit* with wine. These expressions are used when drinking beer or spirits. *Prost* is also used at New Year's when toasting with champagne or *Sekt* (sparkling wine): *Prost Neujahr* (Happy New Year).

12. *Der blaue Portugieser* is the name of a red wine frequently grown and served in Austria. There are other wines that also carry the name *Portugieser* (Portuguese), such as *Portugieser Weißherbst,* a blush wine from *Baden-Württemberg.* None of these wines is actually grown in Portugal, and they only take their name after a grape originating in Portugal.

13. *Das deutsche Weingesetz* (purity law) prohibits additives and dilutive processes. It groups wine into three major categories: 1. *deutscher Tafelwein* (table wine), made from a variety of wine from various legally approved wine-producing areas; sugar is added; 2. *Qualitätswein* (quality wine), made from a variety of wine from one particular wine-producing area; sugar is added; 3. *Qualitätswein mit Prädikat* (special title quality wine), made from wines from one area, no added sugar allowed. *Qualitätswein* can only be bottled after inspection and approval.

   A similar law exists for beer. The beer law is called *das Reinheitsgebot,* limiting the ingredients for beer to hops, water, malt, and barley. These laws are strictly enforced.

14. *Panschen* is a colloquialism meaning "to mush, to mix." In wine terminology, it means "to dilute, to mix, to add."

15. During a mild (and sunny) fall season some grapes will be left on the winestock for *die Spätlese,* a special late gathering for reserve quality wines. If the grapes are still on the winestock during the first night frost, the wine produced from it is called *Eiswein* (ice wine). Frost adds a particular richness to the already ripened grape.

# C. GRAMMATIK UND GEBRAUCH

## 1. ADVERBIEN MIT PRÄPOSITIONEN (ADVERBS WITH PREPOSITIONS)

The case of the object following these adverbs is determined by the preposition.

*FROH ÜBER* (glad about)
*Ich bin froh über Ihren Erfolg bei der Weinmesse.*
  I'm glad about your success at the wine fair.

*GLÜCKLICH ÜBER* (happy about)
*Er ist sehr glücklich über das Ergebnis der Verhandlungen.*
  He is very happy about the outcome of the negotiations.

*FREUNDLICH ZU* (friendly, nice toward)
*Sie waren sehr freundlich zu uns und wir möchten Ihnen danken.*
  You were very nice to us and we wanted to thank you.

*ZUFRIEDEN MIT* (satisfied, happy with)
*Sie war sehr zufrieden mit dem Bericht über die Messe.*
  She was very happy with the report on the fair.

*VOLL VON* (full of)
*Wir waren voll von Begeisterung über die hervorragenden Verkäufe.*
  We were full of enthusiasm about the excellent sales.

*VERRÜCKT NACH* (crazy about)
*Du bist verrückt nach belgischer Schokolade.*
  You're crazy about Belgian chocolate.

*VERWANDT MIT* (related to)
*Sind Sie verwandt mit ihm?*
  Are you related to him?

*ENTSETZT ÜBER* (shocked by)
*Er war entsetzt über die Verkaufszahlen.*
  He was shocked by the sales figures.

*EIFERSÜCHTIG AUF* (jealous of)
*Ihr seid eifersüchtig auf unseren Erfolg.*
  You are jealous of our success.

*BEGEISTERT VON* (to be enthusiastic about)
*Ich war total begeistert von ihren Plänen.*
  I was totally enthusiastic about her plans.

BELEIDIGT ÜBER (insulted by)
*Sie war beleidigt über meine Antwort.*
  She felt insulted by my answer.

BELIEBT BEI (loved/admired by)
*Er ist sehr beliebt bei den Gästen des Hotels.*
  He is much loved by the hotel guests.

BÖSE AUF (angry with, at/mad at)
*Sind Sie böse auf mich?*
  Are you angry with me?

BEKANNT FÜR (well known for)
*Herr Müller ist bekannt für seine Verkäufe.*
  Mr. Müller is well known for his sales.

BEKANNT MIT (acquainted with)
*Wir sind seit Jahren mit Herrn Meibel bekannt.*
  We have been acquainted with Mr. Meibel for years.

## 2. *EIN-WÖRTER ALS PRONOMEN*
   (*EIN*-WORDS AS PRONOUNS)

The possessive adjectives *mein, dein, sein,* as well as the indefinite article *ein* and the negative form *kein* can be used as pronouns. Compare:

| | | |
|---|---|---|
| *Wessen Glas ist das?* | *Das ist seins.* | *Das ist sein Glas.* |
| Whose glass is that? | That's his. | That's his glass. |
| *Ist das Ihr Mantel?* | *Nein, das ist nicht meiner.* | *Nein, das ist nicht mein Mantel.* |
| Is that your coat? | No, that's not mine. | No, that's not my coat. |
| *Ist das euer Schlüssel?* | *Ja, das ist unserer.* | *Ja, das ist unser Schlüssel.* |
| Is that your key? | Yes, that's ours. | Yes, that's our key. |
| *Ist das deine Katze?* | *Ja, das ist meine.* | *Ja, das ist meine Katze.* |
| Is that your cat? | Yes, that's mine. | Yes, that's my cat. |

## 3. WORTBILDUNG AUS ADJEKTIVEN
## (WORD FORMATION FROM ADJECTIVES)

Several verbs derive from adjectives such as *leicht, schwer, schön, klein,* and *groß* plus prefix and ending. The prefixes *er-* and *ver-* indicate a progressive movement or development defined by the comparative form of the adjective that joins the prefix.

LEICHT                     *ERLEICHTERN\** (to make easy[-ier])
*Ihr Preisangebot erleichtert die Sache sehr.*
Your price offer makes the whole thing much easier.

SCHÖN                   *VERSCHÖNERN\** (to improve, to beautify)
*Der Garten wird durch die Rosenbäume verschönert.*
The garden is made more beautiful by the rosebushes.

KLEIN                    *VERKLEINERN\** (to reduce)
*Wir möchten diesen Raum verkleinern. Wir werden Wände ziehen.*
We want to make the room smaller. We will put up walls.

GROSS                   *VERGRÖßERN\** (to increase, to enlarge)
*Seine Firma hat sich in den letzten 3 Jahren um 10 Angestellte vergrößert.*
His company grew by ten employees during the last three years.

DUNKEL                 *VERDUNKELN\** (to darken, to shut out the light)
*Du musst das Zimmer verdunkeln, wenn du dir Dias ansehen möchtest.*
You have to shut out the light if you want to look at slides.

SCHLECHT             *VERSCHLECHTERN\** (to turn bad, to deteriorate)
*Die Lage hat sich extrem verschlechtert.*
The situation drastically deteriorated.

SCHLIMM              *VERSCHLIMMERN\** (to worsen)
*Seine fehlenden Verkäufe verschlimmern die Bilanz.*
His lack of sales worsens the (trade) balance.

---

\* These verbs form feminine nouns with *-ung* endings: *die Verkleinerung, die Beschleunigung, die Erleichterung, die Befähigung, die Verschlechterung,* etc. See Lesson 15 for noun endings and formation.

A few verbs formed from adjectives take the prefix *be-*. They end in *-igen* and describe a falsifying, clarifying, or temporary, sudden change, but no development.

*SCHÖN* (beautiful)                    *BESCHÖNIGEN** (to make something more or better than it is)

*Ich glaube, sie beschönigt die Situation.*
I think she makes the situation look better (than it is).

*REIN* (clean)                    *BEREINIGEN** (to clear up a situation, to resolve)

*Du musst die Angelegenheit mit den 2.000 EUR Schulden noch bereinigen.*
You still have to resolve that matter concerning the €2,000 debt.

*FÄHIG* (capable, able)                    *BEFÄHIGEN** (to enable)

*Mit dieser Prüfung sind Sie befähigt, Weinzertifikate auszustellen.*
This examination enables you to issue wine certificates.

*LUSTIG* (funny)                    *BELUSTIGEN** (to amuse)

*Der Entertainer soll die Gäste belustigen.*
The entertainer is supposed to amuse the guests.

*RUHIG* (quiet, silent)                    *BERUHIGEN** (to calm)

*Sie war ganz aufgeregt und musste sich erstmal beruhigen.*
She was very excited and had to calm down first.

The verbs *beschleunigen* and *beleidigen* are not derived from adjectives and instead form adjectives themselves: *beleidigt* (insulted) and *beschleunigt* (accelerated).

*BESCHLEUNIGEN** (to accelerate)
*Auf der Autobahn können Sie beschleunigen.*
On the highway you can drive faster.

*BELEIDIGEN** (to insult)
*Ich wollte Sie nicht beleidigen.*
I didn't mean to insult you.

## 4. IDIOMATIC EXPRESSIONS

*ROT ANLAUFEN* (to go/turn red with anger)
*Du läufst ja rot an vor Wut!*
You're turning red with anger.

* These verbs form feminine nouns with *-ung* endings: *die Verkleinerung, die Beschleunigung, die Erleichterung, die Befähigung, die Verschlechterung,* etc. See Lesson 15 for noun endings and formation.

*ROT WERDEN* (to blush)
*Als wir ihm sagten, dass wir seinen Plan durchschaut hatten, wurde er rot.*
> When we told him that we saw through his plan, he blushed.

*GRÜN WERDEN VOR NEID* (to turn green with envy)
*Der Inhaber des Cafés nebenan wurde grün vor Neid.*
> The owner of the café next door turned green with envy.

*BLAU SEIN* (to be drunk)
*Wenn Frau Zöllner noch mehr Riesling trinkt, wird sie blau.*
> If Ms. Zöllner drinks more Riesling, she'll get drunk.

*WEIß WIE DIE WAND/WEIß WIE KREIDE* (to turn white as a sheet, a ghost)
*Plötzlich wurde Frau Zöllner weiß wie die Wand.*
> Suddenly Ms. Zöllner turned white as a sheet.

*SCHWARZSEHEN* (to anticipate the worst; lit.: to see black)
*In keiner Situation sollte man schwarzsehen.*
> No situation warrants the anticipation of the worst.

*SICH SCHWARZ ÄRGERN* (to get extremely annoyed/angry)
*Als ich merkte, dass ich zu teuer eingekauft hatte, habe ich mich schwarz geärgert.*
> When I realized that I bought everything at top price, I got extremely annoyed.

*SCHWARZ VOR AUGEN WERDEN* (to pass out; to faint)
*Plötzlich wurde ihm schwarz vor Augen.*
> Suddenly he passed out.

*SCHWARZFAHREN* (to ride public transportation without paying)
*Er ist oft schwarzgefahren, bis er erwischt wurde.*
> He used to ride a lot without paying, until he was caught.

*SICH GRAUE HAARE WACHSEN LASSEN* (to worry excessively; lit.: to let gray hair grow)
*Darüber lasse ich mir keine grauen Haare wachsen, das ist es nicht wert.*
> I won't worry about it; it's just not worth it.

*GRAU IN GRAU . . . SEIN/MALEN* (to be bleak; fig.: to paint a gloomy picture)
*Es regnete seit Tagen, die Stadt war grau in grau.*
> It had been raining for days; the city looked bleak.

*Sie malt immer alles grau in grau.*
> She always paints a gloomy picture.

*DIE WELT DURCH EINE ROSAROTE BRILLE SEHEN* (to see the world through rose-tinted glasses)
*Wir haben die Welt oft durch eine rosarote Brille gesehen, dabei war alles ganz anders.*
We often saw the world through rose-tinted glasses when everything was very different.

# D. REIN GESCHÄFTLICH

## 1. IMPORT AND EXPORT

Germany is a key member of the G7 (the seven strongest economic nations in the world) and maintains strong economic ties to nations around the world. The U.S.A. is one of the most important trading partners of Germany. German exports mostly go to France, Italy, the Netherlands, Great Britain, Belgium and Luxembourg, the U.S.A., Austria, Switzerland, Spain, and Japan. Germany imports from France, the Netherlands, Italy, Belgium and Luxembourg, Great Britain, the U.S.A., Japan, Austria, Switzerland, and Spain.

Since 1993 there are no more customs charges in inter-European trade. Commercial import/export as well as private freight shipping are no longer subject to taxation or lengthy customs declarations. The *Europäischer Binnenmarkt* (European home market) was created for all member countries of the *Europäische Union* (European Union), which was formed out of the former *EWG, Europäische Wirtschaftsgemeinschaft* (European Economic Community). Trade between Europe and non-European countries is, of course, still subject to international trade requirements, customs fees, and import taxes.

The import of most products originating in and purchased from other countries without license is permitted. Certain petroleum products, agricultural commodities, and coal imports from non-EU countries require import licenses. Information and import licenses can be obtained from either the *Bundesamt für Wirtschaft* (Federal Office for Trade and Industry), the *Bundesamt für Ernährung und Forstwirtschaft* (the Federal Office for Food and Forestry), or the *Bundesministerium für Ernährung, Landwirtschaft und Forstwirtschaft* (Ministry of Agriculture), depending on the type of goods you plan to import. The following documents should accompany your import shipment: a *Frachtbrief* (bill of lading), a *Ursprungszeugnis* (certificate of origin), and a *Rechnung* (commercial invoice) containing the following information: name and address of vender and buyer; place and date of invoice; method of shipment; number, kind, and markings of the packages; exact descriptions; quantity; agreed price of the goods; as well as delivery and payment terms.

With few exceptions, German exporters are free to contract and carry out all export transactions. Exports of all goods require an export declaration to be filed with the customs authorities for statistical purposes and as a control for export licensing. Information and licensing can be obtained from the *Bundesamt für Wirtschaft* (Federal Office for Trade and Industry).

## 2. VOCABULARY

| | |
|---|---|
| *die Verzollung* | payment of duty |
| *die Zollbearbeitung, die Zollabfertigung* | customs clearance |
| *die Import-/Exportzollgebühren* | import/export customs fees/duty |
| *das Zollamt* | customs office |
| *die Warenmuster* | sample of goods |
| *Nicht zum Verkauf.* | Not for sale. |
| *Keine Handelsware.* | No commercial value./N.C.V. |
| *die Begleitpapiere* | documentation accompanying the consignment |
| *der Lieferant* | supplier |
| *der Liefertermin* | delivery on |
| *die Versandart* | shipment via (sea, air, truck, rail) |
| *die Menge* | quantity |
| *der Gegenstand* | item |
| *der Einzelpreis* | price per item |
| *der Gesamtpreis* | total |
| *der Lieferschein* | delivery note |
| *die Ausfuhrerklärung* | export declaration |
| *die Einfuhrerklärung* | import declaration |
| *der Ausführer* | exporter |
| *der Versender* | sent by |
| *der Empfänger* | recipient |
| *das Ursprungsland* | country of origin |
| *das Bestimmungsland* | country of destination |
| *das Packstück* | (individual packages/pieces of) consignment |
| *die Warenbezeichnung* | description of goods |
| *die Grenzübergangsstelle* | point of crossing border |
| *die Lieferbedingungen* | terms of delivery |

# ÜBUNGEN

1. *Setzen Sie die richtige Präposition ein.*

   a. *Wir sind _____ unser Angebot von europäischen Importen bekannt.*
   b. *Er ist mit meinem Auto davongefahren, und ich musste zu Hause bleiben. Ich war sehr böse _____ ihn.*
   c. *Sie war ganz neidisch _____ unseren Erfolg.*
   d. *Sind Sie zufrieden _____ dieser Auswahl?*
   e. *Wir sind überzeugt da _____ dass Ihnen unser Wein schmecken wird.*
   f. *Sie sollten _____ ihr neues Haus froh sein.*
   g. *Wir waren entsetzt _____ die schlechten Verkaufszahlen.*
   h. *Er war _____ seinen amerikanischen Kollegen _____ seine gute Arbeit bekannt.*

2. *Übersetzen Sie.*

   a. He was supposed to explain the situation; instead he made it look better than it was.
   b. The financial situation of the company has grown worse.
   c. The weather turned bad.
   d. My computer makes work much easier for me.
   e. You live far away from any major highway or rail station. That makes transportation a lot more difficult. (use *weit entfernt, Autobahn,* and *erheblich*)

3. *Setzen Sie die Farbe ein.*

   a. *Sie wurde _____ vor Neid, als sie mein neues Auto sah.*
   b. *Er hat sich _____ geärgert, dass er sein ganzes Geld verloren hat.*
   c. *Wir sahen wie der Chef _____ vor Wut anlief.*
   d. *Nachdem er seit 3 Wochen immer noch nicht auf unseren Brief geantwortet hat, sehe ich _____, was unsere gemeinsamen Pläne angeht.*
   e. *Irgendwann hörte auch Sybille auf, die Welt _____ zu sehen.*
   f. *Du bist _____, du solltest wirklich nicht Auto fahren.*

# LEKTION 20
KARNEVAL.  Carnival.

## A. DIALOG

*Eine amerikanische Touristin reist durch Deutschland und die Schweiz zur Fastnachtszeit.[1] Sie lernt in Basel[2] einen Fotografen kennen.*

GUIDO BERGER: Was hat Sie denn im Februar nach Europa verschlagen,[3] wo es doch überall so kalt ist?

MARY SWINN: Ich interessiere mich für Karneval und Kostüme. Letztes Jahr war ich in Venedig, das Jahr davor in Rio.

GUIDO BERGER: Haben Sie denn dieses Jahr auch die Baseler Fastnacht[4] mitgemacht?

MARY SWINN: Ja, ich war hier und in Bern, und davor war ich noch in Köln und in Mainz.[5] Es war toll.

GUIDO BERGER: Wo hat es Ihnen am besten gefallen?

MARY SWINN: Überall ist es so anders. In Mainz und Köln war es als wären die Leute auf einmal verrückt geworden.

GUIDO BERGER: Ja, das ist schon phänomenal. Das ganze Jahr über gehen die Menschen zur Arbeit, sind pflicht- und verantwortungsbewusst, und dann plötzlich im Februar sind sie wie ausgewechselt.[6] Für viele ist das die einzige Möglichkeit, aus sich herauszugehen.[7]

MARY SWINN: Ich habe gestaunt, dass der Schweizer Karneval so traditionsreich ist. Es scheint als wäre der Brauch[8] hier noch genau so, wie er ursprünglich einmal war.

GUIDO BERGER: Ja, das stimmt schon. Das liegt daran, dass die Schweiz über die Jahrhunderte unabhängig war und ihre Volksbräuche der Tradition wegen[9] so erhalten hat.

MARY SWINN: Ging es nicht immer darum, böse Geister zu verjagen?

GUIDO BERGER: Nicht immer. Es gibt auch einige Bräuche, die den Winter verabschieden und den Frühling begrüßen, wie z.B. das Verbrennen des Strohmannes in Zürich[10] oder das Glockenläuten am 1. März im Engadin,[11] das sogenannte Chalandamarz.

MARY SWINN: Wir haben das Mardi Gras in New Orleans, und das war's dann auch schon. Ansonsten gibt es nur noch Halloween.

302

GUIDO BERGER: Hätten Sie Interesse daran, sich ein paar meiner Fotos von der Baseler Fastnacht bei mir anzuschauen?

MARY SWINN: Ja, gerne. Wo haben Sie die denn?

GUIDO BERGER: In meinem Studio. Das ist gar nicht weit.

MARY SWINN: Für Ihre Fotos verzichte ich sogar auf meinen morgendlichen Spaziergang.

*Bei Guido Berger zu Hause.*

GUIDO BERGER: So, da sind wir schon. Ich mache uns erst einmal einen Kaffee.

MARY SWINN: Da hängen ja schon die Fotos. Die Masken sind wirklich wunderschön. Aber warum sind alle als Hexen verkleidet?

GUIDO BERGER: Wären Sie nicht auch gerne einmal in Ihrem Leben eine Hexe, die auf ihrem Besen davonreitet?

MARY SWINN: Na ja, so tun als ob[12] wäre schon lustig. Da läuft ja direkt ein Strohmann umher. Und hier das Bild von den bemalten Kindergesichtern ist aber schön.

GUIDO BERGER: Setzen Sie sich. Hier, schauen Sie mal in diese Mappe. Die Sammlung enthält nur Porträts.

MARY SWINN: Sie gehören ja wirklich zu den besten Fotografen, die ich je gesehen habe.

GUIDO BERGER: Danke. Es kommt darauf an, mit wem man mich vergleicht.

MARY SWINN: Sie müssten doch eigentlich gut zu tun haben.

GUIDO BERGER: Na ja, glücklicherweise mache ich schon des öfteren eine Serie für große Zeitschriften. Diese Fastnachtserie wird nächsten Monat in Italien und Frankreich erscheinen.

MARY SWINN: Ich bin von Ihrer Arbeit wirklich sehr beeindruckt.

GUIDO BERGER: Ich überlege gerade, ob ich die nächsten Tage noch nach Biel[13] fahre. Ich muss mich aber erst erkundigen, ob der Tourismusverband noch Interesse an den Bildern hat. Hätten Sie nicht Lust, mitzukommen?

MARY SWINN: Vielen Dank für die Einladung. Aber ich fliege zurück.

GUIDO BERGER: Wann denn?

MARY SWINN: Morgen schon.

GUIDO BERGER: **Ach, wie schade. Kann ich Sie zum Flughafen bringen?**

MARY SWINN: **Das ist nett von Ihnen, aber das brauchen Sie nicht, ich habe eine Taxe[14] bestellt.**

GUIDO BERGER: **Na, dann muss ich Ihnen wohl mein Geschenk jetzt schon geben. Drehen Sie sich mal um und schließen Sie die Augen.**

MARY SWINN: **Wie spannend. Warum um Himmels Willen[15] bekomme ich denn jetzt auch noch ein Geschenk? Das habe ich doch gar nicht verdient.**

GUIDO BERGER: **Fürchten Sie sich vor Geistern?**

MARY SWINN: **Nein. Darf ich mich jetzt umdrehen?**

*Als Mary sich umdreht, sieht sie, dass Guido Berger eine Hexenmaske trägt. Er lacht und reicht sie ihr.*

GUIDO BERGER: **Hier, die ist für Sie. Ich hoffe, Sie kommen bald wieder nach Basel.**

MARY SWINN: **Vielen Dank. Das ist wirklich sehr aufmerksam von Ihnen.**

---

TRANSLATION

An American tourist is traveling through Germany and Switzerland at carnival time. She meets a photographer in Basel.

GUIDO BERGER: What brought you to Europe in February, while it is so cold everywhere?

MARY SWINN: I'm interested in carnival and costumes. Last year I went to Venice and the year before to Rio.

GUIDO BERGER: And did you take part in the Basel carnival this year?

MARY SWINN: Yes, I was here and in Berne. And before that I was also in Cologne and Mainz. It was great.

GUIDO BERGER: Where did you like it best?

MARY SWINN: It's very different everywhere. In Mainz and Cologne it seemed as if people had suddenly gone crazy.

GUIDO BERGER: Yes, that is indeed astounding. Throughout the year, they go to work, are conscientious and responsible, and then suddenly in February it's as if everything's been turned upside down. For many it's the only opportunity to come out of their shell once in a while.

MARY SWINN: I was surprised to see that the Swiss carnival was so full of tradition. It seems as if the custom is still exactly the way it has always been.

GUIDO BERGER: Yes, that's right. That's because Switzerland has been neutral over centuries, and the local customs are kept up for tradition's sake.

MARY SWINN: Wasn't the idea always to chase away evil spirits?

GUIDO BERGER: Not always. There are also many customs that bid goodbye to winter and welcome the spring, as the burning of the straw man in Zurich for example or the bell clattering in Engadin on March 1, the so-called Chalandamarz.

MARY SWINN: We have Mardi Gras in New Orleans, and that's just about it. Apart from that we only have Halloween.

GUIDO BERGER: Would you be interested in seeing some of my photographs of Basel carnival?

MARY SWINN: Yes, I'd love to. Where do you have them?

GUIDO BERGER: At my studio. It's not far.

MARY SWINN: I'll even miss out on my morning walk for your photos.

At Guido Berger's apartment.

GUIDO BERGER: So, here we are. I'll make us some coffee first.

MARY SWINN: Your photos—there they are. These masks are really beautiful. But why is everybody dressed up as a witch?

GUIDO BERGER: Wouldn't you like to be a witch once in your life and ride off on your broomstick?

MARY SWINN: Well, pretending to be, that would be fun. And there's a straw man walking around. And here this picture of the painted children's faces is beautiful.

GUIDO BERGER: Take a seat. Here, look at this folder. This collection is just portraits.

MARY SWINN: You really are one of the best photographers I've ever seen.

GUIDO BERGER: Thanks. It depends who you compare me with.

MARY SWINN: Surely you have plenty of work.

GUIDO BERGER: Well, yes, fortunately I('ll get to) do a series for a big magazine once in a while. This carnival series will be published in Italy and France next month.

MARY SWINN: I'm really very impressed by your work.

GUIDO BERGER: I was just thinking about going to Biel for the next couple of days. I'll just have to check whether the tourist office still wants some photos. Would you like to come along?

MARY SWINN: Thanks for the invitation. But I'm flying home.

GUIDO BERGER: When?

MARY SWINN: Tomorrow already.

GUIDO BERGER: Oh, well, that's too bad. Can I take you to the airport?

MARY SWINN: That's nice of you, but you don't have to, I called a cab.

GUIDO BERGER: Well, then I'm going to have to give you your present now. Turn around and close your eyes.

MARY SWINN: How exciting. Why on earth do I get a present now? I hardly deserve it.

GUIDO BERGER: Are you afraid of ghosts?

MARY SWINN: No. May I turn around now?

When Mary turns around she sees that Guido Berger is wearing a witch's mask. He laughs and hands it to her.

GUIDO BERGER: Here, this is for you. I hope you'll be returning to Basel soon.

MARY SWINN: Thank you so much. That's really very kind of you.

# B. IN KÜRZE

1. *Die Fastnacht* is a regional name for carnival. It literally means "the night of fasting" and is the night before *Aschermittwoch* (Ash Wednesday). The tradition of fasting, however, is rarely adhered to and the term simply refers to celebrating *Karneval*. Another name for *Fastnacht* is *Fasching*. Any of the three terms is equally acceptable. People traditionally dress up as fools, clowns, and witches.

2. *Basel* is a large city in the northwestern corner of Switzerland, located on the Rhine river. Basel's website, www.Basel.ch, offers a lot of interesting information.

3. *Was hat Sie hierher verschlagen?* (What brought you to this neck of the woods) is always used in the passive.

4. *Die Baseler Fastnacht* differs from celebrations in Germany, as it takes place during the week following Ash Wednesday. It is largely dominated by witches' rather than fools' costumes, and the local population wanders through the streets singing and beating drums. Carnival is celebrated throughout Switzerland at various times during the entire month of February.

5. *Mainz,* a city near Frankfurt, is one of the major centers of carnival activities in Germany. The *Mainzer Rosenmontagszug,* a parade with floats and bands and the local population dressed up as fools, is broadcast live from Mainz on *Rosenmontag* (Rose Monday), the day before *Fastnacht.*

6. *Wie ausgewechselt sein* describes people and animals when they are completely different from their usual behavior.

*Nach dem Urlaub war er wie ausgewechselt.*
After vacation he was a new person.

7. *Aus sich herausgehen* (to step outside oneself) is used in a similar way to the English "to loosen up."

8. *Der Brauch* means the tradition, the custom. The term *volkstümlicher Brauch* refers to an ancient custom.

9. *Wegen* (sake) can either follow a noun or join with pronouns: *der Tradition wegen* (for tradition's sake), *meinetwegen* (for my sake), *seinetwegen* (for his sake). *Wegen* always takes the genitive case.

10. *Sechseläuten* in Zurich is the annual spring festival in April centered around *Böögg* burning. The *Böögg* is a large straw figure burned to welcome the spring season.

11. *Chalandamarz* is the name of an ancient spring custom celebrated in the canton *Graubünden* (Grisons) on March 1, when the population take to the streets to welcome spring with the incessant clatter of small bells.

12. *So tun als ob* (to pretend as if) is used with the subjunctive II:

*Er könnte so tun, als ob er ein Fotograf wäre.*
He could pretend he was a photographer.

13. *Biel* is a city in the French-speaking canton *Neuchatel.* Its French name is *Bienne.*

14. *Das Taxi/ein Taxi* is also used in the following spelling and gender change, *die Taxe/eine Taxe.*

15. *Um Himmels Willen* is the German equivalent of "for goodness' sake" or "for heaven's sake."

# C. GRAMMATIK UND GEBRAUCH

## 1. *VERBEN MIT PRÄPOSITIONEN* (VERBS WITH PREPOSITIONS)

Many verbs require a preposition. Some cannot be used without the preposition; others change their meaning when used with the preposition.

*SICH INTERESSIEREN FÜR* (to be interested in something)
*Mary interessiert sich für die Karnevalsbräuche.*
Mary is interested in the carnival customs.

*VERZICHTEN AUF* (to do without/to renounce/to abstain)
*Er hat auf seine Erbschaft verzichtet.*
He renounced his inheritance.

*SICH UNTERHALTEN/SPRECHEN/DISKUTIEREN ÜBER* (to talk about something)
*Wir sprachen drei Stunden über das Problem und fanden keine Lösung.*
We talked about the problem for three hours and found no solution.

*SICH HANDELN UM* (to deal with/to be concerning, regarding something)
*Es handelt sich um 30 Aufnahmen eines Baseler Fotografen.*
It concerns thirty photos of a Basel photographer.

*SICH GEWÖHNEN AN* (to get used to, to become familiar with)
*Ich gewöhne mich langsam an das Wetter.*
I'm slowly becoming accustomed to the weather.

*SICH KONZENTRIEREN AUF* (to concentrate on)
*Bitte konzentrieren Sie sich auf die Bilder.*
Please concentrate on the pictures.

*WARTEN AUF* (to wait for)
*Mary Quinn wartete auf einen Brief aus der Schweiz.*
Mary Quinn waited for a letter from Switzerland.

*SICH WUNDERN ÜBER* (to be puzzled about, to be amazed)
*Ich wundere mich immer wieder über seinen phänomenalen Erfolg.*
Time and time again I'm amazed at his phenomenal success.

*SICH FREUEN ÜBER* (to enjoy)
*Wir haben uns sehr über Ihren Besuch gefreut.*
We very much enjoyed your visit.

*SICH FREUEN AUF* (to look forward to)
*Guido Berger freut sich auf Mary Quinns Besuch.*
    Guido Berger is looking forward to Mary Quinn's visit.

*SICH UNTERHALTEN/SPRECHEN/DISKUTIEREN MIT* (to talk with someone)
*Möchten Sie mit Mary sprechen*
    Would you like to speak to Mary?

*SICH TREFFEN MIT* (to meet with)
*Ich treffe mich jeden Dienstag mit meinem Bruder.*
    I meet my brother every Tuesday.

*GEHÖREN ZU* (to belong to)
*Das Ehepaar gehört zu dieser Reisegruppe.*
    The couple belongs to this tour group.

*VERGLEICHEN MIT* (to compare with/to)
*Das können Sie nicht damit vergleichen.*
    That you cannot compare.

*HANDELN MIT* (to trade)
*Wir handeln mit antiken Uhren.*
    We trade in antique watches and clocks.

*HANDELN VON* (to deal with)
*Der Film handelt von den Karnevalszügen.*
    The film is about carnival processions.

*SICH TRENNEN VON* (to separate)
*Sie trennte sich von ihrem Mann und reichte die Scheidung ein.*
    She separated from her husband and filed for a divorce.

*ZWEIFELN AN* (to doubt)
*Ich zweifle an seinem Geschmack.*
    I doubt his taste.

*LIEGEN AN* (to depend on something, to be due to something)
*Das liegt daran, dass die Schweiz ihre unterschiedlichen Bräuche bewahrt hat.*
    That's due to the fact that Switzerland kept up its various traditions.

The *da*-compound is necessary when the object the preposition relates to is not specifically mentioned in the main clause or when a subordinated clause starting with *dass* is added to introduce another subject and verb.

*Ich verlasse mich auf deine Pünktlichkeit.*
    I'm counting on your punctuality.

*Ich verlasse mich darauf, dass du am Dienstag pünktlich bist.*
I count on your being punctual on Tuesday.

*Ich verlasse mich darauf.*
I am counting on it.

The preposition is a fixed part that resurfaces when asking for the subject:

*Worum handelt es sich?*
What is it regarding?

*Es handelt sich um eine Warensendung aus Luzern.*
It is regarding a shipment from Lucerne.

*Wovon handelt der Film?*
What is the film about?

*Der Film handelt von einem Karnevalszug, der sich verirrt.*
The film is about a carnival procession that gets lost.

## 2. *MODALE ADVERBIEN MIT „-WEISE"* (MODAL ADVERBS WITH -WEISE)

Adverbs such as *glücklich* (glad), *dumm* (stupid, silly), and *nett* (nice) describe the way in which the action occurs. They can form comparative modal adverbs with the suffix *-weise*.

*Sie hat glücklicherweise sofort gemerkt, dass der Fotoapparat weg war.*
Luckily, she noticed immediately that her camera was gone.

*Er hat dummerweise vergessen, ihre Telefonnummer aufzuschreiben.*
He foolishly forgot to write down her telephone number.

*Sie hat netterweise den Koffer der alten Frau getragen.*
She kindly carried the suitcase of the old lady.

## 3. *PARTIZIPIEN DER GEGENWART UND DER VERGANGENHEIT* (PRESENT AND PAST PARTICIPLES)

The present participle is formed with the infinitive plus *d*.

| | |
|---|---|
| *kommen* (to come) | *kommend* (coming) |
| *folgen* (to follow) | *folgend* (following) |
| *singen* (to sing) | *singend* (singing) |
| *lachen* (to laugh) | *lachend* (laughing) |

Present participles are used as adjectives and take adjective endings according to gender, case, and number of the noun they refer to.

*Der schlafende Hund liegt vor der Tür.*
The sleeping dog lies in front of the door.

*Der in Basel lebende Fotograf hat ein Studio.*
The photographer living in Basel has a studio.

*Eine lachende Frau schaut aus dem Fenster.*
A laughing woman looks out of the window.

The present participle describes a current action. As an adjective it can replace a relative clause. Compare:

*Das Kind, das singt, läuft die Straße entlang.*
The child who sings is running along the street.

*Das singende Kind läuft die Straße entlang.*
The singing child runs along the street.

The past participles have already been discussed as part of compound present and past perfect tenses.

| | |
|---|---|
| *kommen* (to come) | *gekommen* (come) |
| *folgen* (to follow) | *gefolgt* (followed) |
| *singen* (to sing) | *gesungen* (sung) |
| *lachen* (to laugh) | *gelacht* (laughed) |

The past participle is used to express actions that have happened in the past. The past participle is only used as an adjective to express actions that would, by necessity, require the passive if expressed in a relative clause.

*Die gesandte Fotografin ist hier.*
*Die Fotografin, die aus Bern gesandt wurde, ist hier.*
The photographer sent from Berne is here.

Participial constructions are commonly used in written text to avoid the addition of subordinated clauses, especially in long sentences. Compare:

*Der Journalist, der vor Jahren arbeitslos geworden war, hatte ein Restaurant eröffnet.*
*Der Journalist, vor Jahren arbeitslos geworden, hatte ein Restaurant eröffnet.*
*Der vor Jahren arbeitslos gewordene Journalist hatte ein Restaurant eröffnet.*
The journalist, who became unemployed years ago, had opened a restaurant.

*Die Frau, die als Katze verkleidet war, stieg in ihr Auto und fuhr davon.*
*Die Frau, als Katze verkleidet, stieg in ihr Auto und fuhr davon.*
*Die als Katze verkleidete Frau stieg in ihr Auto und fuhr davon.*
The woman who was dressed up as a cat got into her car and drove off.

311

# D. REIN GESCHÄFTLICH

## 1. ETIQUETTE

In general, business etiquettes in Germany and in the U.S.A. are virtually identical, yet some subtle differences do exist. The hierarchical structure in any business or company is more clearly defined in Germany than in the United States. While this is easy to perceive and observe as long as people address each other with the formal *Sie* and *Herr* or *Frau,* the invisible boundaries of courtesy and respect are kept up even in the rare case when the employer and employees address each other with the informal *du.* Informality does not wipe out the respect for the other's position, status, and rank. The accepted roles in work situations are carefully maintained.

In general, colleagues don't socialize much after work. It is very common to work with a group of people for years without ever going out for dinner, lunch, or drinks. When they do socialize with business partners and colleagues, Germans tend to avoid physical contact far more than Americans do. Shaking hands usually is as far as it goes. Patting people on the back, hugging them, and play fighting are considered obtrusive or peculiar at best.

Regular breakfast meetings, power lunches, and dinner negotiations, popular in the U.S.A., are uncommon in Germany. Business dinners or lunches are viewed as singular events providing the chance to get to know one another, to reinstate a business relationship previously neglected, or to celebrate a successful business deal. Breakfast meetings are altogether unusual, as there are very few restaurants offering breakfast. Breakfast is considered to be a private meal eaten at home with one's family.

## 2. GIFT GIVING

American business executives marketing in Germany encounter occasional difficulties with the *Zugabeverordnung* (Promotional Gifts Ordinance), which prohibits giveaways except calendars and other promotional material of nominal value, marked with the company's name. A *Zugabe,* or *Werbegeschenk* (promotional gift), directly associated with a single transaction or sales effort, is distinguished from a business gift, which is presented in order to maintain good business relations. Business gifts are generally considered in good taste if their value does not exceed €50, a figure rooted in German income tax law. In any case, a business or advertising gift is in bad taste and against the law if it results in a sense of obligation in the recipient.

Gifts among relatives or friends are given on birthdays and Christmas. There is no such thing as a bridal or baby shower in Germany. Wedding gifts are given on the wedding day, and gifts for the baby are usually given on an individual basis just before or anytime after the child is born. It is certainly possible to give gifts without a particular reason. These gifts, however, should be small, and you should not expect anything in return. Giving roses to a woman always carries romantic overtones, and giving perfume to a woman may be considered inappropriate unless you know her well as a friend or are romantically involved.

## 3. ON THE ROLES OF MEN AND WOMEN

More and more German women have joined the work force and have proceeded to take on key positions in industry, law, and politics. Although *die Gleichberechtigung der Frau* (equal opportunity for women) is widely accepted, women in Germany (as elsewhere) may still face unpleasant reminders of the past in the attitudes of some people. In the wake of the women's liberation movement in Germany the title for young or unmarried women *Fräulein* (Miss) has become obsolete.* Nowadays this title is considered patronizing or even rude. Use *Frau* instead.

Relationships between men and women in Germany are slightly different than in the U.S.A. Platonic friendships between men and women are much more common in Germany. Often these friendships are very close, yet remain without any romantic overtones. In other words, for a man to go out to dinner with a woman does not necessarily constitute a date, and for a woman to go home with a man does not necessarily carry sexual connotations. When going out for lunch, dinner, drinks, or on a date it is far more common in Germany to split the bill or to take turns in paying, regardless of gender or who has invited whom.

## 4. GIVING AND ACCEPTING COMPLIMENTS AND PRESENTS

*Ich habe Ihnen/dir etwas mitgebracht.*
I brought you something.

*Das ist aber nett von Ihnen/dir. Vielen Dank.*
That's really nice of you. Thank you very much.

*Das ist doch nicht nötig./Das wäre doch nicht nötig gewesen.*
You didn't need to./That really wasn't necessary.

*Das ist wirklich sehr aufmerksam von Ihnen.*
That's most kind of you. (formal)

*Das ist sehr lieb von dir./Das ist aber lieb von dir.*
How sweet of you. (informal)

*Ich möchte Sie einladen.*
I'd like to invite/treat you.

* See Lesson 1.

*Vielen Dank für Ihre Einladung. Wir kommen gerne./Leider können wir nicht kommen.*
Thank you very much for your invitation. We'd love to come./Unfortunately we won't be able to come.

*Ich möchte es Ihnen schenken. Ich hoffe, es gefällt Ihnen.*
I would like to give it to you. I hope you like it.

*Sie waren so nett zu uns. Wir möchten uns bei Ihnen für Ihre Gastfreundlichkeit bedanken.*
You were so nice to us. We would like to thank you for your hospitality.

*Vielen Dank. Wir freuen uns, dass es Ihnen so gut gefallen hat.*
Thank you. We are glad that you liked it.

*Wir hatten einen schönen Abend/Tag. Vielen Dank.*
We had a nice evening/day. Thank you so much.

*Es war nett bei Ihnen.*
It was really nice (visiting you).

*Wir haben uns gefreut, Sie kennen zu lernen.*
It was nice to meet you.

*Kommen Sie bitte wieder vorbei, wenn Sie hier sind.*
Please stop by again if you are in the area.

*Kommen Sie uns jederzeit besuchen.*
Please come and see us anytime.

---

# ÜBUNGEN

1. *Setzen Sie die richtigen Präpositionen ein.*

   a. *Wir haben uns _____ Café getroffen und den Tagesplan besprochen.*
   b. *Um 10 Uhr morgens sollen wir _____ einer Tagung teilnehmen.*
   c. *Mittags treffen wir uns _____ Frau Bruck.*
   d. *Mein Kollege bemerkte, dass er _____ zweifelt, dass wir vor 14 Uhr schon wieder _____ Flughafen sein können.*
   e. *Wir sprachen _____ das Treffen um 13 Uhr.*
   f. *Ich vertraue Ihnen diese Unterlagen _____, bitte achten Sie darauf, dass Sie sie nicht verlieren.*
   g. *Kommen Sie, ich sehe Frau Bruck. Ich möchte mich _____ ihr unterhalten.*

**2.** *Übersetzen Sie.*

    a. We are waiting for the bus.
    b. We are looking forward to meeting you on Wednesday.
    c. I have doubts about his plans.
    d. We discussed the trip to Switzerland all weekend.
    e. We were annoyed about the delayed flight.

**3.** *Formulieren Sie die Sätze als Vermutung. Benutzen Sie „müssen" in a bis c, und „können" in d bis f.*

BEISPIEL: *Sie hat viel Geld verdient.*
          *Sie müsste viel Geld verdient haben.*

    a. *Der Bus ist angekommen.* (add *längst*)
    b. *Das Flugzeug ist gelandet.*
    c. *Er kann gut deutsch.*
    d. *Das kann sein.*
    e. *Er ist schon nach Hause gegangen.*
    f. *Frau Bruck ist da.*

**4.** *Setzen Sie die Partizipien der Gegenwart und der Vergangenheit ein.*

    a. *Der Zug hat sich verspätet. Wir haben unseren Flug verpasst.*
    *Wegen des _____ Zug haben wir unseren Flug verpasst.*
    b. *Zum Fasching haben wir unsere Gesichter bemalt. Dann sind wir zur Party gegangen.*
    *Wir sind mit _____ Gesichtern zur Faschingsparty gegangen.*
    c. *Der Herr, der verkleidet ist, sitzt im Sessel.*
    *Der _____ Herr sitzt im Sessel.*
    d. *Die Gäste sind gerade zurückgekehrt. Sie sind auf ihr Zimmer gegangen.*
    *Die _____ Gäste sind auf ihr Zimmer gegangen.*
    e. *Die Musiker stehen auf der Straße und singen. Lasst uns hinuntergehen!*
    *Lasst uns zu den _____ Musikern auf der Straße hinuntergehen!*
    f. *Wir müssen in den Monaten, die folgen, hart arbeiten.*
    *Wir müssen in den _____ Monaten hart arbeiten.*

# ZWEITE WIEDERHOLUNGSAUFGABE

**1.** *Bilden Sie Sätze mit dem Infinitiv.*

   a. *Warum sind Sie nicht gekommen?*
      *Ich habe mich entschlossen, _____ (zu Hause/bleiben).*
   b. *Warum hat er angerufen?*
      *Er hat angerufen, _____ (sich entschuldigen).*
   c. *Wissen Sie, wo Herr Berger ist?*
      *Nein, er ist weggefahren, _____ (eine Adresse hinterlassen).*
   d. *Warum hat Sie das teurere Sofa gekauft?*
      *Sie hat es gekauft, _____ (nicht länger/nach einem
      anderen/suchen/müssen).*
   e. *Warum fliegt Frau Schwert nach Hannover?*
      *Frau Schwert fliegt nach Hannover, _____ (treffen/die neuen
      Kunden).*
   f. *Warum ärgert sich der Kellner?*
      *Ein Gast hat das Restaurant verlassen, _____ (zahlen).*
   g. *Wieso musste Sylvia ins Krankenhaus?*
      *(vorher/zum Arzt gehen) _____, hat sie gewartet, bis sie so
      krank war, dass sie nicht mehr arbeiten konnte.*

**2.** *Setzen Sie das Folgende in die indirekte Rede.*

   a. *Herr Meier fragte: „Wo sind denn die Akten geblieben?"*
   b. *Frau Ranke sagte: „Ich habe sie Ihnen doch schon gestern auf den
      Tisch gelegt."*
   c. *Herr Meier antwortete: „Ich habe die Akten nie gesehen."*
   d. *Herr Wallner sagte: „Tut mir leid. Ich habe die Akten vom Tisch
      genommen, um etwas nachzusehen."*
   e. *Herr Meier sagte: „Das nächste Mal müssen Sie mir Bescheid sagen,
      wenn Sie meine Akten brauchen."*

**3.** *Setzen Sie „lassen", „bekommen", „werden", „lohnen", „leisten", „gehen"
ein.*

   a. *Dieses Haus ist zu teuer. Das können wir uns nicht _____.*
   b. *Wieviel _____ ich für eine Uhr aus dem letzten Jahrhundert?*
   c. *_____ sie denn noch?*
   d. *Wenn sie kaputt ist, _____ sich der Kauf nicht. So ein altes Stück
      _____ sich nicht reparieren.*
   e. *Sie können sie doch schätzen _____.*
   f. *Dann _____ Sie warten müssen, bis ich den Bericht vom
      Gutachter _____ habe.*

**4.** *Setzen sie den richtigen bestimmten Artikel oder das richtige Relativpronomen ein.*

   a. *Wir fuhren wegen _____ Auftrag nach Bern, um mit _____ Kunden zu sprechen.*

   b. *Entlang _____ Straße führt ein Radfahrweg.*

   c. *Wir parkten neben _____ Haus.*

   d. *Gegenüber _____ Bank ist ein Taxistand.*

   e. *Der Auftrag _____ Bern _____ Firma liegt auf _____ Tisch.*

   f. *Das Auto, _____ neben _____ das Fahrrad steht, gehört meinem Kollegen.*

   g. *Der Herr, _____ Visitenkarte ich Ihnen gestern gab, hat gerade angerufen.*

**5.** *Formulieren Sie die folgenden Sätze als Wunsch.*

BEISPIEL: *Ich bin nicht mehr jung.*
          *Wenn ich doch nur jung wäre!*

   a. *Er hat immer noch nicht auf unseren Anruf geantwortet.*

   b. *Wir sind seit 2 Wochen zurück aus der Schweiz. (doch noch)*

   c. *Ich weiß nicht, wo ich mein Auto geparkt habe.*

   d. *Er hat nicht genug Geld. (Er wünschte, _____.)*

**6.** *Setzen Sie das Folgende ins Passiv.*

   a. *Er hat 400 Kataloge bestellt.*

   b. *Wir haben vor drei Jahren zwei neue Häuser gebaut.*

   c. *Wir liefern die Bestellung am 17.05.*

   d. *Der Fahrer holte die Gäste um 11 Uhr vom Hotel ab.*

   e. *Der Kundendienst repariert den Videorecorder.*

   f. *Sie hat die Reparatur ihres Autos beauftragt.*

**7.** *Setzen Sie die folgenden Sätze in die richtige Zeit.*

   a. *Im Jahre 1578 _____ die Stadtmauer _____ (bauen).*

   b. *Wussten Sie, dass die Stadt zuvor mehrere Male _____ (angreifen)?*

   c. *Da _____ (müssen) man ja etwas tun, sonst _____ ständig Krieg _____ (sein).*

   d. *Früher _____ (sein) dies eine sehr erfolgreiche Handelsstadt.*

   e. *Seit wann _____ (sein) diese Stadt nicht mehr so erfolgreich?*

   f. *Oh, das _____ (lassen) sich schlecht sagen. Ich _____ (denken), ab dem 17. Jahrhundert _____ (werden) der Handel immer weniger.*

   g. *Wovon _____ (leben) die Stadt heute?*

   h. *Hauptsächlich vom Fremdenverkehr. _____ (sein) Sie schon einmal in dieser Gegend?*

   i. *Nein, wir _____ (machen) bisher immer Urlaub in Bayern _____.*

**8.** *Setzen Sie die folgenden Sätze in den Konjunktiv II.*

    a. *Er fragte, ob jemand _____ (anrufen).*

    b. *Wenn ich das _____ (wissen), _____ ich nie dorthin _____ (fahren).*

    c. *Es kann nichts passiert sein, sonst _____ wir davon _____ (erfahren).*

    d. *Das _____ (sein) wirklich lustig _____, wenn du uns _____ (überrascht haben).*

    e. *Er sagte, er _____ noch nie in den Alpen _____ (sein).*

**9.** *Setzen Sie die richtige Präposition ein.*

    a. *Ich freue mich sehr _____ unser Treffen.*

    b. *Frau Zell sagte mir, Sie seien inzwischen sehr bekannt _____ die hervorragende Qualität Ihrer Produkte.*

    c. *Ich bin seit einigen Jahren interessiert _____ ihrer Ware.*

    d. *Ich hoffe, dass wir _____ unserem kommenden Treffen _____ Preise sprechen können.*

    e. *Vielen Dank _____ Ihre freundliche Einladung.*

    f. *_____ freundlichen Grüßen.*

**10.** *Bilden Sie Substantive.*

| | |
|---|---|
| a. *besprechen* | j. *schön* |
| b. *mitteilen* | k. *alt* |
| c. *angeben* | l. *krank* |
| d. *anzeigen* | m. *fleißig* |
| e. *verkaufen* | n. *wichtig* |
| f. *reklamieren* | o. *schnell* |
| g. *bedienen* | p. *reich* |
| h. *gehen* | q. *sauber* |
| i. *überweisen* | |

# LESESTÜCK 4

*Die Schwaben[2] sind schon ein ganz besonderes Volk. Sie sind berüchtigt[3] für vieles, unter anderem[4] für den schwäbischen[5] Dialekt, der mit Vorliebe[6] -le ans Ende aller Substantive hängt, und natürlich für den schwäbischen Fleiß[7], der sich am besten im schwäbischen Slogan »Schaffe, schaffe, Häusle baue«[8] zusammenfassen lässt. Und dann war da noch die Sache mit der sprichwörtlichen[9] schwäbischen Sauberkeit.*

*Jeden Samstag Vormittag kann man die Schwaben, egal ob jung oder alt, dabei beobachten, wie sie das Trottoir[10]—zu deutsch: der Gehweg[11]—kehren[12], den Hauseingang[13] wischen[14] und das Treppenhaus[15] bohnern[16]. Dieses für die meisten anderen Deutschen etwas seltsam[17] anmutende[18] Ritual nennt sich Kehrwoche, und ist seit über 500 Jahren gesetzlich verankert[19].*

*Mit einer städtischen Verordnung[20] in Stuttgart im 15. Jahrhundert fing alles an. »Damit die Stadt rein erhalten wird, soll jeder seinen Mist[21] alle Woche hinausführen, jeder seinen Winkel[22] alle 14 Tage, doch nur bei Nacht, sauber ausräumen und an der Straße nie einen anlegen. Wer kein Sprechhaus[23] hat, muss den Unrat in den Bach[24] tragen.« Was nicht in den Bach durfte, musste vor die Tore der Stadt getragen werden. Nur in Kriegszeiten[25], wenn es nicht sicher war, vor die Tore der Stadt zu treten, durfte der Mist innerhalb der Stadtmauern[26] gelagert werden. Mit der Zeit wurde diese Tradition immer mehr perfektioniert[27], bis 1714 die erste organisierte Müllabfuhr[28] entstand. Hatten sich bisher Männer und Frauen gemeinsam um den Dreck[29] gekümmert[30], so war das Kehren jetzt allein Sache der Frau, während Angestellte der Stadt, meistens Männer, den Müll vor die Stadttore transportierten.*

*Da die Schwaben auch sehr gewissenhafte[31] Menschen sind, setzten sie bald einen Gassensäuberungsinspektor[32] ein, der prüfte[33], ob auch ordentlich gekehrt wurde. Wenn es etwas zu bemängeln[34] gab, ging der Inspektor zum Hausbesitzer[35] und schimpfte[36], der wiederum ging zum Mieter und schimpfte, und der wiederum schimpfte mit seiner Frau. Wie so vieles hat sich auch diese werte[37] Tradition erhalten.*

*Wer gerade dran ist[38] mit der Kehrwoche—Kehrwoche wird in einem Haus mit mehr als einer Partei im Rotationsverfahren durchgeführt—kann sicher sein, dass die Mitbewohner im Haus peinlichst[39] darauf achten, dass auch das letzte Staubkörnle[40] sauber weggekehrt wird. Wenn nicht, kann es schon einmal sein, dass auch heute noch geschimpft wird. Schließlich ist die Kehrwoche fester Bestandteil[41] einer jeden Hausordnung im Mietvertrag, und somit selbst heute noch gesetzlich sanktioniert.*

*Tja, die Kehrwoche ist halt einfach eine ernste Angelegenheit[42] im Ländle[43], auch wenn die meisten anderen Deutschen darüber heimlich schmunzeln[44].*

| | | |
|---|---|---|
| 1. | *die Kehrwoche* | weekly cleaning |
| 2. | *der Schwabe* | Swabian |
| 3. | *berüchtigt* | notorious |
| 4. | *unter anderem* | among other things |
| 5. | *schwäbisch* | Swabian (adj.) |
| 6. | *die Vorliebe* | preference |
| 7. | *der Fleiß* | efficiency, industriousness |
| 8. | *Schaffe, schaffe, Häusle baue* | Work, work, building a house. |
| 9. | *sprichwörtlich* | proverbial |
| 10. | *das Trottoir* | sidewalk |
| 11. | *der Gehweg* | sidewalk |
| 12. | *kehren* | to brush, to sweep up |
| 13. | *der Hauseingang* | house entrance |
| 14. | *wischen* | to clean |
| 15. | *das Treppenhaus* | (public) staircase |
| 16. | *bohnern* | to wax (floors) |
| 17. | *seltsam* | strange, odd, weird |
| 18. | *anmuten* | to appear, to seem |
| 19. | *gesetzlich verankert* | regulated by law |
| 20. | *die Verordnung* | regulation, order |
| 21. | *der Mist* | (fig.) dirt; (lit.) dung, manure |
| 22. | *der Winkel* | corner, spot; (math.) angle |
| 23. | *das Sprechhaus* | toilet (antiquated) |
| 24. | *der Bach* | brook, stream |
| 25. | *die Kriegszeiten* | wartimes |
| 26. | *die Stadtmauern* | city fortification, city walls |
| 27. | *perfektionieren* | to perfect |
| 28. | *die Müllabfuhr* | garbage collection |
| 29. | *der Dreck* | dirt, waste |
| 30. | *sich kümmern um* | to take care of, to mind |
| 31. | *gewissenhaft* | conscientious |
| 32. | *der Gassensäuberungsinspektor* | alley cleanup inspector |
| 33. | *prüfen* | to check, to examine |
| 34. | *bemängeln* | to find fault with, to criticize |
| 35. | *der Hausbesitzer* | property owner |
| 36. | *schimpfen* | to scold |
| 37. | *wert* | worth, precious |
| 38. | *dran sein* | to be one's turn |
| 39. | *peinlichst* | meticulously, painstakingly |
| 40. | *das Staubkörnle* | speck of dust |
| 41. | *fester Bestandteil sein* | to be part and parcel |
| 42. | *die Angelegenheit* | matter |
| 43. | *das Ländle* | Swabian diminutive for *das Land* mostly used jokingly only for Baden-Württemberg |
| 44. | *schmunzeln* | to smirk, to smile |

# LÖSUNGEN (ANSWER KEY)

## LEKTION 1

1. a. *Wer hat das Essen gekocht?*   b. *Was hat Kevin Milton mitgebracht?*
c. *Wo ist die Frauenkirche?*   d. *Wann ist Kevin Milton angekommen?*
e. *Wieviele Gäste sind eingeladen?*   f. *Wie heißt die Bekannte der
Obermeiers?*   g. *Was besucht Kevin Milton in München?*   h. *Warum
kann Herr Milton nicht lange in München bleiben?*
2. a. *Ich ging gestern zum Marienplatz.*   b. *Nach einer halben Stunde kam
Bernd.*   c. *Wir gingen am Viktualienmarkt essen.*   d. *Wir fuhren dann
ins Büro und kauften auf dem Weg Blumen für seine Frau.*   e. *Abends
ging ich zu den Obermeiers und gab Anna die Blumen.*
3. a. *Er ist mit dem Zug nach Regensburg gefahren.*   b. *Abends hat er sich mit
einem Geschäftskollegen getroffen.*   c. *Sie sind spazieren gegangen.*   d. *Er
hat die vielen alten Häuser in der Innenstadt gesehen.*   e. *Am nächsten
Tag hat er den Dom besucht und Geschenke für seine Freunde gekauft.*
4. a. *Ich war letztes Jahr nicht in Regensburg.*   b. *Er hat Herrn Obermeier
nicht angerufen.*   c. *Waren Sie nicht in München?*   d. *Wir sind nicht
ins Museum gegangen.*   e. *Bayern ist nicht klein.*   f. *Ich fahre nicht
gerne mit dem Auto.*   g. *Die gothische Kathedrale gefällt mir nicht.*
5. a. *kein*   b. *keine*   c. *Kein*   d. *keine*   e. *keinen*   f. *kein*   g. *kein*
6. 1g/2e/3f/4h/5a/6d/7c/8b

## LEKTION 2

1. a. *Er will den Vermieter treffen, aber er hat die Adresse vergessen.*   b. *Ich
habe eine Wohnung gefunden und kann sofort einziehen.*   c. *Ich wohne
nicht in der Stadt, sondern auf dem Lande.*   d. *Er kann mit dem Taxi
fahren oder den Bus nehmen.*   e. *Sie sucht eine Wohnung in Heidelberg,
denn sie wird dort (or in Heidelberg) studieren.*   f. *Herr Walker hat eine
Wohnung gefunden, aber er muss zwei Wochen warten, bis sie fertig ist.*
2. a. *Ich werde 2006 wahrscheinlich ein Haus kaufen.*   b. *Er ist morgen in
Bonn.*   c. *Wann kommst du zurück?*   d. *Er wird wahrscheinlich im
Dezember in die Staaten zurückfliegen.*   e. *Ich glaube, ich werde am
Wochenende im Hotel sein.*
3. a. *Ich werde viele Möbel brauchen. Ich weiß nicht, wo ich Möbel billig
kaufen kann, aber Herr Meier wird mir helfen. Vielleicht werde ich
hier lange wohnen. Ich werde einen Kühlschrank brauchen, denn die
Wohnung hat keinen. Die Kaution beträgt 2.000 EUR, aber Herr Schaller
gibt mir einen Mietvertrag für 6 Monate und sagt, dass er nur 1.000 EUR
berechnen wird. Er wird mir einen Schlüssel für die Wohnung geben und
einen Hausschlüssel. Wir werden dich in der neuen Wohnung besuchen.*
4. a. *ersten*   b. *siebten*   c. *fünfzehnte*   d. *dritte*   e. *dreißigste*   f. *elfte*
g. *sechsten*

5. a. *altes*   b. *neue, schöne*   c. *blaue*   d. *moderne*   e. *weißen, langen*
6. a. *Ein alter Mann stand an einer großen Ecke.*   b. *Vor einem kleinen Fenster stand ein weißer Kühlschrank*   c. *In modernen Häusern wohnt er nicht lange, er lebt gerne in einer alten Wohnung.*

## LEKTION 3

1. a. *Nein, Daueraufträge sind gebührenfrei.*   b. *Herr Walker wird für einige Monate in Frankfurt bleiben.*   c. *Er kann in London mit Euroschecks bezahlen.*   d. *Er will jeden Monat Geld auf sein Konto in den USA überweisen.*
2. a. *Ich möchte ein Girokonto eröffnen.*   b. *Ich möchte etwas Geld an meine Familie in den USA schicken.*   c. *Ich möchte 500,75 EUR an eine Firma in Hamburg überweisen.*   d. *Können Sie mir einen Überweisungsauftrag geben?*   e. *Ich möchte $600 in Euro wechseln und das Geld auf mein Konto einzahlen.*   f. *Können Sie mir meinen Kontostand sagen?*   g. *Darf ich Ihren Pass sehen?*
3. a. *Ich kann Ihnen beim Ausfüllen des Formulars helfen.*   b. *Er soll morgen zum Arzt gehen.*   c. *Sie kann heute nachmittag schon Geld von ihrem neuen Konto abheben.*   d. *Darf mein Kollege den Überweisungsauftrag unterschreiben?*   e. *Herr Meier und Herr Walker wollen zur Bank gehen.*   f. *Ich muss schon wieder 500 EUR für mein Auto bezahlen.*
4. a. *Zusätzlich bekommen Sie noch eine Euroscheckkarte.*   b. *Jetzt weiß ich, wo die Bank ist, denn Herr Meier hat mir den Weg gezeigt.*   c. *Gestern war ich nicht im Büro.*   d. *Selbstverständlich kann er Geld abheben, er hat doch 500 EUR eingezahlt.*   e. *Leider muss ich unsere Verabredung verschieben, mein Auto ist kaputt.*
5. a. *Wenn Carola mir heute abend den Scheck bringt, kann ich morgen zur Bank gehen und den Scheck einzahlen.*   b. *Wenn mein Gehalt morgen auf meinem Konto ist, kann ich Dir die 300 EUR zurückzahlen.*   c. *Falls ich ihn morgen treffe, sage ich ihm Bescheid.*   d. *Wenn Sie nach Paris fahren, müssen Sie mir ein Photo von der Notre Dame mitbringen.*   e. *Wenn Herr Walker das Geld rechtzeitig in die USA schickt, kommt es pünktlich an.*   f. *Falls die Bankgebühren sehr niedrig sind, möchte ich auch ein Konto bei der Bank eröffnen.*   g. *Vorausgesetzt, dass sein Gehalt rechtzeitig eingeht, bieten wir ihm einen Überziehungskredit von 8.000 EUR an.*   h. *Unter der Bedingung, dass du um 23 Uhr wieder zurück bist, kannst du mein Auto leihen.*

## LEKTION 4

1. a. *Die Lampe, die hinter dem grünen Sessel steht, ist sehr alt.*   b. *Der Auktionär, der ein Büro am Opernplatz hat, hat viele schöne Uhren./ Der Auktionär, der viele schöne Uhren hat, hat ein Büro am Opernplatz.*   c. *Die Sessel, in denen ich sehr gerne sitze, sind grün.*   d. *Die Wohnung,*

322

*in die ich gerne einziehen möchte, liegt sehr zentral.* e. *Herr Hansen, der kein Geld hat, will im Winter Ski fahren./Herr Hansen, der im Winter Ski fahren will, hat kein Geld.* f. *Das Hotel, das billig ist, liegt weit weg von den Sehenswürdigkeiten.*
2. a. *kleiner* b. *breiter* c. *am größten* d. *größeres* e. *weniger* f. *kleiner* g. *meisten*
3. a. *mehr* b. *gerne* c. *lieber* d. *besser* e. *hässlicher* f. *am besten* g. *schneller* h. *höchsten*
4. a. *Das Buch ist genauso teuer wie die Uhr.* b. *Christian hat viel mehr Antiquitäten als ich.* c. *Das antike Sofa kostet viel mehr als die Uhr./ Die Uhr kostet viel weniger als das Sofa.* d. *Kirsten hat (letzten Monat) genauso viel Geld verdient wie ich.* e. *Die Armbanduhr ist viel teurer als die Kette, aber sie ist schöner.*
5. a. *Sie war gestern bei einem Antiquitätenhändler.* b. *Ich muss zur Arbeit gehen.* c. *Wir sind schon zum siebten Mal hier.* d. *Was hast du mit ihm verhandelt?* e. *Ihr habt uns seit eurem Urlaub nicht angerufen.*
6. a. *Das* b. *Den* c. *die* d. *den* e. *Dem, dem*

## LEKTION 5

1. a. *Warum ist Frau Keller zum Hotel Stern gegangen? Sie hat einen Termin für ein Vorstellungsgespräch.* b. *Was hat sie in Dortmund gemacht? Sie hat in einem Hotel gearbeitet.* c. *Wo hat sie in Paris gearbeitet? Sie hat im Hotel du Nord gearbeitet.*
2. a. *Ihnen* b. *mir* c. *Ihnen* d. *mir* e. *ihr*
3. a. *dich* b. *uns* c. *sich* d. *sich, sich* e. *euch* f. *mir* g. *sich* h. *sich* i. *dir*
4. a. *Wenn* b. *Als* c. *Als* d. *Als* e. *Wenn*
5. a. *Sobald er das Abendessen gekocht hat, geht er ins Theater.* b. *Während ich auf meine Eltern warte, lese ich ein Buch.* c. *Sobald wir drei Bewerber ausgewählt haben, rufen wir Sie an.* d. *Ich war schon im Kino, bevor der Film anfing.* e. *Nachdem das Vorstellungsgespräch beendet war, ging ich eine Tasse Tee trinken.*

## LEKTION 6

1. a. *diesem* b. *Diese* c. *diese* d. *diese* e. *diesem* f. *Diese* g. *Dieses* h. *Manche* i. *Welches* j. *jedes* k. *Solche*
2. a. *Das Haus wurde zwischen 1975 und 1977 gebaut.* b. *Das Haus wurde Marina und Gary gezeigt.* c. *Die Kirchen aus dem Mittelalter werden restauriert.* d. *Um 20 Uhr wird die Tür geschlossen.* e. *Das Haus in Berlin wurde verkauft.*
3. a. *Heute hat niemand die Kirche besucht.* b. *Jemand, der Architektur studiert, möchte das Bauhaus-Archiv sehen.* c. *Niemand wusste, wo der Marktplatz war.* d. *Hat niemand angerufen?* e. *Hat jemand den Studenten gesehen?* f. *Hat es dir niemand gesagt?*

4. a. *Die alten Häuser am Marktplatz wurden von der Firma Schobel & Co. gestrichen.* b. *Das Alte Museum wurde von Schinkel gebaut.* c. *Gary wurde von Marina durch Berlin geführt.* d. *Der Bauwettbewerb wurde vom Architektenbüro Schmitt gewonnen.* e. *Die Ausstellung wurde von vielen Touristen besucht.* f. *Viele Stadtpläne wurden von uns gekauft.*
5. a. *Es gibt viele Bäume in Berlin.* b. *Es gab Wildschweine im Tiergarten./Es gab im Tiergarten Wildschweine.* c. *Es gab vor dem 2. Weltkrieg in Berlin viele alte Gebäude.* d. *Es gibt viele Museen in Berlin.* e. *Es gab im lezten Jahrhundert hier einen Markt./Im letzten Jahrhundert gab es hier einen Markt.* f. *Es gibt viele Architekten in Berlin.*
6. a. *Die Kirche von Schinkel ist dahinten.* b. *Der Leierkastenmann steht da drüben.* c. *Der Bus hält da vorne.* d. *Stellen Sie sich dahinter!*

## LEKTION 7

1. a. *Schreib(e) einen Brief an Herrn Weilandt in Hannover!* b. *Sagt ihm um 18 Uhr Bescheid!* c. *Setz dich auf die Bank und warte bis um 4 auf mich!* d. *Stellen Sie die Kisten unter den Tisch!* e. *Vergiss den Hund nicht!* f. *Legt die Bücher auf den Tisch!*
2. a. *dem/das* b. *dem/den* c. *der/dem* d. *die* e. *der*
3. a. *Bitte stellen Sie die Kisten in das linke Büro.* b. *Hat er das Bild schon in den Konferenzraum gehängt?* c. *Der Fernseher steht vor dem Fenster.* d. *Bitte setzen Sie sich, Herr Klimke.* e. *Jens liegt auf dem Boden. Er ist müde.* f. *Legen Sie die Bücher auf den Schreibtisch.* g. *Der LKW steht vor dem Haus.* h. *Jens stellte das rote Auto neben den LKW.*

## LEKTION 8

1. a. *Wir fuhren durch die Stadt.* b. *Um 20 Uhr kamen wir in Luzern an.* c. *Wir konnten das Hotel ohne den Stadtplan nicht finden.* d. *Wir können hier für SF 120 übernachten.* e. *Wir sind immer um das Hotel herum gegangen und haben ein Restaurant gesucht.* f. *Um 22 Uhr gingen wir zum Hotel zurück.* g. *Ich wollte in Luzern bleiben, aber mein(e) Freund(in) war gegen die Idee. (gegen den Gedanken).*
2. a. *seine* b. *Unser* c. *Ihre* d. *meine, meinen* e. *euer* f. *ihren* g. *deine*
3. a. *irgendwer* b. *irgendwo* c. *irgendwann* d. *Irgendwann* e. *Irgendwo*
4. a. Was anyone here? b. Yes, I put the note (piece of paper) somewhere. c. When you find it sometime, let me know. d. I wrote to the Hotel Interlake sometime. e. The letter has to be someplace/somewhere.

## LEKTION 9

1. a. *Miriam Wallstätter kommt aus Wien und ist Regisseurin (von Beruf).* b. *Frau Wallstätter und Herr Clausen haben sich auf der Berlinale*

*getroffen.* c. *Herr Clausen ist Filmkritiker und lebt in Hamburg.*
d. *Dieter Hellberg ist ein Kollege von Herrn Clausen./Dieter Hellberg ist
ein Filmemacher geworden.* e. *Dieter Hellberg ist nicht bei den
Filmfestspielen, weil er viel um die Ohren hat./weil er viel beschäftigt
ist./weil er einen Film dreht./Dieter Hellberg macht eine deutsch-
französische Koproduktion fürs Fernsehen.* f. *In dem Film von Frau
Wallstätter geht es um die Mafia, Interpol und Plutonium Schmuggel.*
2. a. *Beim Zuschauen bin ich eingeschlafen.* b. *Nach dem Spielen gehen
die Kinder nach Hause.* c. *Vor dem Essen geht er in den Garten.*
d. *Vom Laufen wirst du müde.* e. *Beim Telefonieren ging sie in die
Küche.* f. *Nach dem Schwimmen legen wir uns in die Sonne.*
3. a. While watching I fell asleep. b. After playing the kids go home.
c. Before eating he goes into the garden. d. From running/walking
you become tired. e. While on the telephone she walked into the
kitchen. f. After swimming we'll lie in the sun.
4. a. *Obwohl er dich zur Biennale eingeladen hat, kannst du nicht
hinfahren.* b. *Ich habe kein Geld. Trotzdem möchte ich gern nach
Cannes fahren.* c. *Obgleich der Regisseur keinen Preis gewonnen hat,
hat er gefeiert.* d. *Obwohl die Schauspielerin sehr schön war, fand sie
keine Rollen.* e. *Obwohl Gerd schon seit 5 Tagen weg ist, habe ich seinen
Blumen immer noch kein Wasser gegeben.* f. *Wir haben unseren
Stadtplan vergessen. Trotzdem sind wir weiter durch Cannes gegangen
und haben das Kino gesucht.*
5. a. *Das Gute ist stärker als das Böse.* b. *Der Schwarzhaarige bekam die
Rolle.* c. *Die Schlechten gewinnen selten.* d. *Das Neueste ist immer am
interessantesten.*

## LEKTION 10

1. a. *Je langsamer das Auto fährt, desto später kommt er an.* b. *Ich habe
sowohl Tee als auch Kaffee gekauft.* c. *Er hat drei Autos sowie zwei
Fahrräder.* d. *Je länger du wartest, desto teurer werden die Aktien.*
e. *Sobald ich von Ihnen höre, kann ich mich entscheiden.* f. *Je älter die
Ware, desto schwieriger der Verkauf.*
2. a. *angekommen.* b. *ausgestiegen* c. *vorgestellt* d. *unternommen*
e. *eingeschlafen* f. *aufgestanden*
3. a. *Wir kamen gestern an.* b. *Wir stiegen an der Börse aus.* c. *Sie
stellten sich erst einmal vor.* d. *Unternahmt Ihr schon etwas?* e. *Nein,
wir schliefen sofort ein.* f. *Ich stand um 10 Uhr auf.*
4. a. *Es hängt vom Investmentberater ab.* b. *Wir nehmen uns viel für das
nächste Jahr vor.* c. *Frau Keller missachtet das Gesetz.* d. *Bitte rufen
Sie an und beschreiben (Sie) das Haus.* e. *Sie geht aus und sieht sich
die Altstadt an.* f. *Frau Albert bietet Herrn Gersen Aktien an.*

1. a. *alte*   b. *schöne, grüne/kleine*   c. *kaltes*   d. *heißen*   e. *moderne,*
*antike*   f. *viele kleine/großen, kleinen/verschiedene*   g. *flachen*
h. *reichen/zweiten*
2. a. *sind/haben*   b. *hat*   c. *ist/hat*   d. *haben/sind*   e. *Hat*   f. *haben*
g. *Seid*   h. *haben/sind*
3. a. *Die Bücher lagen auf dem Tisch.*   b. *Die Uhren sind zu teuer.*   c. *Die*
*Flüge nach Mailand sind gestrichen worden.*   d. *Häuser mit kleinen*
*Fenstern gefallen mir nicht.*   e. *Er hat unsere Treffen abgesagt.*   f. *Die*
*Überweisungsaufträge wurden erst gestern abgegeben.*   g. *Ich ziehe mich*
*immer gut an, wenn ich zu Vorstellungsgesprächen gehe.*
4. a. *Möchten*   b. *möchte*   c. *Darf/Kann*   d. *können/muss*   e. *Wollen*
f. *soll/muss*   g. *müssen*
5. a. *Ich werde Ski fahren lernen.*   b. *Er wird bestimmt schon angerufen*
*haben.*   c. *Wir werden uns bald wiedersehen.*   d. *Bis dahin wird alles*
*fertig sein.*   e. *Er wird im nächsten Jahr wahrscheinlich mehr Geld*
*haben.*   f. *Sie wird den Koffer vorbeibringen.*   g. *Sie wird wohl nicht*
*mehr kommen.*
6. a. *der*   b. *die/dem/den*   c. *den/den*   d. *den/der*   e. *den/den*
f. *die/der/das/dem/die*
7. a. *mich/mir*   b. *mich/Sie/meinen*   c. *Ihnen/Mein/mir/seine/mir*
8. a. *Nehmen Sie bitte Platz!*   b. *Legen Sie die Bücher auf den Tisch!*
c. *Stellen Sie die Bücher ins Regal!*   d. *Stellen Sie den Fernseher auf den*
*Tisch!*   e. *Hängen Sie die Bilder an die Wand!*
9. a. *Er hat den Schreibtisch, der mir am besten gefiel, verkauft./Den*
*Schreibtisch, der mir am besten gefiel, hat er verkauft.*   b. *Seit wir im*
*letzten Jahr segeln waren, malt meine Tochter nur noch Segelboote.*   c. *Als*
*sie Rom besuchten, lernten sie die Familie Rossa kennen.*   d. *Wenn du zur*
*Arbeit gehst, musst du die Tür abschließen.*   e. *Anette und Jörg Schumann,*
*die in Mannheim leben, fahren jedes Jahr nach München und besuchen die*
*Obermeiers.*   f. *Der Herr mit den braunen Haaren, der gerade ein Konto*
*eröffnet hat und für die DUS Trading in Frankfurt arbeitet, kommt aus*
*Boston.*   g. *Sobald das Geld da ist, gebe ich Ihnen Bescheid.*
10. a. *Bitte legen Sie ab.*   b. *Er unterschreibt den Brief.*   c. *Bei unserem*
*Spaziergang durchquerten wir den Wald.*   d. *Wir haben uns für das*
*nächste Jahr viel vorgenommen.*   e. *Seit fünf Jahren hängt die Firma*
*stark von Exporten ab.*   f. *Wir sehen uns am Sonntag die*
*Gemäldeausstellung an.*   g. *Er stellt uns Herrn Neumeister vor.*

## LEKTION 11

1. a. *dass*   b. *dass*   c. *dass*   d. *Das*   e. *das*   f. *dass*   g. *Dass*   h. *das*
2. a. *Herr Riemers zeigt Adrian das Moderatenband, damit er sich ein*
*Bild vom deutschen Zuschauergeschmack machen kann.*   b. *Adrian*
*McCormick ist in Mainz, um beim ZDF zu arbeiten.*   c. *Herr Riemers*
*freut sich, mit Adrian McCormick zusammenzuarbeiten.*   d. *Es gibt*

*Austauschprogramme für Geschäftsleute, damit sie im Ausland Erfahrungen austauschen können.*

3. a. *Anstatt das Licht anzuschalten, machte sie den Fernseher aus.* b. *Werbung wird gezeigt, ohne die Sendungen zu unterbrechen.* c. *Um Deutsch zu lernen, fliegen wir nach Hannover.* d. *Er ging schlafen, ohne die Tür abzuschließen.* e. *Adrian ist nach Mainz gekommen, um beim ZDF zu arbeiten.* f. *Anstatt uns Schlösser anzusehen, haben wir geschlafen.* g. *Anstatt das Fernsehprogramm zu ändern, senden sie immer dasselbe.*

4. a. *Er entschloss sich, im Rahmen des Austauschprogramms nach Innsbruck zu gehen.* b. *Wir freuen uns, Sie in Freiburg zu sehen.* c. *Ich plane, Programmdirektor bei der ARD zu werden.* d. *Sie entschlossen sich, das Frühstücksprogramm zu ändern.* e. *Wir erwarten, das Programm bis Januar ändern zu können.* f. *Sie hoffen, das Programm bis April fertig zu haben.*

5. a. *Ich habe (mir) den Film immer wieder angesehen.* b. *Ich habe schon immer gewusst, dass er beim Fernsehen arbeiten will.* c. *Was? Er hat immer noch nicht angerufen. Ich warte schon seit Wochen.* d. *Sie fahren immer wieder nach Dänemark.* e. *Ich habe immer noch das gleiche Auto.* f. *Ihr Fernseher ist immer noch nicht repariert. Er ist seit 3 Wochen kaputt.*

## LEKTION 12

1. a. *Sie muss ihre Firma in Deutschland anmelden, damit sie ein Bankkonto aufmachen/eröffnen kann.* b. *Sie will ein Bankkonto aufmachen, weil sie nicht immer Geld nach Kiel schicken will.* c. *Frau Stettner bleibt in Wien, weil sie sich um den Stuttgarter Auftrag kümmern muss (da sie sich um den Stuttgarter Auftrag kümmern muss).*

2. a. *Warum fährst du immer wieder nach Wien?* b. *Weswegen möchten Sie lieber etwas anderes?* c. *Weshalb hast du Kopfschmerzen?* d. *Weswegen brauchen Sie unbedingt Kontakte in Kiel?* e. *Weshalb müssen wir dort hinfahren?*

3. a. *Wissen Sie, ob Herr Mierbach jetzt jede Woche einmal nach Wien fährt?* b. *Wissen Sie, ob die Bau- und Design Messe einmal pro Jahr stattfindet?* c. *Wissen Sie, wann der Brief angekommen ist?* d. *Wissen Sie, ob der Arzt den Kostenvoranschlag schon zuruückgeschickt hat?* e. *Wissen Sie, wo das Fax ist?* f. *Wissen Sie, ob der Vertrag datiert und unterschrieben ist?* g. *Wissen Sie, wieviel Geld Sylvia abgehoben hat?*

4. a. *Frau Stettner fährt nach Stuttgart, weil sie in Stuttgart einen Kunden hat.* b. *Da das Gebäude in Stuttgart nicht fertig ist, muss ich noch nicht an dem Design arbeiten.* c. *Hat er dir gesagt, warum er das glaubt?* d. *Was haben Sie gesagt?* e. *Herr Mierbach, wissen Sie, ob Frau Stettner zu Hause ist?* f. *Ich kann keinen Mietwagen nehmen, zumal ich meine Kreditkarte vergessen habe.*

5. a. *Da* b. *Deswegen/Deshalb* c. *weil/da* d. *Da* e. *Deswegen/Deshalb*

# LEKTION 13

1. a. *Wo war der Unfall? Der Unfall war an der Marburger Ecke Stoltzstraße.* b. *Wer sind die Zeugen? Die Zeugen sind ein Kioskverkäufer und ein Fußgänger.* c. *Was behauptet der Fahrer des BMW? Er behauptet, er sei nicht schneller as 40 km/h gefahren.* d. *Warum ist Marlies Schröder vermutlich schuld an dem Unfall? Marlies Schröder hat die Vorfahrt nicht beachtet.*
2. a. *Das Anwaltsbüro/Das Büro des Anwalts liegt außerhalb der Stadt.* b. *Die Gegendarstellung des Mandanten ist falsch.* c. *Der Kotflügel des Autos ist kaputt.* d. *Frau Schröders Auto ist neu.* e. *Außerhalb der Innenstadt sind die Anwälte billiger.* f. *Binnen eines Monats werden die Bäume geschnitten.*
3. a. *Er sagte, er wisse, dass der BMW Fahrer schneller als 40 gefahren sei.* b. *Wir fragten, ob er uns den Weg zeigen könne.* c. *Herr Hubert sagte, dass der Bericht des Gutachters noch nicht da sei.* d. *Der Mann am Kiosk sagte, dass er sich richtig erschrocken habe.* e. *Frau Schröder sagte, sie habe/hätte noch nie einen Unfall gehabt.* f. *Herr Hubert sagte, dass die Gegendarstellung richtig gewesen sei.*
4. a. *Der Angeklagte ist unschuldig/nicht schuldig.* b. *Ich bin mir nicht sicher.* c. *Der Zeuge hatte gelogen und wurde immer unsicherer.* d. *Das Ende des Gerichtsverfahrens ist ungewiss.* e. *Er zeigte sein Unwissen, indem er alles falsch beantwortete.*
5. a.3. *der Gerichtshof*/the court of law b.4. *die Zeugenaussage*/witness' statement c.1. *die Verkehrsordnung*/traffic regulations d.5. *der Rechtsweg*/legal steps e.6. *der Zeitungsbericht*/newspaper report f.7. *die Anwaltskanzlei*/the law office g.2. *das Verfassungsgericht*/the constitutional court

# LEKTION 14

1. a. *Es wurde bei sechs Angestellten eingebrochen./Bei sechs Angestellten wurde eingebrochen.* b. *Wertgegenstände/Wertsachen wurden entwendet./Es wurden Wertsachen/Wertgegenstände entwendet.* c. *Anita schreibt die Zeitungsberichte für Jens, weil Jens mit den Nachforschungen beschäftigt ist.* d. *Björn glaubt, dass die Einbrecher spionieren, weil die Gö-Bau keine gestohlenen Papiere angibt./ . . . , weil keine Papiere entwendet wurden./ . . . , weil die Einbrecher immer nur bei Führungskräften der Gö-Bau einbrechen.*
2. a. *zerriss* b. *versprochen/abgesagt* c. *sagte . . . aus* d. *trafen . . . ein/bemerkten*
3. a. *Hör bloß auf.* b. *Was ist los?* c. *Er ist sowieso (so oder so) nicht alt genug.* d. *Wir verließen um 1 Uhr morgens das Büro.* e. *Um 23 Uhr 45 trafen die letzten Nachrichten ein.* f. *Der Chef wünschte uns einen schönen Feierabend.* g. *Ich möchte den Einbruch bei der Polizei nachforschen.* h. *Bist du fertig?/Seid ihr fertig?*
4. a.—4 b.—6 c.—8 d.—1 e.—3 f.—7 g.—5. h.—2

# LEKTION 15

1. a. *Die Kaufleute setzten die Peise fest.*   b. *Obwohl wir den Besuch schon lange geplant hatten, mussten wir absagen.*   c. *Das Rathaus wurde umgebaut, darum waren der Bürgermeister und die Stadtverwaltung in ein anderes Haus gezogen.*   d. *Er sollte zuerst nach Kiel und dann nach Magdeburg fahren, obwohl er gar nicht soviel Zeit hatte.*   e. *Waren Sie in Schwerin?*   f. *Ich wusste nicht, wie weit die Stadt entfernt war.*   g. *Sie hatten uns vorher Bescheid gesagt. Darum blieben wir hier.*
2. a. *Früher haben hier die Schiffe angehalten, um die Waren zu liefern.*   b. *Jetzt gibt es das nicht mehr.*   c. *Wir sind 1950 von Friedrichshafen nach Helmstedt umgezogen.*   d. *Die Hansestadt wurde 1143 gegründet.*   e. *Die heutige Stadt wurde 1158 gegründet.*   f. *Da die Stadt oft zerstört wurde, musste sie neu gegründet werden.*   g. *Damals war sie eine der größten Städte Deutschlands.*
3. a. *Vor einigen Jahren besuchte ich das Handelsmuseum in Bremen.*   b. *Wir hatten ihn verloren, aber dann fanden wir ihn (wieder).*   c. *Die Kaufleute besuchten die ehemalige Fabrik.*   d. *Anfangs war es schwierig, aber jetzt ist es einfach.*   e. *Die Kaufleute kamen von überall nach Lübeck zu den Hanse Treffen.*
4. a. *die Schnelligkeit*   b. *die Leichtigkeit*   c. *die Freundlichkeit*   d. *die Sauberkeit*   e. *die Krankheit*   f. *die Gründung*   g. *die Beobachtung*   h. *die Richtigkeit*   i. *die Beschreibung*

# LEKTION 16

1. a. *Du solltest es bis jetzt gelernt haben./Du hättest es bis jetzt lernen sollen.*   b. *Ich wünschte, ich hätte das gestern gewusst.*   c. *Wenn ich nur ein Auto hätte, würde ich morgen nach Augsburg fahren.*   d. *Wenn wir letztes Jahr das Programm gekauft hätten, hätten wir diesen Fehler nicht gemacht.*   e. *Könnten Sie mir sagen, wo die Bushaltestelle ist?*   f. *Wenn ich nur wüsste, wo er ist.*   g. *Wenn ich nur gewusst hätte, wo er gewesen ist.*
2. a. *Sie käme früher/Sie würde früher kommen, wenn sie wüsste, wann die Schulung beginnt.*   b. *Wenn er um 18 Uhr nach Hause gegangen wäre, müsste er längst zu Hause sein.*   c. *Wenn die Firma kein Telefon hätte, gäbe es keine Aufträge/würde es kein Aufträge geben.*   d. *Herr Krüger sagte, sie sei nicht in der Schule gewesen/sie wäre nicht in der Schule gewesen.*   e. *Ich wusste, er würde nicht mehr nach Regensburg kommen.*   f. *Wenn ich Geld hätte, würde ich sofort ein Haus kaufen.*
3. a. *Wenn Sie doch nur Zeit hätten.*   b. *Ich wünschte, es wäre später.*   c. *Ich wünschte, wir hätten das Auto gekauft.*   d. *Wenn du doch nur zum Zahnarzt gegangen wärst.*   e. *Ich wünschte, es würde klappen.*   f. *Wenn ihr doch nur etwas gelernt hättet.*   g. *Ich wünschte, es würde nicht regnen.*
4. a. *Er hat einen Preis gewonnen. Folglich kann er seine Schulden bezahlen.*   b. *Sie hat die statistischen Angaben so verändert, dass man sie viel besser verstehen kann.*   c. *Sie hat 100% im Test bekommen.*

*Demnach hat sie alles richtig gemacht.* d. *Ich weiß, was wir machen müssen, damit wir noch rechtzeitig ankommen.* e. *Ihr verdient viel mehr Geld als wir. Demzufolge habt ihr recht gehabt mit eurer Idee.* f. *Gib ihm alle Unterlagen, damit er die Arbeit fertig stellen kann.* g. *Mir hat es sehr gut in Prag gefallen, deshalb fahre ich nächstes Jahr wieder hin.*

## LEKTION 17

1. a. *Würden Sie sagen, dass die Werbekampagne erfolgreich war?* b. *Das lässt sich leicht machen.* c. *Du hättest ihn vorher anrufen sollen.* d. *Du müsstest die Zeitung anrufen und die Anzeigen ändern (lassen).* e. *Er sollte den Text gestern nachmittag abgeben.*
2. a. *Er ließ die Anzeigen gestern buchen.* b. *Das lässt sich nicht sagen.* c. *Der Marketingchef ließ sich mit dem Auto zum Flughafen fahren.* d. *Lasst uns morgen weiter machen!* e. *Er lässt sich nichts sagen.* f. *Das lässt sich leicht machen.*
3. a. *lasse* b. *hört* c. *helfen* d. *lassen* e. *Lassen* f. *sehe*

## LEKTION 18

1. a. *Herr Köhler brachte das Diktiergerät zum Kundendienst, weil es nicht mehr funktionierte./weil es nicht mehr aufnimmt./weil es nicht mehr geht.* b. *Die Aufnahmevorrichtung ist lose./Es nimmt nicht mehr auf.* c. *Herr Köhler wollte kein neues Gerät kaufen, weil er es umtauschen wollte.* d. *Das Gerät muss zum Hersteller geschickt werden, damit der Hersteller nachsehen kann, ob das Gerät fehlerhaft ist.* e. *Herr Köhler wird in 4 bis 8 Wochen vom Hersteller hören.*
2. a. *Ich möchte mich beschweren.* b. *Sie möchte ihren Videorecorder umtauschen.* c. *Kannst du mein Auto reparieren?/Können Sie mein Auto reparieren?* d. *Mein Auto wird repariert.* e. *Ich möchte die Suppe zurückgehen lassen. Sie ist kalt.* f. *Wir möchten unsere Tickets (or: Karten) umtauschen.*
3. a. *hin* b. *her* c. *hin* d. *her* e. *hin* f. *her* g. *her*
4. a. *Entweder ist das Gerät kaputt gegangen, oder Sie haben es beschädigt.* b. *Ich habe Sie nicht nur angerufen, sondern Ihnen auch geschrieben.* c. *Das Gerät ist nicht nur kaputt, sondern die Batterien sind auch verbraucht.* d. *Weder ich noch jemand anders hat es benutzt.* e. *Entweder geben Sie mir ein besseres Gerät, oder ich beschwere mich.* f. *Wir sind weder nach Mannheim noch nach Ludwigshafen gefahren.*
5. a. *Ich weiß, warum das Gerät repariert werden muss.* b. *Er sagt, er habe den Recorder nicht fallen gelassen./nicht fallen lassen.* c. *Der Hersteller berichtet, das Gerät könne nicht mehr repariert werden.* d. *Frau Kreibach sagte zu ihrem Kollegen, dem anderen Kunden müsse/müsste geholfen werden.* e. *Der Kollege fragte, ob er der Frau helfen könne.*

## LEKTION 19

1. a. *für*  b. *auf*  c. *auf*  d. *mit*  e. *von*  f. *über*  g. *über*  h. *bei, für*
2. a. *Er sollte die Situation erklären, stattdessen hat er sie beschönigt.*
   b. *Die finanzielle Situation der Firma hat sich verschlimmert.*  c. *Das Wetter hat sich verschlechtert.*  d. *Mein Computer erleichtert meine Arbeit sehr.*  e. *Sie wohnen weit von einer Autobahn oder einem Bahnhof entfernt. Das erschwert den Transport erheblich.*
3. a. *grün*  b. *schwarz*  c. *rot*  d. *schwarz*  e. *rosarot*  f. *blau*

## LEKTION 20

1. a. *im*  b. *an*  c. *mit*  d. *daran, am*  e. *über*  f. *an*  g. *mit*
2. a. *Wir warten auf den Bus.*  b. *Wir freuen uns darauf, Sie am Mittwoch zu treffen./Wir freuen uns auf unser Treffen mit Ihnen am Mittwoch.*
   c. *Ich zweifele an seinen Plänen.*  d. *Wir diskutierten das ganze Wochenende über unsere Reise in die Schweiz.*  e. *Wir haben uns geärgert, dass der Flug verspätet war./Wir ärgerten uns über den verspäteten Flug.*
3. a. *Der Bus müsste längst angekommen sein.*  b. *Das Flugzeug müsste gelandet sein.*  c. *Er müsste gut deutsch können.*  d. *Das könnte sein.*
   e. *Er könnte nach Hause gegangen sein.*  f. *Frau Bruck könnte da sein.*
4. a. *verspäteten*  b. *bemalten*  c. *verkleidete*  d. *gerade zurück gekehrten*
   e. *singenden*  f. *folgenden*

## ZWEITE WIEDERHOLUNGSAUFGABE

1. a. *Ich habe mich entschlossen, zu Hause zu bleiben.*  b. *Er hat angerufen, um sich zu entschuldigen.*  c. *Er ist weggefahren, ohne eine Adresse zu hinterlassen.*  d. *Sie hat es gekauft, um nicht länger nach einem anderen suchen zu müssen.*  e. *Frau Schwert fliegt nach Hannover, um die neuen Kunden zu treffen.*  f. *Ein Gast hat das Restaurant verlassen, ohne zu zahlen.*  g. *Anstatt vorher zum Arzt zu gehen, hat sie gewartet, bis sie so krank war, dass sie nicht mehr arbeiten konnte.*
2. a. *Herr Meier fragte, wo die Akten geblieben seien.*  b. *Frau Ranke sagte, sie hätte sie ihm doch gestern schon auf den Tisch gelegt.*  c. *Herr Meier antwortete, dass er die Akten nie gesehen habe/hätte./Herr Meier antwortete, er habe/hätte die Akten nie gesehen.*  d. *Herr Wallner sagte, es täte ihm leid, er habe/hätte die Akten vom Tisch genommen, um etwas nachzusehen.*  e. *Herr Meier sagte, dass Herr Wallner ihm das nächste Mal Bescheid sagen müsse/müsste, wenn er seine Akten brauche.*
3. a. *Das können wir uns nicht leisten.*  b. *Wieviel bekomme ich für eine Uhr aus dem letzten Jahrhundert?*  c. *Geht sie denn noch?*  d. *Wenn sie kaputt ist, lohnt sich der Kauf nicht. So ein altes Stück lässt sich nicht reparieren.*  e. *Sie können sie doch schätzen lassen.*  f. *Dann werden Sie warten müssen, bis ich den Bericht vom Gutachter bekommen habe.*

4. a. *des Auftrages, dem*  b. *der*  c. *dem*  d. *der*  e. *der Berner, dem*
   f. *das, dem*  g. *dessen*
5. a. *Wenn er doch nur geantwortet hätte!/Wenn er doch nur antworten*
   *würde!*  b. *Wenn wir doch noch in der Schweiz wären!*  c. *Wenn ich nur*
   *wüsste, wo ich mein Auto geparkt habe.*  d. *Er wünschte, er hätte genug*
   *Geld.*
6. a. *400 Kataloge sind bestellt worden./400 Kataloge wurden bestellt.*
   b. *Vor drei Jahren wurden zwei neue Häuser (von uns) gebaut.*  c. *Die*
   *Bestellung wird am 17.05. geliefert.*  d. *Die Gäste wurden um 11 Uhr*
   *vom Hotel abgeholt.*  e. *Der Videorecorder wird (vom Kundendienst)*
   *repariert.*  f. *Die Reparatur ihres Autos wurde beauftragt./Die Reparatur*
   *ihres Autos ist beauftragt worden.*
7. a. *Im Jahre 1578 wurde die Stadtmauer gebaut.*  b. *Wussten Sie, dass die*
   *Stadt zuvor mehrere Male angegriffen wurde?/worden war?*  c. *Da*
   *musste man ja etwas tun, sonst wäre ständig Krieg gewesen.*  d. *Früher*
   *war dies eine sehr erfolgreiche Handelsstadt.*  e. *Seit wann ist diese Stadt*
   *nicht mehr so erfolgreich?*  f. *Oh, das lässt sich schlecht sagen. Ich denke,*
   *ab dem 17. Jahrhundert wurde der Handel immer weniger.*  g. *Wovon*
   *lebt die Stadt heute?*  h. *Hauptsächlich vom Fremdenverkehr. Waren Sie*
   *schon einmal in dieser Gegend?/Sind Sie schon einmal in dieser Gegend*
   *gewesen?*  i. *Nein, wir haben bisher immer Urlaub in Bayern*
   *gemacht./Nein, wir machten bisher immer Urlaub in Bayern.*
8. a. *Er fragte, ob jemand angerufen hätte.*  b. *Wenn ich das gewusst hätte,*
   *wäre ich nie dorthin gefahren.*  c. *Es kann nichts passiert sein, sonst*
   *hätten wir davon erfahren.*  d. *Das wäre wirklich lustig gewesen, wenn*
   *du uns überrascht hättest.*  e. *Er sagte, er wäre noch nie in den Alpen*
   *gewesen.*
9. a. *auf*  b. *für*  c. *an*  d. *bei, über*  e. *für*  f. *Mit*
10. a. *die Besprechung*  b. *die Mitteilung*  c. *die Angabe*  d. *die Anzeige*
    e. *der Verkauf*  f. *die Reklamation*  g. *die Bedienung*  h. *der Gang*
    i. *die Überweisung*  j. *die Schönheit*  k. *das Alter*  l. *die Krankheit*
    m. *der Fleiß*  n. *die Wichtigkeit*  o. *die Schnelligkeit*  p. *der Reichtum*
    q. *die Sauberkeit*

# APPENDIXES

## A. PRONUNCIATION GUIDE

### LETTERS AND SOUNDS

### *DAS ALPHABET* (THE ALPHABET)

The German alphabet has 26 regular letters. They are pronounced as follows:

| German Spelling | Approximate Sound in English | Example |
| --- | --- | --- |
| a | f<u>a</u>ther | *Anna, Albert* |
| b | <u>b</u>ed | *Bank, Berlin* |
| c | nu<u>ts</u> | *Celsius* |
| d | <u>d</u>ate; tiger | *Drama, Bad* |
| e | M<u>ay</u>; f<u>ai</u>ry | *Erich, Ende* |
| f | <u>f</u>ly | *Film, Fabel* |
| g | <u>g</u>arden | *Gas, Gustav* |
| h | <u>h</u>ouse | *Hotel, Hunger* |
| i | p<u>i</u>zza | *Idee, Iris* |
| j | <u>y</u>es | *ja, Jaguar* |
| k | <u>k</u>eep | *Karl, Kanal* |
| l | <u>l</u>and | *Lampe, Linie* |
| m | <u>m</u>ile | *Maschine, Martha* |
| n | <u>n</u>ew | *Nation, Natur* |
| o | al<u>o</u>ne | *Oper, Ofen* |
| p | <u>p</u>rice | *Problem, Paul* |
| q | <u>q</u>uality | *Qualität, Quiz* |
| r | <u>r</u>ice | *Rose, Reis* |
| s | rai<u>s</u>e; bo<u>ss</u> | *Signal, See, Reis, Haus* |
| t | <u>t</u>ea | *Tee, Telefon* |
| u | r<u>oo</u>m | *Utopie, gut* |
| v | <u>f</u>air | *Vers, Vater* |
| w | <u>v</u>ain | *Willi, Wolf* |
| x | a<u>x</u> | *Xylophon, Axt* |
| y | n<u>ew</u> | *typisch, Lyrik* |
| z | nu<u>ts</u> | *Zoo, Zone* |

## DIE UMLAUTE UND ß (THE UMLAUTS AND ß)

The letters *a, o,* and *u* can also appear with two dots above them, called umlauts; these letters have a different sound. The ß (called "ess-tsett") is a ligature of the letters *s* and *z*.

| German Spelling | Approximate Sound in English | Example |
|---|---|---|
| ä | f<u>ai</u>r | B<u>ä</u>r |
| ö | M<u>ay</u> | <u>Ö</u>l |
| ü | n<u>ew</u> | gr<u>ü</u>n |
| ß | hi<u>ss</u> | wei<u>ß</u> |

## DIPHTHONGE (DIPHTHONGS)

| German Spelling | Approximate Sound in English | Example |
|---|---|---|
| ai, ei | l<u>i</u>ke | K<u>ai</u>ser, <u>Ei</u>s |
| äu, eu | b<u>oy</u> | H<u>äu</u>ser, d<u>eu</u>tsch |
| au | h<u>ou</u>se | H<u>au</u>s, M<u>au</u>s |

## DIE KONSONANTENVERBINDUNGEN (CONSONANT COMBINATIONS)

| German Spelling | Approximate Sound in English | Example |
|---|---|---|
| ch | lo<u>ch</u> | Ba<u>ch</u>, Bu<u>ch</u>, |
|  | <u>h</u>ue | i<u>ch</u>, Mün<u>ch</u>en, Mil<u>ch</u>, Kir<u>ch</u>e |
| sch | <u>sh</u>oe | <u>Sch</u>uh, <u>Sch</u>iff |
| sp | <u>sh</u>oe | <u>Sp</u>ort, <u>Sp</u>anien |
| st | <u>sh</u>oe | <u>St</u>uhl, <u>St</u>ern |

# B. GRAMMAR SUMMARY

## 1. THE DEFINITE ARTICLE

|        | MASCULINE | FEMININE | NEUTER | PLURAL |
|--------|-----------|----------|--------|--------|
| NOM.   | der       | die      | das    | die    |
| ACC.   | den       | die      | das    | die    |
| DAT.   | dem       | der      | dem    | den    |
| GEN.   | des       | der      | des    | der    |

## 2. *DER*-WORDS: *DIESER, JENER, WELCHER, MANCHE, SOLCHE*

|        | MASCULINE | FEMININE | NEUTER  | PLURAL  |
|--------|-----------|----------|---------|---------|
| NOM.   | dieser    | diese    | dieses  | diese   |
| ACC.   | diesen    | diese    | dieses  | diese   |
| DAT.   | diesem    | dieser   | diesem  | diesen  |
| GEN.   | dieses    | dieser   | dieses  | dieser  |

## 3. THE INDEFINITE ARTICLE

|        | MASCULINE | FEMININE | NEUTER |
|--------|-----------|----------|--------|
| NOM.   | ein       | eine     | ein    |
| ACC.   | einen     | eine     | ein    |
| DAT.   | einem     | einer    | einem  |
| GEN.   | eines     | einer    | eines  |

## 4. EIN-WORDS: *KEIN, MEIN, DEIN, SEIN, IHR, UNSER, EUER, IHR, IHR*

|  | MASCULINE | FEMININE | NEUTER | PLURAL |
|---|---|---|---|---|
| NOM. | mein | meine | mein | meine |
| ACC. | meinen | meine | mein | meine |
| DAT. | meinem | meiner | meinem | meinen |
| GEN. | meines | meiner | meines | meiner |

## 5. MASCULINE *N*-NOUNS

|  | SINGULAR | PLURAL |
|---|---|---|
| NOM. | der Architekt | die Architekten |
| ACC. | den Architekten | die Architekten |
| DAT. | dem Architekten | den Architekten |
| GEN. | des Architekten | der Architekten |

Other masculine *n*-nouns include:

| | | |
|---|---|---|
| der Mensch | der Diplomat | der Zeuge |
| der Bauer | der Fotograf | der Journalist |
| der Jurist | der Experte | der Bursche |
| der Präsident | der Nachbar | |

## 6. PRECEDED ADJECTIVES

|  | MASCULINE | FEMININE | NEUTER |
|---|---|---|---|
| NOM. | der junge Mann | die alte Stadt | das schöne Haus |
|  | ein junger Mann | eine alte Stadt | ein schönes Haus |

| | PLURAL |
|---|---|
| | die guten Weine |
| | keine guten Weine |

| | MASCULINE | FEMININE | NEUTER |
|------|-----------|----------|--------|
| ACC. | *den jungen Mann* | *die alte Stadt* | *das schöne Haus* |
| | *einen jungen Mann* | *eine alte Stadt* | *ein schönes Haus* |

PLURAL
*die guten Weine*
*keine guten Weine*

| | MASCULINE | FEMININE | NEUTER |
|------|-----------|----------|--------|
| DAT. | *dem jungen Mann* | *der alten Stadt* | *dem schönen Haus* |
| | *einem jungen Mann* | *einer alten Stadt* | *einem schönen Haus* |

PLURAL
*den guten Weinen*
*keinen guten Weinen*

| | MASCULINE | FEMININE | NEUTER |
|------|-----------|----------|--------|
| GEN. | *des jungen Mannes* | *der alten Stadt* | *des schönen Hauses* |
| | *eines jungen Mannes* | *einer alten Stadt* | *eines schönen Hauses* |

PLURAL
*der guten Weine*
*keiner guten Weine*

## 7. UNPRECEDED ADJECTIVES

| | MASCULINE | FEMININE | NEUTER | PLURAL |
|------|-----------|----------|--------|--------|
| NOM. | *guter Kuchen* | *gute Torte* | *gutes Brot* | *gute Torten* |
| ACC. | *guten Kuchen* | *gute Torte* | *gutes Brot* | *gute Torten* |
| DAT. | *gutem Kuchen* | *guter Torte* | *gutem Brot* | *guten Torten* |
| GEN. | *guten Kuchens* | *guter Torte* | *guten Brotes* | *guter Torten* |

## 8. PERSONAL PRONOUNS

| SINGULAR | 1ST PERSON | 2ND PERSON | 3RD PERSON MASCULINE | 3RD PERSON FEMININE | 3RD PERSON NEUTER |
|---|---|---|---|---|---|
| NOM. | *ich* | *du* | *er* | *sie* | *es* |
| ACC. | *mich* | *dich* | *ihn* | *sie* | *es* |
| DAT. | *mir* | *dir* | *ihm* | *ihr* | *ihm* |

| PLURAL | 1ST PERSON | 2ND PERSON | 3RD PERSON | POLITE |
|---|---|---|---|---|
| NOM. | *wir* | *ihr* | *sie* | *Sie* |
| ACC. | *uns* | *euch* | *sie* | *Sie* |
| DAT. | *uns* | *euch* | *ihnen* | *Ihnen* |

## 9. INTERROGATIVE PRONOUNS

| | | |
|---|---|---|
| NOM. | *wer* | *was* |
| ACC. | *wen* | *was* |
| DAT. | *wem* | |
| GEN. | *wessen* | |

## 10. QUESTION WORDS

| | | | |
|---|---|---|---|
| *warum* | why | *wieviel* | how much |
| *weshalb* | why | *wer* | who |
| *weswegen* | why | *wie* | how |
| *wieso* | why | *wozu* | what for |
| *wann* | when | *was* | what |
| *wo* | where | | |

## 11. THE DEMONSTRATIVE PRONOUN *DER*

|      | MASCULINE | FEMININE | NEUTER | PLURAL |
|------|-----------|----------|--------|--------|
| NOM. | der       | die      | das    | die    |
| ACC. | den       | die      | das    | die    |
| DAT. | dem       | der      | dem    | denen  |

## 12. RELATIVE PRONOUNS

|      | MASCULINE | FEMININE | NEUTER | PLURAL |
|------|-----------|----------|--------|--------|
| NOM. | der       | die      | das    | die    |
| ACC. | den       | die      | das    | die    |
| DAT. | dem       | der      | dem    | denen  |
| GEN. | dessen    | deren    | dessen | deren  |

## 13. INDEFINITE PRONOUNS

|      |            |              |            |       |       |        |
|------|------------|--------------|------------|-------|-------|--------|
| NOM. | jemand     | niemand      | irgendwer  | etwas | man   | nichts |
| ACC. | jemand(en) | niemand(en)  | irgendwen  | etwas | einen |        |
| DAT. | jemand(em) | niemand(em)  | irgendwem  | —     | einem |        |
| GEN. | jemandes   | niemand(e)s  | —          | —     | eines |        |

## 14. REFLEXIVE PRONOUNS

| SINGULAR   |      | PLURAL |      |
|------------|------|--------|------|
| ich        | mich | wir    | uns  |
| du         | dich | ihr    | euch |
| er/sie/es  | sich | sie    | sich |
|            |      | Sie    | sich |

# 15. VERBS IN THE INDICATIVE

## PRESENT

I ask, I am asking, I do ask

|       |        |     |        |
|------:|--------|----:|--------|
| ich | *frage* | wir | *fragen* |
| du | *fragst* | ihr | *fragt* |
| er/sie/es | *fragt* | sie | *fragen* |
|       |        | Sie | *fragen* |

## PRESENT PERFECT
## WEAK VERBS

I have asked, I asked, I did ask

|       |        |     |        |
|------:|--------|----:|--------|
| ich | *habe gefragt* | wir | *haben gefragt* |
| du | *hast gefragt* | ihr | *habt gefragt* |
| er/sie/es | *hat gefragt* | sie | *haben gefragt* |
|       |        | Sie | *haben gefragt* |

## STRONG VERBS

I have come, I came, I did come

|       |        |     |        |
|------:|--------|----:|--------|
| ich | *bin gekommen* | wir | *sind gekommen* |
| du | *bist gekommen* | ihr | *seid gekommen* |
| er/sie/es | *ist gekommen* | sie | *sind gekommen* |
|       |        | Sie | *sind gekommen* |

## WEAK IRREGULAR (MIXED) VERBS

I have thought

| | | | | |
|---|---|---|---|---|
| ich | habe gedacht | | wir | haben gedacht |
| du | hast gedacht | | ihr | habt gedacht |
| er/sie/es | hat gedacht | | sie | haben gedacht |
| | | | Sie | haben gedacht |

## SIMPLE PAST
## WEAK VERBS

I asked, I was asking

| | | | | |
|---|---|---|---|---|
| ich | fragte | | wir | fragten |
| du | fragtest | | ihr | fragtet |
| er/sie/es | fragte | | sie | fragten |
| | | | Sie | fragten |

## STRONG VERBS

I came, I was coming

| | | | | |
|---|---|---|---|---|
| ich | kam | | wir | kamen |
| du | kamst | | ihr | kamt |
| er/sie/es | kam | | sie | kamen |
| | | | Sie | kamen |

## WEAK IRREGULAR (MIXED) VERBS

I thought

| | | | | |
|---|---|---|---|---|
| ich | dachte | | wir | dachten |
| du | dachtest | | ihr | dachtet |
| er/sie/es | dachte | | sie | dachten |
| | | | Sie | dachten |

## PAST PERFECT
### WEAK VERBS

I had asked

| | | | | |
|---|---|---|---|---|
| ich | hatte gefragt | | wir | hatten gefragt |
| du | hattest gefragt | | ihr | hattet gefragt |
| er/sie/es | hatte gefragt | | sie | hatten gefragt |
| | | | Sie | hatten gefragt |

## STRONG VERBS

I had come

| | | | | |
|---|---|---|---|---|
| ich | war gekommen | | wir | waren gekommen |
| du | warst gekommen | | ihr | wart gekommen |
| er/sie/es | war gekommen | | sie | waren gekommen |
| | | | Sie | waren gekommen |

## WEAK IRREGULAR (MIXED) VERBS

I had thought

| | | | | |
|---|---|---|---|---|
| ich | hatte gedacht | | wir | hatten gedacht |
| du | hattest gedacht | | ihr | hattet gedacht |
| er/sie/es | hatte gedacht | | sie | hatten gedacht |
| | | | Sie | hatten gedacht |

## FUTURE

I will ask

| | | | | |
|---|---|---|---|---|
| ich | werde fragen | | wir | werden fragen |
| du | wirst fragen | | ihr | werdet fragen |
| er/sie/es | wird fragen | | sie | werden fragen |
| | | | Sie | werden fragen |

# 16. VERBS IN THE SUBJUNCTIVE

## PRESENT TIME SUBJUNCTIVE
## SUBJUNCTIVE I

I would say

| | | | |
|---|---|---|---|
| ich | sage | wir | sagen |
| du | sag(e)st | ihr | sage(e)t |
| er/sie/es | sage | sie | sagen |
| | | Sie | sagen |

I would come

| | | | |
|---|---|---|---|
| ich | komme | wir | kommen |
| du | komm(e)st | ihr | komm(e)t |
| er/sie/es | komme | sie | kommen |
| | | Sie | kommen |

## SUBJUNCTIVE II

I would say

| | | | |
|---|---|---|---|
| ich | sagte | wir | sagten |
| du | sagtest | ihr | sagtet |
| er/sie/es | sagte | sie | sagten |
| | | Sie | sagten |

I would come

| | | | |
|---|---|---|---|
| ich | käme | wir | kämen |
| du | käm(e)st | ihr | käm(e)t |
| er/sie/es | käme | sie | kämen |
| | | Sie | kämen |

# PAST-TIME SUBJUNCTIVE
## SUBJUNCTIVE I

I had asked

| ich | habe gefragt | wir | haben gefragt |
|-----|--------------|-----|---------------|
| du | habest gefragt | ihr | habt gefragt |
| er/sie/es | habe gefragt | sie | haben gefragt |
| | | Sie | haben gefragt |

I had come

| ich | sei gekommen | wir | seien gekommen |
|-----|--------------|-----|----------------|
| du | sei(e)st gekommen | ihr | sei(e)t gekommen |
| er/sie/es | sei gekommen | sie | seien gekommen |
| | | Sie | seien gekommen |

## SUBJUNCTIVE II

I would have said

| ich | hätte gesagt | wir | hätten gesagt |
|-----|--------------|-----|---------------|
| du | hättest gesagt | ihr | hättet gesagt |
| er/sie/es | hätte gesagt | sie | hätten gesagt |
| | | Sie | hätten gesagt |

I would have come

| ich | wäre gekommen | wir | wären gekommen |
|-----|---------------|-----|----------------|
| du | wär(e)st gekommen | ihr | wär(e)t gekommen |
| er/sie/es | wäre gekommen | sie | wären gekommen |
| | | Sie | wären gekommen |

## FUTURE-TIME SPECIAL SUBJUNCTIVE

I will ask

| ich | werde fragen | | wir | werden fragen |
|---|---|---|---|---|
| du | wirst fragen | | ihr | werdet fragen |
| er/sie/es | wird fragen | | sie | werden fragen |
| | | | Sie | werden fragen |

## 17. PASSIVE VOICE

## PRESENT TENSE

I am asked

| ich | werde gefragt | | wir | werden gefragt |
|---|---|---|---|---|
| du | wirst gefragt | | ihr | werdet gefragt |
| er/sie/es | wird gefragt | | sie | werden gefragt |
| | | | Sie | werden gefragt |

## SIMPLE PAST

I was asked, I have been asked

| ich | wurde gefragt | | wir | wurden gefragt |
|---|---|---|---|---|
| du | wurdest gefragt | | ihr | wurdet gefragt |
| er/sie/es | wurde gefragt | | sie | wurden gefragt |
| | | | Sie | wurden gefragt |

## PRESENT PERFECT

I was asked, I have been asked

| ich | bin gefragt worden | | wir | sind gefragt worden |
|---|---|---|---|---|
| du | bist gefragt worden | | ihr | seid gefragt worden |
| er/sie/es | ist gefragt worden | | sie | sind gefragt worden |
| | | | Sie | sind gefragt worden |

I had been asked

| ich | war gefragt worden | wir | waren gefragt worden |
|---|---|---|---|
| du | warst gefragt worden | ihr | wart gefragt worden |
| er/sie/es | war gefragt worden | sie | waren gefragt worden |
| | | Sie | waren gefragt worden |

## 18. REFLEXIVE VERBS

| | | | |
|---|---|---|---|
| sich waschen | to wash oneself | sich anziehen | to dress (oneself) |
| sich rasieren | to shave | sich erinnern | to remember |
| sich freuen | to look forward | sich entschuldigen | to apologize |
| sich unterhalten | to converse | sich kämmen | to comb (one's hair) |
| sich leisten + dat. | to afford | sich kaufen + dat. | to buy (for oneself) |
| sich wünschen + dat. | to wish | | |

## 19. STRONG, IRREGULAR WEAK, AND MODAL VERBS

| INFINITIVE | PRESENT | SIMPLE PAST | PAST PARTICIPLE |
|---|---|---|---|
| anfangen to begin | fängt an | fing an | angefangen |
| backen to bake | bäckt | buk (backte) | gebacken |
| beginnen to begin | | begann | begonnen |
| bekommen to receive | | bekam | bekommen |
| beweisen to prove | | bewies | bewiesen |
| bieten to offer | | bot | geboten |
| bleiben to remain | | blieb | ist geblieben |
| brechen to break | bricht | brach | gebrochen |
| bringen to bring | | brachte | gebracht |
| denken to think | | dachte | gedacht |

| | | | |
|---|---|---|---|
| *diskutieren* | | *diskutierte* | *diskutiert* |
| to discuss | | | |
| *dürfen* | *darf* | *durfte* | *gedurft* |
| to be allowed to | | | |
| *einladen* | *lädt ein* | *lud ein* | *eingeladen* |
| to invite | | | |
| *empfehlen* | *empfiehlt* | *empfahl* | *empfohlen* |
| to recommend | | | |
| *essen* | *isst* | *aß* | *gegessen* |
| to eat | | | |
| *fahren* | *fährt* | *fuhr* | *ist gefahren* |
| to drive | | | |
| *fallen* | *fällt* | *fiel* | *ist gefallen* |
| to fall | | | |
| *finden* | | *fand* | *gefunden* |
| to find | | | |
| *fliegen* | | *flog* | *ist geflogen* |
| to fly | | | |
| *frieren* | | *fror* | *gefroren* |
| to freeze | | | |
| *geben* | *gibt* | *gab* | *gegeben* |
| to give | | | |
| *gefallen* | *gefällt* | *gefiel* | *gefallen* |
| to please | | | |
| *gehen* | | *ging* | *ist gegangen* |
| to go | | | |
| *genießen* | | *genoss* | *genossen* |
| to enjoy | | | |
| *gewinnen* | | *gewann* | *gewonnen* |
| to win | | | |
| *greifen* | | *griff* | *gegriffen* |
| to seize | | | |
| *haben* | *hat* | *hatte* | *gehabt* |
| to have | | | |
| *halten* | *hält* | *hielt* | *gehalten* |
| to hold, to stop | | | |
| *hängen* | | *hing* | *gehangen* |
| to hang, to be hanging | | | |
| *heißen* | | *hieß* | *geheißen* |
| to be called | | | |
| *helfen* | *hilft* | *half* | *geholfen* |
| to help | | | |

| | | | |
|---|---|---|---|
| *kennen* | | *kannte* | *gekannt* |
| to know | | | |
| *kommen* | | *kam* | *ist gekommen* |
| to come | | | |
| *können* | *kann* | *konnte* | *gekonnt* |
| to be able to, can | | | |
| *lassen* | *lässt* | *ließ* | *gelassen* |
| to let | | | |
| *laufen* | *läuft* | *lief* | *ist gelaufen* |
| to run, to walk | | | |
| *leiden* | | *litt* | *gelitten* |
| to suffer | | | |
| *leihen* | | *lieh* | *geliehen* |
| to lend, to borrow | | | |
| *lesen* | *liest* | *las* | *gelesen* |
| to read | | | |
| *liegen* | | *lag* | *gelegen* |
| to lie (down) | | | |
| *mögen* | *mag* | *mochte* | *gemocht* |
| to like | | | |
| *müssen* | *muss* | *musste* | *gemusst* |
| to have to, must | | | |
| *nehmen* | *nimmt* | *nahm* | *genommen* |
| to take | | | |
| *nennen* | | *nannte* | *genannt* |
| to name, to call | | | |
| *raten* | | *riet* | *geraten* |
| to advise, to guess | | | |
| *rennen* | | *rannte* | *ist gerannt* |
| to run | | | |
| *reservieren* | | *reservierte* | *reserviert* |
| to reserve | | | |
| *rufen* | | *rief* | *gerufen* |
| to call | | | |
| *schaffen* | | *schuf* | *geschaffen* |
| to create | | | |
| *schlafen* | *schläft* | *schlief* | *geschlafen* |
| to sleep | | | |
| *schließen* | | *schloss* | *geschlossen* |
| to close | | | |
| *schneiden* | | *schnitt* | *geschnitten* |
| to cut | | | |
| *schreiben* | | *schrieb* | *geschrieben* |
| to write | | | |

| | | | |
|---|---|---|---|
| *schreien*<br>to scream | | *schrie* | *geschrien* |
| *schwimmen*<br>to swim | | *schwamm* | *ist geschwommen* |
| *sehen*<br>to see | *sieht* | *sah* | *gesehen* |
| *sein*<br>to be | *ist* | *war* | *ist gewesen* |
| *senden*<br>to send | | *sandte* | *gesandt* |
| *sitzen*<br>to sit | | *saß* | *gesessen* |
| *sollen*<br>to be supposed to | *soll* | *sollte* | *gesollt*<br>(uncommon) |
| *sprechen*<br>to speak | *spricht* | *sprach* | *gesprochen* |
| *springen*<br>to jump | | *sprang* | *ist gesprungen* |
| *stehen*<br>to stand | | *stand* | *gestanden* |
| *steigen*<br>to climb | | *stieg* | *ist gestiegen* |
| *sterben*<br>to die | | *starb* | *ist gestorben* |
| *stoßen*<br>to push, to run into | | *stieß* | *hat/ist gestoßen* |
| *streiten*<br>to fight | | *stritt* | *gestritten* |
| *tragen*<br>to carry, to wear | *trägt* | *trug* | *getragen* |
| *treffen*<br>to meet | *trifft* | *traf* | *getroffen* |
| *treten*<br>to walk, to tread, to kick | *tritt* | *trat* | *getreten* |
| *trinken*<br>to drink | | *trank* | *getrunken* |
| *tun*<br>to do | | *tat* | *getan* |
| *verbieten*<br>to forbid | | *verbot* | *verboten* |
| *verbinden*<br>to connect | | *verband* | *verbunden* |
| *vergessen*<br>to forget | | *vergaß* | *vergessen* |

| | | | |
|---|---|---|---|
| *verlieren* | | *verlor* | *verloren* |
| to lose | | | |
| *verschwinden* | | *verschwand* | *ist verschwunden* |
| to disappear | | | |
| *wachsen* | *wächst* | *wuchs* | *ist gewachsen* |
| to grow | | | |
| *waschen* | *wäscht* | *wusch* | *gewaschen* |
| to wash | | | |
| *werden* | *wird* | *wurde* | *ist geworden* |
| to become, to get | | | |
| *wissen* | *weiß* | *wusste* | *gewusst* |
| to know | | | |
| *wollen* | *will* | *wollte* | *gewollt* |
| to want, to wish, intend to | | | |
| *ziehen* | | *zog* | *gezogen* |
| to pull | | | |

## 20. COMPARATIVE AND SUPERLATIVE

| POSITIVE | COMPARATIVE | SUPERLATIVE |
|---|---|---|
| *gut* | *besser* | *beste, -r, -s* <br> *am besten* |
| *groß* | *größer* | *größte, -r, -s* <br> *am größten* |
| *hoch* | *höher* | *höchste, -r, -s* <br> *am höchsten* |
| *nahe* | *näher* | *nächste, -r, -s* <br> *am nächsten* |
| *viel* | *mehr* | *meiste, -r, -s* <br> *am meisten* |
| *gern* | *lieber* | *liebste, -r, -s* <br> *am liebsten* |

# 21. IMPERATIVE

| INFINITIVE | 2ND PERSON SINGULAR | 2ND PERSON PLURAL | *WIR*-FORM | POLITE |
|---|---|---|---|---|
| *geben* | *Gib mir!* | *Gebt mir!* | *Geben wir!* | *Geben Sie mir!* |
| *sein* | *Sei so gut!* | *Seid so gut!* | *Sind wir so gut!* | *Seien Sie so gut!* |
| *lassen* | *Lass mich!* | *Lasst mich!* | *Lasst uns!* | *Lassen Sie mich!* |

# 22. PUNCTUATION

### PERIODS

A period is set after each completed statement.

*Nun machen Sie aber mal einen Punkt.*
Just stop right here.

### EXCLAMATION MARKS

The imperative in German is often followed by an exclamation mark.

*Kommen Sie bitte herein!*
Please come in.

### QUESTION MARKS

Question marks denote the end of a question.

*Woher kommen Sie?*
Where are you from?

### COMMAS

All subordinated subclauses are separated from the main clause by a comma.

*Sie weiß, dass ihr Hund im Garten ist.*
She knows that her dog is in the garden.

Multiple subordinated clauses are separated from the main clause and each other by a comma.

*Ich wusste nicht, wo mein Auto steht, weil meine Freundin es geparkt hat.*
I didn't know where my car was because my girlfriend had parked it.

Two independent main clauses linked with *aber* are also separated by a comma.

*Es hat geregnet, aber wir sind trotzdem ans Meer gefahren.*
It was raining, but we went to the ocean anyway.

When listing nouns or attributes, set a comma between each except the last and second to last, which are linked with *und* or *oder.*

*Ich war in Italien, in Griechenland, in der Schweiz und in Belgien.*
I was in Italy, Greece, Switzerland and Belgium.

Infinitive constructions with *zu* may be separated with a comma.

*Er bat mich (,) ihn im Herbst zu besuchen.*
He asked me to visit him in the fall.

Indirect speech is separated from the introductory phrase by a comma.

*Der Rechtsanwalt sagte, Frau Schulz sei nicht zu Hause gewesen.*
The lawyer said that Mrs. Schulz was not at home.

Relative clauses are always separated from the main clause by commas.

*Der Mann, der den Briefumschlag brachte, ist schon wieder weg.*
The man who brought the envelope left already.

No comma is set between sentence structures with conjunctions like *und* or *oder.*

*Abends kam ich nach Hause und setzte mich auf das Sofa.*
I came home in the evening and sat down on the sofa.

*Sind Sie nach Regensburg oder nach Hannover gefahren?*
Did you go to Regensburg or to Hannover?

QUOTATION MARKS

When quoting direct speech, German uses quotation marks. Please note that the beginning quotation mark in German is set at the bottom of the line and that the quotation marks are inverted.

*Frau Meier sagte: „Meine Tochter studiert."*
Mrs. Meier said, "My daughter is going to the university."

# 23. CAPITALIZATION

All nouns, regular as well as adjectival and verbal nouns, are capitalized.

*das Haus*                         *der Jüngere*
*beim Schwimmen*               *das Gute*

The formal "you" is always capitalized in all pronouns, except the reflexive pronoun.

*Setzen Sie sich!*
Take a seat.

*Kann ich Ihnen helfen?*
Can I help you?

*Haben Sie Ihre Frau nicht gefunden?*
You didn't find your wife?

Names of people and places are always capitalized.

*Rainer Berger*            *Deutschland*          *Amerika*

Contrary to English, adjectives of nationalities, regions, and languages are not capitalized:

*der französische Wein*         *das bayerische Essen*
*die italienischen Kunden*      *die schwäbische Sauberkeit*
*die deutsche Sprache*          *das amerikanische Fernsehen*

Adjectives formed from names of places, landmarks, and set terms are always capitalized.

*die Münchner Filmfestwochen*    *der Schweizer Käse*
*das Salzburger Schloss*         *der Kölner Dom*
*der Hamburger Hafen*            *die Wiener Cafés*

# C. LETTER WRITING

## 1. BUSINESS LETTERS

*AktivChic • Große Kirchstraße 35 • 52078 Aachen*
*Tel.: 07653/372568 · Telefax: 07653/372569*

*Margot Walther*
*Walther & Schirmer Werbeagentur*
*Dorfstraße 14*
*52076 Aachen*

*18.9.03*

*Sehr geehrte Frau Walther,*

*hiermit bestätigen wir den Eingang Ihres Entwurfes für unsere Werbekampagne. Wir haben das Konzept bereits mit der Geschäftsleitung und dem Verkaufspersonal besprochen und sind mit Ihren Vorschlägen sehr zufrieden.*

*Wie bereits telefonisch besprochen, möchten wir in den Anzeigen noch einige geringe Änderungen vornehmen. Wir würden uns freuen, wenn unser Verkaufsleiter Herr Schliehmer diese mit Ihrer Agentur direkt besprechen könnte. Er wird diesbezüglich Kontakt mit Frau Ranke und Herrn Meier aufnehmen.*

*Wir freuen uns auf gute Zusammenarbeit.*

*Mit freundlichen Grüßen*
*i.A. Kohlke*
*Geschäftsleitung AktivChic*

AktivChic • Große Kirchstraße 35 • 52078 Aachen
Phone: 07653/372568 • Fax: 07653/372569

Margot Walther
Walther & Schirmer Werbeagentur
Dorfstraße 14
52076 Aachen

September 18, 2003

Dear Ms. Walther:

We hereby confirm receipt of your proposal for our advertising campaign. We immediately discussed your suggestions with our management and the sales staff and are quite pleased with your ideas.

As briefly discussed over the phone, we would like to make some minor changes in the print ads. We would appreciate if our sales director Mr. Schliehmer could discuss these with your agency directly. He will contact Ms. Ranke and Mr. Meier regarding these changes.

We are looking forward to working with you.

Sincerely,
(signed: Kohlke)
(for)
Management AktivChic

———————

## 2. THANK-YOU NOTES

*21.12.03*

*Sehr geehrter Herr Schneider,*

*ich möchte Ihnen noch einmal für Ihre freundliche Hilfe danken. Sie haben mir den Aufenthalt in Deutschland durch Ihre vielseitigen Hinweise und Hilfeleistungen sehr erleichtert.*

*Auch danke ich Ihnen herzlich für Ihre Einladung zu Ihrer Weihnachtsfeier. Leider werde ich nicht kommen können, da ich morgen bereits nach Boston zurückfliege.*

*Ich hoffe, dass wir uns bei meinem nächsten Besuch in Frankfurt wiedersehen, und wünsche Ihnen alles Gute und viel Erfolg für das Neue Jahr.*

*Mit freundlichen Grüßen,*
*Martin Brenner*

---

December 21, 2003

Dear Mr. Schneider,

I would like to thank you again for your kind assistance. Your helpful tips and advice made my stay in Germany much easier.

I would also like to thank you for your kind invitation to your Christmas party. Unfortunately I won't be able to attend, as I will already be on my way back to Boston.

I hope we will see each other again during my next visit to Frankfurt, and I'd like to wish you all the best and a successful New Year.

Sincerely,
Martin Brenner

---

## 3. INFORMAL LETTERS

*30. September 2003*

*Liebe Gabriele!*

*Herzlichen Dank für deinen Brief. Euer Urlaub in der Schweiz war wohl sehr schön. Ich wünschte, ich hätte Zeit, dieses Jahr nochmal in Urlaub zu fahren.*

*Unser Sommerurlaub an der Nordsee war viel zu kurz. Leider hat es auch oft geregnet. Nächstes Jahr möchte ich wieder nach Griechenland fahren. Dort regnet es wenigstens nicht so viel.*

*Aber zunächst wollen wir die Umbauten im Haus zu Ende bringen. Ich glaube, ich habe dir bereits geschrieben, dass wir den Dachboden für unseren Sohn ausgebaut haben. Nun ist die Küche dran. Wir hoffen, dass wir Ende des Jahres fertig sind. Vielleicht kannst du ja deinen Weihnachtsurlaub bei uns verbringen und dir unser 'neues' Haus anschauen? Wie wär's? Sylvia und ich würden dich dieses Jahr gerne noch einmal sehen. Bitte, sag' einfach ja.*

*Viele liebe Grüße, auch an deine Familie,*

*dein Jürgen*

September 30, 2003

Dear Gabriele,

Thank you for your letter. Apparently your vacation in Switzerland was very nice. I wish I had time to go on another vacation this year.

Our summer vacation at the North Sea was much too short. Unfortunately it rained a lot, too. Next year I want to go to Greece again. At least there it won't rain as much.

But first of all we want to finish renovating our house. I think I already mentioned to you that we renovated the attic for our son. Now we're working in the kitchen. We hope to be finished by the end of the year. Perhaps you could spend your Christmas vacation with us, and take a look at our "new" house. How about it? Sylvia and I would love to see you again this year. Please say you'll come.

Best regards, also, to your family,

Yours Jürgen

---

# 4. SALUTATIONS AND COMPLIMENTARY CLOSINGS

## FORMAL SALUTATIONS

| | |
|---|---|
| *Sehr geehrter Herr Holl,* | Dear Mr. Holl: |
| *Sehr geehrte Frau Holl,* | Dear Mrs. Holl: |
| *Sehr geehrte Damen und Herren,* | Dear Madam, dear Sir: |
| *Sehr geehrter Herr Doktor,* | Dear Dr. (Kuhn): |
| *Sehr geehrter Herr Dr. Kuhn,* | Dear Dr. Kuhn: |
| *Sehr geehrte Frau Doktor,* | Dear Doctor (Merz): |
| *Sehr geehrte Frau Dr. Merz,* | Dear Dr. Merz: |
| *Sehr geehrter Herr Professor,* | Dear Professor (Mai): |
| *Sehr geehrter Herr Professor Mai,* | Dear Professor Mai: |
| *Sehr geehrter Herr Bürgermeister,* | Dear Mayor (Linnert): |

## INFORMAL SALUTATIONS

| | |
|---|---|
| *Lieber Karl,* | Dear Karl, |
| *Liebe Else,* | Dear Else, |
| *Lieber Karl, liebe Else,* | Dear Karl and Else, |
| *Mein lieber Karl,* | My dear Karl, |
| *Meine liebe Else,* | My dear Else, |
| *Meine Lieben,* | Dear Ones, |
| *Mein Liebling,* | My Darling (m. and f.) |
| *Mein Liebster,* | My Darling (m.) |
| *Meine Liebste,* | My Darling (f.) |

## FORMAL CLOSINGS

| | |
|---|---|
| *Mit freundlichen Grüßen,* | Sincerely, ("With friendly greetings,") |
| *Mit freundlichem Gruß,* | Sincerely, ("With a friendly greeting,") |
| *Mit vorzüglicher Hochachtung,* | Very respectfully yours, ("With the most excellent and highest regard,") |
| *Hochachtungsvoll,* | Respectfully yours, ("With high respect,") |

| | |
|---|---|
| *Mit besten Grüßen,* | Best regards, |
| *Mit herzlichem Gruß,* | Love, ("With a hearty greeting,") |
| *Mit herzlichen Grüßen* | Love, ("With hearty greetings,") |
| *Grüße und Küsse,* | Love, ("Greetings and kisses,") |
| *Mach's gut,* | Take care, |

## 5. FORMS OF ADDRESS

*Herr* and *Frau* are not to be abbreviated in forms of address.

The academic titles *Professor* and *Doktor* are considered part of the name and are written before the name. Diplomas and vocational and occupational job titles are used in the written address, but not in the salutation:

| ADDRESS | SALUTATION |
|---|---|
| *Herrn Professor* | *Sehr geehrter Herr Professor,* |
| *Dr. Erich Weimer* | *Sehr geehrter Herr Professor Weimer,* |
| *Herrn Rechtsanwalt* | *Sehr geehrter Herr Dr. Baum,* |
|   *Dr. Friedrich Baum* | |
| *Herrn Dipl. Ing. Helmut Kern* | *Sehr geehrter Herr Kern,* |
| *Frau Direktor Ilse Rau* | *Sehr geehrte Frau Rau,* |
| *Herrn Bürgermeister Kirchner* | *Sehr geehrter Herr Kirchner,* |

## 6. INTERNET ETIQUETTE

E-mail correspondence follows common German rules of writing. It is not appropriate to use only lower case or only upper case letters in an e-mail. E-mail correspondence, particularly business correspondence, follows the basic etiquette of letter writing. Use the same form of address you would in a letter, such as *Liebe Frau Meier, Lieber Herr Bauer, Sehr geehrte Frau Schneider, Sehr geehrter Herr Sommer.* End the e-mail as you would a letter. For example: *Mit freundlichem Gruß, Herzliche Grüsse.* In business e-mails, note your contact information below your signature at the end of the e-mail.

## 7. STANDARD FORMAT FOR STREET ADDRESSES, TELEPHONE NUMBERS, DATES, AND TIME

STREET ADDRESSES

  a.  The street name precedes the house number. For example: *Momm-senstraße 85.*

  b.  The ZIP code precedes the city name. For example: *509337 Köln.*

c. The word *Straße* can be abbreviated as *Str.,* and is often written together with the proper name of the street as one word. For example: *Mommsenstr.*

d. A comma is used to separate the details of an address.

*Seine Addresse lautet: Mommsenstr. 85, 509337 Köln.*
His Address is Mommsenstraße 85, 509337 Cologne.

### TELEPHONE NUMBERS

Telephone numbers consist of *Vorwahl* (area code) and *Rufnummer* (telephone number). Most area codes begin with a '0'. For example: *0711 (Stuttgart), 089 (Munich), 030 (Berlin).* Depending on the size of the city, most telephone numbers consist of at least five numbers. They are arranged in pairs of two. When writing telephone numbers, a space may be left between the pairs. Do not use a hyphen, backslash, or period to separate the pairs of numbers. For example: *31 78 79* or *317879.* In speech, you can recite the numbers separately, or in pairs of two: *drei eins sieben acht sieben neun* or *einunddreißig, achtundsiebzig, neunundsiebzig.*

### DATES

a. Dates are written in the following order: day, month, year. For example: *31.12.00* or *31. Dezember 2000.*

b. A comma is used to separate the details of dates in sentences.

*Ich bin von Montag, 6. Januar bis Mittwoch, 8. Januar im Urlaub.*
I'll be on vacation from Monday, January 6 through Wednesday, January 8.

### TIME

German-speaking countries use the 24-hour clock for official time. When writing in German, use either *h* or *Uhr* after the hour to indicate "o'clock." For example: *Um 23h30 fährt der Zug ab.* or *Um 23 Uhr 30 fährt der Zug ab.*

# THE GERMAN SPELLING REFORM

This book abides by the rules and regulations of the German spelling reform. Even though the new orthographic rules became mandatory in 2000, don't be surprised to encounter written materials with the old spellings.

a. The most important change deals with the German *ß*. The general rule reads that from now on *ß* will only be used after a long vowel, a long Umlaut, or a diphthong. *ß* is, however, replaced by *ss* after a short and stressed vowel. For example: *Fass* instead of *Faß*, *Kuss* instead of *Kuß*, *Boss* instead of *Boß*, *Reisepass* instead of *Reisepaß*, and *dass* instead of *daß*. BUT: *Fuß* and *Gruß* keep the *ß*, since the preceding vowel is long, as well as *weiß* and *heiß*.

b. If, in compound words, three identical letters meet, all three are kept. For example: *Kaffeeernte, Bestellliste, Schifffahrt, Hawaiiinseln, Teeei*. Alternatively it is possible to separate these compounds with a hyphen. For example: *Kaffee-Ernte, Bestell-Liste, Schiff-Fahrt, Hawaii-Inseln, Tee-Ei*.

c. Consonants are doubled after a short vowel. For example: *Tipp, Ass, Stopp*.

d. Foreign words are adapted to German rules. This means that *ph* can be replaced by *f*; *–tial* and *–tiell* can be replaced by *–zial* and *–ziell*; *gh, rh*, and *th* can be simply *g, r, t*. For example: *Delphin* or *Delfin*, *Photo* or *Foto*, *Geographie* or *Geografie*; *essentiell* or *essenziell*, *substantiell* or *substanziell*; *Spaghetti* or *Spagetti*, *Thunfisch* or *Tunfisch*, *Panther* or *Panter*, *Katarrh* or *Katarr*.

e. Combinations of noun and verb are separated. For example: *Rad fahren* instead of *radfahren, Maschine schreiben* instead of *maschineschreiben, Halt machen* instead of *haltmachen*.

f. Combinations of two verbs, verb and participle are always separated. For example: *fallen lassen, kennen lernen, sitzen bleiben* as well as *getrennt leben, verloren gehen*.

g. Combinations of the verb *sein* are always separated. For example: *an sein, auf sein, beisammen sein*.

h. Combinations of verb and adjective are separate, if the adjective can form a comparative. For example: *gut gehen (besser gehen)* BUT: *fernsehen*.

# GLOSSARY

## ABBREVIATIONS

| | | | |
|---|---|---|---|
| acc. | accusative | lit. | literal |
| adj. | adjective | m. | masculine |
| adv. | adverb | neu. | neuter |
| art. | article | n. | noun |
| coll. | colloquial | obj. | object |
| conj. | conjunction | pl. | plural |
| dat. | dative | pol. | polite |
| def. | definite | prep. | preposition |
| dir. | direct | pron. | pronoun |
| fam. | familiar | poss. | possessive |
| f. | feminine | sing. | singular |
| gen. | genitive | | |

# DEUTSCH—ENGLISCH

## A

**der Abbau** *mining, dismantling*
    **abbauen** *to mine, to dismantle*
    **abbuchen** *to debit the account*
**die Abbuchung, -en** *debit*
**der Abend, -e** *evening*
    Abend *evening, hello (fam.)*
    guten Abend *good evening (pol.)*
    Heiligabend *Christmas Eve*
    zu Abend essen *to have supper*
**das Abendessen, -** *dinner*
    zum Abendessen *for supper*
**das Abendgymnasium, -en** *night school*
**der Abendkurs, -e** *evening class, evening course*
    **abends** *in the evening, evenings*
    **aber** *but*
    **abfahren** *to depart, to leave*
    **abfliegen** *to depart (by airplane)*
**der Abflug, ⁻e** *departure (by airplane)*
    **abgeben** *to hand in*
    **abhängen von** *to depend upon*
**das Abitur, -e** *high school examination, diploma*
    Abitur machen *to take the high school examination*
**der Abiturient, -en** *high school graduate*

**die Ablage, -en** *a shelf or board given room for temporary storage, office: filing*
    **ablegen** *to take off (coat, jacket), to put down*
    **abmelden** *to sign off, to log off (comp.)*
    **abnehmen** *to lose weight; to buy*
**der Abnehmer, -** *buyer*
    **abrasieren** *to shave off*
    **absagen** *to cancel (a meeting, an appointment)*
    **abschicken** *to send off*
    **abschließen** *to lock up, to close, (insurance, agreement) to enter into, to start up*
**der Absender, -e** *return address, sender of mail*
**die Absicht** *intention*
    **absteigen** *to descend, to go down; to stay (in a hotel)*
    In welchem Hotel ist er abgestiegen? *Which hotel is he staying at?*
**der Abstellraum, ⁻e** *storage space, storage room*
**der Abstieg, -e** *descent*
**das Abteil, -e** *compartment*
**die Abteilung, -en** *department (section of a museum)*
    **abtrocknen** *to dry dishes*

abtrocknen (sich) *to dry oneself*
abwarten *to wait, to bide one's time*
abwechseln *to take turns*
abwechselnd *one then the other, taking turns*
acht *eight*
die Achtung *attention, respect, esteem*
    Alle Achtung! *I compliment you.*
achtzehn *eighteen*
achtzig *eighty*
die Adresse, -n *address*
    Ade! *Good-bye! Bye!*
der Affe, -n *ape*
die Ahnung, -en *idea, clue*
die Akademie, -n *academy*
der Akt, -e *act*
die Akte, -n *file*
die Aktenablage, -n *filing shelf*
der Aktenschrank, ¨e *filing cabinet*
die Aktie, -n *(stock market) share*
die Aktiengesellschaft (die AG), -en
    *stock company*
aktuell *current, topical*
das Aktuelle *current events*
das Album, -ben *album*
alle *all*
allein *alone*
die Allergie, -n *allergy*
allergisch *allergic*
    Sind Sie gegen irgendetwas
    allergisch? *Are you allergic to anything?*
alles *all*
die Alm, -en *Alpine pasture*
die Alpen *the Alps*
das Alphabet *alphabet*
als *when, as, than*
alt *old*
der Altbau, -ten *old building*
altertümlich *old-fashioned*
altmodisch *old-fashioned*
die Altstadt, ¨e *old town, city*
    Amerika *America*
an *at, at the side of, to, on*
anbauen *to grow, to produce; to build on*
anbieten *to offer*
das Andenken, - *souvenir*
andere *others*
ändern *to change, to alter*
anders *different*
andrehen *to sell something of inferior quality/value to someone*
die Anerkennung, -en *respect, recognition*
anfangen *to begin, to start*
das Angebot, -e *offer*

der Angeklagte, -n/-n *accused*
angenehm *pleasant*
    Angenehm! *Pleased to meet you*
angesichts (+ gen.) *in view of*
angestellt sein *to be employed*
der/die Angestellte, -n/-n *clerk, employee*
angewandt *applied*
angreifen *to attack*
angrenzen *to border on*
der Anhänger, - *trailer*
ankommen *to arrive*
die Ankunft, ¨e *arrival*
die Anlage, -n *investment*
anlassen *to start (a car)*
der Anlasser, - *starter*
anlegen *to invest money; to land (a boat)*
das Anmeldeformular, -e *registration form*
anmelden *to register, to log on (comp.)*
die Anmeldung, -en *registration*
die Annahme, -n *assumption; also: receiving (goods)*
annehmen *to assume, to presume*
anonym *anonymous*
der Anruf, -e *telephone call*
anrufen *to call, to telephone*
ansagen *to announce*
anschauen *to look at, to review*
    sich etwas anschauen *to look at something*
der Anschluss, *connection*
die Anschrift, -en *address*
ansehen *to look at*
ansehen (sich) *to look at; to look at oneself*
die Ansichtskarte, -n *postcard*
anspringen *to start (car)*
anspruchsvoll *demanding, sophisticated*
die Anstalt, -en *institution*
(an)statt *instead of*
anstellen *to employ someone*
die Anstellung, -en *job, employment*
anstoßen *to toast (with a drink), to bump into, to run into*
anstrengend *strenuous*
die Antiquität, -en *antique object*
der Antiquitätenladen, *antique store, also: second-hand store*
der Anwalt, ¨e *lawyer*
antworten *to answer*
anwenden *to use, to apply, to put into effect*
die Anzahl *number of*

die Anzahl der Einwohner *the number of inhabitants*

die **Anzeige, -n** *advertisement*

    eine Anzeige aufgeben *to file a classified ad*

    eine Anzeige machen *to report someone (to the police)*

    **anzeigen** *to report; to show*

    **anziehen** *to put on, to dress*

    **anziehen (sich)** *to get dressed*

der **Anzug, ¨e** *suit (male)*

der **Apfel, ¨** *apple*

die **Apfelsine, -n** *orange*

der **Apfelstrudel** *apple strudel*

die **Apotheke, -n** *pharmacy*

    In der Apotheke *at the pharmacy*

der **Apotheker, -** *pharmacist*

der **Apparat, -e** *telephone; machine*

    Wer ist am Apparat? *Who is on the phone?*

der **Aquisateur, -e** *someone soliciting new clients (esp. advertising)*

der **April** *April*

die **Arbeit, -en** *work*

    **arbeiten** *to work*

der **Arbeitseifer** *love of work, love of efficiency*

die **Arbeitslosigkeit** *unemployment*

der **Arbeitsplatz, ¨e** *position, job*

die **Arbeitsplatzbeschaffung** *job creation (program)*

das **Archiv, -e** *archive(s)*

der **Architekt, -en/-en** *architect*

die **Architektur** *architecture*

der **Ärmel, -** *sleeve*

    etwas aus dem Ärmel schütteln *to come up with something off-handedly*

    **arrangieren** *to arrange*

die **Art, -en** *type, kind*

der **Artikel, -** *article; object*

der **Arzt, ¨e** *physician (m.)*

    beim Arzt *at the physician's*

die **Ärztin, -nen** *physician (f.)*

der **Aschermittwoch** *Ash Wednesday*

das **Aspirin, -** *aspirin*

die **Assistentin, -nen** *(fem) assistant*

die **Attraktivität** *attractiveness, attraction*

    **auch** *also*

    **auf** *on top of, onto, on*

    auf Wiederhören *good-bye (on the telephone)*

    auf Wiedersehen *good-bye*

der **Aufenthalt, -e** *stay*

    Ich wünsche einen angenehmen Aufenthalt. *Have a pleasant stay.*

die **Aufgabe, -n** *task, duty*

    **aufhören** *to stop*

    **aufladen** *to load*

    **auflegen** *to hang up (the telephone)*

die **Aufnahme, -n** *photo; recording*

    **aufnehmen** *to take down, to take in*

    **aufpassen** *to pay attention*

    **aufregen (sich)** *to get excited, to be upset*

    **aufregend** *exciting*

der **Aufschlag, ¨e** *surcharge*

der **Aufschnitt** *cold cuts*

    **aufstehen** *to get up*

    **aufsteigen** *to ascend, to climb*

der **Aufstieg, -e** *ascent*

der **Auftrag, ¨e** *order*

der **Auftraggeber, -** *person who places order, here: person authorized to sign on account*

    **aufwachen** *to wake up*

die **Aufwendung, -en** *cost, (raised) funds*

    **aufziehen** *to parade, to march*

der **Aufzug, ¨e** *elevator; act (in a play)*

der **Augenblick, -e** *moment*

    **augenblicklich** *current, currently, just now*

der **August** *August*

der **Auktionär, -e** *auctioneer*

    **aus** *out, from (is a native of)*

    **ausbauen** *to expand, to add (to a building)*

die **Ausbildung** *professional training, education*

der **Ausblick** *view*

    **ausbrechen** *to escape, to break out*

die **Ausdauer** *perseverance*

die **Ausfahrt, -en** *highway exit*

der **Ausgang, ¨e** *exit*

    **ausgebucht** *booked, sold out*

    **ausgehen** *to go out*

    **ausgezeichnet** *excellent*

der **Ausguss** *sink*

    **aushalten** *to endure*

die **Aushilfearbeit** *temporary employment*

    **auskennen (sich)** *to be well versed in, to know well*

die **Auskunft, ¨e** *information*

    **ausladen** *to unload*

das **Ausland** *abroad, foreign territories*

    **ausländisch** *foreign*

die **Auslandsüberweisung, -en** *transfer (to foreign bank)*

die **Ausnahme, -n** *exception*

    **ausräumen** *to clear out*

    **ausruhen (sich)** *to rest, to relax*

    **aussagen** *to testify*

der **Ausschlag** *rash*

das Außenfach, ¨e *outside compartment*
ausschließlich *exclusively*
ausschreiben *to advertise*
aussehen *to look like, to resemble*
außer *except for, besides*
außerhalb (+ gen.) *outside of*
das Aussichtsdeck *observation deck*
aussteigen *to get off, to deboard, to leave (also fig.)*
ausstellen *to exhibit*
die Ausstellung, -en *exhibition*
das Ausstellungsstück, -e *displayed item, exhibit*
aussuchen *to pick, to choose*
der Austausch *exchange*
der Ausverkauf, ¨e *sale*
im Ausverkauf sein *to be on sale*
ausverkauft *sold out*
die Auswahl *selection, choice*
auszahlen *to pay out*
das Auszahlungsformular, -e *withdrawal slip*
ausziehen *to undress, to take off*
ausziehen (sich) *to get undressed*
der Auszubildende, -n/-n *trainee, intern*
das Auto(mobil), -s(e) *car*
die Autobahn, -en *highway, freeway*
auf der Autobahn *on the highway*
der Automechaniker, - *auto mechanic*
die Autoreparaturwerkstatt, ¨en *automobile repair shop*
in der Autoreparaturwerkstatt *at the automobile repair shop*
der Autor, -en *author*

# B

der Bach, ¨e *brook, stream*
backen *to bake*
der Backenzahn, ¨e *molar*
das Bad, ¨er *bathroom; bath*
der Bademantel, ¨ *bathrobe, beach robe*
die Bademütze, -en *bathing cap*
baden *to bathe*
der Badeort, -e *spa, health resort*
das Badetuch, ¨er *bath towel, beach towel*
das Badezimmer, - *bathroom*
die Bahn, -en *railroad*
die Deutsche Bundesbahn (DB) *German National Railway*
der Bahnhof, ¨e *train station*
am Bahnhof *at the train station*
der Bahnsteig, -e *platform*
bald *soon*
der Balkon, -e *balcony, deck*
der Ball, ¨e *ball*

das Band, ¨er *tape, ribbon*
die Bank, -en *bank*
auf der Bank *at the bank*
der/die Bankangestellte, -n, -n *bank clerk, teller*
die Bankgebühr, -en *charge, fee*
die Bankleitzahl (BLZ), -en *sorting code*
die Banküberweisung, -en *bank transfer*
das Bargeld *cash*
der Bart, ¨e *beard*
die Batterie, -n *battery*
bauen *to build*
das Bauhaus *German design group, 1919–1933*
der Bauherr, -en *(architectural) client for whom something is built*
der Baumeister, - *(antiqu.) architect*
der Bau, Bauten *building*
der Bauzaun, ¨e *construction site, fence*
bayerisch *Bavarian*
Bayern *Bavaria*
beachten *to watch out for, to bear in mind*
der Beamte, -n/-n *official, civil servant*
die Beamtin, -nen *official, civil servant*
beanspruchen *to demand*
beantworten *to answer*
die Bearbeitungsgebühr, -en *administrative fee*
beauftragen *to order, to engage*
der Becher, - *cup, beaker*
bedanken (sich) *to thank*
bedauerlich *sad, regretful, regrettable*
die Bedienung *service, operation; waiter/waitress*
die Bedienungsanleitung, -en *operational manual, owner's manual*
bedrohlich *threatening*
bedürfen *to require*
beeilen (sich) *to hurry*
beeindrucken *to impress*
beeindruckend *impressing*
beenden *to end, to shut down (comp.)*
befähigen *to enable*
befördern *to promote*
befragen *to question*
der/die Befragte, -n, -n *the one questioned, participant*
begrüßen *to greet*
die Begrüßung, -en *greeting*
behandeln *to treat*
behilflich sein *to help someone, to lend a hand*
bei *with; at; near; during*
beide *both*

das **Bein, -e** *leg*
    **bekannt sein** *to be known, familiar,*
        *accustomed to*
der **Bekannte, -n** *acquaintance*
die **Belastung, -en** *pressure*
die **Beilage, -n** *insert*
das **Beispiel, -e** *example*
    zum Beispiel (z.B.) *for example*
der **Beitrag, ⸚e** *entry, share, participant's*
    *share*
    **bekannt** *well-known*
    **beklagen** *to lament*
    **beklagen (sich)** *to complain*
    **bekommen** *to get*
    **beleidigen** *to insult*
die **Beleidigung, -en** *insult*
    **beliebt** *beloved, much loved*
    **belustigen** *to amuse*
    **bemerken** *to observe, to notice*
    **bemerkenswert** *noteworthy*
    **benachrichtigen** *to inform*
die **Benachrichtigung, -en** *information,*
    *message, memorandum*
    **benötigen** *to need, to require*
das **Benzin** *gas*
    **beobachten** *to watch*
die **Beratung, -en** *consultation*
die **Beratungskosten** *consultancy fee*
    **berechnen** *to charge (interest or fees)*
der **Bereich, -e** *area, field (fig. rather than*
    *geographically)*
    **bereinigen** *to clear, clean up*
der **Berg, -e** *hill, mountain*
die **Bergbahn, -en** *mountain railway*
der **Beruf, -e** *profession, job*
    **beruflich** *professionally*
die **Berufsaussicht, -en** *professional*
    *prospects*
die **Berufsschule, -en** *vocational school*
    **beruhigen** *to quiet, to calm*
    sich beruhigen *to calm down*
    **berühmt** *famous*
    **beschädigt** *damaged*
    **beschäftigen** *to employ, to occupy time*
der **Bescheid** *notification*
    Bescheid geben *to inform someone,*
    *to let someone know*
    Bescheid wissen *to be informed, to be*
    *familiar with*
    **bescheinigen** *to certify, to guarantee*
die **Bescheinigung, -en** *certificate*
    **beschönigen** *to make more than it is*
    **beschreiben** *to describe*
die **Beschwerde, -n** *complaint*
    **beschweren (sich)** *to complain*
    **besetzt** *busy, occupied*

    **besichtigen** *to view*
die **Besichtigung, -en** *sightseeing;*
    *inspection*
    **besonders** *especially*
    **besorgt** *worried*
    **besprechen** *to discuss*
die **Besprechung, -en** *meeting; review*
    **bestätigen** *to confirm*
die **Bestätigung, -en** *confirmation,*
    *acknowledgment*
    **bestehen** *to pass*
    **bestellen** *to order*
    **bestimmt** *certain(ly)*
der **Bestimmungsort, -e** *destination*
der **Besuch, -e** *visit, visitor*
    zu Besuch kommen *to come for a*
    *visit*
das **Beispiel, -e** *example*
    **besuchen** *to visit*
    **betäuben** *to numb; to anesthetize*
die **Betäubung, -en** *anesthesia*
    die örtliche Betäubung *local*
    *anesthesia*
    **betonen** *to emphasize; to add inflection*
die **Betonung, -en** *emphasis, inflection*
der **Betrag, ⸚e** *amount*
das **Bett, -en** *bed*
    **bevor** *before*
die **Bevölkerung** *population*
    **bewerben (sich)** *to apply*
der **Bewerber, -** *applicants*
die **Bewerbung, -en** *(job) application*
    **bewundern** *to admire*
    **bewusst** *conscious; aware*
das **Bewusstsein** *consciousness; awareness*
    **bezahlen** *to pay (someone or for*
    *something)*
    **beziehen** *to receive (money)*
das **Bier, -e** *beer*
der **Biergarten, ⸚** *beer garden*
    **bieten** *to offer*
die **Bilanz, -en** *(financ., statist.) balance*
das **Bild, -er** *picture, print*
der **Bildschirm, -e** *monitor, screen*
der **Bildhauer, -** *sculptor*
die **Bildhauerei** *(the art of) sculpture*
der **Bildungsweg, -e** *educational track*
    **billig** *cheap*
die **Binde, -n** *bandage*
    die elastische Binde *elastic bandage*
der **Binnenmarkt** *home market (as*
    *opposed to export market)*
    **bis** *until*
    Bis bald. *See you soon.*
    bis Montag *until Monday; by*
    *Monday; See you Monday.*

bis morgen *until tomorrow; by
tomorrow; See you tomorrow.*
**bitten** *to ask, to request*
**bitter** *bitter*
**blasen** *to blow*
**blass** *pale*
**blau** *blue*
blau sein, betrunken sein *to be
drunk*
**bleiben** *to stay, to remain*
Bleiben Sie am Apparat. *Hold on.
Stay on the line.*
Wie lange bleiben Sie? *How long will
you stay?*
**blond** *blond*
**die Blume, -n** *flower*
**das Blumengeschäft, -e** *flower shop*
**die Bluse, -n** *blouse*
**der Boden, ⁻n** *floor, base, attic*
**die Bohne, -n** *bean*
**bohnern** *to clean; to wax*
**bohren** *to drill*
**die Bombardierung, -en** *bombardment*
**der Bote, -n** *messenger (m.)*
**die Botin, -nen** *messenger (f.)*
**das Boxen** *boxing*
**der Boxkampf, ⁻e** *boxing match*
**brauchen** *to need*
**braun** *brown*
**die Bräune** *suntan*
**die Bremse, -n** *brake*
**bremsen** *to brake*
**das Bremspedal, -en** *brake pedal*
**brennen** *to burn*
**der Bretzel** (hochdtsch.), **-n** *pretzel*
**die Brezen** (bay.), **-** *(large) pretzel*
**der Brief, -e** *letter*
**der Briefkasten, ⁻** *mailbox*
**die Briefmarke, -n** *stamp*
**die Brille, -n** *glasses*
**bringen** *to bring*
**das Brot, -e** *bread*
das belegte Brot *open-faced sandwich*
das Brötchen, - *roll*
die Brotzeit *snack meal, dinner*
**der Bruder, ⁻** *brother*
**brünett** *brunette*
**das Buch, ⁻er** *book*
**buchen** *to book*
**das Bücherregal, -e** *bookshelf*
**der Buchhalter, -** *accountant*
**die Buchung, -en** *booking, here:
transaction*
**das Bügeleisen, -** *iron*
**bügeln** *to iron*
**die Bühne, -n** *attic; stage*

**die Bundesrepublik (Deutschland)**
*Federal Republic (of Germany)*
**das Bundesland, ⁻er** *state*
**die Bundesbahn** *the Federal Railroad
System*
**der Bundestag** *House of Representatives*
**die Bundestagswahl, -en** *federal election*
**die Burg, -en** *castle*
**der Bürger, -** *burgher, citizen*
**das Büro, -s** *office*
**der Bus, -se** *bus*
**die Buslinie, -n** *bus line*
**die Bushaltestelle, -n** *bus stop*
**die Butter** *butter*
das Butterbrot, -e *a slice of bread and
butter*

# C

**das Café, -s** *café, coffee shop*
im Café *in a café*
**der Cent, -** *cent*
**die Chemie** *chemistry*
**der Chemiker, -** *chemist*
**die Christlich-Demokratische Union
(CDU)** *the Christian Democratic
Union*

# D

**da** *there*
da oben *up there*
**das Dach, ⁻er** *roof*
**der Dachboden, ⁻en** *attic*
**die Dachterrasse, -n** *roof terrace*
**dahinter** *behind, beyond*
**damals** *back then*
**die Dame, -n** *lady*
**der Damenfriseur, -e (der Damenfrisör,
-e)** *lady's hairdresser*
**der Damenfriseursalon, -s (der
Damenfrisörsalon, -s)** *lady's
hairdresser's; salon*
**damit** *so that*
**dampfen** *to steam*
**der Dampfer** *steamboat*
**die Dampferfahrt, -en** *steamboat trip*
**danach** *following that, afterward*
**der Dank** *thanks; gratitude*
Recht herzlichen Dank! *Thank you
very much.*
**die Dankbarkeit** *gratitude*
**danken** *to thank*
**Danke.** *Thanks. Thank you.*
**Dankeschön.** *Thanks a lot.*
**dann** *then*

darüber *about that*
das *the (neuter)*
dass *that (conj.)*
die Datei, -en *(computer) file*
die Datenverarbeitung, -en *data processing*
der Dauerauftrag, ⸚e *automatic bank transfer (for regular monthly payments)*
dauern *to last*
die Dauerwelle, -n *permanent wave*
davor *before*
die Decke, -n *blanket*
der Deckel, - *lid*
dein *your (fam. sing.)*
die Delikatesse, -n *delicatessen, gourmet food*
demnach *therefore, thus*
die Demokratie *democracy*
die Demokratisierung *change into a democracy*
denken *to think*
denken an (+ acc.) *to think of*
denn *because, since*
das Deodorant, -s *deodorant*
der *the (masculine)*
der -, die -, dasselbe *same (as in identical items)*
deren *whose, their*
deshalb *that's why*
deswegen *because of that*
deutlich *clearly visible, recognizable*
deutlich werden *to become clear, to crystallize, to emerge*
Deutschland *Germany*
der Dezember *December*
das Dia, -s *color slide*
der Dialog, -e *dialogue*
der Diaprojektor, -en *slide projector*
die *the (feminine)*
der Dieb, -e *thief (m.)*
die Diebin, -nen *thief (f.)*
der Diebstahl, ⸚e *theft*
die Diele, -n *hallway*
der Dienst, -e *service*
der Dienstag *Tuesday*
diese -r, -s *this*
die Differenz, -en *difference*
direkt *directly*
der Dirigent, -en *conductor*
die Diskussion *discussion*
diskutieren *to discuss*
doch *of course*
der Dokumentarfilm *documentary*
der Dom, -e *cathedral*
der Donnerstag *Thursday*

doppelt *double*
das Doppelzimmer, - *double room*
das Dorf, ⸚er *village*
dort *there*
dort drüben *over there*
dorthin *there (to)*
die Dose, -n *tin, jar, box*
der Dramatiker, - *playwright*
draußen *outside*
das Drehbuch *script*
der Drehort *(film) location, set*
am Drehort *(film) on location*
drei *three*
dreimal *three times*
dreißig *thirty*
dreizehn *thirteen*
dringend *urgent(ly)*
die Drogerie, -n *drugstore*
in der Drogerie *at the drugstore*
der Drogeriemarkt, ⸚e *self-service drugstore*
der Drogist, -en, -en *drugstore employee*
drüben *over there, there*
der Drucker, - *printer*
du *you (fam.)*
dumm *stupid; silly*
Wie dumm! *How silly!*
das Duplikat, -e *carbon copy, duplicate*
durch *through*
durchkommen *to get through, to make it, to survive*
durchleben *to survive, to overcome*
durchqueren *to cut through*
der Durchschlag *carbon copy, duplicate*
durchschneiden *to cut through (paper)*
der Durchschnitt *average*
durchsetzen *to push through, to enforce*
durchsichtig *transparent*
dürfen *may, to be allowed to*
die Dusche, -n *shower*
duschen *to shower*
duschen (sich) *to take a shower*

# E

ebenfalls *equally, also*
echt *real, genuine*
die Ecke, -n *corner*
der Edelstahl *stainless steel*
ehe *before*
eher *sooner*
ehemalig *former*
das Ei, -er *egg*
eigen *own*

das Eigenheim, -e *house (owned)*
   eigenständig *independent(ly), under*
      *no supervision*
   eigentlich *actually*
das Eigentum, ⁻er *belongings*
die Eigentumswohnung, -en
      *condominium*
die Eile *hurry*
   Ich bin in Eile. *I'm in a hurry.*
   einbrechen *to break in*
der Einbrecher, - *burglar*
der Einbruch, -e *break-in, burglary*
   eindämmen *to halt, to block*
   eindrucksvoll *striking*
   einfach *simple, easy*
der Eingang, ⁻e *entrance*
   eingeber *to enter (comp.)*
der/die Einheimische, -n, -n *local*
      *resident*
   einige *several*
der Einkauf, ⁻e *purchase*
   Einkäufe machen *shopping*
   einkaufen *to shop*
die Einkaufsliste, -n *shopping list*
   einladen *to load; to invite*
die Einladung, -en *invitation*
   einmal *once*
      noch einmal *once more*
   einmalig *unique, once*
   einnehmen *to take, to swallow*
   einreiben *to rub*
   einreiben (sich) *to rub oneself*
   einreichen *to present check for payment*
   eins *one*
   einschalten *to switch on*
die Einschaltquote, -en *viewer rating*
das Einschreiben, - *registered letter*
   eintragen *to register*
   eintragen (sich) *to register oneself*
   eintreffen *to arrive*
   einverstanden *okay, agreed*
   einzahlen *to pay in, to deposit*
das Einzahlungsformular, -e *deposit slip*
die Einzelheit, -en *detail*
   einzeln *piece by piece, singly*
das Einzelzimmer, - *single room*
   einzig *sole*
   einzigartig *unique*
das Eis *ice; ice cream*
   eisig *icy*
das Elektrogerät, -e *electrical appliance*
   elf *eleven*
die Eltern *parents*
die E-Mail, -s *e-mail*
   empfangen *to receive, to greet*
der Empfang *reception*

in Empfang nehmen *to receive (both*
      *people as well as objects or delivery)*
der Empfänger, - *receiver of mail*
der Empfangschef, -s *reception clerk*
   empfehlen *to recommend*
   empfindlich *sensitive*
das Ende *end*
   endlich *finally*
   endlos *endless*
   eng *narrow*
   England *England*
der Enkel, - *grandson*
die Enkelin, -nen *granddaughter*
   enorm *vast, far-reaching*
   entfernen *to remove*
   entfernt *distant, far away*
die Entfernung, -en *distance*
   entkommen *to get away*
   entscheiden *to decide*
   entschließen (sich) *to decide (to do*
      *something)*
   entschuldigen *to apologize, to excuse*
   Entschuldigen Sie. *Excuse me.*
die Entschuldigung, -en *excuse*
   entsprechend *equivalent*
   entstehen *to come up, to arise*
   entwenden *to steal, to remove*
      *(illegally)*
   entwickeln *to develop*
der Entwurf, ⁻e *draft, rough draft, rough*
      *drawing, design*
die Entzündung, -en *inflammation*
er *he*
der Erbe, -n *heir*
   erben *to inherit*
   erbrechen *to vomit*
die Erbschaft, -en *inheritance*
die Erbse, -n *pea*
das Erbstück, -e *heirloom*
die Erdbeermarmelade, -n *strawberry*
      *jam*
das Erdgeschoss *first floor*
   erfahren *to find out, to experience*
   erfolgen *to occur, to result*
   erfrischend *refreshing*
das Ergebnis, -se *result, outcome*
   erhalten *to receive; to maintain*
   erholen (sich) *to relax, to recuperate*
   erinnern (sich) *to remember*
die Erinnerung, -en *memory*
   zur Erinnerung *in memory of*
   erkälten (sich) *to catch a cold*
die Erkältung, -en *cold*
   erkennen *to recognize*
   erleichtern *to facilitate, to make easier*
   ermüdend *tiring*

erneuern *to redefine, to renew*
die Erneuerung, -en *renovation,*
    *renewal*
eröffnen *to open up (an account)*
erreichen *to reach*
errichten *to erect (building)*
der Ersatz *replacement, substitute*
erschöpft *exhausted*
erschrecken *to scare someone*
erschweren *to complicate, to make*
    *more difficult*
ersetzen *to replace*
erst *only (in reference to time)*
erstaunlich *amazing*
erster, -e, -es *first*
die Erststimme *first vote*
erwarten *to await*
die Erwartung, -en *expectation,*
    *anticipation*
erweitern *to expand, to extend*
erwerben *to acquire*
erzählen *to tell; narrate*
    erzählen von (+ dat.) *to tell about*
es *it*
das Essen *food, meal*
essen *to eat*
etwas *some, a little*
euer *your (fam. pl.)*
der Euro, - *euro*
Europa *Europe*
europäisch *European*
    Europäische Union *European Union*
die Euroscheckkarte, -n *checking card*

# F

die Fabel, -n *fable*
fabelhaft *fabulous*
der Fabrikant, -en *manufacturer (m.)*
das Fach, ̈er *compartment, subject*
die Fachkenntnis, -se *knowledge in a*
    *particular field*
der Faden, ̈ *thread*
die Fahne, -n *flag*
fahren *to drive, to go, to travel*
    fahren mit (+ dat.) *to go by means of*
die Fahrkarte, -n *ticket*
fallen *to fall*
falsch *wrong*
die Familie, -n *family*
fangen *to catch*
fantastisch *fantastic*
die Farbe, -n *color, paint*
färben *to dye*
das Färben *coloring, dyeing*
der Fasching *carnival*

die Fassung, -en *version*
die Fastenzeit, -en *Lent*
faszinierend (adj./adv.) *fascinating*
das Faxgerät, -e *fax machine*
der Februar *February*
fehlen *to be absent, to be missing*
    Was fehlt? *What's missing?*
    Was fehlt denn? *What is wrong?*
    Was fehlt dir? *What's wrong with*
    *you?*
die Feier, -n *celebration, ceremony*
feiern *to celebrate*
der Feiertag, -e *holiday, day of rest*
    der kirchliche Feiertag, -e *Christian*
    *holiday*
fein *fine, precious*
    vom feinsten *at its best*
der Felsen, - *rock*
das Fenster, - *window*
der Fensterrahmen, - *windowframe*
die Feriensaison *vacation season*
fern *distant, far away*
die Ferne *far distance*
die Fernbedienung, -en *remote control*
das Ferngespräch, -e *long distance call*
fernsehen *to watch TV*
das Fernsehen *TV (the media)*
der Fernseher, - *TV (the set)*
fertig *ready, finished*
fest *firm*
das Fest, -e *party, celebration, festival*
die Festplatte, -n *hard drive*
die Festspiele *(plural) festival*
der Festtag, -e *holiday, festivity*
die Filiale, -n *branch*
der Film, -e *film, movie*
der Film-Enthusiast, -en *movie fan*
der Filmemacher, - *filmmaker*
finden *to find*
der Fisch, -e *fish*
der Fischer, - *fisherman*
der Fischmarkt, ̈e *fish market*
die Fläche, -n *plane, surface*
die Flasche, -n *bottle*
der Fleck, -en *mark, spot, stain*
das Fleisch *meat*
die Fliege, -n *fly*
fliegen *to fly*
flink *quick*
flirten *to flirt*
der Flohmarkt, ̈e *flea market*
floppen *to flop*
die Flucht *flight (escape)*
flüchten *to escape*
der Flug, ̈e *flight*
der Fluggast, ̈e *airplane passenger*

der Flughafen, ⁔ *airport*
    auf dem Flughafen *at the airport*
das Flugzeug, -e *airplane*
der Flur, -e *hallway*
die Förderung, -en *mining (raw material); sponsoring, subsidization (financial)*
das Förderungsprojekt, -e *subsidized project*
die Form, -en *form, shape*
das Format, -e *format*
das Formular, -e *form, document*
das Foto, -s *photograph*
der Fotoapparat, -e *camera*
der Fotograf, -en, -en *photographer*
die Frage, -n *question*
die Frankiermaschine, -n *postage meter*
Frankreich *France*
französisch *French*
die Frau, -en *woman, wife, Ms. (used as a form of address)*
die Freie Demokratische Partei (FDP) *the Free Democratic Party*
Freitag *Friday*
die Fremdwährung, -en *foreign currency*
die Fremdsprache, -en *foreign language*
freuen (sich) *to be happy about something, to be joyful*
der Freund, -e *male friend, boyfriend*
die Freundin, -nen *female friend, girlfriend*
frieren *to freeze*
    Es friert. *It's freezing.*
frisch *fresh*
der Friseur, -e (der Frisör, -e) *male hairdresser*
der Friseursalon, -s (der Frisörsalon, -s) *barbershop, hairdresser's salon, beauty parlor*
    im Friseursalon *at the barbershop/hairdresser*
die Friseuse, -n (die Frisöse, -n) *female hairdresser*
frisieren *to do someone's hair*
die Frucht, ⁔e *fruit*
der Frühling *spring*
das Frühstück *breakfast*
    inklusive Frühstück *including breakfast*
    zum Frühstück *for breakfast*
führen *to lead, to guide*
die Führung, -en *guided tour*
das Führungsteam, -s *management team*
füllen *to fill*
die Füllung, -en *filling*

das Fundbüro, -s *lost and found*
    auf dem Fundbüro *at the lost and found*
fünf *five*
fünfzehn *fifteen*
fünfzig *fifty*
die Funktion, -en *function*
funktionieren *to function, to work*
für *for*
furchtbar *terrible*
fürchten *to fear*
der Fuß, ⁔sse *foot*
der Fußball, ⁔e *soccer*
das Fußballspiel, -e *soccer match*
der Fußboden, ⁔ *floor*
der Fußgänger, - *pedestrian*
die Fußgängerzone, -n *pedestrian zone*
der Fußnagel, ⁔ *toenail*
die Fußpflege *pedicure*
der Fußpfleger, - *male pedicurist*
die Fußpflegerin, -nen *female pedicurist*
die Fußzeile, -n *footer (comp.)*

# G

gähnen *to yawn*
die Gallerie, -n *gallery*
der Gang, ⁔e *aisle, hallway, corridor*
ganz *very, whole*
    ganz im Gegenteil *quite to the contrary*
    ganz und gar *utterly, totally*
die Garage, -n *garage*
die Garantie, -n *guarantee*
garantiert *warranted, guaranteed*
der Garantieschein, -e *warranty*
die Garderobe, -n *cloakroom, coatrack, wardrobe*
das Gartencafé, -s *garden café*
das Gaspedal, -e *gasoline pedal*
der Gastarbeiter, - *foreign worker*
der Gastgeber, - *host*
die Gastronomie *catering, restaurant trade*
das Gebäck *pastry*
das Gebäude, - *building*
geben *to give*
    es gibt *there is, there are*
das Gebiet, -e *area*
das Gebirge, - *mountains, mountain*
    im Gebirge *in the mountains*
der Gebirgsverein, - *hiking and climbing club*
das Gebiss, -e *set of teeth*
der Gebrauch *usage*

gebrauchen *to use*
die Gebrauchsanweisung, -en *owner's manual, operational manual*
der Gebrauchtwagen, - *used car*
die Gebühr, -en *charge*
gebührenfrei *free of charge, no fee payable*
der Gedanke, -n *thought*
die Geduld *patience*
gefallen (+ dat.) *to please, to like*
das Gefängnis, -se *prison, jail*
gegen *against, around*
    gegen zehn Uhr, *around ten o'clock*
gegenseitig *each other, one another, reciprocal*
der Gegenstand, ¨e *object*
    persönliche Gegenstände *personal items*
das Gegenteil, -e *the direct opposite (to something)*
gegenüber *opposite (only with location)*
gehen *to go, to leave*
    Wie geht es Ihnen? *How are you? (pol.)*
    Wie geht's? *How are you? (fam.)*
    Mir geht's nicht so gut. *I'm not feeling so well.*
gehören *to belong*
gelb *yellow*
das Geld, -er *money*
der Geldautomat, -en *automatic teller machine*
die Geldbörse, -n *purse*
das Gemälde, - *painting*
gemischt *mixed*
das Gemüse *vegetable(s)*
gemütlich *cozy*
genau *exact, exactly*
genauso *exactly like, just as*
genießen *to enjoy*
geöffnet *open*
das Gepäck *luggage cart*
der Gepäckwagen, - *baggage cart*
gerade *straight*
geradeaus *straight ahead*
das Gerät, -e *device, appliance, machine*
die Gerechtigkeit *justice*
das Gericht *court of law*
der Gerichtshof *court of law*
gern *gladly, willingly*
das Geschäft, -e *store; business; deal*
die Geschäftsbesprechung, -en *business discussion*
der Geschäftsführer, - *manager*
das Geschenk, -e *gift*

der Geschenkeinkauf, ¨e *gift purchases*
geschlossen *closed*
die Geschwindigkeitsbegrenzung *speed limit*
der/die Geschworene, -n *jury*
das Gespräch, -e *conversation, talk*
die Gesprächsrunde *panel (discussion)*
gestatten *to allow, to permit*
    Gestatten Sie? *Permit me. May I introduce myself?*
gestern *yesterday*
gesund *healthy*
das Getränk, -e *beverage*
das Getreide *grain*
das Gewerbe, - *line of business, line of manufacturing*
die Gewerbeanmeldung, -en *business registration*
die Gewerkschaft, -en *union*
gewinnen *to win*
das Gewürz, -e *spice*
der Gipfel, - *summit, mountaintop*
die Girlande, -n *garland*
das Girokonto, -en *checking account*
der Glanz *shine*
glänzend *splendid*
die Glanzzeit *peak period*
das Glas, ¨er *glass*
der Glasbläser, - *glassblower*
glatt *smooth*
die Glatze, -n *bald head*
glauben *to believe*
gleich *in a minute; equal*
der Gleichstrom *direct current (DC)*
gleichzeitig *simultaneous(ly)*
der Gletscher, - *glacier*
glücklich *happy*
das Gold *gold*
golden *golden*
die Goldfüllung, -en *gold filling*
der Goldhenkel, - *gold handle*
die Goldkrone, -n *gold crown*
die Grafik, -en *graphic, illustration*
der Grafiker, - *graphic designer*
das Gramm *gram*
die Grammatik *grammar*
das Gras, ¨er *grass*
grau *gray*
greifen *to grasp*
die Grenze *border*
Griechenland *Greece*
die Grippe, -n *flu*
groß *big, large*
großartig *magnificent*
die Größe, -n *size*
der Größenwahn *delusions of grandeur*

der Großkonzern, -e *large concern,*
    *company*
die Großmutter, ¨ *grandmother*
der Großvater, ¨ *grandfather*
    Gruetzi *hello (Swiss)*
    grün *green*
die Grünen *the Green Party*
die Grünanlage, -n *green space/area,*
    *park, recreational facility*
die Grünfläche, -n *green space, lawn, park*
    gründen *to found*
das Grundstück, -e *land, estate*
der Grundstückspreis, -e *cost of land*
die Gruppentour, -en *group tour*
der Gruß, ¨sse *greeting*
    Mit freundlichen Grüßen *Sincerely*
    grüßen *to greet*
        Grüß Gott! *Hello (So. German)*
    gucken *to look*
        Guck mal! *Look!*
    gültig *valid*
die Gunst, ¨ *favor*
    zu Ihren Gunsten *in your favor*
der Gürtel, - *belt*
    gut *good, well*
der Gutachter, - *evaluator*
die Gutschrift, -en *credit (form)*
das Gymnasium, Gymnasien *high school*
die Gymnastik *gymnastics, calisthenics*
    Gymnastik machen *to do calisthenics*

# H

das Haar, -e *hair*
die Haarfarbe, -n *hair color*
der Haarschnitt *haircut*
der Haartrockner, - *hair dryer*
das Haarwuchsmittel, - *hair growth*
    *product*
    haben *to have*
der Hafen, ¨ *harbor*
    haften *to be liable*
die Haftung, -en *liability*
    Haftung übernehmen *to accept*
    *liability*
die Halbzeit, -en *halftime*
die Hälfte, -n *half*
    zur Hälfte *by half*
die Halle, -n *hall*
    hallo *hello*
der Hals, ¨e *throat*
die Halsschmerzen (pl.) *sore throat*
    halten *to hold, to stop*
        sich auf dem Laufenden halten *to*
        *keep abreast of the news, to stay*
        *informed*

    halten von *to think of, to evaluate*
die Haltestelle, -n *stop (as in*
    *bus/tram/subway stop)*
die Hand, ¨e *hand*
    handeln von *to be about, deal with*
    *(topic)*
    handeln mit *to deal with (goods)*
    handeln *to bargain*
der Händler, - *trader, shopkeeper*
die Handlung, -en *story, action*
der Handschuh, -e *glove*
das Handtuch, ¨er *towel*
das Handwerk *handicraft, trade*
der Handwerker, - *handyman, workman,*
    *craftsman*
    handwerklich *manual*
    handwerkliches Geschick *manual*
    *dexterity, skilled hands*
das Handy, -s *cell phone*
    hängen *to hang*
    hängen bleiben *to be stuck with*
    *something, to be left with*
der Hanseat, -en *person of old lineage*
    *from a Hanseatic city*
    hart *hard*
der Hass *hate, hatred*
    hassen *to hate*
    häßlich *ugly*
der Hauptbahnhof, ¨e *main, central*
    *railroad station*
der Hauptdarsteller, - *protagonist,*
    *lead/main character*
die Hauptpost *main post office*
die Hauptrolle, -n *lead, main role*
    hauptsächlich *mainly,*
    *predominantly*
das Haus, ¨er *house*
    heben *to lift*
    heilbar *curable*
    heilen *to heal*
die Heilquelle, -n *medicinal spring*
das Heimatland *homeland*
    Mein Heimatland ist . . . *My*
    *homeland is . . .*
    heiß *hot (temperature only)*
    heißen *to be named, to be called*
    helfen *to help*
        helfen bei (+ dat.) *to help with*
    hell *light, pale*
das Hemd, -en *shirt*
    heraus *out(ward)*
    herausbrechen *to break off*
der Herbst *autumn*
der Herd, -e *stove*
der Herr, -en, -en *gentleman, mister*
    *(usually used only in address)*

der Herrenfriseursalon, -s (der
  Herrenfrisörsalon, -s)
  *barbershop*
herrlich *glorious, wonderful*
herumsprechen (sich) *to be talked
  about, to become common knowledge*
herunter *down(ward)*
herunterladen *to download*
herüber *across, over*
hervorheben *to point out, to
  emphasize*
hervorragend *excellent*
heute *today*
heutzutage *nowadays*
die Hexe, -n *witch*
hier *here*
hierzulande *in this country*
die Hilfe *help*
die Hilfeleistung, -en *aid, support*
hilfreich *helpful*
hilfsbereit *willing to help*
der Himmel, - *sky, heaven*
  Himmelfahrt *Ascension Day*
  hin *(to) there*
    hin und zurück *round trip*
  hinaus *out(ward)*
  hinten *at the back*
  hinter *behind*
  hintereinander *one behind the other*
der Hintergrund, ⁓e *background,
  backdrop*
  hinterlegen *to leave (a note, document,
    etc.) for someone*
  hinüber *across, over*
  hinunter *down(ward)*
  hinweg *over, beyond*
der Hirtenjunge, -n, -n *shepherd boy*
  hoch *high (up), tall*
der Hochbetrieb *rush hour, busy season,
  rush*
das Hochdeutsch *High German, Standard
  German*
die Hochschule *university, academy*
der Hof, ⁓e *court, yard*
  hoffen *to hope*
  hoffentlich *hopeful*
die Hoffnung, -en *hope*
das Hoftheater *court theater*
  höher *higher*
  die Homepage, -s *homepage*
  hören *to hear, listen*
    Auf Wiederhören. *Good-bye. (on the
      telephone)*
der Hörer, - *receiver*
die Hose, -n *pants, slacks*
das Hotel, -s *hotel*

  im Hotel *in the hotel*
der Hotelpage, -n *bellhop*
  hübsch *pretty*
das Huhn, ⁓er *hen*
das Hühnchen, - *chicken*
  hundert *hundred*
    hunderteins *one hundred one*
    zweihundert *two hundred*
der Hunger *hunger*
  Hunger haben *to be hungry*
  hungrig *hungry*
die Hupe, -n *horn*
  husten *to cough*
der Husten *cough*
der Hut, ⁓e *hat*
die Hütte, -n *shelter, hut*

# I

  ich *I*
die Idee, -n *idea*
  ihr *you (fam.pl.), her, their*
  Ihr *your (pol.)*
  immer *always*
  immerhin *still, after all, if nothing else*
die Immobilie, -n *real estate*
der Immobilienmakler, - *real estate agent*
der Immobilienmarkt, ⁓e *real estate
  market*
die Impfung, -en *vaccination*
  imposant *impressive*
  in *in, inside, into*
  indem *in such a way that*
  individuell *individual*
die Industrie, -n *industry*
der Industrielle, -n *industrialist*
  industriell *industrial*
das Industrieprojekt, -e *industrial project*
der Industriezweig, -e *industrial branch*
  informieren *to inform*
    sich informieren über (+ acc.) *to
      inform oneself about, to stay
      informed*
die Infrastruktur, -en *infrastructure*
der Inhalt, -e *contents*
die Initiale, -n *initials*
  innen *inside, interior*
der/die Innenausstatter/in, -, -nen
  *interior designer*
das Innenfach, ⁓er *inside compartment*
  innerhalb (+ gen.) *inside*
die Innenstadt, ⁓e *center of town,
  downtown district*
die Insel, -n *island*
das Inserat, -e *the advertisement*
  inserieren *to place an ad*

**insgesamt** *altogether, sum total*
**der Intendant, -en** *director*
**interessieren für (sich)** *to be interested in*
**interessant** *interesting*
**das Internet** *Internet*
**die Internetadresse, -n** *Internet address*
**das Internet-Café, -s** *Internet Café*
**das Interview, -s** *interview*
**interviewen** *to interview*
**der Interviewleiter, -** *interview director*
**investieren** *to invest*
**die Investition, -en** *investment*
**das Investment, -s** *investment*
**irgendwann** *sometime*
**irgendwas** *something*
**irgendwo** *somewhere*
**Italien** *Italy*

# J

**die Jacht, -en** *yacht*
**die Jacke, -n** *jacket*
**das Jahr, -e** *year*
**die Jahreszeit, -n** *season*
**das Jahrhundert, -e** *century*
**die Jahrhundertwende, -n** *turn of the century*
**jährlich** *yearly, every year*
**der Januar** *January*
**je** *ever; each; respectively*
    **je . . . desto** *the more . . . the more, the . . . the . . .*
    **je nachdem** *depends on, depending upon*
**jedenfalls** *anyway, in any case*
**jede, -r, -s** *each, every*
**jederzeit** *anytime*
**jeder** *each, every*
**jener** *that*
**jemals** *ever*
**jetzt** *now*
**der Jog(h)urt** *yogurt*
**die Jugend** *youth*
**jugendlich** *young, adolescent*
**der Jugendstil** *Art Nouveau*
**der Juli** *July*
**jung** *young*
**der Junge, -n/-n** *boy*
**der Juni** *June*
**Jura** *the study of law*
    **Er studiert Jura.** *He is studying law.*
**der Jurist, -en** *lawyer, attorney at law*

# K

**das Kabel, -** *cable*
**die Kabelfabrik, -en** *cable factory*
**das Kabelfernsehprogramm, -e** *cable program*
**der Kabelsender, -** *(TV) cable station*
**der Kaffee, -s** *coffee*
    **Kaffee trinken** *to have coffee*
**der Kahn, ¨e** *barge*
**der Kaiser, -** *emperor*
**die Kaiserzeit** *imperial times*
**das Kalbfleisch** *veal*
**kalt** *cold*
**die Kamera, -s** *camera*
**kämmen** *to comb*
    **sich (die Haare) kämmen** *to comb (one's hair)*
**kämpfen** *to fight*
**Kanada** *Canada*
**der Kandidat, -en** *candidate*
**die Kanne, -n** *pot (as in coffeepot), pitcher*
**die Kapelle, -n** *band*
**das Kapital** *capital, assets*
**die Kapitalangabe, -n** *details on assets or profit and loss (of a company)*
**kaputt** *broken, tired*
    **Ich bin kaputt.** *I'm exhausted.*
**der Karfreitag** *Good Friday*
**die Karies** *periodontal disease, cavity, caries*
**der Karneval** *carnival (period before Lent)*
**das Kartentelefon, -e** *public telephone operated with telephone cards*
**die Kartoffel, -n** *potato*
**der Karton, -s** *box, cardboard box, carton*
**der Käse** *cheese*
**die Kasse, -n** *cash till, cashier's desk*
**der Kassierer, -** *cashier*
**die Kathedrale, -n** *cathedral*
**kaufen** *to buy*
**das Kaufhaus, ¨er** *department store*
    **im Kaufhaus** *in the department store*
**kaum** *hardly, barely*
**kein** *no, not any, not a*
**keinerlei** *none*
**der Keller, -** *cellar, basement*
**kennen** *to know, to be familiar with*
**die Kenntnis, -se** *knowledge*
**die Keramik** *ceramics*
    **das Keramikstück, -** *ceramic piece*
**der Kiez** *old inner city residential area*
**das Kilo, -s** *kilo*
**der Kilometer, -** *kilometer (km)*
**das Kind, -er** *child*
**das Kinderzimmer, -** *child's room*

kindhaft *childlike*
der **Kineast, -en** *film enthusiast*
das **Kino, -s** *movie theater*
das **Kinopublikum** *moviegoers, movie theater audience*
der **Kiosk, -s** *kiosk, newsstand*
die **Kirche, -en** *church*
die **Kirsche, -n** *cherry*
der **Kirschstrudel** *cherry strudel*
die **Kiste, -n** *box, container*
der **Kittel, -** *gown, apron*
die **Klage, -n** *complaint, (jur.) lawsuit*
der **Kläger, -** *plaintiff*
  **klappen** *to work, to happen (successfully)*
  **klar** *clear*
    **Klar!** *Certainly! Of course!*
die **Klasse, -n** *class*
    die erste Klasse *the first class*
    erster Klasse *first class*
das **Kleid, -er** *dress*
die **Kleidung** *clothing*
  **klein** *small*
das **Kleingeld** *coins, change*
die **Kleinstadt, ¨e** *small town*
  **klemmen** *to jam*
das **Kloster, ¨** *cloister*
der **Knopf, ¨e** *button*
  **knusprig** *crunchy, crispy*
  **kochen** *to cook*
der **Kode** *code*
der **Kodename** *codeword*
das **Kodewort** *codeword*
der **Koffer, -** *suitcase*
das **Kofferfließband, ¨er** *baggage conveyor belt*
der **Kollege, -n** *co-worker, colleague*
das **Kombinationsschloss, ¨er** *combination lock*
  **kommen** *to come*
    Ich komme aus (+ dat.) *I come from (with locations)*
die **Kommunalwahl, -en** *local election*
der/die **Komparse, -n** *(film) extra*
die **Konditorei, -en** *confectionary, café with bakery and pastry shop*
die **Konferenz, -en** *conference*
der **Konferenzraum, ¨e** *conference room*
der **Kongress, -e** *convention*
  **können** *to be able to, can (ability)*
der **Konkurrent, -en** *competitor*
die **Konkurrenz** *competition*
  **konkurrenzfähig** *competitive*
der **Konsul, -n** *consul*
das **Konsulat, -e** *consulate*
der **Kontakt, -e** *connection, contact*

das **Konto, Konten** *account*
    ein Konto einrichten *to open an account*
    ein Konto eröffnen *to open an account*
der **Kontoauszug, ¨e** *bank statement*
der **Kontostand** *balance (of account)*
der **Kontrast, -e** *contrast*
der **Konzern, -e** *company, corporation*
das **Konzert, -e** *concert*
der **Konzertveranstalter, -** *concert promoter*
  **kooperieren** *to cooperate*
das **Kopfrechnen** *mental arithmetic*
der **Kopf, ¨e** *head*
  **kopflos** *headless*
die **Kopfschmerzen** *(pl.) headache*
das **Kopfweh** *headache*
die **Kopfzeile, -n** *header (comp.)*
die **Koproduktion, -en** *co-production*
der **Körper, -** *body*
die **Körperpflege** *personal hygiene*
der **Körperpuder, -** *dusting powder*
die **Kosten** *(plural) costs*
  **kosten** *to cost*
    Was kostet das? *How much does it cost?*
der **Kragen, ¨** *collar*
  **krank** *ill*
    Ich bin krank. *I am ill.*
  **krankhaft** *pathological*
die **Krankheit, -en** *illness, disease*
der **Kranz, ¨e** *circle, frame, wreath*
  **kraus** *wavy, frizzy*
die **Kreditkarte, -n** *credit card*
der **Kreis, -e** *circle*
das **Kreuz, -e** *cross*
die **Kreuzung, -en** *intersection, cross breed*
der **Krieg, -e** *war, (often) World War II*
der **Kriminalfall, ¨e** *criminal case*
das **Kriminalgericht, -e** *criminal court*
der **Krimskrams** *knickknacks, odds and ends*
die **Kritik, -en** *criticism*
der **Kritiker, -** *critic, reviewer*
die **Krone, -n** *crown*
der **Kronzeuge, -n** *main witness*
die **Küche, -n** *kitchen*
der **Kuchen, -** *cake*
der **Kugelschreiber, -** *ballpoint pen*
die **Kuh, ¨e** *cow*
der **Kühlschrank, ¨e** *refrigerator*
der **Kuli, -s** *ballpoint pen*
die **Kultur, -en** *culture*
die **Kulturnotiz, -en** *cultural note*
der **Kunde, -n/-n** *customer*

die Kunst, ⁓e *art, the arts*
der Künstler, - *artist*
das Künstlerviertel, - *artists' district, district inhabited by artists*
die Kunstausstellung, -en *art exhibition*
die Kunstbibliothek, -en *art library*
das Kunstmuseum, Kunstmuseen *art museum*
das Kunstwerk, -e *work of art*
die Kur, -en *cure, treatment*
    eine Kur machen *to take a cure*
der Kurfürst, -en *elector, electoral prince*
der Kurgast, ⁓e *spa visitor*
das Kurkonzert, -e *concert at a spa*
der Kurort, -e *spa, health resort*
    in einem Kurort *in a spa*
der Kurs, -e *exchange rate*
    Der Kurs ist niedrig/hoch. *The exchange rate is low/high.*
der Kurswagen, - *through coach (on a train)*
die Kurtaxe, -n *spa surcharge*
kurz *short*
    in Kürze *shortly*
die Kurzfassung, -en *synopsis, short version*
der Kurzfilm -e *short feature, short film*
kurzfristig *on short notice*
die Kusine, -n *cousin (f.)*

# L

labil *unstable*
laden *to load*
der Laden, ⁓ *store*
der Ladenschluss *(store) closing time*
    vor Ladenschluss *before the store closes*
der Ladentisch, -e *(store) counter*
die Lage, -n *location, position*
die Lampe, -n *lamp*
der Lampenschirm -e *lampshade*
das Land, ⁓er *country; state*
    auf dem Land *in the country*
die Landtagswahl, -en *state election*
landesweit *statewide; all across the country*
lang *long (adj.)*
lange *long (adv.)*
    Es dauert lange. *It takes a long time.*
langfristig *long-term*
langsam *slow, slowly*
längst *for long, already; longest*
langweilig *boring*
lassen *to leave, to let*
der Lastkraftwagen, -en *truck*

der Lastwagen, - *truck*
laufen *to run, to walk*
    jemandem auf dem Laufenden halten *to keep someone posted or informed*
im Lauf(e) (+ gen.) *in the course of*
laut *loud*
läuten *to ring*
leben *to live*
das Leben, - *life*
der Lebenslauf, ⁓e *résumé*
die Lebensmittel *(pl.) groceries*
der Lebensretter, - *life-saver*
lecker *delicious*
    Die Kuchen sind lecker. *The cakes are delicious.*
das Leder *leather*
    aus Leder *made from leather*
leer *empty*
legen *to put down, to lay down*
legen (sich) *to lie down*
die Legende, -n *legend*
der Lehm *mud*
die Lehmpackung, -en *mud pack*
lehren *to teach*
die Lehre, -n *(vocational) training (in trade or crafts)*
der Lehrling, -e *trainee*
der Lehrer, - *teacher*
leicht *light, easy*
die Leichtathletik *track and field*
leid: Es tut mir leid. *I'm sorry.*
leiden *to suffer*
    leiden an (+ dat.) *to suffer from*
leider *unfortunately*
leid tun *to be sorry, to feel sorry for someone*
der Leierkasten, ⁓ *barrel organ*
der Leierkastenmann, ⁓er *organ-grinder*
leihen *to lend*
das Leinen *linen*
das Leinenkleid *linen dress*
die Leinwand, ⁓e *canvas, (cinemat.: screen)*
leisten (sich) *to afford*
leiten *to lead, manage*
die Leitung, -en *cable, pipe; leadership, management; line*
    Die Leitung ist besetzt. *The line is busy.*
    Die Leitung ist gestört. *The line is temporarily out of order.*
lernen *to learn*
die Leselampe, -en *reading lamp*
letzte, -r, -s *last*
der Leuchttisch, -e *light box, illuminated screen, slide table*

die Leute *people*
das Licht, -er *light*
das Lieblingsstück, -e *favorite piece*
der Lieferant, -en, -en *supplier, deliverer*
die Lieferung, -en *delivery*
der Lieferschein, -e *delivery note*
der Lieferwagen, - *delivery van*
die Liegehalle, -n *lounge*
   liegen *to lie*
der Liegewagen, - *couchette (on a train)*
die Liga, -s *league*
   links *to the left, on the left*
der Liter, - *liter*
das Lizenzrecht, -e *licensing right*
der LKW, -s *truck*
das Loch, ˙-er *hole*
   ein Loch im Zahn *cavity*
die Locke, -n *curl*
   lockig *curly*
der Logensitz, -e *box seat*
   lohnen *to reward*
   Es lohnt sich. *It's worthwhile.*
   los *loose*
   Was ist los? *What's the matter?*
   löschen *to delete*
   lösen *to solve*
   losrennen *to dash off*
die Lösung, -en *answer, solution*
   luftdicht *airtight*
   luftig *breezy*
die Luftpost *air mail*
   mit Luftpost *by airmail*
die Lunge, -n *lung*
die Lust, ˙-e *pleasure, delight*
   Lust haben *to feel like*

# M

   machen *to do, to make*
   (Es) macht nichts. *(It) doesn't matter.*
   Das macht 125 Euro. *That'll be 125 euros.*
die Magenschmerzen (pl.) *stomachache*
der Mai *may*
   mal *once, x-times*
   malen *to paint*
der Maler, - *painter*
die Malerei, -en *painting*
der Makler, - *broker, real estate agent*
   manche *some (usually pl.)*
   manchmal *sometimes*
der Mann, ˙-er *man*
   männlich *male*
die Mannschaft, -en *team*
der Markt, ˙-e *market*

die Marktanalyse, -n *market analysis*
das Marzipan *marzipan*
der März *march*
die Massage, -n *massage*
das Maßband, ˙-er *tape measure*
der Maskenball, ˙-e *costume ball*
die Massenmedien *mass media*
das Material, -ien *material*
die Matinée, -s *matinee*
die Maus, ˙-e *mouse*
das Medikament, -e *medication*
das Meer, -e *ocean, shore*
   mehr *more*
   mehrere *several*
das Mehl *flour*
   mehrmals *several times*
   mein *my*
die Menge *quantity, a lot*
der Mensch, -en *human being*
die Menschheit *mankind*
die Messe, -n *trade fair, exhibition*
   auf der Messe *at the trade fair*
das Messegelände, - *exhibition grounds*
   messen *to measure*
der Messestand, ˙-e *booth*
das Metall, -e *metal*
der Metallfaden, ˙- *metal thread*
die Miete, -n *rent*
   mieten *to rent*
   ein Segelboot mieten *to rent a sailboat*
die Mietpreisbindung, -en *rent control*
das Mietshaus, ˙-er *tenement building, apartment complex*
der Mietvertrag, ˙-e *rental agreement*
die Million, -en *million*
   mindestens *at least, minimal*
das Mineralwasserbad, ˙-er *bath or pool with mineral water*
die Minute, -n *minute*
der Mist *manure, garbage*
   mit *with, by means of (transportation)*
der Mitarbeiter, - *colleague, co-worker*
   mitbringen *to bring along, to take with you*
   mitmachen *to participate*
   mitnehmen *to bring along, to take with*
der Mittag, -e *noon*
das Mittagessen, - *lunch (main meal)*
   zum Mittagessen *for lunch*
   mittags *at noon*
die Mitte, -n *middle*
   mitteilen *to inform*
die Mitteilung, -en *message, information*
die Mittel, - *medicine*

das **Mittelalter** *the Middle Ages, medieval times*
der **Mittelgang, ⁻e** *middle aisle*
das **Mittelmeer** *Mediterranean Sea*
die **Mittelmeerinsel, -n** *Mediterranean island*
    **mitten: mitten auf** (+ dat.) *in the middle of*
die **Mitternacht, ⁻e** *midnight*
    **mitwirken** *to participate, to take part in*
die **Mitwirkenden** *(theater, film) participants*
der **Mittwoch** *Wednesday*
die **Möbel** *(plural) furniture*
der **Möbelstile, -** *furniture style*
das **Möbelstück, -e** *piece of furniture*
das **Modell, -e** *model*
    **mögen** *to like (inclination), may (possibility)*
die **Möglichkeit, -en** *possibility*
die **Mohrrübe, -n** *carrot*
der **Moment, -e** *moment*
    **im Moment** *at the moment, at the present time*
der **Monat, -e** *month*
der **Monitor, -e** *computer monitor, screen*
    **monströs** *monstrous, gigantic (ugly)*
der **Montag** *Monday*
    **morgen** *tomorrow*
    **morgen früh** *tomorrow morning*
der **Morgen** *morning*
    **Guten Morgen.** *Good morning. (pol.)*
    **Morgen** *morning, hello (fam.)*
    **morgens** *in the morning*
das **Motorrad, ⁻er** *motorcycle*
    **müde** *tired*
    **Ich bin müde.** *I am tired.*
der **Müll** *garbage*
das **Müllfahrzeug, -e** *garbage truck*
das **Mundwasser, ⁻** *mouthwash*
der **Münzfernsprecher, -** *coin-operated public telephone*
die **Musik** *music*
das **Museum, -een** *museum*
    **im Museum** *at the museum*
der **Musiker, -** *musician*
das **Müsli, -s** *muesli*
    **müssen** *to have to, must (necessity)*
die **Mutter, ⁻** *mother*
die **Mütze, -n** *cap*

# N

    **nach** *after, to*
der **Nachbar, -n** *neighbor*
    **nachdem** *after that*
    **nachfragen** *inquire*
    **nachmittags** *during the afternoon*
die **Nachricht, -en** *news item*
    **eine Nachricht hinterlassen** *to leave a message*
die **Nachrichten** *news broadcast*
    **nachsehen** *to look up*
die **Nacht, ⁻e** *night*
    **Gute Nacht.** *Good night.*
der **Nachtisch, -e** *dessert*
    **nachts** *at night*
der **Nacken, -** *neck*
    **nah(e)** *near, close*
der **Nahverkehrszug, ⁻e** *short distance train*
    **nächste** *next*
der **Name, -n** *name*
    **nass** *wet*
der **Nationalfeiertag, -e** *national holiday*
    **natürlich** *of course, natural*
    **neb(e)lig** *foggy*
    **neben** *next to*
die **Nebenrolle, -n** *supporting role*
der **Neffe, -n, -n** *nephew*
    **nehmen** *to take*
    **nein** *no*
    **nennen** *to call, to address, to name*
der **Nerv, -en** *nerve*
der **Nervenkitzel** *thrill, suspense*
    **nett** *nice*
das **Netz, -e** *net, network, system*
    **neu** *new*
der **Neue, -n** *the new person*
das **Neujahr** *New Year*
    **neulich** *recently*
    **neun** *nine*
    **neunzehn** *nineteen*
    **neunzig** *ninety*
    **nicht** *not*
die **Nichte, -n** *niece*
das **Nichtraucherabteil, -e** *the non-smoking compartment*
    **nichts** *nothing*
    **nie** *never*
die **Niederlage, -n** *defeat*
    **niemals** *never*
    **niemand** *no one, nobody*
    **nirgendwo** *nowhere*
    **noch** *still, yet*
    **noch nicht** *not yet*
    **nochmal** *once again, one more time*

nördlich *northerly*
die Nordsee *North Sea*
normal *standard, normal*
normalerweise *normally, generally*
der Notausgang, ¨e *emergency exit*
die Note, -n *grade*
die Notiz, -en *note*
    das Notizbuch, ¨er *notebook*
    Notizen machen *to take (a few) notes*
der Notruf, -e *emergency call*
der November *November*
    Numerus Clausus *"closed numbers"*
    *system limiting university*
    *admissions*
die Nummer, -n *number*
nur *only*
nützlich *useful*
nutzlos *useless*
der Nutznießer, - *beneficiary*
    einen Nutznießer einsetzen *to name*
    *a beneficiary*

# O

ob *if, whether*
der Obdachlose, -n *homeless person*
das Obdachlosenheim, -e *homeless*
    *shelter*
obgleich *although*
das Obst *(singular) fruit*
obwohl *although, despite*
der Ochse, -n *ox*
oder *or*
offenbar *obviously*
offensichtlich *obvious(ly)*
öffentlich *public, open*
oft *often*
ohne *without*
das Ohr, -en *ear*
    viel um die Ohren haben *to be*
    *occupied with something, to be busy*
das Öl, -e *oil, ointment*
der Oktober *October*
der Omnibus, -se *bus*
der Onkel, - *uncle*
online *online*
die Oper, -n *opera, opera house*
die Ordnung, -en *order*
    Alles ist in Ordnung. *Everything is*
    *all right.*
    Etwas ist nicht in Ordnung.
    *Something is wrong.*
orientieren *to inform, to instruct*
die Originalverpackung, -en *factory*
    *box/wrapping*
der Ort *place, location, town*

Ostern *Easter*
Österreich *Austria*
östlich *easterly*
die Ostsee *Baltic sea*
der Overheadprojektor, -en *overhead*
    *projector*

# P

das Paar, -e *pair*
    ein paar *a few*
das Päckchen, - *package*
die Packung, -en *box*
    Es steht auf der Packung. *It's written*
    *on the box.*
das Paket, -e *parcel*
das Panorama *panorama*
die Parade, -en *parade*
der Park, -s *park (recreational area)*
das Parkett, -s *parquet, orchestra*
    parkieren *to park one's car*
die Parknähe *adjacent to a park*
der Parkplatz, ¨e *parking lot, parking*
    *space*
die Partei, -en *political party*
das Parterre *first floor*
der Pass, ¨e *passport*
    die Passkontrolle, -n *passport control*
    passen *to fit, to suit*
    Der Mantel passt mir. *The coat fits*
    *me.*
    passend *fitting, suitable*
der Patient, -en *patient (m.)*
die Patientin, -nen *patient (f.)*
die Pause, -n *intermission*
    perfekt *perfect*
das Perlmutt *mother of pearl*
die Person, -en *person*
das Personal *personnel*
der Personenzug, ¨e *passenger train*
der Pfad, -e *path, trail*
der Pfadfinder, - *boy scout*
der Pfandbrief, -e *(financ.) bond*
die Pfeife, -n *pipe*
    Pfingsten *Pentecost, Whitsuntide*
das Pfund, -e *pound, half a kilo*
die Pizzeria, Pizzerien *pizza shop*
das Photo, -s *photo*
der Photoapparat, -e *camera*
der Photograph
der Plan, ¨e *plan*
    planen *to plan*
die Plastik, -en *sculpture*
der Platz, ¨e *seat, square, place*
der Platzanweiser, - *usher*
    plaudern *to chat*

plötzlich *suddenly*
die Politik *politics*
die Polsterung *upholstery*
portugiesisch *Portuguese*
die Position, -en *position*
die Post *post office, mail*
das Postamt, ⁻er *post office*
die Postkarte, -n *postcard*
die Postleitzahl, -en *ZIP code*
das Postscheckkonto *postal checking account*
das Postsparkonto *postal savings account*
das Porzellan *china, porcelain*
die Pracht, - *splendor, pomp*
prachtvoll *splendid*
praktisch *practical, convenient*
das Präparat, -e *medical or chemical preparation, medication*
der Präsident, -en *president*
der Preis, -e *price, prize*
preisgünstig *reasonable*
die Preisverleihung, -en *award ceremony*
die Presse, -n *press*
pressieren *to be urgent*
prima *excellent, great*
der Privatgegenstand, ⁻e *personal belongings*
das Problem, -e *problem*
die Produktion, -en *production*
der Produzent, -en/-en *producer*
das Programm, -e *program*
das zweite Programm *Channel Two*
promenieren *to stroll about, to promenade*
das Projekt, -e *project*
prüfen *to assess, to test, to check, to examine*
die Luft prüfen *to check the air*
die Prüfung, -en *test, examination*
das Publikum *audience*
der Pullover, - *sweater*
pünktlich *on time, punctual*
putzen *to clean*
sich die Zähne putzen *to brush one's teeth*

# Q

das Quadrat, -e *square*
quadratisch *square*
der Quadratmeter, - *square meter*
die Qualität *quality*
qualitativ *qualitywise*
die Quantität *size, quantity*
quantitativ *sizewise, (rich in) quantity*
der Quark *(fresh/curd) cheese*

das Quartier *quarter, accommodations*
quer *across, diagonal, sideways*
die Quelle, -n *spring, well*
der Querulant, -en *grumbler, querulous person*
quietschen *to screech, to squeak*
quittieren *to give a receipt for; discharge*
die Quittung, -en *receipt*

# R

das Rad, ⁻er *bicycle*
Rad fahren *to bicycle, to cycle*
das Radio, -s *radio*
im Radio *on the radio*
der Radsport *cycling*
der Rahmen, - *frame*
im Rahmen *as part of . . . , within the framework*
der Rand, ⁻er *edge, border*
der Rang, ⁻e *dress circle*
rar *rare*
die Rarität, -en *rarity*
rasen *to speed*
der Rasierapparat, -e *electric razor*
die Rasiercreme, -s *shaving cream*
rasieren *to shave*
sich rasieren *to shave oneself*
die Raststätte, -n *rest area, service station (along Autobahn)*
der Rat *advice; senate, committee*
raten *to guess*
das Rathaus, ⁻er *town hall*
der Raucher, - *smoker*
der Raum, ⁻e *room*
die Realität, -en *reality*
rechnen *to count*
die Rechnung, -en *check, invoice*
Die Rechnung bitte! *The check please!*
der Rechnungseingang, ⁻e *receipt of invoice*
das Recht *right, law*
Recht haben *to be right*
rechts *to the right, on the right*
der Rechtsanwalt, ⁻e *lawyer (m.)*
die Rechtsanwältin, -nen *lawyer (f.)*
rechtzeitig *in time*
die Redaktion, -en *editorial department*
der Redaktionsschluss, *time to go to press*
der Redakteur, -e *editor*
reell *real*
das Regal, -e *shelf*
regelmäßig *regular(ly)*
der Regen *rain*

der Regenmantel, ⸚ *raincoat*
die Regie *(film) direction*
   Regie führen *to direct*
der Regisseur, -e *film director*
   regnen *to rain*
      Es regnet. *It's raining.*
   reichen *to be sufficient*
      Es reicht. *It's enough.*
der Reifen, - *tire*
   reinigen *to clean*
      chemisch reinigen *to dry clean*
die Reinigung, -en *cleaning*
      die chemische Reinigung *dry*
        *cleaning*
die Reise, -n *journey, trip*
      Gute Reise. *Have a nice trip.*
das Reisebüro, -s *travel agency*
der Reiseführer, - *travel guide (book)*
die Reisegruppe, -n *travel group*
   reisen *to travel*
der/die Reisende, -n, -n *traveler*
der Reisepass, ⸚e *passport*
der Reisescheck, -s *traveler check*
die Reisetasche, -n *traveling bag*
das Reiseziel, -e *destination*
der Reißverschluss, ⸚e *zipper*
   rennen *to run*
   renommiert *renowned*
   renovieren *to renovate*
   reparieren *to repair*
die Reportage, -n *(TV/film) report*
   reservieren *to reserve*
   reserviert *reserved*
die Reservierung, -en *reservation*
das Restaurant, -s *restaurant*
      im Restaurant *in a restaurant*
das Rezept, -e *prescription, recipe*
die Rheintour *Rhine tour*
   richtig *correct, accurate*
das Rindfleisch *beef*
das Ritual, -e *ritual*
der Rock, ⸚e *skirt*
die Rolle, -n *role*
der Rollstuhl, ⸚e *wheelchair*
die Röntgenaufnahme, -n *X ray*
das Röntgenbild, -er *X-ray*
der Rosenmontag *Rose Monday (Monday*
      *before Lent)*
   rot *red*
die Rotation, -en *rotation*
das Rotationsverfahren, - *taking turns, in*
      *rotation*
   rötlich *reddish*
die Routine, -n *routine*
der Rückflug, ⸚e *return flight*
der Rucksack, ⸚e *backpack*

der Rücksitz, -e *backseat*
der Ruf *reputation*
   rufen *to call*
   ruhig *calm*
die Ruine, -n *ruin*

# S

die S-Bahn, -en *subway*
die Sache, -n *thing, item, stuff*
      die Sachen *belongings*
die Sachertorte, -n *Sacher torte*
der Sachschaden, ⸚ *damage to property*
   sagen *to say*
die Sahne *cream*
der Salat, -e *salad*
die Salbe, -n *salve*
der Samstag *Saturday*
der Sammler, - *collector*
die Sammlung, -en *collection*
das Sammlungsstück, -e *collection piece*
der Sand *sand*
   sandig *sandy*
der Sänger, - *singer*
   sanktionieren *to sanction, to stipulate*
   sauber *clean*
die Sauberkeit *cleanliness*
   sauer *sour*
die Säule, -n *column; pillar*
   Schade! *Too bad!*
der Schaden, ⸚ *damage*
      Personenschaden *personal injury*
      Sachschaden *material damage*
der Schadstoff, -e *harmful substance,*
      *hazardous waste*
   schaffen *to accomplish, to create; to*
      *work*
der Schal, -s *scarf*
der Schalter, - *desk, customer service desk,*
      *teller*
der Schalterbeamte, -n *postal clerk at the*
      *window*
die Schalterstunden, - *opening hours*
der Schauspieler, - *actor*
der Scheck, -s *check*
      einen Scheck einlösen *to cash a*
      *check*
die Scheckkarte, -n *checking card*
das Scheckkonto, -konten *checking*
      *account*
der Schein, -e *bill (money)*
   scheinen *to shine, to seem*
   schenken *to give*
die Schere, -n *pair of scissors*
   schicken *to send, to ship*
das Schiff, -e *ship, boat*

schießen *to shoot*
das **Schild, -er** *sign*
schimpfen mit *to scold*
schlafen *to sleep*
der **Schlafsack, ⸚e** *sleeping bag*
der **Schlafwagen, -** *sleeping car*
das **Schlafzimmer, -** *bedroom*
schlagen *to beat*
die **Schlagfertigkeit, -en** *wit, ready wit*
die **Schlagsahne** *whipped cream*
die **Schlagzeile, -n** *(newspaper) headline*
schlecht *bad, badly*
    Es geht mir schlecht. *I'm not feeling well.*
schleppen *to haul*
schleudern *to skid, to spin*
schließen *to close*
schließlich *finally, eventually*
der **Schlüssel** *key*
die **Schmerzen** *pain, hurt*
schmerzen *to hurt*
der **Schmuck** *jewelry*
das **Schmuckstück, -e** *piece of jewelry, treasure*
der **Schmuggel** *smuggling*
schmunzeln *to smirk, to smile*
der **Schnee** *snow*
der **Schneefall, ⸚e** *snowfall*
schneiden *to cut*
schneien *to snow*
    Es schneit. *It's snowing.*
schnell *quick, fast*
der **Schnellimbiss, -e** *snack bar*
die **Schnellreinigung, -en** *express dry cleaning*
das **Schnitzel, -** *cutlet*
der **Schnupftabak** *snuff*
die **Schnupftabakdose, -n** *snuffbox*
der **Schnurrbart, ⸚e** *mustache*
der **Schöffe, -n** *jury*
die **Schöffin, -en** *jury*
die **Schokolade** *chocolate*
schon *already*
schön *beautiful*
der **Schrank, ⸚e** *wardrobe, cupboard, armoire, closet*
schrecklich *horrible*
schreiben *to write*
    schreiben an (+ acc.) *to write to*
    schreiben über (+ acc.) *to write about*
die **Schreibmaschine, -n** *typewriter*
der **Schreibtisch, -e** *desk*
schrecklich *horrible*
schreien *to scream, to yell*
der **Schriftverkehr** *correspondence*

die **Schublade, -n** *drawer*
die **Schule, -n** *school*
der **Schulabgänger, -** *graduate*
der **Schüler, -** *(school) student*
der **Schwabe, -n** *Swabian*
schwäbisch *Swabian (adj.)*
schwach *weak*
der **Schwager, ⸚** *brother-in-law*
die **Schwägerin, -nen** *sister-in-law*
schwarz *black*
die **Schwarzwälderkirschtorte, -n** *Black Forest cake*
das **Schwein, -e** *pig, pork*
    Schwein haben *to be lucky (undeservedly)*
das **Schweinefleisch** *pork*
die **Schweiz** *Switzerland*
der **Schweizer, -** *Swiss (person)*
schweizerisch *Swiss (adj.)*
    schwyzerdütsch *Swiss German*
die **Schwellung, -en** *swelling*
die **Schwester, -n** *sister*
schwimmen *to swim*
das **Schwimmen** *swimming*
schwindlig *dizzy*
schwül *muggy*
sechs *six*
sechzehn *sixteen*
sechzig *sixty*
der **See, -n** *lake*
die **See** *ocean*
das **Segel, -** *sail*
das **Segelboot, -e** *sailing boat*
segeln *to sail*
das **Segelschiff, -e** *sailing ship*
das **Seerecht** *maritime rights*
der **Seetang** *seaweed*
der **Segelanzug, ⸚e** *sailing suit*
sehen *to see*
    auf Wiedersehen *good-bye (pol.)*
die **Sehenswürdigkeit, -en** *sight, point of interest*
die **Sehne, -n** *tendon*
die **Seide, -n** *silk*
die **Seife, -n** *soap*
sein *his, its*
sein *to be*
    frei sein *to be available*
    fertig sein *to be ready*
seit *since, for (time expressions)*
die **Seite, -n** *page*
der **Sekretär, -e** *male secretary*
selber (colloquial) *self*
selbst *self*
selbstverständlich *naturally, of course*
seltsam *strange, odd*

das Seminar, -e *seminar, seminary*
die Semmel, -n *bread roll*
die Sendeanstalt, -en *(radio, TV) station, network*
senden *to send*
der Sender, - *station (radio, TV)*
der September *September*
servieren *to serve*
Servus *good-bye (Austrian)*
der Sessel, - *armchair*
die Sesselbahn, -en *chair lift*
setzen *to sit down, to set, to place, to put*
sicher *sure, safe, secure; certain(ly)*
der Sicherheitsgurt, -e *safety belt*
sicherlich *certainly*
die Sicht *view*
die Sicherheit, -en *security, safety*
mit Sicherheit *absolutely, definitely*
sicherlich *certainly*
sie *she, they*
Sie *(formal) you*
sieben *seven*
siebzehn *seventeen*
siebzig *seventy*
der Sieg, -e *victory*
siegen *to win*
das Silber *silver*
sitzen *to sit*
der Sitzplan, ⸚e *seating plan*
die Sitzung, -en *meeting*
der Ski, -er *ski(s)*
skilaufen, skifahren *skiing*
die Skulptur, -en *sculpture*
der Slogan, -s *slogan*
so *so*
so dass *so that*
die Socke, -n *sock*
ein Paar Socken *a pair of socks*
das Sofa, -s *sofa, couch*
sogar *even*
der Sohn, ⸚e *son*
solch, -e, -r, -s *such*
sollen *to be supposed to (obligation)*
somit *thus, therefore*
der Sommer *summer*
das Sonderangebot, -e *special offer*
die Sonderausstellung, -en *special exhibition*
sondern *but, on the contrary, rather*
nicht nur . . . sondern auch *not only . . . but also*
die Sonderschule, -n *special needs school*
der Sonnabend *Saturday*
die Sonne, -n *sun*
der Sonnenbrand, ⸚e *sunburn*

die Sonnenschutzcreme, -s *sunscreen lotion*
das Sonnenschutzöl, -e *sun protection oil*
der Sonntag *Sunday*
sonst *otherwise*
Sonst noch was? *Anything else?*
die Sorge, -n *worry*
sorgen (sich) *to worry about*
sorgen für *to care for, to look after, to see to something*
Sorgen haben *to be worried, to worry*
sowieso *in any case, anyhow*
sozial *social, (concerning) community*
die Sozialdemokratische Partei Deutschland (SPD) *the Social Democratic Party of Germany*
die Sozialwissenschaften *social sciences*
die Spalte, -n *(newsprint) column*
Spanien *Spain*
spannend *thrilling*
das Sparbuch, ⸚er *passbook, savings*
sparen *to save*
der Spargel, - *asparagus*
das Sparkonto, Sparkonten *savings account*
der Spaß, ⸚e *fun*
Spaß machen *to have fun, to enjoy; to kid, to make a joke*
spät *late*
Wie spät ist es? *What time is it?*
der Spaziergang, ⸚e *walk*
spazieren gehen *to go for a walk*
der Spediteur, -e *moving, shipping agent*
die Spedition, -en *carrier, shipping company*
speichern *to save (comp.)*
die Speisekarte, -n *menu*
der Speisewagen, - *dining car*
der Spekulant, -en *speculator (stock market)*
spekulieren *to speculate*
das Spiel, -e *game*
der Spieler, - *male player*
der Spielfilm, -e *feature film*
das Spielkasino, -s *gambling casino*
die Spielzeit, -en *season*
der Spion, -e *spy*
die Spionage *espionage*
spionieren *to spy*
die Spitze, -n *top*
die Splitterpartei, -en *splinter party*
der Sponsor, -en *sponsor*
der Sport *sports*
der Sportverein, -e *sports club*
sprechen *to talk*
sprechen über (+ acc.) *to talk about*

das Sprechzimmer, - *consulting room*
das Sprichwort, -e *proverb*
  sprichwörtlich *proverbial*
die Spritze, -n *shot*
  eine Spritze geben *to give a shot*
die Spur, -en *trace*
  spüren *to feel, to sense*
der Staat, -en *state (as in country)*
  staatlich *stately, the State's . . .*
das Staatstheater, - *federal theater*
  stabil *stable*
die Stadt, :e *city*
das Städtchen, - *small city*
die Stadtgrenze, -n *city border*
die Stadtmauer, -n *city fortification*
die Stadtmitte, -n *city center*
der Stadtplan, :e *city map*
die Stadtplanung, -en *city planning*
das Stadttheater, - *municipal theater*
das Stadtzentrum, Stadtzentren *city center*
der Stahl *steel*
die Stahlindustrie *steel industry*
der Stamm, :e *stem*
der Stammkunde, -n *regular customer*
der Stammtisch, -e *regular customer's table at bar/restaurant*
  ständig *constantly*
der Ständer, - *stand*
der Stapel, - *stack*
  stark *strong*
  stattfinden *to occur, to take place*
die Statue, -n *statue*
der Stau, -s *traffic jam*
der Staub *dust*
das Staubkorn, :er *speck of dust*
die Stehlampe, -n *torch lamp, freestanding lamp*
die Steckdose, -n *power socket, outlet*
  stecken *to stick, to put*
der Stecker, - *plug*
  stehen *to stand*
  in Schlange stehen *to stand in line*
  stehen bleiben *to stop, to stall*
  stehend *standing, (waterway) still*
  stehlen *to steal*
  steigen *to climb*
  steil *steep*
der Stein, -e *stone, rock*
die Stelle, -n *spot, place*
  stellen *to place, to put*
  stellen *to place*
die Stellenanzeige, -n *employment ad*
die Stellung, -en *position*
die Steuer, -n *tax*
der Steuerberater, - *C.P.A.*

die Steuererhöhung, -en *tax increase*
die Steuersenkung, -en *tax decrease*
  stiften *to donate*
die Stimme, -n *voice, vote*
  stimmen *to vote*
  seine Stimme abgeben *to cast one's vote*
  stimmen *to be correct, to be true*
  Das stimmt. *That's right.*
der Stock, :e *floor*
  der erste Stock *the second floor*
der Stoff, -e *material*
die Strafe, -n *penalty, punishment*
der Strand, :e *beach*
  am Strand *at the beach*
der Strandkorb, :e *large wicker beach chair*
die Straße, -n *street*
die Straßenbenutzungsgebühr, -en *toll*
das Straßencafé, -s *street café*
die Straßenwachthilfe, -n *highway assistance service*
  streng *strict*
  streuen *to sprinkle*
der Strom *electricity; (wide) river*
  stromlinienförmig *streamlined*
der Strudel, - *strudel*
das Stück, -e *piece*
der Student, -en *student*
  studieren *to go to college*
das Studium, Studien *study course*
der Stuhl, :e *chair*
  stundenlang *for hours*
der Sturm, :e *storm*
  stürmen *to storm*
  Es stürmt. *It's stormy.*
  stürmisch *rough, stormy*
die Sturmwarnung, -en *storm warning*
  stutzen *to trim*
  suchen *to search for, to look for*
  Südamerika *South America*
  südlich *southerly*
das Substantiv, -e *noun*
  süddeutsch *Southern German*
  sündigen *to sin*
  super *great, super*
der Supermarkt, :e *supermarket*
die Suppe, -n *soup*
  süß *sweet*
  sympathisch *likable*
  Er ist mir sympathisch. *I like him.*
  sympatisch sein *to be likable*
das Symptom, -e *symptom*
die Szene, -n *scene*

# T

die Tabaksdose, -n *tobacco box, snuffbox*
die Tablette, -n *pill*
der Tacho, -s *speedometer*
der Tachometer, - *speedometer*
die Tafel, -n *announcement board*
    die Tafel Schokolade *bar of chocolate*
der Tag, -e *day*
    Guten Tag. *Hello. (pol.)*
    Tag. *Hello. (fam.)*
    tagein tagaus *day in, day out*
    täglich *daily*
die Tagesroutine *daily routine*
die Tagesschau *daily news program*
    täglich *daily*
    dreimal täglich *three times a day*
die Tagung, -en *conference, convention*
das Tal, ¨er *valley*
    tanken *to get gas*
die Tankstelle, -n *gas station*
die Tante, -n *aunt*
die Tapete, -n *wallpaper*
    tapezieren *to hang wallpaper*
die Tasche, -n *bag, purse*
der Taschenrechner, - *pocket calculator*
die Taschenuhr, -en *pocket watch*
die Tasse, -n *cup*
    eine Tasse Kaffee *a cup of coffee*
die Tastatur, -en *(computer, typewriter) keyboard*
die Taste, -n *button, key*
der Täter, - *culprit, wrongdoer*
    tatsächlich *actually, in fact*
    tausend *thousand*
das Taxi, -s *taxi*
die Teekanne, -n *teapot*
das Teil, -e *piece*
der Teil, -e *part*
    teilnehmen *to participate*
der Teilnehmer, - *participant*
die Teilnahme *participation*
    teilweise *partly, partially*
das Telefon, -e *telephone*
der Telefonanschluss, ¨e *telephone connection*
das Telefonbuch, ¨er *telephone book*
die Telefongesellschaft, -en *telephone company*
das Telefongespräch, -e *telephone conversation*
    telefonieren *to call, to telephone*
    telefonisch *by telephone, over the telephone*
    telefonisch erreichen *to reach by telephone*

die Telefonkarte, -n *telephone card*
die Telefonnummer, -n *telephone number*
die Telefonrechnung, -en *telephone bill*
die Telefonzelle, -n *telephone booth*
der Teppich, -e *carpet, rug*
der Termin, -e *date, meeting, appointment*
    einen Termin haben *to have an appointment*
die Terrasse, -n *terrace, deck, patio*
    teuer *expensive*
das Theater, - *theater*
der Theaterbesucher, - *theatergoer*
die Theaterkasse, -n *theater box office*
    an der Theaterkasse *at the theater box office*
das Theaterstück, -e *play*
das Thema, -en *subject*
    tief *deep*
die Tiefgarage, -n *subterranean parking*
der Tisch, -e *table*
der Titel, - *title*
die Tochter, ¨er *daughter*
    toll *great (coll.)*
der Töpfer, - *potter*
die Töpferei *pottery*
das Tor, -e *gate, goal*
die Torte, -n *cake, (fruit) tart*
der Tourist, -en *tourist*
der Tourismus *tourism*
die Tournee, -n *tour*
die Tracht, -en *regional dress, costume*
die Tradition, -en *tradition*
    traditionsreich *traditional, steeped in tradition*
    tragen *to wear*
der Transformator, -en *transformer*
der Transport, -e *transport*
die Transportmöglichkeit, -en *means of transport*
    treffen *to meet*
das Treffen, - *meeting*
der Treffpunkt, -e *meeting point*
    treiben *to do (an activity)*
    Sport treiben *to engage in sports*
    trennen *to separate*
    sich trennen *to part*
die Treppe, -n *stairs*
    Nehmen Sie die Treppe! *Take the stairs!*
das Treppenhaus, ¨er *(public) staircase*
    treten *to step*
    trinken *to drink*
das Trinkgeld, -er *tip*
    trocknen *to dry*
    sich die Haare trocken *to dry one's hair*

der Tropfen, - *drop*
trotz *despite*
trotzdem *in spite of, despite, although*
Tschau. *Good-bye. (fam.)*
tschechisch *Czech*
Tschüss. *Good-bye. (fam.)*
tun *to do, to make*
  gut tun *to do good*
  Schwimmen tut ihr gut. *Swimming is good for her.*
  weh tun *to hurt*
  Es tut weh. *It hurts.*
die Tür, -en *door*
der Turm, ⸚e *tower*
turnen *gymnastics*
das Turnen *gymnastics*
die Tüte, -n *bag*

# U

über *over, above, across*
überall *all over, everywhere*
das Überangebot *surplus offer, offer (on saturated market)*
der Überblick, -e *overview*
übereinstimmen *to agree*
  nicht Übereinstimmen *to disagree*
überflüssig *superfluous, redundant*
überholen *to overtake (another vehicle)*
überlegen *to contemplate*
übernehmen *to take over, to accept*
überqueren *to cross over*
überprüfen *to check, to double-check*
übertragen *to broadcast*
die Überschwemmung, -en *flood, flooding*
übersehen *to estimate, to evaluate*
übersetzen *to translate*
überwechseln *to change, to transfer*
überweisen *to transfer*
die Überweisung, -en *(bank) transfer*
der Überweisungsauftrag, ⸚e *(bank) transfer form, remittance order*
überziehen *to overdraw, to pull over, to put on*
die Uhr, -en *clock, watch*
  Wieviel Uhr ist es? *What time is it?*
der Uhrmacher, - *watchmaker*
um (zu) *in order to*
um *around (time expressions)*
  Um wieviel Uhr? *At what time?*
der Umbau, -ten *redesign, renovation*
umbauen *to rebuild, to remodel*
die Umfrage, -n *survey, poll*
umgehen *to handle, to deal with; to avoid*

die Umgehungsstraße, -n *city highway diverting traffic from the center*
die Umhängetasche, -n *shoulder bag*
die Umkleidekabine, -n *fitting room*
umschalten *to switch, to convert*
umsetzen *convert*
  in die Realität umsetzen *to implement, to realize (an idea)*
umsonst *without charge, free*
umsteigen *to change trains*
der Umtausch, ⸚e *exchange*
umtauschen *to exchange*
die Umwelt *environment*
die Umweltforschung *environmental research*
der Umweltschutz *environmental protection*
umziehen *to move*
umziehen (sich) *to change one's clothes*
der Umzug, ⸚e *move*
unangenehm *unpleasant*
die Unannehmlichkeit, -en *inconvenience*
unbedingt *absolutely, without fail*
unbekannt *unknown*
und *and*
der Unfall, ⸚e *accident*
unglaublich *unbelievable*
uninteressant *uninteresting*
die Universität, -en *university*
unklar *unclear*
unmodern *old-fashioned*
unordentlich *untidy, unorganized*
der Unrat *waste, garbage*
unruhig *restless*
unsachgemäß *inappropriately, insufficiently, improperly*
unschlagbar *invincible*
unser *our*
unsichtbar *invisible*
unter *under, beneath, underneath*
unter anderem *among other things*
untereinander *among (themselves)*
unterhalten (sich) *to talk, to chat; to enjoy oneself*
unternehmen *to go and do something, to venture out*
das Unternehmen, - *company; venture, plan*
der Unternehmer, - *entrepreneur*
die Unternehmensberatung, -en *management consultancy*
die Unterlagen *documents, papers, records, files*
unterschreiben *to sign*
die Unterschrift, -en *signature*

**unterstellen** *to assume, to presume (with bad intent); to seek shelter; to place under/beneath*
**unterstützen** *to support*
die **Unterstützung** *support*
**untersuchen** *to examine closely, to investigate*
das **Unwetter, -** *violent storm*
**unzählig** *numerous, innumerable*
der **Urlaub** *vacation*
   in Urlaub fahren *to go on vacation*
das **Urlaubsziel, -e** *destination*
die **Urne, -n** *ballot box*
   zur Urne gehen *to cast one's vote*
die **USA** *the U.S.A.*

# V

der **Vater, ̈er** *father*
der **Vatikan** *Vatican*
der **Vegetarier, -** *vegetarian*
   **verabschieden (sich)** *to say good-bye*
   Ich verabschiede mich. *I'm saying good-bye.*
die **Verabschiedung, -en** *good-bye, leave-taking*
   **veranstalten** *to host, to organize*
die **Veranstaltung, -en** *event*
   **verantworten** *to be responsible*
   **verantwortlich** *responsible*
die **Verantwortung, -en** *responsibility*
der **Verbandkasten, ̈** *first-aid kit*
der **Verbandstoff** *bandage*
   **verbessern** *to improve*
   **verbieten** *to forbid*
   **verbinden** *to connect*
   falsch verbunden *wrong number*
die **Verbindung, -en** *connection*
das **Verbrechen, -** *crime*
   **verbringen** *to spend (time)*
   **verdienen** *to earn*
   **verdoppeln** *to double*
der **Verein, -e** *club, organization*
die **Vereinbarung, -en** *agreement*
   **vergessen** *to forget*
   **vereint** *united*
   **verfallen** *to expire, to become void*
die **Verfassung** *constitution*
das **Verfassungsgericht** *constitutional court*
die **Verfügung, -en** *decree, order, instruction*
   zur **Verfügung stellen** *to provide, to supply*
   zur **Verfügung stehen** *to be available, to be at someone's disposal*
   **vergangen** *passed, past (time)*

**vergeben** *to give away, to forgive*
**vergessen** *to forget*
der **Vergleich, -e** *comparison*
   einen Vergleich ziehen *to draw a comparison*
   im Vergleich zu *compared with/to, in comparison with*
**vergleichen** *to compare*
das **Vergnügen, -** *pleasure*
   viel Vergnügen *enjoy yourself*
**vergrößern** *to enlarge, to increase*
**verhandeln** *to negotiate*
der **Verkäufer, -** *salesman*
der **Verkehr** *traffic*
die **Verkehrsregel, -n** *traffic rule*
das **Verkehrsschild, -er** *traffic sign*
der **Verkehrsstau, -s** *traffic congestion*
der **Verkehrsunfall, ̈e** *traffic accident*
**verkehrswidrig** *in violation of traffic regulations*
**verkleinern** *to reduce, to decrease, to make smaller*
**verleihen** *to award*
die **Verleihung, -en** *award ceremony*
**verlieren** *to lose*
**vermerken** *to note (only in writing)*
der **Vermieter, -** *landlord*
**veröffentlichen** *to publish*
die **Veröffentlichung, -en** *publication*
**verordnen** *to rule, to order*
die **Verordnung, -en** *rule, regulation*
**verpacken** *to pack*
**verpackt** *packed*
die **Verpackung, -en** *packaging, packing material*
**verpassen** *to miss*
**verringern** *to decrease, to reduce*
**verrückt** *crazy*
**versagen** *to fail*
der **Versammlungsraum, ̈e** *meeting room, conference room, hall*
**versäumen** *to miss, to omit, to fail to do something*
**verschlafen** *to oversleep*
**verschreiben** *to prescribe*
**versichert** *injured*
die **Versicherung, -en** *insurance*
**versiert** *fluent, familiar with, experienced*
**versprechen** *to promise*
   das Blaue vom Himmel versprechen *to promise the moon*
die **Versorgung, -en** *supply, provision, care*
das **Versorgungsnetz, -e** *supply system, network*

die Verstärkung, -en *intensification, support, backup*
verstehen *to understand*
versteigern *to auction*
die Versteigerung, -en *auction*
verstoßen (gegen) *to break a law, rule*
versuchen *to try*
der Vertrag, ⸚e *contract*
vertragen *to tolerate*
vertreten *to represent*
der/die Verwandte, -n, -n *relative*
die Verwaltung *administration*
die Verwaltungshilfe *administrative aid*
verwenden *to use*
die Verwendung, -en *use*
für etwas Verwendung haben *to have use for something*
der Vetter, -n *cousin (m.)*
der Verzehr *(food) consumption*
die Videokassette, -n *video tape*
das Videogerät, -e *VCR*
der Videorekorder - *VCR*
viel *much, many*
vielleicht *perhaps, maybe*
vielseitig *versatile, many (different), multifaceted*
die Vielseitigkeit *versatility, various aspects*
vier *four*
vierzehn *fourteen*
vierzig *forty*
die Visitenkarte, -n *business card*
die Vokabel, -n *vocabulary word*
das Volk, ⸚er *people, nation*
die Völkerverständigung *the communication between nations*
das Volkslied, -er *folk song*
voll *full*
die Vollbeschäftigung *full employment*
völlig *totally, completely*
die Vollreinigung, -en *dry cleaning*
vollständig *complete*
das Volt, - *volt*
von *from, by (the agent of the action)*
von morgens bis abends *from morning to evening*
vor *in front of, before*
vor allem *above all, predominantly, primarily*
voraus *ahead*
voraussichtlich *probably*
vorbeifahren *to drive by*
vorbeikommen *to come by*
der Vordersitz, -e *front seat*
der Vorderzahn, ⸚e *front tooth*

die Vorfahrt *right of way*
der Vorfall, ⸚e *occurrence*
die Vorführung, -en *show, showcase, presentation*
vorhaben *to intend, to plan*
vorhanden *present, available*
vorlegen *to present, to submit*
vorletzter, -e, -es *the one before last*
die Vorliebe, -n *preference*
vorne *in the front*
der Vorort, -e *suburb*
vorrätig *available*
vorrätig sein *to be in stock*
Die Ware ist nicht vorrätig. *The merchandise isn't in stock.*
der Vorsatz, ⸚e *intention, intent*
der Vorschlag, ⸚e *suggestion*
vorschreiben *to prescribe*
die Vorschrift, -en *rule, law, regulation*
die Vorsicht *caution*
der Vorstand, ⸚e *board of directors*
das Vorstandsmitglied, -er *board member*
vorstellen *to introduce*
vorstellen (sich) *to imagine, to conjure; to introduce oneself*
die Vorstellung, -en *introduction, performance*
das Vorstellungsgespräch, -e *(job) interview*
der Vortrag, ⸚e *speech, lecture*
vorteilhaft *advantageous, flattering*
vorzeigen *to show, to present*

# W

wachhalten *to keep awake*
wachsen *to grow*
der Wagen, -e *car*
die Wahl, -en *choice, election*
die Wahlbeteiligung *voter turnout*
wählen *to choose, to vote*
der Wähler, - *male voter*
die Wählerin, -nen *female voter*
das Wahlergebnis, -se *election result*
der Wahlkampf, ⸚e *political campaign*
das Wahlrecht *right to vote*
wahr *true, genuine*
Das ist wahr. *That's true.*
während (+ gen.) *while, during, in the course of*
währenddessen *meanwhile*
wahrscheinlich *probably*
der Wald, ⸚er *forest, woods*
die Wand, ⸚e *wall (in a house or room)*
wandern *to wander, to walk*
die Wanderung, -en *hike*

die **Wandmalerei,** -en *mural*
das **Wandregal,** -e *wall (shelf) unit*
  **wann** *when*
die **Ware,** -n *goods, product*
das **Warenmuster,** - *sample (of product, merchandise)*
  **warm** *warm*
  **warten** *to wait*
    warten auf (+ acc.) *to wait for*
  **warum** *why*
  **was** *what*
  **waschen** *to wash*
    mit der Hand waschen *to wash by hand*
    sich waschen *to wash oneself*
die **Waschküche,** -n *laundry room*
das **Wasser** *water*
    Wasser brauchen *to need water*
  **weben** *to weave*
der **Weber,** - *weaver*
die **Weberei** *weaving*
die **Web-Seite,** -n *web page*
der **Wechselkurs** *exchange rate*
  **wechseln** *to change*
der **Wechselstrom** *alternating current (AC)*
die **Wechselstube,** - *money changing establishment*
  **wecken** *to wake*
    Wecken Sie mich um . . . *Wake me at (time)*
der **Wecker,** - *alarm clock*
  **weg** *away, gone*
der **Weg,** -e *way*
  **wegdenken** *to unthink, to imagine it weren't there*
  **wegen** (+ gen.) *because of*
  **weich** *soft*
  **Weihnachten** *Christmas*
  **weil** *because*
die **Weile** *while, short time*
der **Wein,** -e *wine*
der **Weinberg,** -e *vineyard*
die **Weinlese** *vine (grape) gathering*
die **Weinprobe,** -n *wine tasting*
der **Weisheitszahn,** ⁼e *wisdom tooth*
  **weiß** *white*
der **Weißwein,** -e *white wine*
  **weit** *far*
  **weitere** *further, additional*
  **weitergeben** *to hand on, to pass on*
  **welche** *which*
die **Welle,** -n
der **Weltkrieg,** -e *world war*
  **wem** *whom*
  **wenig** *little*

  **weniger werden** *to become less, to decrease*
  **wenigstens** *at least*
  **wenn** *when, as, if, whenever*
  **wer** *who*
die **Werbeeinnahmen** *income from commercials or advertising*
der **Werbeslogan,** -s *advertising slogan*
die **Werbung** *advertising, commercials, advertisement*
  **werden** *to become*
das **Werk** *a) plant, factory b) the works, oeuvre*
der **Werkzeugkasten,** *toolbox*
der **Wert,** -e *value*
    wert sein *to be worth*
das **Wertpapier,** -e *bond, security*
  **westlich** *westerly*
    weiter westlich *farther west*
der **Wettbewerb,** -e *competition, contest*
  **wettbewerbsfähig** *competitive*
das **Wetter** *weather*
  **wichtig** *important*
  **wider** *in contrast to*
der **Widerstand,** ⁼e *resistance*
  **widerstehen** *to resist*
  **wie** *how*
  **wieder** *again*
der **Wiederaufbau** *restoration*
  **wiederkommen** *to return, to come back*
  **wiederholen** *to repeat*
die **Wiederholung,** -en *repetition*
die **Wiederholungsaufgabe,** -n *review quiz*
  **wiederum** *then again*
  **wieso** *why*
die **Wiedervereinigung** *reunification*
die **Wiese,** -n *meadow*
  **wieviel** *how much/many*
der **Wind** *winter*
  **wir** *we*
der **Wille** *will*
  **Willkommen!** *Welcome!*
  **willkommen (heißen)** *to welcome someone*
der **Winkel,** - *corner*
der **Wintermorgen** *winter morning*
der **Winzer,** - *wine grower, vineyard owner*
die **Wirtschaft** *economy*
  **wirtschaftlich** *economic(ally)*
das **Wirtschaftswachstum** *economic growth*
  **wissen** *to know (a fact)*
    Das sollten Sie wissen. *You should know this.*

die Wissenschaftler, - *scientist*
witzig *witty, funny*
wo *where*
die Woche, -n *week*
das Wochenende, -n *weekend*
die Wochenschau, -en *weekly news program*
der Wochentag, -e *day of the week*
woher *from where*
wohin *to where*
wohl *probably*
wohnen *to reside, to live*
die Wohnung, -en *apartment*
sozialer Wohnungsbau *subsidized apartments*
das Wohnviertel, - *residential area, residential quarter(s)*
das Wohnzimmer, - *living room*
die Wolke, -n *cloud*
wollen *to want (intention)*
Wie Sie wollen. *As you wish.*
wozu *what for*
wunderschön *beautiful, wonderful*
der Wunsch, "e *wish*
auf Wunsch *if so desired, upon request*
wünschen *to wish*
die Wurst, "e *sausage*
die Wurzel, -n *root*
die Wurzelbehandlung, -en *root canal*
wütend *furious*
wütend sein *to be furious*

# X

x-mal *umpteen times*

# Y

Ypsilon *the letter Y*

# Z

die Zahl, -en *number*
zahlen *to pay*
zahllos *numerous*
die Zahlung, -en *payment*
der Zahn, "e *tooth*
zahnlos *toothless*
der Zahnarzt, "e *male dentist*
beim Zahnarzt *at the dentist's*
die Zahnärztin, -nen *female dentist*
der Zahnbelag *plaque*
die Zahnbürste, -n *toothbrush*
das Zahnfleisch *gum*
die Zahnmedizin *dentistry*
die Zahnpasta, Zahnpasten *tooth paste*

die Zahnschmerzen *toothache*
der Zeh, -en *toe*
zehn *ten*
das Zeichen *sign, reference, signal*
zeichnen *to draw*
die Zeichnung, -en *drawing*
zeigen *to show*
die Zeit, -en *time*
die Zeitschrift, -en *magazine*
die Zeitung, -en *newspaper*
der Zeitungsverlag, -e *newspaper publisher*
der Zement *cement*
das Zementwerk, -e *cement factory*
zentral *central*
das Zentrum, Zentren *center*
das Stadtzentrum *city center*
zerbrechen *to break*
zerfallen *to decay, to rot, to fall apart*
zerren *to sprain, to tear*
zerreißen *to tear apart*
die Zerrung, -en *sprain*
zersetzen *to decompose*
sich zersetzen *to dissolve, to disintegrate*
zerstören *to destroy*
die Zerstörung, -en *destruction*
der Zettel, - *(scrap) piece of paper*
der Zeuge, -n *witness*
das Zimmer, - *room*
das Zimmermädchen, -n *maid*
die Zimmernummer, -n *room number*
die Zinsen *(plural) interest*
der Zinssatz, "e *interest rate*
die Zivilisation, -en *civilization*
der Zoll *customs*
die Zollerklärung, -en *customs declaration*
die Zone, -n *zone, area*
zu *at, to, too*
der Zucker *sugar*
zuerst *at first*
der Zug, "e *train*
der Zugang, "e *access*
zugreifen *to take the opportunity, to take advantage*
zuhören *to listen*
die Zündkerze, -n *spark plug*
der Zündschlüssel, - *ignition key*
die Zündung, -en *ignition*
die Zukunft *future*
zukünftig *in the future*
der Zukunftsplan, "e *future plan*
zuletzt *last of all*
zuliebe *in love of, for . . . sake*
zurück *back*

**zurückgehen lassen** *to return food at a restaurant*
**zurückgeben** *to give back*
**zurücklassen** *to leave behind*
**zurückzahlen** *to reimburse*
**zunächst** *first, first of all*
**zusammen** *together*
**die Zusammenarbeit** *cooperation, collaboration*
**zusammenbrechen** *to break down, to collapse*
**zusammenfassen** *to sum up*
**die Zusammenfassung, -en** *sum, result, synopsis*
**die Zusammenkunft, ⸚e** *meeting*
**zusammenlegen** *to lay together, to put together*
zusammen liegen *to lie together*
**zusätzlich** *additional*

**der Zuschauer** *(TV) viewer*
**die Zuschauer** *audience, viewers*
**der Zuschlag, ⸚e** *surcharge*
**der Zuschuss, ⸚e** *subsidy*
**der Zustand, ⸚e** *state (of being)*
**zustoßen** *to be afflicted, to be injured*
**zuviel** *too much*
**zuvor** *previously*
**zwanzig** *twenty*
einundzwanzig *twenty-one*
**zwei** *two*
**die Zweigstelle, -n** *branch office*
**zweiter, -e, -es** *second*
**die Zweitstimme, -n** *second vote*
**zwingen** *to force*
**zwischen** *between, among*
**die Zwischenzeit** *meantime*
in der Zwischenzeit *in the meantime*
**zwölf** *twelve*

# ENGLISH–GERMAN

## A

about *über*
above *über*
academy *die Hochschule*
to accept *akzeptieren, annehmen*
to access *Zugang haben zu*
access *der Zugang*
account *das Konto, die Konten*
  checking account *das Scheckkonto,*
  *das Girokonto*
  savings account *das Sparkonto*
to acquire *erwerben*
across *über*
act (in a play) *der Akt, -e*
actor *der Schauspieler*
actually *tatsächlich, wirklich*
to adapt *adaptieren, sich anpassen*
address *die Adresse, -n*
  return address *der Absender, -*
to address (person, audience) *ansprechen,*
  (letter) *beschriften*
adjacent *nahegelegen, nebenan, in der*
  *Nähe liegend*
to admire *bewundern*
advantageous *vorteilhaft*
advertising *die Werbung, -en*
  advertising slogan *der Werbespruch, ̈-e*
to afford *sich leisten*
after *nach, nachdem*
afterward *danach*
again *wieder*
against *gegen*
age *das Alter*
ago *vor*
to agree *übereinstimmen, einverstanden*
  *sein*
agreed *einverstanden*
agreement *der Vertrag, ̈-e*
ahead *voraus*
airplane *das Flugzeug, -*
  airplane passenger *der Fluggast, ̈-e*
airport *der Flughafen, -*
airtight *luftdicht*
aisle *der Gang, ̈-e*
  middle aisle *der Mittelgang, ̈-e*
album *das Album, -s*
alive *lebendig*
all *alle, alles*
allergy *die Allergie, -n*
to allow *gestatten*
alone *allein*

alphabet *das Alphabet*
Alps (the) *die Alpen*
already *schon, bereits*
also *auch*
to alter *ändern, abändern*
always *immer*
amazing *erstaunlich*
America *Amerika*
among *unter*
and *und*
anesthesia *die Betäubung, -en*
  local anesthesia *die örtliche*
  *Betäubung*
answer *die Antwort, -en, die Lösung, -en*
to answer *antworten*
antique *die Antiquität, -en*
anyhow *sowieso*
anyone *jemand, irgendwer,*
  *irgendjemand*
apartment *die Wohnung, -en*
  subsidized apartments *sozialer*
  *Wohnungsbau*
to apologize *sich entschuldigen*
apparently *scheinbar*
appetite *der Appetit*
apple *der Apfel, ̈*
  apple strudel *der Apfelstrudel, -*
appliance (electrical) *das Elektrogerät, -*
  *e*
application *die Bewerbung, -en; der*
  *Antrag, ̈-e*
to apply *sich bewerben; anwenden*
appointment *der Termin, -e*
apprentice *der Lehrling, -e*
apprenticeship *die Lehre, -n*
April *der April*
apron *der Kittel, die Schürze*
area *die Gegend, -en; die Umgebung, -en;*
  *der Bereich, -e*
to arrange *arrangieren*
to arrive *ankommen, eintreffen*
arrival *die Ankunft, ̈-e*
art *die Kunst, ̈-e*
  art museum *das Kunstmuseum,*
  *Kunstmuseen*
  work of art *Kunstwerk, -e*
artist *der Künstler, -*
article *der Artikel, -*
Ascension Day *Himmelfahrt*
ascent *der Aufstieg, -*
to ascent *aufsteigen*
Ash Wednesday *der Aschermittwoch*

ask *fragen*
asparagus *der Spargel*
aspirin *das Aspirin, -*
at *bei*
  at a place of business *bei*
  at the side of *an der Seite von*
to attack *angreifen*
to attend *besuchen, teilnehmen*
attention *die Aufmerksamkeit, -en*
Attention! *Achtung!*
attic *der Dachboden, ⁻*
attire *die Bekleidung, -en*
auction *die Auktion, -en*
auctioneer *der Auktionär, -e*
audience *die Zuschauer, das Publikum*
August *der August*
aunt *die Tante, -n*
Austria *Österreich*
author *der Autor, -en*
automatic *automatisch*
automobile *das Auto, -s*
  automobile mechanic *der Automechaniker, -*
  automobile repair shop *die Autoreparaturwerkstatt, ⁻en*
autumn *der Herbst*
available *verfügbar, vorrätig*
average *der Durchschnitt*
awake
  to keep awake *wachhalten*
aware *bewusst*

# B

back *zurück*
background *der Hintergrund, ⁻e*
backpack *der Rucksack, ⁻e*
bad *schlecht, böse*
bag *die Tasche, -n; die Tüte*
  shoulder bag *die Umhängetasche*
  sleeping bag *der Schlafsack, ⁻e*
to bake *backen*
balcony *der Balkon, -e*
bald (head) *die Glatze, -n*
ball *der Ball, ⁻e*
  costume ball *der Maskenball, ⁻e*
Baltic *die Ostsee*
to ban *verbieten*
band *die Kapelle, -n*
bandage *die Binde, -n, der Verbandsstoff*
  elastic bandage *die elastische Binde*
bank *die Bank, -en*
  bank transfer *die Banküberweisung, -en*
  bank account *das Bankkonto, -en*

bar *die Tafel, -en*
  snack bar *der Schnellimbiss, -e*
barbershop *der Friseursalon, -s; der Frisörsalon, -s; der Herrenfriseursalon, -s; der Herrenfrisörsalon, -s; der Friseur, -e; der Frisör, -e*
to bargain *handeln*
basic(ally) *grundsätzlich, grundlegend*
basis *die Basis, die Grundlage, -n*
bath *das Bad, ⁻er*
  mineral bath *das Mineralwasserbad, ⁻er*
to bathe *baden*
bathrobe *der Bademantel, ⁻*
bathroom *das Badezimmer, -*
battery *die Batterie, -n*
to be *sein*
  to be available *frei sein*
  to be in stock *vorrätig sein*
  to be ready *fertig sein*
beach *der Strand, ⁻e*
beaker *der Becher, -*
bean *die Bohne, -n*
beard *der Bart, ⁻e*
to beat *schlagen*
beautiful *schön*
to beautify *verschönern*
beauty *die Schönheit*
because *weil, denn*
  because of *wegen*
to become *werden*
bed *das Bett, -en*
bedroom *das Schlafzimmer, -*
beef *das Rindfleisch*
beer *das Bier, -e*
before *bevor, davor, vor*
behind *dahinter, hinter*
  one behind the other *hintereinander*
to believe *glauben*
bell *die Glocke, -n*
bellhop *der Hotelpage, -n*
to belong *gehören*
belonging (personal) *der Privatgegenstand, ⁻e*
belt *der Gürtel, -*
  baggage conveyor belt *das Kofferfließband, ⁻er*
beneath *under*
beside *neben*
besides *(ganz) abgesehen davon, dass . . . ; außer*
best *am besten, der/die/das Beste, beste*
better *besser*

between *zwischen*
beverage *das Getränk, -e*
beyond *dahinter*
bicycle *das Rad, ¨er*
to bicycle *Rad fahren*
big *groß*
bill (money) *der Schein, -e*
bitter *bitter*
black *schwarz*
blond *blond*
blouse *die Bluse, -n*
to blow *blasen*
blue *blau*
board *die Tafel, -n*
boat *das Boot, -e; das Schiff, -e*
body *der Körper, -*
book *das Buch, ¨er*
to book *buchen*
booked *ausgebucht*
bookshelf *das Bücherregal, -e*
booth *die Kabine, -n; der Messestand, ¨e*
border *die Grenze, -n; der Rand, ¨er*
boring *langweilig*
to borrow *leihen, borgen*
both *beide*
to bother *stören*
bottle *die Flasche, -n*
box *die Kiste, -n; der Karton, -s; die Packung, -en*
   ballot box *die Wahlurne, -n*
   box seat *der Logensitz, -e*
   factory packing *die Originalverpackung, -en*
boxing *das Boxen*
   boxing match *der Boxkampf, ¨e*
boyfriend *der Freund, -e*
brake *die Bremse, -n*
   brake pedal *das Bremspedal, -e*
to brake *bremsen*
bread *das Brot, -e*
to break *zerbrechen*
breakfast *das Frühstück, -e*
   including breakfast *inklusive Frühstück*
to breakfast *frühstücken*
breezy *luftig*
bright *hell*
to brighten *erhellen*
to bring *bringen*
   to bring along *mitbringen*
to broadcast *übertragen*
broken *kaputt*
brook *der Bach, ¨e*
brother *der Bruder, ¨*
   brother-in-law *der Schwager, ¨*
brown *braun*

brunette *brünett*
to burden *beschweren*
to burn *brennen*
bus *der Bus, -se; der Omnibus, -se*
   bus line *die Buslinie, -n*
business *das Geschäft, -e; die Firma, Firmen*
   business card *die Visitenkarte, -n*
   business discussion *die Geschäftsbesprechung, -en*
busy *beschäftigt, besetzt*
but *aber, sondern*
butter *die Butter*
button *der Knopf, ¨e*
to buy *kaufen*
buyer *der Käufer, -; der Abnehmer, -*
by *bei, von, bis*
phone booth *die Telefonzelle, -en*

# C

cab *die Taxe, -n; das Taxi, -s*
café *das Café, -s*
   garden café *das Gartencafé, -s*
   sidewalk café *das Straßencafé, -s*
calculator (pocket) *der Taschenrechner, -*
to calculate *berechnen*
call *der Anruf, -s*
   long-distance call *das Ferngespräch, -e*
to call *anrufen, rufen*
   to be called *heißen*
calm *ruhig*
to calm *beruhigen*
   to calm down *sich beruhigen*
camera *der Fotoapparat, -e; der Fotoapparat, -e*
campaign (political) *der Wahlkampf, ¨e*
can *die Büchse, -n*
can (to be able to) *können*
Canada *Kanada*
candidate *der Kandidat, -en*
cap *die Mütze, -n*
   bathing cap *die Bademütze, -n*
car *das Auto, -s, der Wagen, -*
   dining car *der Speisewagen, -*
   sleeping car *der Schlafwagen, -*
   used car *der Gebrauchtwagen, -*
card (credit) *die Kreditkarte, -n*
card (post) *die Postkarte, -n*
care *die Sorge, -n*
to care *sich sorgen, sich interessieren*
carnival *der Karneval, Fasching*
carpet *der Teppich*
carrot *die Mohrrübe, -n*

case *der Fall, -̈e*
case (in any) *sowieso*
cash *das Bargeld, -er*
cashier *der Kassierer, -*
casino (gambling) *das Spielkasino, -s*
castle *die Burg, -en*
to catch *fangen*
cathedral *der Dom, -e; die Kathedrale, -n*
cause *der Grund, -̈e*
cavity *Karies*
ceiling *die Decke, -n*
to celebrate *feiern*
celebration *die Feier, -n*
cell phone *das Handy, -s*
cellar *der Keller, -*
cent *der Cent, -*
center *das Zentrum, Zentren, der Mittelpunkt, -e*
ceramics *die Keramik*
ceremony *die Zeremonie, -n; die Feier, -n*
change *die Veränderung, -en; die Änderung, -en, der Wechsel, -*
to change *überwechseln, umsteigen, wechseln*
   to change one's clothes *sich umziehen*
   to change reservations *umbuchen*
Channel Two *das Zweite Programm, ZDF*
chapel *die Kirche, -n; die Kapelle, -n*
charge *die Gebühr, -en*
   to charge extra *einen Aufschlag berechnen*
to charge *berechnen*
cheap *billig*
cheaper *billiger*
check *der Scheck, -s; die Rechnung, -en*
   to cash a check *einen Scheck einlösen*
to check *prüfen, überprüfen*
   to check the air *die Luft prüfen*
cheese *der Käse*
cherry *die Kirsche, -n*
chicken *das Huhn, -̈er*
child *das Kind, -er*
childlike *kindhaft*
chocolate *die Schokolade*
   bar of chocolate *die Tafel Schokolade*
choice *die Wahl*
to choose *wählen, auswählen*
Christmas *Weihnachten*
   Christmas Eve *der Heiligabend*
city *die Stadt, -̈e*
   city center *die Stadtmitte, -n; das Stadtzentrum, Stadtzentren*
   city map *der Stadtplan, -̈e*

city wall *die Stadtmauer, -n*
   small city *das Städtchen*
civilization *die Zivilisation, -en*
class *die Klasse, -n*
   first class *erster Klasse, die erste Klasse*
to clean *putzen, reinigen*
   to clean (brush) one's teeth *sich die Zähne putzen*
   to dry clean *chemisch reinigen*
cleaning *die Reinigung, -en*
   dry cleaning *die chemische Reinigung, -en*
   express dry cleaning *die Schnellreinigung, -en*
clear *klar*
clerk *der/die Angestellte, -n, -n*
   bank clerk *der Bankangestellte, -n, -n*
   postal clerk *der Postangestellte, -n, -n*
   reception clerk *der Empfangschef, -s*
to climb *aufsteigen, steigen*
clock *die Uhr, -en*
   alarm clock *der Wecker, -*
cloister *das Kloster, -̈*
close *nahe, eng verbunden*
to close *schließen*
closed *geschlossen*
clothing *die Kleidung*
cloud *die Wolke, -n*
coach (through) *der Kurswagen, -*
coast *die Küste, -n*
coat *der Mantel, -̈*
coatrack *die Garderobe, -n*
code *der Kodename, -n; das Kodewort, -̈er; die Kodierung, -en*
coffee *der Kaffee*
coin *die Münze, -n*
coins *das Kleingeld*
cold *die Erkältung, -en; die Kälte; kalt*
collar *der Kragen, -*
college *die Universität, -en*
   to go to college *studieren*
color *die Farbe*
coloring *das Färben*
to comb *kämmen*
   to comb one's hair *sich die Haare kämmen*
to come *kommen*
   to come by *vorbeikommen*
   to come for a visit *zu Besuch kommen*
   to come from (with locations) *kommen aus (+ dat.)*
company *der Konzern, -e*
   large company *der Großkonzern, -e*
comparable *vergleichbar*
to compare *vergleichen*

comparison *der Vergleich, -e*
compartment *das Abteil, -e; das Fach, -̈ er*
   inside compartment *das Innenfach, -̈er*
   non-smoking compartment *das Nichtraucherabteil, -e*
   outside compartment *das Außenfach, -̈er*
compatible *kompatibel, vereinbar*
to compete *wetteifern*
competition *der Wettbewerb, -e; die Konkurrenz*
to complain *sich beklagen, sich beschweren*
concern *der Konzern, -e*
   large concern *der Großkonzern, -e*
concert *das Konzert, -e*
   concert at a spa *das Kurkonzert, -e*
conductor *der Dirigent, -en*
confectionary *die Konditorei, -en*
conference *die Konferenz, -en; die Tagung, -en; die Besprechung, -en*
to connect *verbinden, Kontakt aufnehmen*
connection *der Anschluss, -̈e*
constantly *ständig*
consul *der Konsul*
consulate *das Konsulat, -e*
contents *der Inhalt, -e*
contrary (on the) *sondern*
contrast *der Kontrast, -e*
convenience *die Annehmlichkeit, -en; die Bequemlichkeit, -en*
convenient *angenehm*
convention *die Konferenz, -en; die Tagung, -en*
conversation *die Unterhaltung, -en; das Gespräch, -e*
to converse *sich unterhalten*
converter *der Umschalter, -; der Transformator, -en*
cook *der Koch, -̈e*
to cook *kochen*
to cooperate *kooperieren, zusammenarbeiten*
corner *die Ecke, -n; der Winkel, -*
correct *richtig, korrekt*
   to be correct *stimmen, Recht haben*
cost *die Kosten*
to cost *kosten*
couchette *der Liegewagen, -*
cough *der Husten*
to cough *husten*
to count *rechnen*
country *das Land, -̈er*
cousin (f.) *die Kusine, -n*
cousin (m.) *der Vetter, -n*

cozy *gemütlich*
craft *das Handwerk, -e*
cream (whipped) *die Schlagsahne*
credit card *die Kreditkarte, -n*
crisp *knusprig*
cross *das Kreuz, -e*
crown *die Krone, -n*
   gold crown *die Goldkrone, -n*
crunchy *knusprig, knirschend*
culture *Kultur, -en*
cup *der Becher, -; die Tasse, -n*
   a cup of coffee *eine Tasse Kaffee*
curable *heilbar*
cure *die Heilung, -en*
curl *die Locke, -n*
curly *lockig*
currency *die Währung, -en*
current *laufend, z.Zt.*
current (electrical) *der Strom, -̈e*
   alternating current (AC) *der Wechselstrom*
   direct current (DC) *der Gleichstrom*
current(ly) *aktuell, augenblicklich*
custom *die Sitte, -n; die Tradition, -en; der Brauch, -̈e; die Gewohnheit, -en*
customer *der Kunde, -n*
customs *der Zoll*
   customs declaration *die Zollerklärung, -en*
customary *gewöhnlich*
to cut *schneiden*
cutlet *das Schnitzel, -*

# D

daily *täglich*
   daily news broadcast *die Tageschau*
   daily routine *die Tagesroutine, -n*
damage *der Schaden, -̈*
to damage *schaden, beschädigen*
to be damaged *beschädigt sein*
dark *dunkel*
to darken *verdunkeln*
to dash off *los rennen*
daughter *die Tochter, -̈*
day *der Tag, -e*
   Good Day. *Guten Tag.*
debt *die Schulden*
December *der Dezember*
deck (observation) *das Aussichtsdeck, -s*
to decompose *zersetzen*
defeat *die Niederlage*
to define *definieren*
definitely *sicher, bestimmt*
to delete *löschen*
delicate *empfindlich*

delicious *lecker*
delight *die Lust, ¨e*
delivery *die Lieferung, -en*
  delivery van *der Lieferwagen, -*
democracy *die Demokratie*
dentist (f.) *die Zahnärztin, -nen*
dentist (m.) *der Zahnarzt, ¨e*
dentistry *die Zahnmedizin*
deodorant *das Deodorant, -s*
to depart *abfahren*
  to depart by airplane *abfliegen*
department *die Abteilung, -en*
departure *der Abflug, ¨e*
to deposit *einzahlen*
to descend *absteigen*
descend *der Abstieg*
to describe *beschreiben*
desk *der Schreibtisch, -e*
dessert *der Nachtisch, -e*
destination *das Reiseziel, -e*
detail *die Einzelheit, -en*
devil *der Teufel, -*
dialogue *der Dialog, -e*
difference *die Differenz, -en, der
  Unterschied*
diploma *das Abitur, das Diplom*
direction *die Gebrauchsanweisung,
  -en*
to do *tun*
to direct (cinemat.) *Regie führen*
direct *direkt*
directly *direkt*
director (cinemat.) *der Regisseur, -e; der
  Direktor, -en (gen.)*
to disagree *nicht übereinstimmen*
to discuss *diskutieren*
discussion *die Diskussion, -en*
disease *die Krankheit, -en*
to disintegrate *sich zersetzen*
to dissolve *sich zersetzen, sich auflösen*
district *das Viertel*
dizzy *schwindlig*
to do *machen, tun*
  to do calisthenics *Gymnastik
    machen*
  to do good *gut tun*
  to do someone's hair *frisieren*
door *die Tür, -en*
doorbell *die Türklingel, -n*
double *doppel*
double room *das Doppelzimmer, -*
down *herunter*
download *herunterladen*
draft *der Entwurf, ¨e*
to draw *zeichnen*

drawing *die Zeichnung, -en*
dress *das Kleid, -er*
to dress *anziehen*
  local dress (costume) *die Tracht, -en*
  to get dressed *sich anziehen*
to drill *bohren*
to drink *trinken*
to drive *fahren, treiben*
drop *der Tropfen, -*
druggist *der Drogist, -en, -en*
drugstore *die Drogerie, -n*
  self-service drugstore *der
    Drogeriemarkt, ¨e*
dry *trocken*
to dry *abtrocknen*
  to dry oneself *sich abtrocken*
due *auf Grund von; wegen; fällig am*
during *während*
dumpling *der Knödel, -*
dye *die Farbe, -n*
to dye *färben*
dyeing *das Färben*

# E

each *jede, -r, -s*
early *früh*
to earn *verdienen*
Easter *Ostern*
easterly, eastern *östlich*
to eat *essen*
edge *der Rand, ¨er*
editor *der Redakteur, ¨e; (publ.) der
  Lektor, -en*
editorial *die Redaktion, -en*
effect *der Effekt, -e*
egg *das Ei, -er*
either *entweder*
to elect *wählen*
election *die Wahl, -en*
  federal election *die Bundestagswahl,
    -en*
  local election *die Kommunalwahl,
    -en*
  state election *die Landtagswahl, -en*
elevator *der Fahrstuhl, ¨e*
else *noch*
embassy *die Botschaft, -en*
to emerge *aufkommen, geschehen*
emergency *der Notfall, ¨e*
  emergency call *der Notruf, -e*
  emergency exit *der Notausgang, ¨e*
emphasis *die Betonung, -en; die
  Hervorhebung, -en*
to emphasize *betonen, hervorheben*

**employment** *die Beschäftigung, -en; die
  Stellung, -en*
  full-time employment *die
  Vollbeschäftigung, -en; die
  Ganztagsbeschäftigung, -en*
  part-time employment *die
  Teilzeitbeschäftigung, -en; die
  Halbtagsbeschäftigung, -en*
  temporary employment *die
  Aushilfsarbeit*
**empty** *leer*
**encyclopedia** *das Lexikon, Lexika; die
  Enzyklopädie, -n*
**to end** *enden, beenden*
**end** *das Ende, der Schluss*
**endless** *endlos*
**to endure** *aushalten*
**to enforce** *durchsetzen, festlegen*
**England** *England*
**to enjoy** *genießen*
  enjoy yourself *viel Vergnügen*
**to enter** *eintreten, hineinkommen, eingeben
  (comp.)*
**entrance** *der Eingang, ¨e*
**environment** *die Umwelt*
**equal** *gleich*
**escalator** *die Rolltreppe, -n*
**to escape** *entkommen, fliehen*
**especially** *besonders*
**esteem** *die Achtung*
**euro** *der Euro, -*
**even** *sogar, gerade*
**evening** *der Abend, -e*
  Good evening. *Guten Abend.*
  in the evening *am Abend*
**eventually** *endlich, letztendlich*
**ever** *schon*
**every** *jede, -r, -s*
**everybody** *jeder*
**everything** *alles*
**everywhere** *überall*
**examination** (high school) *das Abitur*
**example** *das Beispiel, -e*
  for example *zum Beispiel, -e*
**to examine** *prüfen*
**excellent** *ausgezeichnet*
**except for** *außer*
**exchange** *der Umtausch, ¨e*
**to exchange** *umtauschen, eintauschen*
**exchange rate** *der Wechselkurs, -e*
**exciting** *spannend*
**to excuse** *entschuldigen*
**excuse** *die Entschuldigung, -en*
**exhausted** *erschöpft*
  to be exhausted *erschöpft sein*

**exhibition** *die Ausstellung, -en*
  special exhibition *die
  Sonderausstellung, -en*
  exhibition grounds *das Messegelände, -*
**exit** *der Ausgang, ¨e*
**to expect** *erwarten*
**expensive** *teuer*
**eye** *das Auge, -n*
**eyeglasses** *die Brille, -n*

## F

**fable** *die Fabel, -n*
**fabulous** *fantastisch, großartig*
**fair** (trade) *die Messe, -n*
**to fall** *fallen*
**false** *falsch*
**family** *die Familie, -n*
**famous** *berühmt*
**fantastic** *fantastisch*
**far** *weit, fern*
**far away** *weit weg, weit entfernt*
**fast** *schnell*
**father** *der Vater, ¨er*
**favorite** *liebste, -r, -s*
**February** *der Februar*
**fee** (bank) *die Bankgebühr, -en*
**to feel like** *Lust haben*
**festival** *das Fest, -e*
**few** (a) *ein paar*
**to fight** *kämpfen*
**file** *die Datei, -en*
**to fill** *füllen*
**filling** *die Füllung, -en*
  gold filling *die Goldfüllung, -en*
**film** *der Film, -e*
**finally** *endlich*
**to find** *finden*
**fine** *fein, gut*
**first** *zuerst, als erstes, erste, -r, -s*
**fish** *der Fisch, -e*
**fish market** *der Fischmarkt, ¨e*
**to fit** *passen*
**flag** *die Fahne, -n*
**flattering** *vorteilhaft*
**flea market** *der Flohmarkt, ¨e*
**flight** *der Flug, ¨e; die Flucht*
  return flight *der Rückflug, ¨e*
**to flirt** *flirten*
**flood** *die Überschwemmung, -en*
**floor** *der Boden, ¨; der Fußboden, ¨; der
  Stock*
  first floor *das Erdgeschoss; das
  Parterre*
  second floor *der erste Stock*

flour *das Mehl*
flower *die Blume, -n*
to fly *fliegen*
fly *die Fliege, -n*
foggy *neblig*
to follow *folgen*
    as follows *wie folgt*
foot *der Fuß, ⸚e*
footer *die Fußzeile, -n*
for *für*
to forbid *verbieten*
force *der Zwang, ⸚e*
to force *zwingen*
foreign *ausländisch*
forest *der Wald, ⸚er*
forever *für immer, ewig*
to forget *vergessen*
form *das Formular, -e*
    deposit slip *das Einzahlungsformular, -e*
    registration form *das Anmeldeformular, -e*
    withdrawal slip *das Auszahlungsformular, -e*
formal *förmlich*
former *ehemalig*
France *Frankreich*
to freeze *frieren*
fresh *frisch*
Friday *der Freitag*
    Good Friday *Karfreitag*
friend (f.) *die Freundin, -nen*
friend (m.) *der Freund, -e*
frizzy *kraus*
from *von, aus*
    from morning to evening *von morgens bis abends*
front of (in) *vor*
fruit *das Obst, die Frucht, ⸚e*
to fulfill *erfüllen*
full *voll*
fun *der Spaß, ⸚e*
function *die Funktion, -en*
to function *funktionieren*
funny *witzig*
furious *wütend*
    to be furious *wütend sein*
furniture *die Möbel (pl.)*
    furniture style *der Möbelstil, -e*

# G

gallery *die Gallerie, -n*
game *das Spiel, -e*
garage *die Garage, -n*
garden *der Garten, ⸚*

to get gas *tanken*
gasoline *das Benzin*
    gasoline pedal *das Gaspedal, -e*
    gasoline pump *die Tanksäule, -n*
    gasoline station *die Tankstelle, -n*
gentleman *der Herr, -en, -en*
genuine *wahr*
geranium *die Geranie, -n*
German *Deutsch (n.), deutsch (adj.)*
    High German *Hochdeutsch*
    Standard German *Hochdeutsch*
Germany *Deutschland*
to get *bekommen*
    to get up *aufstehen*
giant *der Gigant, -en;* (adj./adv.) *gigantisch*
gift *das Geschenk, -e*
    gift purchase *der Geschenkeinkauf, ⸚e*
girlfriend *die Freundin, -nen*
to give *geben*
    to give a shot *eine Spritze geben*
glacier *der Gletscher, -*
glad *froh*
gladly *gern*
glass *das Glas, ⸚er*
    glassblower *der Glasbläser*
glasses (eye) *die Brille, -n*
glorious *herrlich*
glove *der Handschuh, -e*
to go *gehen*
    to go by (means of) *fahren mit*
    to go on vacation *in Urlaub fahren*
goal *das Tor, -e; das Ziel, -e*
gold *das Gold*
golden *golden*
good *gut*
good-bye *Ade; auf Wiederhören; auf Wiedersehen; Servus; Tschau; Tschüss*
gown *der Kittel, -*
grade *die Note, -n*
graduate (high school) *der Abiturient, -en*
to grant *bewilligen, gewähren*
grant *die Förderung, -en; das Stipendium, Stipendien*
gram *das Gramm, -e*
grammar *die Grammatik*
granddaughter *die Enkeltochter, ⸚*
grandfather *der Großvater, ⸚*
grandmother *die Großmutter, ⸚*
grandson *der Enkelsohn, ⸚e*
grass *das Gras, ⸚er*
gratitude *der Dank*
gray *grau*
great *groß, großartig, prima!, schön, fantastisch*

Greece *Griechenland*
green *grün*
to greet *grüßen*
greeting *die Begrüßung, -en; der Gruß, ¨e*
to grasp *begreifen*
gravel *der Kies*
groceries *die Lebensmittel*
ground *der Boden, ¨en; die Erde*
to grow *wachsen, anbauen*
guest *der Gast, ¨e*
gums *das Zahnfleisch*
gymnastics *die Gymnastik, das Turnen*
   to do gymnastics *turnen*

# H

hair *das Haar, -e*
   hair color *die Haarfarbe, -n*
   hair dryer *der Haartrockner, -*
   hair growth product *das Haarwuchsmittel*
haircut *der Haarschnitt, -e*
hairdresser (female) *die Friseuse, -n; die Frisöse, -n*
hairdresser (male) *der Friseur, -e; der Frisör, -e*
hairdresser's (shop) *der Friseursalon, -s; der Frisörsalon, -s*
hall *die Halle, -n*
   city hall *das Rathaus, ¨er*
hallway *die Diele, -n; der Flur, -e; der Gang, ¨e*
hand *die Hand, ¨e*
to hand in *abgeben*
handicraft *das Handwerk, -e*
   to hang up *auflegen, aufhängen*
   to hang wallpaper *tapezieren*
handshake *der Handschlag, die Hand geben*
harbor *der Hafen, ¨*
hard *hart, schwer*
hard drive *die Festplatte, -n*
hardly *kaum*
hat *der Hut, ¨e*
to haul *schleppen*
to have *haben*
   to have a right *ein Recht haben*
   to have an appointment *einen Termin haben*
   to have supper *zu Abend essen*
   to have use for something *für etwas Verwendung haben*
head *der Kopf, ¨e*
headache *die Kopfschmerzen*
header *die Kopfzeile, -n*

headless *kopflos*
to heal *heilen*
healthy *gesund*
to hear *hören*
heaven *der Himmel, -*
heavy *schwer*
hello *Gruezi, Grüß Gott, Hallo*
to help *helfen*
   to help with *helfen bei (+ adj.)*
help *die Hilfe*
Help (me)! *Hilfe!, Hilf mir!*
here (adverb) *da*
high *hoch, groß*
higher *höher*
highway *die Autobahn, -en*
   highway assistance *die Straßenwacht*
hike *die Wanderung, -en*
   hike and climbing club *der Gebirgsverein, -e*
hill *der Hügel, -; der Berg, -e*
historic *geschichtlich*
history *die Geschichte*
hole *das Loch, ¨er*
holiday *der Feiertag, -e; der Festtag, -e;*
   Christian holiday *der Kirchliche Feiertag*
   national holiday *der Nationalfeiertag*
home *das Heim, das Zuhause, das Haus*
home country *die Heimat*
homeland *das Heimatland*
homepage *die Homepage, -s*
homework *die Aufgabe, -n*
to hope *hoffen*
hope *die Hoffnung, -en*
hopefully *hoffentlich*
horn *die Hupe*
horrible *schrecklich*
host *der Gastgeber, -*
hot *heiß*
hotel *das Hotel, -s*
hour *die Stunde, -n*
hours (for) *stundenlang*
house *das Haus, ¨er*
how *wie*
however *aber*
hundred *hundert*
   one hundred *einhundert*
   two hundred *zweihundert*
hunger *der Hunger*
hurry *die Eile*
to hurry *sich beeilen*
to hurt *schmerzen, weh tun*
   to hurt somebody *schaden*
husband *der Mann, ¨er; der Ehemann, ¨er*
hygiene (personal) *die Körperpflege*

# I

I *ich*
ice (cream) *das Eis*
icy *eisig*
idea *die Idee, -n*
if *wenn*
ignition *die Zündung, -en*
    ignition key *der Zündschlüssel, -*
ill *krank*
illegal *illegal*
illness *die Krankheit, -en*
to imagine *sich vorstellen*
immediate(ly) *sofort*
immense *immens, groß*
to implement *in die Realität umsetzen*
impressive *imposant*
in *in*
inconvenience *die Unannehmlichkeit, -en*
to increase *erweitern*
individual *individuell*
industrial *industriell*
industrialist *der Industrielle, -n*
industry *die Industrie, -n*
inflammation *die Entzündung, -en*
information *die Information, -en*
to inform *informieren*
    to inform oneself about *sich informieren über*
    initial *die Initiale, -n*
    injured *beschädigt*
to inquire *nachfragen*
inside *innen, innerhalb*
inspection *die Besichtigung, -en*
instead (of) *(an)statt*
to instruct *orientieren, lehren*
insurance *die Versicherung, -en*
insured *versichert*
interest *das Interesse, -n*
interest *die Zinsen*
interesting *interessant*
interest rate *der Zinsatz, ¨e*
intermission *die Pause, -n*
Internet *das Internet*
    Internet address *die Internetadresse, -n*
    Internet café *das Internet-Café, -s*
intersection *die Kreuzung, -en*
interview *das Interview, -s*
    interview director *der Interviewleiter*
    interviewee *der/die Befragte, -n, -n*
to interview *interviewen*
interior *innen*
interior design *die Innenausstattung, -en; das Interior Design, -s*

into *hinein, herein, in*
to introduce *vorstellen, einleiten*
    introduction *die Einleitung, -en; die Vorstellung, -en*
to invest *investieren*
    investment *die Investition, -en; das Investment, -s; die Anlage, -n*
iron (electrical) *das Bügeleisen, -*
to iron *bügeln*
island *die Insel, -n*
to issue *ausstellen*
Italy *Italien*

# J

jacket *die Jacke, -n*
to jam *klemmen*
jam *die Marmelade, -n*
January *der Januar*
jewelry *der Schmuck*
job *die Arbeit, der Arbeitsplatz, ¨e; der Job, -s; die Stellung, -en*
jobless *arbeitslos*
to join *mitmachen, Mitglied werden*
journalism *der Journalismus*
journalist *der Journalist, -en*
journey *die Reise, -n*
judge *der Richter, -*
judgment *das Urteil, -e*
July *der Juli*
June *der Juni*
jury *die Geschworenen, die Schöffen*
to justify *rechtfertigen*
just *einfach, gerade, gerecht*
just now *gerade eben*
justice *die Gerechtigkeit*
juvenile court *Jugendgericht*
juvenile *der/die Jugendliche, -n*

# K

to keep *behalten*
key *der Schlüssel, -*
keyring *das Schlüsselbund, ¨e*
kilo *das Kilo, -s*
    half a kilo *das Pfund, -e*
kilometer (km) *der Kilometer*
kind *die Art, -en; der Typ, -en; freundlich, nett, aufmerksam*
kindness *die Freundlichkeit, -en; die Güte*
kiosk *der Kiosk, -e*
kit (first-aid) *der Verbandskasten, ¨*
kitchen *die Küche, -n*
to knock *(an)klopfen*

to know *wissen, kennen*
knowledge *das Wissen, die Kenntnis, -se*
known *bekannt*

# L

to lament *klagen*
lamp *die Lampe, -n*
reading lamp *die Leselampe, -n*
to land (boat) *anlegen; landen*
to last *dauern*
late *spät*
large *groß*
law *das Recht, -e*
lawyer *der Jurist, -n, -n; der Rechtsanwalt, ¨e*
to lay *legen*
to lead *führen*
lead role *die Hauptrolle, -n*
league *die Liga, -en*
to learn *lernen*
at least *wenigstens*
leather *das Leder, -*
(made) of leather *aus Leder*
to leave *weggehen; lassen*
to leave behind *zurück lassen*
left (direction) *links*
leg *das Bein, -e*
legend *die Legende, -n*
to lend *leihen*
lent *die Fastenzeit*
to let *lassen*
letter *der Brief, -e*
express letter *der Eilbrief, -e*
registered letter *das Einschreiben, -*
level *die Ebene, -n*
library *die Bibliothek, -en*
art library *die Kunstbibliothek, -en*
license *die Lizenz, -en*
licensing rights *die Lizenzrechte, -*
to lie *liegen*
life *das Leben*
lifesaver *der Lebensretter*
lift (chair) *die Sesselbahn, -en*
light (n) *das Licht, -er;* (adj.) *leicht*
lightbulb *die Glühbirne, -en*
likable *sympathisch sein*
to like *mögen*
liked *beliebt*
likelihood *die Wahrscheinlichkeit, -en*
likely *wahrscheinlich, möglich*
line *die Leitung, -en*
linen *das Leinen*
linen dress *das Leinenkleid*
to listen *hören*
liter *der Liter*

little *klein*
to live *leben*
to load *aufladen, einladen, laden*
location (film) *der Drehort, -e*
lock *das Kombinationsschloss, ¨er*
to log on/off *an (ab) melden (comp.)*
long *lang*
to look *gucken*
to look at *ansehen; anschauen; besichtigen*
to look at oneself *sich ansehen*
to look at something *sich etwas anschauen*
to look for *suchen*
to lose *verlieren*
lot (a) *eine Menge, viel*
loud *laut*
lounge *die Liegehalle, -n*
luggage *das Gepäck*
luggage cart *der Gepäckwagen, -*
lunch *das Mittagessen, -*

# M

magazine *die Zeitschrift, -en*
magnificent *großartig*
maid *das Zimmermädchen, -*
mail *die Post*
air mail *die Luftpost*
e-mail *die E-Mail, -s*
mailbox *der Briefkasten, ¨*
major *bedeutend; der/die/das Haupt-...*
majority *der Hauptteil, -e; die Mehrheit, -en*
to make *machen, tun*
man *der Mann, ¨er; der Ehemann, ¨er*
manager *der Geschäftsführer, -*
manual *handwerklich*
manual dexterity *handwerkliches Geschick*
manufacturer *der Fabrikant, -en, -en*
many *viele*
to march *aufziehen*
mark *der Fleck, -en*
market *der Markt, ¨e*
market analysis *die Marktanalyse, -en*
mass media *die Massenmedia*
massage *die Massage, -n*
material *das Material, -ien*
matinee *die Matinée, -n*
May *der Mai*
may (to be allowed to) *dürfen*
meadow *die Wiese, -n*
me *mich, mir*
meat *das Fleisch*

**medication** *das Medikament, -e; das Präparat, -e*
**medicine** *das Mittel, -*
**medieval** *mittelalterlich*
**Mediterranean Sea** *das Mittelmeer*
    Mediterranean island *die Mittelmeerinsel, -n*
**to meet** *treffen*
    to meet one another *sich treffen*
**meeting** *die Verabredung, -en; das Treffen, die Zusammenkunft, ¨e*
**member** *das Mitglied, -er*
**membership** *die Mitgliedschaft, -en*
**memory** *die Erinnerung, -en*
    in memory of *zur Erinnerung an*
**menu** *die Speisekarte, -n*
**merchandise** *die Ware, -n*
**message** *die Nachricht, -en*
**messenger** *der Bote, -n*
**metal** *das Metall*
**middle** *die Mitte, -n*
    in the middle of *mitten auf (+ dat.)*
**Middle Ages** *das Mittelalter*
**midnight** *die Mitternacht, ¨e*
**million** *die Million, -en*
    a million *eine Million*
**mine** *meins*
**minimal** *minimal, mindestens*
**minute** *die Minute, -n*
**to miss** *verpassen*
    to be missing *fehlen*
**Mister** *der Herr, -en, -en*
**mixed** *gemischt*
**model** *das Modell, -e*
**molar** *der Backenzahn, ¨e*
**moment** *der Moment, -e*
**Monday** *der Montag*
**money** *das Geld, -er*
**monstrous** *monströs*
**month** *der Monat, -e*
**more** *mehr*
**morning** *der Morgen, -de*
    good morning *guten Morgen*
    in the morning *morgens*
**mornings** *morgens*
**mother** *die Mutter, ¨*
**motorcycle** *das Motorrad, ¨er*
**mountain** *der Berg, -e*
    the mountains *das Gebirge*
    mountain railway *die Bergbahn, -en*
**mouse** *die Maus, ¨e*
**mouthwash** *das Mundwasser, -*
**to move** *bewegen; umziehen*
**move** *der Umzug, ¨e*
**mover** *der Spediteur, -e*
    moving company *die Spedition, -en*

**movie** *der Film, -e*
    movie fan *der Film Enthusiast, -en, -en*
**much** *viel*
    too much *zu viel*
**mud** *der Lehm*
    mud pack *die Lehmpackung, -en*
**muggy** *schwül*
**mural** *die Wandmalerei, -en*
**museum** *das Museum, Museen*
**music** *die Musik*
**musician** *der Musiker, -*
**must** (to have to) *müssen*
**mustache** *der Schnurrbart, ¨e*
**my** *mein*

# N

**name** *der Name, -n*
**to name** *nennen*
    to name a beneficiary *einen Nutznießer einsetzen*
**to narrate** *erzählen*
**narrow** *eng*
**near** *bei, nahe*
**neck** *der Nacken, -*
**to need** *brauchen*
**negotiation** *die Verhandlung, -en*
**neighbor** *der Nachbar, -n*
**neighborhood** *die Nachbarschaft, -en*
**nephew** *der Neffe, -n*
**net** *das Netz, -e*
**new** *neu*
    New Year *das Neujahr*
**news** *die Nachrichten*
    news broadcast *die Nachrichten*
**newspaper** *die Zeitung, -en*
**newsstand** *der/das Kiosk, -e*
**never** *niemals, nie*
**next** *nächste, -r, -s; neben*
**nice** *nett, schön*
**niece** *die Nichte, -n*
**night** *die Nacht, ¨e*
    at night *nachts; in der Nacht*
    Good night. *Gute Nacht.*
**no** *nein*
**nobody** *niemand*
**noon** *der Mittag, -e*
**normally** *normalerweise*
**north** *der Norden; nördlich*
**North Sea** *die Nordsee*
**northerly, northern** *nördlich*
**not** *nicht*
    not only . . . but also *nicht nur . . . sondern auch*
**note** *die Notiz, -en*
    notebook *das Notizbuch, ¨er*

nothing *nichts*
to notify *benachrichtigen*
notification *die Benachrichtigung, -en*
to notify *benachrichtigen*
November *der November*
now *jetzt*
nowadays *heutzutage*
nowhere *nirgendwo*
to numb *betäuben*
number *die Nummer, -n; die Zahl, -en;*
   room number *die Zimmernummer, -n*
   wrong number *falsch verbunden*
numerous *zahllos*
nurse *die Krankenschwester, -en*

# O

object *der Artikel, -; der Gegenstand, ¨e*
obvious *offensichtlich*
obviously *offensichtlich, offenbar*
ocean *das Meer, -e*
October *der Oktober*
odd *seltsam*
   odd number *die ungerade Zahl*
of *von*
   of course *selbstverständlich*
   in the course of *während*
offer *das Angebot, -e*
   special offer *das Sonderangebot, -e*
to offer *anbieten*
office *das Büro, -s*
   main post office *die Hauptpost*
   post office *die Post, das Postamt, ¨er*
official *der Beamte, -n; die Beamtin, -nen*
oil *das Öl*
ointment *das Öl, -e; die Salbe, -n*
old *alt*
   old-fashioned *altertümlich; unmodern*
on *an; auf*
   on top of *auf*
   onto *auf*
once *einmal*
   once more *noch einmal*
oneself *selber; selbst*
only *nur*
open *geöffnet*
   to open an account *ein Konto*
     *einrichten/eröffnen*
operator *die Vermittlung; (usage) der*
   *Bedienende*
operation *die Bedienung; (med.) die*
   *Operation*
operation manual *die*
   *Gebrauchsanweisung, die*
   *Bedienungsanleitung*
option *die Option*

or *oder*
orange *die Apfelsine, -en*
order *der Auftrag, die Ordnung, -en*
to order *beauftragen, bestellen*
order confirmation *die*
   *Auftragsbestätigung*
to orient oneself *sich orientieren*
others *andere*
otherwise *sonst*
out *hinaus/heraus*
out of *aus*
outside *draußen, außerhalb (+ gen.)*
over *über*
to oversleep *verschlafen*
overview *der Überblick, -e*
own *eigen*

# P

package *das Päckchen, -*
pain *die Schmerzen*
to paint *malen*
painter *der Maler, -*
painting *das Gemälde, -; die Malerei, -en*
pair *das Paar, -e*
   a pair of socks *ein Paar Socken*
pale *blass*
panorama *das Panorama, -s*
pants *die Hose, -n*
paper (slip of) *der Zettel, -*
parade *der Umzug, ¨e*
to parade *aufziehen*
parents *die Eltern*
park *der Park, -s*
part *der Teil, -e*
participant *der Teilnehmer, -; der*
   *Befragte, -n, -n*
to participate *mitmachen*
particular *besonders*
partial(ly) *anteilig, teilweise*
party *das Fest, -e*
party (political) *die Partei, -en*
   splinter party *die Splitterpartei, -en*
to pass *bestehen* (exam); *überholen* (traffic)
   to pass by *vorbeigehen*
   to pass one's time *verbringen*
passport *der Pass, ¨e; der Reisepass,*
   *¨e*
   passport control *die Passkontrolle*
pastime *die Freizeit*
pastry *das Gebäck*
path *der Pfad, -e*
pathological *krankhaft*
patience *die Geduld*
patient (female) *die Patientin, -nen*
patient (male) *der Patient, -en*

to pay *bezahlen*
    to pay back *zurückzahlen*
    to pay out *auszahlen*
pea *die Erbse, -n*
peculiar *seltsam*
pedestrian *der Fußgänger, -*
    pedestrian zone *die Fußgängerzone, -n*
pedicure *die Fußpflege*
pedicurist (female) *die Fußpflegerin, -nen*
pedicurist (male) *der Fußpfleger, -*
Pentecost *Pfingsten*
people *die Leute*
performance *die Vorstellung, -en*
perhaps *vielleicht*
permanent wave *die Dauerwelle, -n*
to permit *gestatten*
perseverance *die Ausdauer*
pharmacist *der Apotheker, -*
pharmacy *die Apotheke, -n*
photo *die Aufnahme, -n; das Photo, -s,*
    *das Foto, -s*
photographer *der Photograph, -en, -en*
    *der Fotograf, -en, -en*
physician (female) *die Ärztin, -nen*
physician (male) *der Arzt, ¨e*
to pick *aussuchen*
picture *das Bild, -er*
piece *das Stück, -e*
pill *die Tablette, -n*
place *der Platz, ¨e*
to place *setzen, stellen*
plan *der Plan, ¨e*
    seating plan *der Sitzplan, ¨e*
to plan *planen*
plaque *der Zahnbelag*
platform *der Bahnsteig, -e*
play *das Theaterstück, -e*
player (female) *die Spielerin, -nen*
player (male) *der Spieler, -*
to play *spielen*
playwright *der Dramatiker, -*
pleasant *angenehm*
please *bitte*
to please *gefallen*
pleasure *die Lust, ¨e; das Vergnügen, -*
plug (spark) *die Zündkerze, -n*
point *der Punkt, -e*
to point *zeigen*
to point out *hervorheben*
politician *der Politiker, -*
politics *die Politik*
popular *beliebt*
population *die Bevölkerung, -en*
pork *das Schweinefleisch*
post office *die Post*
possibility *die Möglichkeit, -en*

postcard *die Ansichtskarte, -n*
potato *die Kartoffel, -n*
potential (adj.) *potentiell*
potential (noun) *das Potential, die*
    *Möglichkeit, -en*
potter *der Töpfer, -*
pottery *die Töpferei*
pound *das Pfund, -e*
powder *der Körperpuder, -*
preparation *das Präparat, -e*
to prescribe *verschreiben, vorschreiben*
to preserve *erhalten*
to pretend *so tun als ob, vortäuschen*
president *der Präsident, -en*
press *die Presse*
pretty *hübsch*
price *der Preis, -e*
    price range *die Preislage, -n*
probably *wahrscheinlich, wohl*
profession *der Beruf, -e*
program *das Programm, -e*
    cable program *das*
    *Kabelfernsehprogramm, -e*
to promenade *promenieren, spazieren*
    *gehen*
to promise *versprechen*
prospect (for a profession) *die*
    *Berufsaussicht, -en*
public *öffentlich*
punctual *pünktlich*
purchase *der Einkauf, ¨e*
purse *die Geldbörse, -n; die Tasche, -n*
to put *setzen, stecken, stellen*
    to put on (clothes) *anziehen*

# Q

quadruple *vierfach*
quality *die Qualität*
quantity *die Quantität, -en*
query *die Anfrage, -en*
to question *fragen*
question *die Frage, -en*
quick *schnell*
quiet *ruhig, still*
to quiet *beruhigen*
quite *ganz, ziemlich*
quiz (review) *die Wiederholungsaufgabe,*
    *-en*

# R

radio *das Radio, -s*
railroad *die Bahn, -en; die Eisenbahn, -en*
rain *der Regen*
to rain *regnen*

raincoat *der Regenmantel,* ⸚

rapid *rapide, schnell*

rare *selten, rar*

rarety *die Rarität, -en*

rash *der Ausschlag,* ⸚e

rather *sondern*

razor (electric) *der Rasierapparat, -e*

real *real, reell*

reality *die Wirklichkeit, -en*

really *wirklich*

reasonable *preisgünstig*

to rebuild *umbauen*

receipt *die Quittung, -en*

reception *der Empfang,* ⸚e

to receive *empfangen*

receiver (telephone) *der Hörer, -*

receiver (of mail) *der Empfänger, -*

recipe *das Rezept, -e*

recognition *die Anerkennung, -en*

to recognize *erkennen, wiedererkennen*

to recommend *empfehlen*

to recuperate *erholen*

red *rot*

reddish *rötlich*

refreshing *erfrischend*

refrigerator *der Kühlschrank,* ⸚e

refund *die (Kosten)erstattung, -en; die Rückerstattung, -en*

to refund *zurückzahlen*

to register *eintragen*

   to register oneself *sich eintragen*

regular(ly) *regelmäßig*

to reimburse *zurückzahlen*

relative *der/die Verwandte, -n, -n*

to relax *sich ausruhen, erholen*

reliable *zuverlässig*

to rely upon *sich verlassen auf*

remarkable *bemerkenswert*

remittance order *der Überweisungsauftrag*

to remodel *umbauen*

to remove *entfernen*

to renovate *renovieren*

to repair *reparieren*

to replace *ersetzen*

to report *berichten*

to represent *vertreten*

Republic (Federal) *die Bundesrepublik*

reputation *der Ruf*

to request *bitten, anfordern*

request *die Bitte, -n; die Anfrage, -n*

to require *benötigen*

to reserve *reservieren*

reservation *die Reservierung, -en*

reserved *reserviert*

to reside *wohnen*

resident (local) *der/die Einheimische, -n*

resort (health) *der Badeort, -e; der Kurort, -e*

respect *die Achtung*

responsible *verantwortlich*

responsibility *die Verantwortung, -en*

to rest *sich ausruhen*

restaurant *das Restaurant, -s*

restless *unruhig*

to restore *restaurieren*

restoration *die Restaurierung, -en*

result *das Ergebnis, -se*

   election result *das Wahlergebnis, -se*

return *die Retoure, die Rückkehr*

to return *zurückkommen, zurückkehren*

reunification *die Wiedervereinigung*

to reward *lohnen*

rice *der Reis*

rich *reich*

to ride *fahren,* (horse) *reiten*

ridiculous *lächerlich*

right *rechts, richtig*

right (noun) *das Recht, -e*

right (direction) *rechts*

right (to be) *Recht haben*

rightfully *rechtmäßig*

to ring *läuten*

river *der Fluss,* ⸚e; *der Strom,* ⸚e

rock *der Felsen, -, der Stein, -e*

role *die Rolle, -n*

roll *das Brötchen*

roof *das Dach,* ⸚er

room *der Raum,* ⸚e; *das Zimmer, -*

   child's room *Kinderzimmer, -*

   consulting room *das Sprechzimmer, -*

   double room *das Doppelzimmer, -*

   fitting room *die Umkleidekabine, -n*

   laundry room *die Waschküche, -n*

   living room *das Wohnzimmer, -*

   single room *das Einzelzimmer, -*

   waiting room *das Wartezimmer, -*

root *die Wurzel, -n*

   root canal *die Wurzelbehandlung, -en*

Rose Monday (Monday before Lent) *der Rosenmontag*

rough *stürmisch*

routine *die Routine, -n*

to rub *einreiben*

rug *der Teppich, -e*

ruin *die Ruine, -n*

to run *laufen, rennen*

# S

safe *sicher*

safety *die Sicherheit, -en*

sailboat *das Segelboot, -e*
salad *der Salat, -e*
sale *der Verkauf, ̈-e*
salesman *der Verkäufer, -*
saleswoman *die Verkäuferin, -nen*
salve *die Salbe, -n*
sample *das Beispiel, -e; das Muster, -*
sand *der Sand*
sandwich *das Butterbrot, -e*
sandy *sandig*
Saturday *der Samstag, Sonnabend*
sausage *die Wurst, ̈-e*
to save *sparen, speichern* (comp.)
to say *sagen*
scarf *der Schal, -s*
scene *die Szene, -n*
school *die Schule, -n*
   high school *das Gymnasium,*
     *Gymnasien*
   special needs school *die Sonderschule,*
     *-n*
scientist *der Wissenschaftler, -*
scissors *die Schere, -n*
to scold *schimpfen mit*
score *das Ergebnis, -se*
scream *der Schrei, -e*
to scream *schreien*
screw *die Schraube, -n*
sculptor *der Bildhauer, -*
sculpture *die Bildhauerei, die Plastik*
   *-en, die Skulptur, -en*
sea *die See, das Meer, -e*
seaside *am Meer*
to search for *suchen*
season *die Jahreszeit, -en;* (Sport) *die*
   *Spielzeit, -en*
   vacation season *die Feriensaison*
seat *der Platz, ̈-e*
   backseat *der Rücksitz, -e*
   front seat *der Vordersitz, -e*
seaweed *der Seetang*
second *die Sekunde, -n*
secretary (female) *die Sekretärin, -nen*
secretary (male) *der Sekretär, -e*
secure *sicher*
securities (stock exchange) *die*
   *Pfandbriefe*
security *die Sicherheit, -en*
to see *sehen*
   seldom *selten*
   self *selbst; selber*
to sell *verkaufen*
to send *schicken; senden*
   to send off *abschicken*
   to send to *schicken an (+ acc.)*

sender *der Absender, -*
sensitive *empfindlich*
to separate *teilen, trennen*
September *der September*
serious *ernst*
to serve *servieren*
service *der Dienst, -e*
to set *setzen*
several *einige*
severe *streng, hart*
shall (to be supposed to) *sollen*
to share *teilen*
to shave *rasieren*
   to shave off *abrasieren*
   to shave oneself *sich rasieren*
   to shave the neck *ausrasieren*
shaving cream *die Rasiercreme, -s*
shelf *das Regal, -e*
shelter *der Schutz, das Heim*
shepherd (boy) *der Hirtenjunge, -n*
to shine *scheinen*
ship *das Schiff, -e*
shirt *das Hemd, -en*
shop *das Geschäft, -e*
   coffee shop *das Café, -s*
   flower shop *das Blumengeschäft, -e*
   pizza shop *die Pizzeria, Pizzerien*
to shop *einkaufen*
shopping *Einkäufe machen*
   shopping list *die Einkaufsliste, -n*
shore *die Küste, n*
short *kurz*
   on short notice *kurzfristig*
short list *die engere Auswahl, -en*
shot *die Spritze, -n*
to show *zeigen*
shower *die Dusche, -n*
to shower *duschen*
   to take a shower *sich duschen*
to shut *zumachen, schließen*
to shut down (comp.) *beenden*
sick *krank*
side *die Seite, -n*
sight *die Sicht; der Ausblick, -e*
sights *die Sehenswürdigkeiten*
sightseeing tour *die Besichtigungstour, -*
   *en*
sign *das Schild, -er*
silk *die Seide*
silly *dumm*
silver *das Silber*
similar *ähnlich*
simple *einfach*
to sin *sündigen*
since *seit*

sincerely *Mit freundlichen Grüßen*
singer *der Sänger*
singly (piece by piece) *einzeln*
sink *der Ausguss, ⸚e*
sister *die Schwester, -n*
    sister-in-law *die Schwägerin, -nen*
to sit *sitzen*
    Sit down! *Setzen Sie sich!*
    size *die Größe, -n*
skiing *skilaufen; skifahren*
skill *die Fähigkeit, -en; die Kenntnis,*
    *-se*
skirt *der Rock, ⸚e*
sky *der Himmel, -*
slacks *die Hose, -n*
slight *wenig, nur, gering(fügig)*
small *klein*
to smile *lächeln, schmunzeln*
smoker *der Raucher, -*
smooth *glatt*
snow *der Schnee*
to snow *schneien*
snowfall *der Schneefall, ⸚e*
snuff *der Schnupftabak*
soap *die Seife, -n*
soccer *der Fußball, ⸚e*
    soccer match *Fußballspiel, -e*
social sciences *die Sozialwissenschaft,*
    *-en*
sock *die Socke, -n*
socket (elec.) *die Steckdose, -n*
sofa *das Sofa, -s*
soft *weich*
sold out *ausgebucht; ausverkauft*
solution *die Lösung, -en*
some *einige, ein paar, etwas*
someone, somebody *jemand,*
    *irgendwer*
something *etwas, irgendetwas*
sometimes *manchmal*
somewhere *irgendwo*
son *der Sohn, ⸚e*
soon *bald*
sorrow *die Sorge, -n*
soup *die Suppe, -n*
sour *sauer*
southerly, southern *südlich*
souvenir *das Andenken, -*
spa *der Badeort, -e; der Kurort, -e*
Spain *Spanien*
to speed *rasen*
speed limit *die Geschwindig-*
    *keitsbegrenzung*
speedometer *der Tacho, -s; der*
    *Tachometer, -*

to spend *ausgeben (Geld); verbringen*
    *(Zeit)*
splendid *glänzend*
splendor *die Pracht*
sport *der Sport*
    sports club *der Sportverein, -e*
    to engage in sports *Sport treiben*
spot *der Fleck, -en*
sprain *die Zerrung, -en*
to sprain *zerren*
spring *der Frühling; die Quelle, -n*
    medicinal spring *die Heilquelle, -n*
to sprinkle *streuen*
square *der Platz, ⸚e*
stable *stabil*
stability *die Stabilität*
stack *der Stapel, -*
stage *die Bühne, -n*
stain *der Fleck, -en*
stair *die Treppe, -n*
staircase *das Treppenhaus, ⸚er*
stamp *die Briefmarke, -en*
to stand *stehen*
to start *beginnen, anfangen, starten*
starter *der Anlasser, -*
state *der Staat, -en*
statement (bank) *der Kontoauszug, ⸚e*
station (train) *der Bahnhof, ⸚e*
station (radio or TV) *der Sender, -*
stay *der Aufenthalt, -e*
to stay *bleiben*
to steam *dampfen*
steamboat *der Dampfer, -*
    steamboat trip *die Dampferfahrt, -en*
steel (stainless) *der Edelstahl*
steep *steil*
to stick to *stecken, kleben*
still *trotzdem, immer noch*
still water(way) *stehendes Gewässer, -*
to stipulate *verordnen, festsetzen*
stock exchange *die Börse, -n*
stock *die Aktie(n)*
stomachache *die Magenschmerzen*
to stop *halten; stehen bleiben*
storage (room/space) *der Abstellraum, ⸚*
    *e*
storm *der Sturm, ⸚e*
    storm warning *die Sturmwarnung, -en*
    violent storm *das Unwetter, -*
to storm *stürmen*
stormy *stürmisch*
stove *der Herd, -e*
straight *gerade*
    straight ahead *geradeaus*
strange *seltsam*

strenuous *anstrengend*
strike *der Streik, -s*
striking *eindrucksvoll*
strong *stark, kräftig*
strudel *der Strudel, -*
to struggle *kämpfen*
student *der Student, -en, -en*
studies *das Studium, Studien*
to study *studieren*
stupid *dumm*
style *der Stil*
subject *das Fach, ¨-er*
subordinate *untergeordnet*
to subsidize *fördern, unterstützen*
subsidy *die Förderung, -en*
subway *die S-Bahn, -en; die U-Bahn, -en*
such *solche*
suddenly *plötzlich*
to suffer *leiden*
    to suffer from *leiden an*
sugar *der Zucker*
summer *der Sommer*
summit *der Gipfel, -*
sun *die Sonne, -n*
    sun protection oil *das Sonnenschutzöl, -e*
sunburn *der Sonnenbrand, ¨-e*
Sunday *der Sonntag*
sunscreen (lotion) *die Sonnenschutzcreme, -s*
suntan *die Bräune*
superfluous *überflüssig*
to supervise *überwachen, beaufsichtigen*
supermarket *der Supermarkt, ¨-e*
supper *das Abendessen, -*
supplier *der Lieferant, -en*
to support *unterstützen*
support *die Unterstützung, -en*
supporting role *die Nebenrolle, -n*
surcharge *der Aufschlag, ¨-e; der Zuschlag, ¨-e*
    spa surcharge *die Kurtaxe, -n*
surface *die Fläche, -n*
surplus *das Überangebot, der Überschuss*
surprise *die Überraschung*
to surprise *überraschen*
to swallow *einnehmen, schlucken*
to swamp *überschütten*
swamp *der Sumpf*
sweater *der Pullover, -*
sweet *süß*
swelling *die Schwellung, -en*
swimming (to go) *schwimmen gehen*
to switch (channels) *umschalten*
Switzerland *die Schweiz*
syllable *die Silbe*
symptom *das Symptom, -e*

# T

table *der Tisch, -e*
table lamp *die Tischlampe, -n*
to take *bringen; einnehmen; nehmen*
    to take a picture *aufnehmen*
    to take a seat *sich setzen*
    to take advantage *zugreifen*
    to take off *ausziehen*
    to take out (stains) *entfernen*
    to take place *stattfinden*
    to take opportunity *zugreifen*
to talk *reden, sprechen*
    to talk about *sprechen über (+ acc.)*
talk *das Gespräch, -e*
task *die Aufgabe, -n*
tax *die Steuer, -n*
    tax decrease *die Steuersenkung, -en*
    tax increase *die Steuererhöhung, -en*
taxi *das Taxi, -s*
tea *der Tee, -s*
to teach *lehren, unterrichten*
teacher *der Lehrer, -*
team *die Mannschaft, -en*
to tear *zerren*
teeth (set of) *das Gebiss, -e*
telephone *das Telefon, -e; der Apparat, -e*
    by telephone *telefonisch*
    coin-operated telephone *der Münzfernsprecher, -*
    over the telephone *telefonisch*
    telephone book *das Telefonbuch, ¨-er*
    telephone conversation *das Telefongespräch, -e*
    telephone card *die Telefonkarte, -n*
    telephone number *die Telefonnummer, -n*
to telephone *telefonieren*
    to reach by telephone *telefonisch erreichen*
television *das Fernsehen, -*
television set *der Fernsehapparat, -e*
to tell *erzählen*
    to tell about *erzählen von (+ dat.)*
    Tell me! *Sag mal!*
teller *der/die Bankangestellte, -n, -n*
tendon *die Sehne, -n*
terrace *die Terrasse, -n*
terrible *furchtbar*
to test *überprüfen*
than *als*
to thank *danken*
    thank you *Danke*
thanks *der Dank*
that *dass, jener*
theater *das Theater, -*

court theater *das Hoftheater, -*
federal theater *das Staatstheater, -*
municipal theater *das Stadttheater, -*
theater box office *die Theaterkasse, -n*
**theatergoer** *der Theaterbesucher, -*
**theft** *der Diebstahl, -̈e*
**then** *dann*
**there** *da; dort*
over there *dort drüben*
(to) there *hin*
up there *da oben*
**thereafter** *danach*
**therefore** *darum; deswegen; deshalb*
**these** *dieser*
**thief** (male) *der Dieb, -e*
**thief** (female) *die Diebin, -nen*
**thing** *die Sache, -n*
to **think** *denken*
to think of *denken an (+ acc.)*
**this** *dieser, diese, dieses*
**thorough** *sorgfältig, genau*
**those** *jener, jene, jenes*
**thought** *der Gedanke, -n*
**thousand** *tausend*
**thread** *der Faden, -̈*
**threatening** *bedrohlich*
**thrilling** *spannend*
**throat** *der Hals, -̈e*
sore throat *die Halsschmerzen*
**through** *durch*
**throughout** *überall, in ganz . . .*
**thunder** *der Donner*
**thunder and lightning** *Gewitter*
**Thuringia** *Thüringen*
**Thursday** *der Donnerstag*
**thus** *somit, so, auf diese Art*
**ticket** *die Fahrkarte, -n*
**time** *die Zeit*
closing time (store) *der Ladenschluss*
halftime *die Halbzeit, -en*
many times *x-mal*
several times *mehrmals*
short time *die Weile*
three times a day *dreimal täglich*
**tip** *das Trinkgeld, -er*
**tire** *der Reifen, -*
**tired** *müde; erschöpft*
**tiring** *ermüdend*
**title** *der Titel, -*
**to** *an; nach; zu*
to **tip over** *umstoßen*
**today** *heute*
**toe** *der Zeh, -en*
toenail *der Fußnagel, -̈e, der Zehnagel*
to **tolerate** *vertragen*

**toll** *die Straßenbenutzungsgebühr*
**tomorrow** *morgen*
tomorrow morning *morgen früh*
**toolbox** *der Werkzeugkasten, -*
**tooth** *der Zahn, -̈e*
front tooth *der Vorderzahn, -̈e*
wisdom tooth *der Weisheitszahn, -̈e*
**toothache** *die Zahnschmerzen (pl.)*
**toothbrush** *die Zahnbürste, -n*
**toothless** *zahnlos*
**toothpaste** *die Zahnpasta, Zahnpasten*
**top** *die Spitze, -n; der Gipfel, -*
**topical** *aktuell*
**torte** *die Torte, -n*
**tour** (group) *die Gruppentour, -en*
**tour** (guided) *die Führung, -en*
**tourism** *der Tourismus, der Fremdenverkehr*
**tourist** *der Tourist*
**tourist center** *das Touristenzentrum*
**toward** *nach*
**towel** (bath/beach) *das Handtuch, -̈er; das Badetuch, -̈er*
**tower** *der Turm, -e*
**town** *die Stadt, -̈e*
old town *die Altstadt, -̈e*
small town *die Kleinstadt, -̈e*
**town hall** *das Rathaus, -̈er*
**totally** *absolut, total*
**trace** *die Spur, -en*
**track** (educational) *der Bildungsweg, -e*
**track** (and field) *die Leichtathletik*
**trade** *das Handwerk*
**traffic** *der Verkehr*
**traffic jam** *der Verkehrsstau, -s*
**traffic rule** *die Verkehrsregel, -n*
**traffic sign** *das Verkehrsschild, -er*
**trail** *der Pfad, -e*
**trailer** *der Anhänger, -*
**train** *der Zug, -̈e; die Bahn, -en*
short distance train *der Nahverkehrszug, -̈e; der Personenzug, -̈e*
to **train** (prof.) *ausbilden,* (sport) *trainieren*
**trainee** *der Auszubildende, -n*
**training** *die Ausbildung, -en*
to **transfer** (money) *überweisen*
**transformer** *der Transformator, -en*
**transport** *der Transport, -e*
**transportation** (means of) *die Transportmöglichkeit, -en*
**travel** *die Reise, -n*
travel agency *das Reisebüro, -s*
travel bag *die Reisetasche, -n*
travel guide (book) *der Reiseführer, -*

to travel *reisen*
  traveler *der/die Reisende, -n, -n*
  treasure *der Schatz, ¨e*
to treat *behandeln*
  treatment *die Kur, -en*
  trial *(jur.) das Verfahren, -; die Verhandlung, -en*
to trim *stutzen*
  trip *die Reise, -n*
    round-trip *hin und zurück*
  triple *dreifach*
  truck *der Lastwagen, -*
  true *wahr*
to be true *stimmen*
  Tuesday *der Dienstag*
to turn on *einschalten*

# U

unacceptable *nicht akzeptabel*
unable *unfähig*
unbelievable *unglaublich*
uncle *der Onkel, -*
unclear *unklar*
under *unter*
to understand *verstehen*
  understanding *das Verständnis, -se*
to undress *ausziehen*
    to get undressed *sich ausziehen*
unemployment *die Arbeitslosigkeit*
unfortunate *schade, unglücklich*
unfortunately *leider, unglücklicherweise*
unhappy *unglücklich*
unification *der Vereinigung, -en*
uninteresting *uninteressant*
union *die Gewerkschaft, -en*
unit *die Einheit, -en*
united *vereint*
unity *die Einigkeit*
university *die Universität, -en; die Hochschule, -n*
to unload *ausladen*
unknown *unbekannt*
unpleasant *unangenehm*
until *bis*
unique *einzigartig*
up *auf, her-/hinauf*
upholstery *die Polsterung*
upper *obere, -r, -s*
upstairs *oben*
urgent *dringend*
us *uns*
usage *der Gebrauch, ¨e*
to use *benutzen, gebrauchen*

useful *nützlich*
useless *nutzlos*
user *der Benutzer, -; der Gebraucher, -*
user-friendly *benutzerfreundlich*
usual *normal, gewöhnlich*
utilities *Strom-, Heiz- und Telefonkosten*
utmost *äußerste*

# V

vacation *der Urlaub, -e; die Ferien (pl.)*
vaccination *die Impfung, -en*
valid *gültig*
validity *die Gültigkeit, -en*
valley *das Tal, ¨er*
value *der Wert, -e*
varied *unterschiedlich*
variety *die Vielfalt, -en; die Vielzahl, -en*
various *verschieden, unterschiedlich*
vase *die Vase, -n*
VCR *das Videogerät, -e; der Videorekorder, -*
veal *das Kalbfleisch*
vegetarian *der Vegetarier, -*
vegetable *das Gemüse*
to verify *(auf seine Richtigkeit) prüfen, überprüfen*
versatile *vielseitig*
versatility *die Vielseitigkeit*
very *sehr*
victory *der Sieg, -e*
to view *besichtigen*
  village *das Dorf, ¨er*
  vine *die Rebe, -n*
  vineyard *das Weingut, ¨er*
  vintage *Prädikatswein, -e; Jahreswein, -e; Antik-, Sammlerstück, -e*
to visit *besuchen*
  visit *der Besuch*
  visitor *der Besucher, -*
  visitor (spa) *der Kurgast, ¨e*
vocabulary *die Vokabel, -n*
void *ungültig*
volt *das Volt, -*
vote *die Stimme, -n*
to vote *wählen*
  right to vote *das Wahlrecht*
  election result *das Wahlergebnis, -se*
  vote (to cast one's) *seine Stimme abgeben; zur Urne gehen*
  voter (female) *die Wählerin, -nen*
  voter (male) *der Wähler, -*
  voter turnout *die Wahlbeteiligung*

# W

**to wait** *warten*
    to wait for *warten auf (+ acc.)*
**to wake** *wecken*
    to wake up *aufwachen*
**to walk** *gehen, spazieren gehen*
  **walk** *der Spaziergang, ⁼e*
  **wall** *die Wand, ⁼e*
  **wallpaper** *die Tapete, -n*
**to wander** *wandern*
**to want to** *wollen*
  **warm** *warm*
**to warn** *warnen*
  **warranty** *der Garantieschein, -e*
**to wash** *waschen*
    to wash by hand *mit der Hand waschen*
    to wash oneself *sich waschen*
**to watch** *beobachten, (zu)sehen*
  **watch** *die Armbanduhr, -en*
**to watch** *beobachten*
**to watch TV** *fernsehen*
  **water** *das Wasser, ⁼*
  **waterway** *das Gewässer, -*
  **wave** *die Welle, -n*
  **wavy** *wellig*
  **way** *der Weg, -e*
    one way *einfach*
    one-way street *die Einbahnstraße*
**weak** *schwach*
**weather** *das Wetter*
**weaver** *der Weber, -*
**weaving** *die Weberei*
**web page** *die Web-Seite, -n*
**Wednesday** *der Mittwoch*
**week** *die Woche, -n*
    day of the week *der Wochentag, -e*
    weekly news broadcast *die Wochenschau, -en*
**well** *gut; die Quelle, -n*
**westerly, western** *westlich*
    farther west *weiter westlich*
**wet** *nass*
**what** *was*
**when** *als; wann; wenn*
**whenever** *wenn*
**where** *wo*
    from where *woher*
    where (to) *wohin*
**whether** *ob*
**which** *welche, -r, -s*
**while** *die Weile, während*
**white** *weiß*
**Whitsuntide** *Pfingsten*

**who** *wer*
**whom** *wem*
**why** *warum*
**wide** *weit*
**wife** *die Frau, -en; die Ehefrau, -en*
**will** *der Wille*
**willing** *bereit*
**willingly** *gern*
**to win** *gewinnen*
  **wind** *der Wind, -e*
  **window** *das Fenster, -*
    window (bank, post office) *der Schalter, -*
  **wine** *der Wein, -e*
  **winter** *der Winter, -*
    winter morning *der Wintermorgen*
**to wish** *wünschen*
  **wit** *die Schlagfertigkeit, -en*
  **witch** *die Hexe, -n*
  **with** *bei; mit*
  **without** *ohne*
  **witty** *witzig*
  **woman** *die Frau, -en*
  **woods** *der Wald, ⁼er*
  **word** *das Wort, -e*
  **world** *die Welt, -en*
  **worldwide** *weltweit*
  **work** *die Arbeit, -en*
**to work** *arbeiten*
  **worker** (foreign) *der Gastarbeiter, -*
**to be worried** *besorgt sein*
**to worry** *Sorgen haben*
**to be worth** *wert sein*
  **wrapping** *die Verpackung, -en*
**to write** *schreiben*
    to write about *schreiben über (+ acc.)*
    to write to *schreiben an (+ acc.)*

# X

**Xmas** *Weihnachten*
**X ray** *die Röntgenaufnahme, -n; das Röntgenbild, -er*

# Y

**yacht** *die Jacht, -en*
**to yawn** *gähnen*
  **year** *das Jahr, -e*
  **yearly** *jährlich*
  **yeast** *die Hefe*
**to yell** *schreien*
  **yellow** *gelb*

yes *ja*
yesterday *gestern*
yet *schon, noch*
   not yet *noch nicht*
to yield *Vorfahrt gewähren*
   Yield *Vorfahrt achten!*
yield *die Rendite*
yogurt *das/der Jog(h)urt*
you *du, Sie, ihr*

young *jung*
your *dein, Ihr*
youth *die Jugend*

# Z

zero *null*
ZIP code *die Postleitzahl, -en*
zipper *der Reißverschluss, ¨-e*

# INDEX